In memory of Prof. Dwijendra Tripathi,
whose work introduced me to business history.

India's New Capitalists

Harish Damodaran is National Editor (Rural Affairs and Agriculture Editor) at the *Indian Express*. A journalist with over 27 years of experience as a reporter and editorial analyst, he has also previously been with *The Hindu BusinessLine* and the Press Trust of India. The present book won Damodaran the Ramnath Goenka Excellence in Journalism Award under the Non-Fiction (Books) category in 2008.

Praise for the book

'Full marks to Harish Damodaran for a book that those interested in the dynamics of capitalist development in India must read. It's not just good journalism but the work of a profoundly talented observer of social change in India.' – *Outlook*

'A pioneer in its treatment of an issue critical to the present trajectory of development... This is an elegantly produced work that will stand the test of time.' – *Telegraph*

'To Harish Damodaran goes the credit of successfully filling the void in our understanding of the process of the emergence of the new "wealth creators" as well as bridging the hiatus between the past and the present.' – *The Hindu*

'The richness of the book lies in the multi-level structure it adopts. From secondary sources, primary material and interviews the author has garnered a wealth of material...that identify India's diverse capitalists, their origins, their, often unusual, traverse to industry, the factors that influenced their success and the role of community links and organizations in ensuring the success of those who did succeed.' – *Frontline*

'It's no secret that some communities have predominated in India's business and trading history. That's changing now, and Damodaran captures that change and the rise of new entrepreneurial groups in the 15 case studies in this book.' – *Business Standard*

'An essential reference work for anyone conducting research on this subject. *India's New Capitalists* is also a good read, and provides a number of surprises to readers who are not familiar with the social background of many of today's prominent businessmen.' – *Economic and Political Weekly*

'Structural change has created new economic opportunities over the past 25 years... Harish Damodaran's fascinating book on Indian entrepreneurs documents the movement of castes from agriculture and administrative occupations into business in recent decades.' – *Mint*

'Caste familiarity generates trust, and...turns into an open-air business school of self-learning for entrepreneurs, teaching them to build businesses... Harish Damodaran, in his book, calls this the "Field to Factory" movement, signifying the expansion of the social base of Indian business "beyond the Baniya".' – *The Hindu BusinessLine*

'Harish Damodaran investigated the caste origins of many of India's industrialists. He identified three trends...The third trajectory, "field to factory", is the transition into the business world of members of India's middle and lower-peasant castes. This must be the path of India's *dalits*, too. But they have not trodden it yet.'– *The Economist*

'To call this work a fascinating collage of business biographies would best describe the experience of reading it, though perhaps at the risk of undermining the rigour with which its material has been assembled.' – *Seminar*

India's New Capitalists

CASTE, BUSINESS, AND INDUSTRY IN A MODERN NATION

HARISH DAMODARAN

With a Foreword by

NANDAN NILEKANI

THE NewIndia FOUNDATION

hachette INDIA

First published in hardback by Permanent Black in association with
The New India Foundation in 2008
First paperback printing 2009
Sixth Impression 2017

This revised and updated edition first published in 2018 by Hachette India
(Registered name: Hachette Book Publishing India Pvt. Ltd)
An Hachette UK company
www.hachetteindia.com

SRD

ISBN 978-93-5195-279-4

Hachette Book Publishing India Pvt. Ltd
4th & 5th Floors, Corporate Centre,
Plot No. 94, Sector 44, Gurugram 122003, India

Typeset in Adobe Garamond 11/14.8
by InoSoft Systems Noida

Printed and bound in India
by Manipal Technologies Limited, Manipal

FSC
www.fsc.org
MIX
Paper from
responsible sources
FSC™ C043100

Contents

Author's Preface to the New Edition

The first edition of this book was written in the middle of the last decade. It was a period that, as I have described elsewhere, marked 'the high noon of Indian capitalist enterprise'. Gross fixed capital formation in the private sector, which averaged between 6.4 per cent and 9.6 per cent of the country's GDP from the 1950s through the 1980s, rose to 14.5 per cent during the 1990s and, then, soared to 21.1 per cent in the first decade of this century, before peaking at 24.7 per cent in 2011–12.[1]

This was, moreover, a period that saw an unleashing of the 'animal spirits' of entrepreneurs. The primary driver here was the economic reforms launched after 1991 and also a new language welcoming private initiative that accompanied it. As industries hitherto reserved for the public sector were opened up and entry barriers imposed by licensing and related restrictions – obtaining government approvals for starting and expanding factories, importing capital equipment, entering into foreign collaborations or raising monies from the capital markets – were dismantled, it led to the emergence of a host of 'new capitalists'. And they came from diverse social backgrounds. This book's central theme was the evolution of India's capitalist class since Independence, specifically the widening of its social base beyond traditional mercantile communities. Liberalization, in a sense, provided further impetus to this process of 'democratization of capital'.

Since this book was written when the last boom had just taken off, there are many 'new capitalists' who did not find mention in it. But to begin with I must rectify the errors in the first edition – they shouldn't have happened. Chinni Krishnan Ranganathan of CavinKare – whose brother Rajkumar pioneered the sale of shampoo in sachets before Hindustan Unilever and others latched on to the idea – is from the Mudaliar, not the Nadar, community. Even more glaring was the observation that India hasn't (rather, hadn't, at that point) produced a single Dalit industrialist of note, although I did refer to reports suggesting the rise of a nascent bourgeoisie – promoters of hospitals, commercial complexes, shoe and leather upholstery units, and other small to medium-scale establishments – from the ranks of this historically disadvantaged community.

It is possible, however, to identify at least four *major* Dalit capitalist names today.

The first is Gaddam Vivekanand, the son of former union minister for labour and textiles G. Venkat Swamy. A medical doctor by training, he heads Visaka Industries Limited, the country's second-largest asbestos fibre cement sheets producer (after the C.K. Birla Group's Hyderabad Industries Ltd) and also a maker of blended synthetic yarns. With profits after tax of Rs 66.56 crore on net sales of Rs 1,043.24 crore for the year ended 31 March 2018, it is the only publicly listed company promoted by a Dalit.[2]

The second is Rajesh Saraiya, whose father Nattha Ram was a central government employee hailing from Saraiya Sana, a village in Sitapur district of Uttar Pradesh. Saraiya, in the late 1980s, went to the Soviet Union on a scholarship to study aeronautical engineering at the National Aviation University in Kiev, Ukraine. The dissolution of the USSR in the early 1990s forced him to take up odd jobs, including as a translator for steel baron Lakshmi Niwas Mittal, who was then eyeing acquisition of plants in the erstwhile republics. Saraiya apparently learnt the tricks of steel trading during this period and went on to start his own business in 1993. Steel Mont, the name of his Dusseldorf-based company, is into global trading of finished steel as well as sourcing of raw material (iron ore, pig iron, coal, coke and ferro-alloys), with operations in some nine countries. Its website claims a group turnover of $350 million and trading one million tonnes of products annually.[3]

The third big Dalit entrepreneur is Ashok Khade of DAS Offshore Engineering Pvt. Ltd. Born to a poor cobbler at Ped village in Maharashtra's Sangli district, his is a true rags-to-riches story – of someone also escaping caste oppression through migration to Bombay (now Mumbai) in 1975. Khade initially worked as a welder at the Mazagon Dock, while simultaneously doing a part-time diploma in mechanical engineering. In 1992, Khade, along with his brothers Datta and Suresh, established the engineering and fabrication firm bearing the initials of their first names. The first contract they got was from Mazagaon Dock itself, on the recommendation of Captain P.V. Nair, a former chairman of the government-owned shipbuilder. It was a Rs 1.82 crore job, to finish a project that the original contractor had abandoned midway. Their company has since grown to be a specialized fabricator of oil well platforms, helipads, jackets and other offshore structures for the petroleum and natural gas industry.[4]

The fourth entrepreneur is Bhagwan Dharmaji Gawai, who owns Citax Energy DMCC, a Dubai-headquartered company trading in crude oil, gas and refined products. From a family of migrant construction workers living in the Hanuman Nagar slum of Mumbai's Kandivali area – they belonged to Buldhana in rural Maharashtra – Gawai managed to complete his school as well as college education. In 1982, he joined the Hindustan Petroleum Corporation Ltd as an officer-trainee, availing the benefit of reservations in public-sector jobs for Scheduled Castes. In 1991, Gawai quit to take up a work offer with the oil major Caltex at Bahrain, and, about seven years later, with the Emirates National Oil Company in Dubai. The experience he had gained from the sourcing of crude and shipping of products led him to launch his own trading operation, first with a local Arab partner in 2002 and, by 2008, as an independent venture.[5]

Dalits apart, there are industrialists from other communities, too, who did not figure in the first edition, some due to oversight and others because they weren't all that big then. Two prominent Parsis who should have found mention are Cyrus Poonawalla of Serum Institute of India Pvt. Ltd, the world's biggest vaccine manufacturer, and Rohinton Soli 'Ronnie' Screwvala, who founded the media firm UTV Software Communications in 1990 and sold it, in 2012, to the Walt Disney Company for $454 million. The same goes for the two Brahmins, T.S. (Trikkur Seetharamaiyer) Kalyanaraman and Virendra Dattatray Mhaiskar. The former controls Kalyan Jewellers, India's largest jewellery store chain, which he set up in 1993 after his father partitioned the family's textile retailing business. That business now includes Kalyan Silks and Kalyan Sarees, which are with Kalyanaraman's brothers T.S. Pattabhiraman and T.S. Ramachandran, respectively. The Kalyan name derives from their grandfather, a priest who, in 1909, relocated from Kumbakonam in Thanjavur (Tamil Nadu) to Thrissur in Kerala, where he set up a textile mill.[6] Mhaiskar controls IRB Infrastructure Developers, a leading highways construction and toll concessionaire company. Founded in 1977 as Ideal Road Builders by his father Dattatray

Pandurang Mhaiskar, it has been linked to union minister and former Bharatiya Janata Party (BJP) president Nitin Gadkari, also a Maharashtrian Brahmin.[7]

Among other communities, some of the prominent businessmen left out were Bhavarlal Hiralal Jain of Jain Irrigation Systems and Badrinarayan Ramulal Barwale of Maharashtra Hybrid Seeds Company (both Marwaris: the former pioneered drip irrigation and commercial tissue culture planting in India, while the latter fathered the country's private seed industry) and Rahul Bhatia of IndiGo airlines, Rana Kapoor of Yes Bank and Kapil Wadhawan of Dewan Housing Finance (Punjabi Khatris).

Coming to the so-called non-traditional business communities – the real focus of this book – the most significant Kamma magnate of today is, perhaps, Chinta Visweswara Rao. His Navayuga Group's rise from a pile foundation and marine berthing structures contractor to full-fledged infrastructure developer – with works spanning highways, bridges, flyovers and metro rail stations, and building and operating the Krishnapatnam Port near Nellore in Andhra Pradesh – is a phenomenon of the last 10 to 15 years. The other major Kammas that I missed mentioning were the construction barons Rajendra Prasad Maganti of Soma Enterprise, Vallurupalli Nageswara Rao of SEW Infrastructure (Southern Engineering Works) and Sridhar Cherukuri of Transstroy India, besides Dasari Jai Ramesh of Vijai Electricals (transformers and switchgears), Alluri Venkateswara Rao of Avanti Feeds (aqua feed and shrimp processing), Yalamanchili Satyanarayana Chowdary of Sujana Group (steel, transmission towers and appliances), and Krishna Prasad Tripuraneni of Spartek Ceramics (vitrified tiles).

This preface, likewise, provides an opportunity to add to the list of Patidar entrepreneurs Vasant Gajera of Laxmi Diamond, Vallabhbhai Shamjibhai Patel of Kiran Gems, Laljibhai Tulsibhai Patel of Dharmanandan Diamonds (he paid Rs 4.31 crore for the famous monogrammed *bandhgala* suit that Prime Minister Narendra Modi had worn during the US President Barack Obama's visit in January 2015), Kishorkumar Bhikhalal Virani of KARP Impex, Naresh Ravjibhai Patel (head of the engineering components firm Patel Brass Works and also the Shree Khodaldham Trust, an influential social and religious institution of Saurashtra Leva Patels), Chandubhai Virani of Balaji Wafers Private Ltd (potato chips and snacks), and Dhanjibhai Anandjibhai Makasana of the Makson Group (confectionary machines and products). All of them are from Gujarat's Saurashtra region and with predominantly agricultural backgrounds.[8]

Among Gounders, two notable inclusions would be Balasubramanian Prabhakaran of Thriveni Earthmovers (an upstart private iron ore, coal and barite mines developer from Salem in Tamil Nadu, with operations in Odisha, Mozambique and Indonesia) and Kandasamy Chandramohan of Namakkal Transport Carriers (now NTC Logistics India). The community's role in developing cluster-based industries of Tamil Nadu beyond knitwear and textiles – lorry/bulk cargo transport and layer poultry in Namakkal, bus body fabrication in Karur, and borewell drilling services in Tiruchengode (the contractors here take their truck-mounted rigs all over India) – is also something that this book did not highlight, and deserves separate documentation.[9]

In addition to the above are assorted industrialists from other communities: Sameer Gehlaut of Indiabulls (finance and real estate: Jat), Hem Singh Bharana of Era Infra Engineering (civil construction: Gujjar), Vazhappully Padmanabhan Nandakumar of Manappuram Finance (gold lending: Ezhava), Veerappa Gangaiah Siddhartha of Cafe Coffee Day (cafe chain with integrated coffee plantations, processing and trading operations: Vokkaliga), Kulandaivel Mudaliar of The Chennai Silks (textile and jewellery retail: Kaikolar Mudaliar[10]) and Manuel Gnanaoli Muthu of MGM

Group (port cargo handling, hotels, resorts and liquor: Nadar).

All these previously left-out/new names, however, do not take away from the key arguments made in the book. Business in India is definitely no longer the preserve of the 'Bania'. The social profile of its capitalist class is far more diversified than at the dawn of Independence (women are still notably under-represented, though). Even if one looks at the *Forbes* list of Indian billionaires by net worth for 2018, only 65 out of the total 119 are from the traditional mainstream mercantile castes: 38 non-Gujarati Bania/ Marwari, 10 Gujarati Bania/Jain, 8 Parsi, 6 Sindhi, 2 Kutchi Bhatia and one Lohana. The remaining 54 represent a mix bag: 15 Brahmin (including 3 Bhumihars, a caste that claims Brahmin status), 12 Khatri/Arora, 5 Muslim, 4 Patidar, 3 Christian, 2 Jats, 2 Nadar and one Nair, Kayastha, Bunt, Konkanastha Vaishya Vani, Lingayat, Kamma, Reddy, Saini, Ezhava, Ramgarhia and Isai Vellalar each.[11] The fact that there are successful entrepreneurs now among Dalits, nevertheless, does not point to the emergence of a business community in the truest sense. For the average Dalit, government service remains the preferred avenue of upward mobility; the businessman is nowhere near being the role model that an IAS bureaucrat or career politician is.

This book's contents cover business developments and events until around 2006. But the defining development since then – more specifically, in the current decade – has been the destruction of capital alongside a drying up of the supply and growth of *new* entrepreneurs.

The first two decades after economic reform, as already alluded to, was a time when private capital came into its own in India. The overall environment was one of optimism, conducive for risk-taking and investments by entrepreneurs, both old and new. Between 1991–92 and 2011–02, gross fixed capital formation in the private sector more than doubled from 12.1 per cent to 24.7

per cent of the GDP, based on the Central Statistics Office's old series of national accounts statistics with 2004–05 as the base year. The same ratio, as per the new 2011–12 base national accounts series, peaked at 27 per cent in 2011–12. However, that year also marked the end of the post-liberalization investment boom, with the private sector gross fixed capital formation-to-GDP ratio declining steadily to reach 21.4 per cent by 2016–17.[12]

Like all booms built on the back of excessive risk-taking and debt pileup, this one, too, has left behind a trail of destruction. Its obvious manifestation has been the collapse of corporates that had taken on too much debt to implement capital-intensive projects, which either got grounded or failed to generate the anticipated cash flows. There are many such houses/companies, including those in this book, which have gone belly-up or been reduced to a pale shadow of their past. And they cut across communities: Essar, Videocon, Bhushan, Ruchi Soya, Alok Industries, Monnet Ispat, Electrosteel, Braj Binani, JBF Industries, Usha Martin and Bajaj Hindusthan (all non-Gujarati Bania/Marwari); Hindustan Construction, Gitanjali Gems and Su-Raj/Winsome Diamonds (Gujarati Bania/Jain); Jaypee, UB, GTL Infrastructure and Orchid Chemicals (Brahmin); Unitech (Sindhi); Ballarpur Industries, Amtek Auto, Moser Baer, Samtel, Punj Lloyd and Uttam Galva Steels (Khatri/Arora); Lanco Infratech, Soma Enterprise, Madhucon, Progressive Constructions, Transstroy India and Sujana Group (Kamma); GVK, IVRCL and Ramky Infrastructure (Reddy); Nagarjuna Group (Raju); GMR (Komati); Era Infra Engineering (Gujjar); Suzlon and Patel Engineering (Patidar); Shree Renuka Sugars (Vaishya Vani); and many more.

Capital destruction at the end of a two-decade-long expansion cycle is only one part, though. Of equal, if not more, interest to us is the supply of 'new capitalists' – there have been far fewer of them in this decade compared to the preceding two. The ones readily identifiable, whose growth is largely a phenomenon of the last ten years, are: Acharya Balkrishna (and Baba Ramdev) of Patanjali Ayurved, Sachin and Binny Bansal of Flipkart, Vijay Shekhar Sharma of Paytm, Kunal Bahl of Snapdeal, Bhavish Aggarwal of Ola Cabs, Naveen Tewari of InMobi, Hari Menon of BigBasket, Deepinder Goyal of Zomato, Ritesh Agarwal of OYO Rooms, Chandra Shekhar Ghosh of Bandhan Bank and Manish Sabharwal of TeamLease Services.

Two things are worth noting about these companies. The first is that they are – with the exception of Patanjali (FMCG), Bandhan (banking) and TeamLease (human resources outsourcing) – confined to a narrow business segment of e-commerce or mobile-enabled services. Secondly, their promoters are all Upper Caste Hindu: Bania/Marwari (Flipkart, Ola, Zomato and OYO), Brahmin (Patanjali, Paytm and InMobi), Khatri (Snapdeal and TeamLease), Nair (BigBasket) and Bengali Kayastha (Bandhan).

The period between 1991 and 2011, in hindsight, was a phase that can be described as coming closest to being synonymous with free-market entrepreneurial capitalism. The lifting of entry barriers and opening up of a host of industries for private-sector participation basically allowed new players to come in. They were from diverse ethnic and community backgrounds, which was, no doubt, helped by the fact that liberalization also coincided with coalition governments and regional parties taking over the reins both at the Centre and in states. The new entrants included regional capitalists who had invested in provincial parties and politicians. Those very connections could now be leveraged, especially when many of the industries being opened up were new – telecom, aviation, power, highways, ports, mines, etc. – and afforded opportunities for capital accumulation, non-existent in the earlier centralized Licence Raj. The new capitalists opened their own channels to the state for land acquisition, obtaining environment clearances and construction permits, securing concessions/leases and bank loans, and bagging public contracts – areas where the scope for patronage and executive discretion has hardly reduced even with liberalization.[13]

But cut to the present. What we are witnessing is more and more sectors being taken over by fewer and bigger players. This process of consolidation isn't limited to telecom, aviation, steel, cement, aluminium, FMCG, consumer electronics and electricals, synthetic fibres, polymers and such 'mature' industries. It extends even to 'start-up' sectors like online retail. Flipkart, for instance, was founded in 2007. Between 2014 and 2016, it acquired two other e-commerce companies, Myntra and Jabong, before itself being bought over two years later by the US retail giant Walmart. China's Alibaba Group is, similarly, the biggest shareholder in Paytm and BigBasket, which were both started between 2010 and 2011. Industrial consolidation is gaining further momentum via 'insolvency resolutions'– banks taking debt-laden companies to court and initiating recovery by sale of their underlying assets to new promoter-investors. In 2018 alone, we have had many such bankruptcy resolutions through acquisitions: Monnet Ispat by JSW Steel, Electrosteel by Vedanta, Bhushan Steel and Usha Martin by Tata Steel, Alok Industries by Reliance, and Ruchi Soya by Adani Wilmar.

In the pre-liberalization era, entry barriers mainly took the form of licence permits and helped perpetuate the dominance of entrenched 'Big Bania' capital. In the new post-GST/IBC (Goods and Services Tax/Insolvency and Bankruptcy Code) order, it is simply market-led consolidation that's going to be a deterrent for new entrants, as the higher investment requirements in mature industries makes it all the more difficult for them to put in the matching promoters' equity. The old model of fund-raising – selling land, pawning the wife's jewellery or borrowing from relatives, friends and clansmen – will not work, when projects are turning increasingly capital-intensive and demand deeper pockets. The loss of flexibility that small businesses had by dealing in cash and not paying full taxes – not possible any longer with GST, which leaves a paper trail for the authorities to track any evasion – would only accelerate the movement towards industrial concentration and market dominance by large firms. Rules-based, tax-compliant capitalism may well end up favouring Big Capital, while foreclosing accumulation possibilities for Small Capital and the prospect of becoming big down the line.[14]

Related to the above is a last point – about politics and 'crony capitalism'. There's nothing new per se to the intermeshing of business interests and politics. This is more so in a competitive democracy like India, where every party/politician may have a chosen set of businessmen for bestowing favours and receiving funding in turn. The appeal of coalition politics and growth of regional parties lay in the fact that it opened up avenues for the emergence of new 'crony capitalists'. To that extent, it translated into a capitalism fairly dynamic and socially diverse, even if crony.

The rise to power of a national party with a monolithic leadership such as the BJP, both at the Centre and most states, naturally begs the question: What does it hold for the future of capitalist enterprise in India? There has been lot of criticism over the Narendra Modi government promoting 'crony capitalism' and being, in the words of Congress President Rahul Gandhi, a 'suit-boot *ki sarkar*'. The real danger of crony capitalism, though, may be when the 'cronies' remain the same and there is no frequent shuffling of their ranks as before. 'Big' becoming bigger and 'Small' not being able to grow is what one needs to be most concerned about today.

Notes

1. Harish Damodaran, 'From Creation to Destruction of Capital' in Niraja Gopal Jayal (edited), *Re-Forming India: The Nation Today*, Gurgaon: Penguin Random House India (2019 forthcoming).
2. Vivekanand was Congress Member of Parliament from Peddapalli (Andhra Pradesh) in 2009-14. This constituency (now in Telangana) was represented earlier by his father. Vivekanand lost in the 2014 Lok Sabha polls and subsequently joined the ruling Telangana Rashtra Samithi.
3. www.steelmont.co.uk and www.steelmont.de (downloaded on 8 September 2018). Also, Prerna Katiyar, 'SteelMont's Rajesh Saraiya to set up cooperative unit in food processing industry', *Economic Times*, 14 August 2016; Aditi Phadnis, 'Dalit Padma Shri winners walk down memory lane', *Business Standard*, 1 April 2014; and Swaminathan S. Anklesaria Aiyar, 'Capitalism's Assault on the Indian Caste System: How Economic Liberalization Spawned Low-Caste Dalit Millionaires', *Policy Analysis*, 21 July 2015, Number 776, Cato Institute.
4. Kruttika Nadig, 'Ashok Khade: Man who built most sought-after offshore fabrication company DAS Offshore', *Economic Times*, 26 July 2011.
5. Naren Karunakaran, 'Bhagwan Gawai: From slum boy to millionaire, a true global citizen', *Economic Times*, 24 July 2011. Gawai and Khade are, interestingly, co-promoters of a separate Abu Dhabi-registered company called DASOFF Petroleum Services LLC, which seems to be largely an operational arm of DAS Offshore Engineering in the West Asian region (http://www.dasoffpetroleum.com/index.html, downloaded on 10 September, 2018). Gawai and Khade are also among the 21 businessmen profiled in Devesh Kapur, D. Shyam Babu and Chandra Bhan Prasad, *Defying the Odds: The Rise of Dalit Entrepreneurs*, New Delhi: Random House India, 2014.
6. Bhima Jewellers, named after its founder Bhima Bhattar, is another example of a migrant Brahmin business family of Kerala. They are Alappuzha (Alleppey)-settled Madhwa or Shivalli Brahmins, with roots in Udupi, Karnataka.

7. Prafulla Marapakwar, 'Infra company rose when Nitin Gadkari was in power', *The Times of India*, 25 October 2012 and Cuckoo Paul, 'Not So Ideal Road Builders', *India Forbes*, 24 October 2012. The Mhaiskars are Chitpavan, while Gadkari is a Deshastha Brahmin.
8. The emergence of 'Kathiawaris' (as Saurashtra Patidars are often called) and the weakening of the Palalpuri Jain hold over the Indian diamond industry is well captured by Kaivan Munshi, 'From Farming to International Business: The Social Auspices of Entrepreneurship in a Growing Economy', NBER Working Paper No. 13065, National Bureau of Economic Research, Cambridge, MA (April 2007). Also, Summit Khanna, 'After years, Kathiawaris outshine Palanpuris in India diamond biz', *Daily News and Analysis*, 18 March 2008.
9. I have dwelt a little on this subject in Harish Damodaran, 'How Tamil Nadu's rural industry model can keep farm unrest at bay', *The Indian Express*, 27 September 2016.
10. Kaikolar or Sengunthar Mudaliars are a community of weavers, to which the former Tamil Nadu chief minister and Dravida Munnetra Kazhagam party founder C.N. Annadurai also belonged. Siddhartha, incidentally, is also the son-in-law of former Karnataka chief minister and union minister for external affairs S.M. Krishna.
11. For the full list, see https://www.forbes.com/billionaires/list/#version:static_country:India (downloaded on 14 September 2018). The 12 Brahmins include Acharya Balkrishna (Patanjali Ayurved), Kiran Mazumdar-Shaw (Biocon), four Infosys promoters (N.R. Narayana Murthy, Nandan Nilekani, Kris Gopalakrishnan and K. Dinesh), Arvind Tiku (AT Holdings), Ranjan Pai (Manipal Group), Vijay Shekhar Sharma (Paytm), T.S. Kalyanaraman (Kalyan Jewellers), Dinesh Nandwana (Vakrangee Ltd) and Sheela Gautam (Sheela Foam), while the 3 Bhumihars are Mahendra Prasad (Aristo Pharmaceuticals) and Basudeo Narain Singh and Samprada Singh of Alkem Laboratories. The 12 Khatris/Aroras are Rahul & Kapil Bhatia (IndiGo), Pawan Munjal (Hero), Kuldip & Gurbachan Singh Dhingra (Berger Paints), Vikas Oberoi (Oberoi Realty), the promoters of Dabur (Vivek Chand, Anand and Amit Burman), Ramesh Juneja (Mankind Pharma), Anand Mahindra (Mahindra Group), Rana Kapoor and Madhu Kapur (Yes Bank), and Analjit Singh (Max

Group). The five Muslims, three Christians and four Patidars are Azim Premji (Wipro), M.A. Yusuff Ali (LuLu Group), Yusuf Hamied (Cipla), Habil Khorakiwala (Wockhardt) and Shamsheer Vayalil (VPS Healthcare); Sunny Varkey (GEMS Education), Joy Alukkas (Joyalukkas India) and Kochouseph Chittilappilly (V-Guard Industries); and Pankaj Patel (Cadila Healthcare), Karsanbhai Patel (Nirma), Achal Bakeri (Symphony Ltd) and Chirayu Amin (Alembic Pharmaceuticals), respectively. The rest comprise Kushal Pal Singh of DLF and Sameer Gehlaut of Indiabulls (Jats), Shiv Nadar of HCL and R.G. Chandramogan of Hatsun Agro Product (Nadars), Ravi Pillai of RP Group (Nair), Ravindra Kishore Sinha of Security & Intelligence Services (Kayastha), B.R. Shetty of NMC Healthcare (Bunt), Leena Gandhi Tewari of USV Private Ltd (Vaishya Vani), Baba Kalyani of Bharat Forge (Lingayat), Murali Divi of Divi's Laboratories (Kamma), P.V. Ramprasad Reddy of Aurobindo Pharma (Reddy), Harindarpal Singh Banga of Noble Group (Saini), S.D. Shibulal of Infosys (Ezhava), Ajay Kalsi of Indus Gas (Ramgarhia) and Kalanithi Maran of Sun Network (Isai Vellalar).

12. I have elaborated more on this in Damodaran 2019 (Note 1).
13. On this, see Kanchan Chandra, 'The New Indian State: The Relocation of Patronage in the Post-Liberalisation Economy', *Economic & Political Weekly*, Vol. L No. 14, 10 October 2015, pp. 46–58.
14. On the impact of GST on Small Capital, see Harish Damodaran, 'Losing the middle', *The Indian Express*, 22 July 2017.

Acknowledgements

This book is the product of a generous fellowship grant that I received from the New India Foundation, Bangalore, in late 2004. I am grateful to the foundation's trustees, especially Ramachandra Guha and Nandan Nilekani, for backing an academic greenhorn who had done very little outside of journalistic writing at that point in time. I feel even more indebted about 14 years later now, when the foundation – including its new trustees, Manish Sabharwal and Srinath Raghavan – considered this book worthy of re-publication with a new preface incorporating more recent developments and fresh insights, if any.

I would like to also specifically thank Rukun Advani and Anuradha Roy of Permanent Black, my original publisher, and Poulomi Chatterjee and Ansila Thomas of Hachette India, who have taken pains to bring out this new edition of *India's New Capitalists*.

Foreword

Post-Independence India has had a complicated and often tense relationship with its entrepreneurs. Only in the last two and a half decades has India's business community begun to recover from an image whiplashed, tarred and feathered by the whimsy of politicians. At the time of Independence the Indian government sought to throw the baby out with the bathwater: the forces of imperialism and capitalism were seen as inextricably linked, and entrepreneurship dismissed as a dangerous disease which worked to the detriment of the common people. The young nation sought its economic roots in so-cialism, whereby the state would hold the commanding heights of the economy and business was relegated to a relatively minor role.

For India in the 1950s this new system was an important part in the casting off of colonial chains, a spirited response, in Nehru's words, to the 'cut-throat civilization of the West'. With its promise of addressing inequality, the state-regulated economy of socialism also seemed parti-cularly suited to India, a country made up of starving masses substantially under the thumb of zamindars and princes. The necessity of providing a dominant role for a state that promised benevolence and paternal government was consequently in the nature of a national belief. It was a belief shared by India's businessmen, as evident from the Bombay Plan which was formulated as early as 1944.

But in the decades that followed – bleak in both economic growth and poverty alleviation – the notion that governments can achieve economic goals better than businesses turned out to be more myth, less truth. And, despite India's focus on creating a casteless society, the Indian state had scarcely understood the role that business can play in enabling and nurturing such a society. There is an old Roman saying to the effect that private capital 'has no smell'; in a free market, success-ful investment is untainted by ideology, caste, and even family loyal-ties, and is a strong driver of secular growth.

Despite this inherent liberating potential of business, the mixed economy pursued by Nehru lurched even further leftwards in the 1960s, and then in the same direction with Indira Gandhi and her various populist policies. The excessive policy controls that were put in place over this period rapidly led to the misdirection of entrepre-neurship. The capitalist's access to political power and the goodwill of ministers for the cornering of licenses required to conduct business became far more important than organizational efficiency and customer satisfaction. Indian business had to wait until the 1980s to see the emergence of pro-business policies by the state. The financial crisis of 1991 led to the emergence of pro-competition annual budgets and policies, and the first decade of the twenty-first century saw Indian business becoming truly global.

During the travails of these decades, India's business communities, even when suppressed and undervalued, played an important role in preserving and nurturing the country's entrepreneurial traditions. In this sense, Harish Damodaran's book is a very important contribution to understanding the development of entrepreneurs in independent India, and I am particularly pleased that it has emerged from a New India Foundation Fellowship.

As Damodaran has shown so well, business in India has grown today to being no longer limited to a few castes or families. While busi-ness was an occupational silo in the caste system, over the years more and more caste groups got into business, moving away from their traditional occupations. This trend became more prevalent with the liberalization of the economy after 1991, which opened the floodgates for new entrepreneurs; and with the rise of the knowledge-based economy, which brought in a whole new breed of businessmen from a variety of backgrounds and mindsets.

In an immature market economy, being part of a business family or a business community remained a key source of competitive advantage. It provided access to capital, and it caused trusted family members to be seen as a source of management talent as well as of market and tech-nical knowledge within an industry. This is evident, for example, among the Gounders of Tirupur in the knitwear business, and in the Palanpur Jains who run the diamond business. In addition, if buyers and sellers were from the same community, it created an environment of trust which lowered transaction costs and time.

This dynamic of family-run businesses was turned on its head by the 1991 reforms. These, apart from generally creating an environment that supported business and competition, also led to the creation of a more mature market infrastructure. The abolition of wealth tax on productive assets in the 1991 budget removed the incentive to hide assets and led to the rapid growth of wealth in stocks. The remarkable modernization of the Indian stock markets through the rise of the National Stock Exchange and the National Stock Depository Limited (NSDL), which created the platform for paperless trading, led to a single efficient national market for both raisers of capital as well as in-vestors. The arrival of Foreign Institutional Investors (FIIs) in the early 1990s led to a new source of capital for companies to raise money. The demand of the new investors for greater transparency, along with the efforts of the stock exchange regulator SEBI and the voluntary actions of leading companies, led to a rapid improvement in corporate govern-ance standards. In the meantime, as banks took to computerization and automation, the individual retail investor got easy access to stock markets through online retail trading applications.

In this environment, kinship and family ties became greatly reduced factors as the keys to a market. The need for informal family- and com-munity-based capital were reduced with the rise of various forms of early financing such as angel funding, venture capital, and private equ-ity. The culture of a father figure who managed and directed business practices has in fact now been replaced with a wide pool of professional managerial talent emerging out of India's management institutions, and these MBAs have been exposed to the global management prac-tices of MNCs and international business houses.

The improvement in access, an effective regulatory environment, and the capabilities of a modern market economy have greatly lower-ed the barriers of entry into business, as well as created the space for a whole new set of entrepreneurs from both traditional and non-traditional backgrounds. The market has in short been opened up to anyone with the talent and energy to take advantage of it. And existing business houses based within traditional communities have had to adapt in order to make the necessary transition from a 'community bazaar' to a modern global and structured marketplace. This has only served to increase the diversity and depth of India's business ethos.

This changing depth, this new diversity among India's capitalists, are features which Damodaran's book has captured quite exceptional-ly well. His work shows us what is now a crucially important part of India's social capital. As India relies more and more on its entrepreneurs to invest in infrastructure, create jobs, and globalize operations, they will occupy an increasingly critical role in the development of the Indian nation. Their diversity and numbers are the best bulwark against the capture of the state by a few big businesses; this massively enhanced collectivity is essential for the elimination of crony capitalism.

Damodaran's book also makes a seminal contribution to understand-ing the link between diverse entrepreneurial capital and the development of societies. The relative absence of entrepreneurs from non-business backgrounds in North India, as well as the non-existence of Dalit en-trepreneurs nationwide, is a very penetrating piece of analysis. For all of us who are concerned with enabling a more equitable society and broad-based growth, addressing such lacunae is probably more impor-tant than all the other measures and public policies being contemplated. Economic freedom is essential for people to experience larger free-doms – for it is the dynamism that is generated when people leverage economic opportunity, and when they fight in a fair competitive market, which breaks down hierarchies and creates inclusive systems.

Harish Damodaran's book succinctly and beautifully captures this transformation, as well as the wide-ranging impact of India's business community on the subcontinent's society and state. It is a work that should be read by all those who wish to understand the evolution of Indian business, and what it portends for the future of South Asia.

NANDAN NILEKANI

Series Editors' Preface to the First Edition

Our aim in 'The Indian Century' is to publish works of impeccable research that are not narrow or monographic and which illuminate, in some large and broad way, the historical shifts in modern India's economy, polity, society, and culture.

Through the twentieth century and beyond, four profound transformations have worked their way across the land and people of India. In the economic realm, India is moving from a near-total dependence on agriculture to an increasing reliance on industry and services. In the realm of politics, India has gone from being a colony of the British to becoming a sovereign nation. Sociologically speaking, India no longer 'lives in her villages' (as Mahatma Gandhi said it did); more and more Indians now base themselves in cities and towns. And in the domain of culture, India is changing from a society based on feudal, hierarchical values to a society that more fully reflects the ambitions and aspirations of modern, participatory democracy.

To be sure, none of these transformations are thoroughgoing.

Many Indians still live in the villages, live off the land, and are deferential to those they consider their social superiors. Nor are any of these transformations smooth – on the contrary, they have given rise to a series of social conflicts that can sometimes be productive and necessary, and which at other times exact a heavy human cost. But however halting, conflict-ridden, and uncertain, it is the simultaneous convergence of these four transformations, in this large and diverse country, that makes India such a compelling place to live in and write about.

The first books in our series presented original and provocative interpretations of the life and legacy of two most remarkable and influential Indians – Gandhi and Ambedkar – by distinguished senior scholars who had an impressive list of publications behind them. Our next offering is a first book by a gifted younger scholar, and with it our series extends from biography to encompass social history. In *India's New Capitalists* Harish Damodaran presents a richly insightful analysis of the deepening of India's business class in recent decades. The study of Indian business history has typically focused on the colonial period, and on the role played by traditional mercantile communities such as the Parsis and the Marwaris. While hagiographic works on entrepreneurs abound, *India's New Capitalists* is the first serious study of Indian business in the period since Independence. Damodaran's book is pioneering in a second respect as well: it explores the transformation of the Indian entrepreneurial class through the entry into it of large numbers of farmers-turned-capitalists.

Harish Damodaran is a journalist with many years of experience in one of India's premier business newspapers. His professional background is manifest in this book – the close attention to detail, to 'thick description', and in the directness and lucidity of his prose. But *India's New Capitalists* is astonishingly better than the work of the standard Indian journalist. It is rigorously researched, based on a wide range of published and unpublished materials, and on many interviews. And it displays a keen sociological sensibility. As Damodaran demonstrates, the success of these farmer-capitalists in the thrusting modern world of industry was made possible only through the skilful use of premodern networks of kin and caste.

Damodaran's fine study greatly enhances our understanding of the social bases of Indian business, while drawing out the political and social implications of the entry into the entrepreneurial class of castes and communities previously excluded. As India's growing economic vigour excites ever greater global attention, this book will, we believe, be a continuous reference point for later studies.

We are delighted to publish it in this series of books on 'The Indian Century'.

RAMACHANDRA GUHA AND
SUNIL KHILNANI

1

Introduction

There is a substantial literature analysing the evolution of business enterprise in India with reference to particular communities and castes. Organized research in this direction is traceable to Dhananjaya Ramchandra Gadgil's two oft-cited mimeographs of the 1950s and an article by Helen B. Lamb during the same decade.[1] These preliminary inquiries led to more comprehensive studies, including Dwijendra Tripathi's edited volume emanating from a business history seminar at the Indian Institute of Management, Ahmedabad, in 1982, and Thomas Timberg's treatise on the industrial transition of the Marwaris.[2]

The interest in exploring business communities has an obvious connection with the belief that economic behaviour is embedded in concrete social relations, wherein actors are seldom atomized individuals or anonymous buyers and sellers with no past record of interaction. Even the most rational and self-seeking businessman prefers to transact with those whom he knows either directly or through existing contacts. That does not rule out impersonal exchange but merely emphasizes the proclivity of people to exercise discrimination when choosing trading partners and not to transact randomly. Dealing with known parties drawn from existing networks of kin, extended families, fellow ethnics, and friends makes it seem relatively possible to avoid breach of contract – via invoking damage to one's reputation within the social circle. Such self-monitoring extra-legal networks are seen as alternatives to contract law in 'generating trust and discouraging malfeasance'.[3] Appealing to reputation entails lower transaction costs than getting embroiled in legal battles with unknown parties.[4]

In the Indian case, the above tendency has manifested itself in the association of business with distinct communities, and capitalism developing correspondingly through a number of business communities rather than an integrated business class.[5] Part of this association, no doubt, is also rooted in religious sanction, by which trading and banking functions were assigned to certain Vaishya castes in the Hindu chatur-varna (four-order) hierarchy. Moreover, business was not considered a particularly honourable vocation. The Vaishya held a higher position than the Shudra (peasant and manual labourer), but was vastly inferior to the Brahmin (priest) and the Kshatriya (warrior). Kautilya's *Arthashastra* indeed derided merchants as 'thieves, in effect, if not in name' and prone to 'harassing the people'. Accordingly, it laid down an elaborate structure of fines for traders resorting to fraud in weights and measures, adulteration, hoarding, cartelisation, charging higher-than-authorized prices, and earning profit margins in excess of 5 per cent.[6]

But such injunctions provide only partial explanation for the evolution of businesses on community lines. There is enough historical material to show that prescriptive codes regulating occupational choices were not always rigidly enforced and, by the seventeenth and eighteenth centuries, business was no longer frowned upon even by Brahmins.[7] Economic stimuli resulting from colonial rule and the opening up of avenues for material reward outside the traditional occupational mould gave impetus to this process. That still did not mean anyone could elevate himself into an entrepreneur: the hereditary mercantile order continued to enjoy a head start because aspirant businessmen from these castes could leverage their existing connections to obtain credit and mobilize capital. These thick networks were also sources of information and markets for their products, besides providing implicit guarantees against trade default and opportunistic behaviour. Those outside such ethnically homogeneous resource groups faced higher transaction costs, although they too could develop similar trust-based arrangements and emerge as 'business communities' in due course.[8] Once a business had reached a certain threshold level, its locus of transactions invariably crossed ethnic boundaries. The firm would eventually corporatize itself or even become a publicly listed entity, formally subservient to company law and other modern secular instrumentalities. The business community would, nevertheless, endure and reproduce itself through the institutions of marriage and kinship.[9] These institutions would reinforce the tendency of class divisions to be articulated through traditional ethnic cleavages and businessmen being identified with particular communities, and vice versa.

The existing scholarship on business communities in India, though rich and insightful, suffers from three broad limitations. The first is lack of contemporary focus in much of the economic history writing, which tends to ignore the significant changes that have impacted upon the structure of Indian industry since Independence. Being stuck in the world of cotton textiles, jute, sugar, paper and iron and steel (that too only in so far as it relates to the Tatas or Martin Burn), the literature does not shed light on the extent to which the growth of sectors like chemicals, plastics, synthetic fibres, pharma, automobiles, consumer electronics, information technology (IT), telecom, media, entertainment and other services have transformed the overall business landscape.[10] Indeed, there is no single work that systematically classifies India's leading companies and conglomerates according to their community/caste origins and provides reasonably up-to-date information capturing the changed industrial profile in today's globalised scenario. In India, historians tend notoriously to shy away from developments after 1947.

The second major shortcoming of the extant research – of direct relevance to us – is its obsessive preoccupation with traditional merchant-banking communities: the Parsis, Gujarati Banias, Jains, Marwaris, Sindhis (Lohanas), Nattukottai Chettiars, Memons, Khojas, and Bohras.[11] This, in a way, reflects the old association of business with an exclusive Vaishya order. The inability to see beyond the Bania has its imprint in smash business histories,[12] self-image conjuring hagiographies in which 'no one drank, cursed, cheated or philandered... workers were all part of the family... everyone lived an abstemious vegetarian life, accumulating wealth only to give it away to temples, hospitals and schools'.[13] Occasionally, this perspective has found expression even in the popular musings of eminent scholars.[14] In the present book we shall consider entrepreneurial groups drawn from not just the old hereditary mercantile order but also from castes with no established pedigree or culture of trading. These new business communities include both those with agricultural and allied backgrounds (Kammas, Reddys, Rajus, Naidus, Gounders, Nadars, Ezhavas, Patidars, Marathas, Hindu and Sikh Jats, Yadavs, etc.) as well as the so-called scribal castes (Brahmins, Khatris, Kayasthas, and the Bengali bhadralok) that have historically dominated the bureaucracy and various white-collar professions. The large-scale entry of these sections into corporate boardrooms is basically a post-Independence phenomenon that has, for reasons earlier alluded to, not received adequate academic attention. No doubt there has been pretty extensive documentation on the rise of non-traditional business communities, especially of rural origins, in specific regional settings.[15] However, these scattered empirical studies have generally confined themselves to small-scale industrialists. The big picture, the pan-Indian perspective, has remained hazy.[16]

The third lacuna that this book will seek to address is the cursory treatment given, in most history writing, to southern India. This again has something to do with the colonial-period hangover: it is a fact that Madras pre-1947 was industrially not on par with Bombay, Bengal, or even Ahmedabad and Kanpur; and hence, perhaps less worthy of investigation. All the same, this has unwittingly contributed to a distorted view of a homogeneous 'South Indian' business class that is typically Tamil-speaking or Chettiar by caste.[17] Nothing can be further from this narrow 'Madrasi' stereotype. Industrialization in the South and the social base of its businessmen extended beyond Madras city and the Nattukottai Chettiars – for that matter, the powerful European agency houses of the Parrys, Binnys, Harveys or Arbuthnots – even prior to Independence.[18] The last fifty-odd years have seen an intensification of this trend, with Coimbatore and its surrounds becoming the country's pre-eminent light engineering, cotton textiles and knitwear centre, and Bangalore and Hyderabad emerging as topnotch IT and pharma destinations. The South, we shall see, has also exhibited greater dynamism with regard to the incorporation of new business communities and the creation of a more socially diverse and heterogeneous capitalist class.

Chapters 2 and 3 of this book will examine savarna (upper-caste) business communities. They include, on the one hand, the entrenched mercantile castes and, on the other, the Brahmins, Khatris, and other 'upstart' savarna elements whose engagement with business is fairly recent. If the industrial transition of the former corresponds to the familiar 'bazaar-to-factory' trajectory, the same may be labelled 'office-to-factory' in respect of the latter. The subsequent five chapters will focus on intermediate castes: the progressive peasantry and other 'rural middle class' strata, from which a new breed of businessmen have arisen, especially in post-Independence India. For a better understanding of their 'farm-to-factory' journey – which has not followed a uniform pattern across regions – we shall take up illustrative case studies to supplement the general analysis. Chapter 9 will look at minorities, while the last chapter is a summing-up exercise aimed at placing our findings upon a wider canvas.

A final comment: throughout this book the businessmen and companies referred to are mainly those with an annual turnover of Rs 100 crore or more. This minimum cutoff, not to be applied rigidly, makes us exclude small-scale enterprises – a seemingly arbitrary move in the light of our earlier observation that firms, on graduating to a certain size, do not restrict their dealings to just their fellow clansmen. In other words, the entrepreneurs under consideration, having transcended their primary caste loyalties, provide poor base material for studying business communities. But this line of reasoning is misplaced, simply because the big businessman today may not have been all that big at an earlier point in time. Moreover, during the incubation phase of his business, community connections would have played a vital role in securing him access to credit, raw materials, information, marketing channels, government contracts, and trading licences. The fact that he manages over a sustained period to outgrow these connections does not undermine the business community from which he emerged and which he outgrew. On the contrary, it is perhaps a measure of the strength or vitality of a business community to throw up entrepreneurs, who, after an initial grounding through kinship and caste backing, are able to operate independently of such thick networks.[19] Successful industrialists, in their turn, produce a demonstration effect and become role models for others within the community.

2

The Old Merchant Communities

Mandi House in Lutyens' Delhi is a converging point for dilettante artists, amorous poets, budding musicians, and radical playwrights: understandable, as the area is home to institutions like the National School of Drama, Kathak Kendra, Shri Ram Centre for Art and Culture, Sahitya Akademi, Sangeet Natak Akademi, and Triveni Kala Sangam. In this very high culture zone, standing out like clear soup in a grand Mughal banquet, is Federation House. Headquarters of the Federation of Indian Chambers of Commerce and Industry (FICCI), this sombre and stolid four-storeyed building epitomizes the country's old business establishment. As one ascends its narrow, neatly-tiled stairs leading to its offices and conference halls, there are black-and-white pictures of FICCI's presidents from 1927 onwards, down to the most recent incumbent. Their profile says it all: four out of every five are from traditional merchant communities.

When we say 'old' or 'traditional', the reference is to mainstream trading castes with a reasonably national, and sometimes limited overseas presence going back to at least the nineteenth century. Such castes include Gujarati Banias/Jains, Marwaris and other non-Gujarati Banias/Jains, Parsis, Nattukottai Chettiars, and the Lohanas and Bhatias of the Kutch–Kathiawar–Sindh belt. These are communities whose trading and banking networks have historically extended over widely dispersed territories beyond their home base, and this characteristic sets them apart from the Subarnabaniks and Sahas of Bengal, the Vanis of Maharashtra, the Komatis of Andhra, the Nadars of Tamil Nadu, the Syrian Christians of Kerala, and even the Punjabi Khatris and Aroras: people with operations localized in particular regions. The distinction is all the more stark in relation to the mass of peddlers, itinerant traders, cattle dealers, fishmongers, vegetable sellers, and wine distillers across the country. Some of the regional merchant groups – especially Khatris and, to a lesser extent, Nadars and Syrian Christians – have undoubtedly gone on to establish themselves on an all-India scale. But, as we shall see in the coming chapters, this is a phenomenon fairly recent from the historical standpoint.

The traditional business communities, on the other hand, form the crust of what is known in Marxian literature as the 'national bourgeoisie'. Through their long-distance networks of trade and finance, these groups have inherited over the ages a wondrous propensity to 'nestle everywhere, settle everywhere, establish connections everywhere'.[1] FICCI, in a sense, was the product of this pan-Indian capitalist class that developed a self-conscious, independent identity in the post-World War I period. Its main drivers were Ghanshyam Das (G.D.) Birla, a Marwari settled in Kolkata; Purshotamdas Thakurdas, a Gujarati Bania and Mumbai's leading cotton merchant; and Lala Shri Ram, a Punjabi Agarwal Bania heading the Delhi Cotton Mills (DCM) group. FICCI's first president, in 1927, Dinshaw Petit, was a Parsi textile tycoon of Mumbai, whose daughter, Ruttenbai, married the founder of Pakistan, Mohammad Ali Jinnah. Two other prominent figures in FICCI's formation were Kasturbhai Lalbhai, a Gujarati Jain representing Ahmedabad's mill owners, and M.C.T. Muthiah Chettiar, a Chennai-based banker who controlled the United India Life Assurance Company. When, on 7 December 1923, G.D. Birla wrote 'it would be a great glory to see merchants from all parts of India standing on one platform',[2] he was not simply drawing a blueprint for FICCI. He was also reflecting the aspirations of dominant trading communities to carve out an autonomous national space for capital accumulation, which the prevailing imperial framework denied. How this class achieved the objective, by closely liaising with the top leadership of the Indian National Congress and evolving a sophisticated and progressive anti-colonial stance without compromising its basic interests, is pretty well documented.[3]

Besides their spatially diversified trading and banking connections, the other distinguishing feature of the old merchant communities is the superior caste status enjoyed by them *vis-à-vis* multitudes of ritually less orthodox local peddlers and retailers. The principal element in them is united under a common Bania caste cluster owing allegiance to either the Jain or the Vaishnav faith of the early-sixteenth-century saint Vallabhacharya. To this cluster belong the Gujarati Banias/Jains, the Marwaris of Rajasthan, and the Agarwal and Vaish Banias of the main Hindi heartland covering Delhi–Haryana, the Upper Gangetic Plain, and Bundelkhand. The Banias, by common consent, are closest to the ideal type Vaishya (mercantile) order in the classical Hindu social hierarchy. There is no such consensus with regard to the Chettiars or the dominant Hindu business castes of Sindh–Kutch–Kathiawar, despite their adherence to strict religious and social practices. Part of this ambiguity derives from the imperfect articulation of the fourfold varna hierarchy in their regions: the absence of Rajputs and like castes with undisputed Kshatriya legacy has, by natural association, undermined the existence of a clearly defined Vaishya order. The confusion is perhaps reproduced when it comes to the Parsis or the great Muslim commercial communities of Sindh–Gujarat: the Memons, Khojas, and Bohras, who were originally converts from Lohanas and other Hindu trading castes. But the common thread through all these communities – Hindu, Parsi, or Muslim – is their rigid rules of marriage and commensality and conservative social values, whether manifested in vegetarianism or by their conspicuous endowments to charitable and religious institutions.[4]

The current chapter on the Vaishya communities includes their non-Bania extensions such as the Chettiars, Sindhis, and Parsis. The Memons, Khojas, and Bohras have, however, been left out: they feature in Chapter 9, which looks exclusively at minorities in Indian business. Finally, given the considerable literature on hereditary merchant communities, we shall limit ourselves to broad observations and to taking note of changes in the composition of Vaishya business houses over the past five decades: the fading away of the old heavyweights and the rise of new groups.

General Trajectories of the Traditional Merchant Communities

A key prerequisite for forging long-distance merchant networks and stimulating goods traffic from upcountry to the main marketing centres was a mechanism for remitting large sums of money to remote corners. The facilitating financial instrument here was the hundi, a centuries-old Bania innovation akin to a bill of exchange. A merchant from Vidarbha bringing raw cotton to Mumbai could, instead of taking payment in cash with attendant risks during transit, be issued a hundi of equivalent amount drawn by the buyer in his favour. The hundi entitled the seller to present it before the Mumbai buyer's agent or correspondent in Vidarbha and collect his money there. This system made it possible to transfer funds without having to physically carry money. While the hundi served initially as a pure remittance facility, over time it also graduated into a credit instrument. In this case, the holder, rather than waiting to present it before the drawer's agent, used the hundi to take a loan by transferring it through endorsement to the lender. The latter would extend the loan amount at a discount on the value of the hundi and subsequently encash the hundi at par. In short, the hundi, to use modern legal jargon, became a 'negotiable instrument'.

In Gujarat, Rajasthan, and the Hindi mainland, Banias controlled the levers of business at all levels: from the village shopkeeper-money-lender to the arhatia (commission agent) handling produce at the katcha (primary procurement) as well as pucca (wholesale brokerage) stages, and the shroffs and bankers who financed inland trade and discounted hundis. The integration tool for this vast bazaar network was the hundi. It was in fact the vital lubricant that greased the wheels of commerce and enabled the merchant castes to spread their tentacles on a national scale. Community links could be leveraged to open as many branches and offices as the number of sons, nephews, in-laws, and loyal clerks permitted. The entire system, including the issuance and encashing of hundis, worked on trust, which, in turn, drew on community resource connections extending from the rural arhatia to the big city merchant and financier. As the Banias broke fresh ground, they simultaneously advanced the economic frontier of the hundi.[5]

Related to the above process was the creation of a formidable merchant diaspora. The Marwaris are, as we noted, originally a group of Bania castes from Rajasthan where they, besides being involved in local trade and moneylending, acted as modis (army provision suppliers) and bankers for various Rajput princely regimes. As ration suppliers and paymasters of the army, they often accompanied troops on war missions, while lending against the security of land revenue or ijara (tax-farming) rights bought at a discount.[6] By the eighteenth century there were also Marwari banking firms outside Rajasthan, financing the numerous cash-strapped independent principalities that had arisen on the ruins of the Mughal empire. The most notable was the house of the Jagat Seths, whose members became bankers to the nawab of Bengal and were even given charge of the treasury and right to mint coins. The Pittys and Ganeriwalas similarly bankrolled the Nizam Asaf Jahi dynasty of Hyderabad in return for farming the revenue of Berar province. The firm of Gopaldas Manohardas enjoyed a like status *vis-à-vis* the maharaja of Benares, whose kingdom was a breakaway from Awadh. Once the English East India Company began making inroads, these merchant princes seamlessly switched sides: the perfidy of the Jagat Seths in Nawab Sirajuddaula's defeat by Robert Clive's men at the Battle of Plassey in 1757 is part of historical folklore.

The real impetus to Marwari out-migration on an organized scale came during British rule. At the turn of the nineteenth century there were many settlers in Delhi, in the grain markets of western Uttar Pradesh (UP) – Hapur, Khurja, and Hathras – and in the river ports of Farrukhabad, Mirzapur, Patna, and Bhagalpur along the Ganges. The commissioning of the rail line from Delhi to Kolkata in 1860 led to a further movement eastwards all the way to Bangladesh, and from there up the Brahmaputra valley into Assam and across the Bay of Bengal into Burma. Within this overall eastern direction, there were sideward forays into northern Bihar, Nepal, Jharkhand, Orissa, and the highlands of Jalpaiguri, Darjeeling, and Kalimpong. Another large migration stream was to Central India (particularly to the princely states of Gwalior, Bhopal, and Indore, and also Jabalpur and Chhatisgarh), Vidarbha (Nagpur), and the Maratha hinterland. Some of this spilt over to the Deccan – mainly Marathwada and Hyderabad city – before tailing off to a trickle at Madras and Mysore.[7]

By the middle of the nineteenth century a pan-Indian Marwari–Bania business community had truly come into being: a commercial resource group networked through the indigenous hundi as well as modern-day railway and telegraph infrastructure. Also, conditions were laid for the emergence of large multi-branch trading firms, such as Tarachand Ghanshyamdas of Kolkata, Sevaram Ramrikhdas of Mirzapur, Bansilal Abirchand of Nagpur, and Sevaram Khushalchand of Jabalpur. In 1868–72, Tarachand Ghanshyamdas had offices at the port cities of Kolkata and Mumbai, in the opium belt of Malwa (Mandsaur, Ratlam, Ujjain, and Indore), and at Amritsar in Punjab, not to speak of related entities or correspondents in other parts of the country. These 'great firms', as one writer called them, were magnets attracting fellow Rajasthani clansmen: many of today's famous Marwari industrial houses began as brokers, partners, and even clerks to them. G.D. Birla's grandfather, Shiv Narain, was a clerk in a Hyderabad firm where Tarachand Ghanshyamdas had a share. The grandfather of the steel tycoon L.N. Mittal too worked for this firm. Likewise Ramdutt Goenka – great-grandfather of the RPG group patriarch Rama Prasad Goenka – was Sevaram Ramrikhdas' chief clerk in Kolkata. Sevaram Ramrikhdas's division in 1847 resulted in independent firms at Kanpur, Mirzapur, Farrukhabad, and Kolkata. The Singhanias happen to be descendants of the Kanpur line.[8]

Wherever they settled, such Marwaris rose to be pre-eminent money-lenders and merchants, financing the growth of cash crops for the world market. Their peak migration to Central India during 1820–60 coincided with the zenith of the Malwa opium trade. With its decline from the latter half of the century, the community shifted to cotton, grains, and oilseeds. Indore became a leading Marwari money and commodity speculation centre. In eastern India the community's main business was providing intermediary services to British agency houses: using their extensive upcountry network to finance and forward raw produce for exports and redistribute imported products on behalf of these firms. The Marwaris owned the bulk of commission agencies in major upcountry raw jute markets like Sirajganj, Narainganj, Madaripur, and Goalundo (all now in Bangladesh), and in the terminal markets of Kolkata preceding the final stages of manufacture or export.[9] By 1900 half of the jute balers were Marwaris, as were those who captured the trade in imported cotton piece goods. Control over the hinterland supply chain helped the community cultivate close links with expatriate firms as their banians (guaranteed brokers). The Goenkas were banians to Ralli Brothers, Onkarnath Jatia to Andrew Yule, Surajmal Jhunjhunwala to Graham & Company, Lakshmi Narain Kanoria to McLeod & Company, Tarachand Ghanshyamdas to Shaw Wallace, and so on. When the British set up tea gardens in Assam after that region's incorporation into the empire in 1818, the Marwaris moved in there as well, opening stores and financing planters through hundis, and remitting money to and from Kolkata. They soon acquired a monopoly on trade in all products, barring tea (which, like coal and jute exports, remained an English preserve).[10]

However, the community which made the most out of colonial circumstances was the Parsis. Right from the late seventeenth century – when a majority of Parsis inhabited the Surat–Navsari stretch of southern Gujarat as agriculturists, artisans, small-time coastal traders and shipbuilders – they evolved a collaborative working relationship with the British, in which cultural factors played a considerable role. Being part of neither the Hindu nor Muslim mainstream, nursing no political ambition, and exposed to commercial influences because of their proximity to the ports of Bharuch, Surat, and Daman, the Parsis seemed ideal for recruitment as native brokers, agents, and shippers. One Rustam Manak Seth became not just broker, banker, and money-changer to the East India Company; in 1660 he was even dispatched to Delhi for making representations against the nawab of Surat. After the Maratha empire fell to the British in 1818, two Parsi brothers – Vicaji and Pestonji Meherji – were entrusted with farming the land and sea customs of Konkan, Pune, and Ahmednagar. Earlier, Dorabji Nanabhai, a middleman, was appointed as Mumbai's first patel (tax farmer), when the Portuguese ceded what was then a minor trading outpost to the Crown in 1655. Even more famous was Lowji Nusserwanji Wadia, a shipbuilder from Surat who, in 1735, was invited by the Company to Mumbai to set up a dock at Mazagaon. Between 1735 and 1913 some seven generations of Wadias built over 400 ships at the Mazagaon and Bombay dockyards.

So intimately was Mumbai's growth tied to Parsi migration – almost as part of a deliberate settlement policy – that by 1800 the community owned half of the city and was even renting out properties to Europeans. Again, when the Company prised open the Chinese market for opium and cotton – to pay for its tea exported to Britain in a beneficial triangular trading arrangement – the Parsis gained enormously. A number of them were in fact imprisoned by the Chinese authorities during the Opium War of 1839–42: among them, Jamshedji Rustomji Irani, Dadabhai Rustomji Banaji, Hirjibhai Rustomji Patel, Nusserwanji Bomanji Mody, and Ardeshir Furdoonji Panday. Significantly, unlike the Marwaris operating between the interior and the ports, the Parsis were direct participants in the export trade as shippers of their own cargo as well as goods belonging to various British consignors. Jamsetjee Jejeebhoy used to send opium and cotton from Mumbai and Kolkata to Canton, export Chinese tea and silk from there to London, and re-route funds from China to India by importing textile and iron goods from Britain. In these he was almost an equal partner of Jardine Matheson, Canton's most powerful mercantile house. From Jejeebhoy (the first Indian to be conferred a baronetcy in 1857) to the Ready-moneys, the Kamas, the Petits, and the Tatas

– Parsis accumulated capital from trade with China. After Sindh's annexation in 1843 they also went to Karachi, initially as military contractors to the British, progressively becoming its dominant domestic trading community. The other symbol of Anglo-Parsi business collaboration was the joint-stock banks of the 1840s: Bank of Bombay, Bank of Western India, and Commercial Bank of India. Once again, the Parsis were active junior promoters in these ventures.[11]

As communities with a global reach, the Gujarati Vaishnav Banias/Jains, alongside the Lohanas and Bhatias, rank possibly higher than even the Parsis. With its long coastline and great ports – like Surat, Bharuch, Porbandar, Mandvi, and Diu – Gujarat has for centuries, had a vigorous maritime engagement across the Indian Ocean. The establishment of colonies by Gujarati Banias in the Red Sea ports of Mocha and Aden (Yemen), Berbera (Somalia), and Massawa (Eritrea) – later extending to the East African inland of Ethiopia, Tanzania, Uganda, and Kenya – predates British arrival. The Banias in Yemen were thought by locals to be unclean infidels and were not allowed to conduct religious rituals in public, being forced to bury (not cremate) their dead, and frequently overassessed at the customs. Yet, despite this second-class-citizen treatment, they controlled the commercial and financial life of the area.[12] Besides Surat (India's busiest port till well into the eighteenth century), Ahmedabad was Gujarat's other prominent commercial centre – stemming from its location on major routes connecting the port towns with the principal markets of the northern hinterland. In this city, too, business leadership was vested in the big Gujarati Bania/Jain merchants and pedhis (banking firms) such as Vakhatchand Khushalchand and Karamchand Premchand – respective forerunners to the Lalbhai and Sarabhai business houses. Mumbai's exceptional growth from the nineteenth century, both as a port city as well as a financial metropolis, lured many Gujarati

Banias/Jains to follow the lead of the Parsis. They made a killing during the American Civil War of 1861, when a disruption in cotton supplies to Britain's textile mills caused a spiralling of global prices. The resultant boom in cotton exports brought substantial wealth into the city, fuelling all-round commodity, stock, and real estate speculation. Among those who amassed fortunes were Premchand Roychand, a Jain cotton, bullion, and stock trader of Surat origin. His myriad public floatations – from the Asiatic Banking Corporation to the Back Bay Reclamation Company for filling and developing land from Mumbai's foreshore – presaged the adventures of latter-day scamsters like Harshad Mehta and Ketan Parekh.[13] Even while entrenching themselves in the city's commodity and financial markets – the Bombay Stock Exchange was founded in 1875 – the Gujarati Banias/Jains did not cut off links with their home the way the Parsis did. On the contrary, as time went by, the Mumbai–Ahmedabad connection only became stronger.

The Lohanas and Bhatias include those native to Gujarat (more so Kutch) and also to the Sindh province of present-day Pakistan. The Kutchi Bhatias were largely traders operating out of Mandvi seaport, from where they spread out into the Persian Gulf and all along the Malabar coast up to Kerala. Khimji Ramdas, one of Oman's premier trading houses today, has its origins in 1870, when Ramdas Thackersey voyaged from Mandvi. From the early nineteenth century the Bhatias and Lohanas also began moving into Mumbai, establishing a stranglehold over the city's wholesale cotton and textile goods market. Like their Kutchi counterparts, the Bhatias from the town of Thatta in Lower Sindh had commercial colonies in Muscat and Bahrain, where they financed the lucrative trade in pearls. But the most ubiquitous of global businessmen have been the Hindu Lohanas of Shikarpur in Upper Sindh and Hyderabad in Lower Sindh. It is they who have come to be known the world over as 'Sindhi Hindus' or simply 'Sindhis'.

The Shikarpuri Lohanas gained prominence as financiers and tax-farmers to the Durrani empire that ruled Afghanistan between 1747 and 1823. The regime's collapse did not really affect the Shikarpuris, as they redeployed their funds to the caravan trade between northern India and Central Asia through Afghanistan. The whole organization and financing of the movement of silk from Bukhara (Uzbekistan) to India and loading indigo on return cargo was done through hundis circulating within the Shikarpuri network. By the 1870s, when the Uzbek khanates were firmly under Russian influence, the community's network encompassed most of Central Asia. They had also diversified into rural moneylending, borrowing from Russian banks at around 6 per cent and on-lending to peasants at 40 to 60 per cent. This suited the banks, as they were spared the trouble of directly dealing with countless small borrowers. Outside of Russian Central Asia, there were Shikarpuris at Sinkiang on Chinese Turkestan territory and in Bandar Abbas and Kerman province of southern Iran, where they were mainly agents for big British firms at Karachi and Mumbai. The Russian Revolution of 1917 resulted in an exodus of the community from Central Asia. A new Shikarpuri indigenous banking network was thereby created, extending from Karachi and Mumbai all the way to South India (under the appellation of 'Multanis') and Burma (where they specialized in re-discounting bills with banks in India).[14]

Even more spectacular has been the international diaspora of the Hyderabadi Lohanas, or 'Sindworkies', a name deriving from the local craft products of Sindh ('Sindwork') marketed by them. What began in the 1850s as peddling operations targeting a narrow European clientele in Mumbai expanded over the ensuing five decades into a worldwide oriental curios and silk textiles trading network. It coincided with an explosion in travel and tourism following the steamship revolution and the opening of the Suez and Panama canals. The Sindworkies basically followed the major maritime trade routes, setting up shop in all the ports of call for travellers: first Egypt (Cairo and Alexandria), and from there the Mediterranean (Malta, Algiers, Gibraltar, Canary Islands, Sicily, and Naples), Africa (Sierra Leone, Lagos, Durban, Mozambique, Harare), and Latin America (Rio de Janeiro, Buenos Aires, Chile, and Panama). Moreover, the sourcing base for silk and craft wares was no longer merely Sindh, but the entire subcontinent and the Far East, where community members opened branches in Singapore, Malaysia (Penang, Malacca), Indonesia (Surabaya, Medan), Philippines (Manila), China (Canton, Shanghai), Hong Kong and Japan (Kobe, Yokohama). In the process, the Sindworkies emerged as important conduits for marketing Japanese goods in the whole South East Asian region. For all their globally dispersed businesses, though, these networks were highly centralized at Hyderabad, and it was there that the yearly accounts of all branches were settled. The usual model was a contract between the principal 'capitalist partner' (shah) in Hyderabad and several 'working partners' *(gumasthas)* who sailed abroad to sell goods that were either supplied by the shah or bought with credit lines arranged by him. The principal firms regularly used the services of exchange banks, especially the Bank of Taiwan and the Hong Kong and Shanghai Bank for Far East operations, and Barclays Bank in Egypt and West Africa.[15]

While the Parsis had trading and financial wires running into China – just as the Gujarati merchants had in the Persian Gulf and the Red Sea, the Shikarpuris in Central Asia, and the Sindworkies in every conceivable port outside North America and mainland Europe – for the Nattukottai Chettiars the chief investment destination was South East Asia. Hailing from Chettinad, a cluster of 75-odd villages in Sivaganga district of Tamil Nadu, the community's forté was moneylending. From around the 1830s the Chettiars, whose operations till then were confined to the Madras Presidency, began increasingly exporting their capital to Ceylon, Burma, the Straits Settlement (Singapore, Malacca, and Penang), and Indo-China (Vietnam, Laos, and Cambodia). So prodigious was this phenomenon – more so in the latter half of the century – that, as per an official estimate for 1929–31, out of the total Rs 120 crore working funds of Chettiar banking firms, only a crore or so was deployed in Madras. The bulk was invested in Burma (Rs 75–80 crore), Malaya (Rs 25 crore), Ceylon (Rs 14 crore), and Indo-China (Rs 5 crore). Partly, this capital pullout reflected the lack of investment outlets in a region where organized industry and foreign trade were mostly in European hands. Neither were the Chettiars steeped in hinter-land trading the way the Marwaris were. Even in their specialized sphere of moneylending, they faced keen, if not threatening, competition from the Kallidaikuruchi Brahmins, the Marwaris, and later also the 'Multanis'. But more than 'push' factors, it was the 'pull' of financial opportunities in Ceylon and South East Asia – virgin areas opened up for colonial exploitation and the introduction of rice, tea, coffee, rubber, and other cash crops – that really induced the export of Chettiar capital. Between 1852–3 and 1932–3 the area under paddy in Lower Burma rose from 6 lakh acres to 97.11 lakh acres. Much of this was bankrolled by Chettiars, who directly or indirectly provided two-thirds of the crop loans at interest rates ranging from 18 to 45 per cent. In 1929 there were some 1650 Chettiar firms all over Burma, with their head offices or proprietors typically based in Chettinad. There was even a Burma Nattukottai Chettiar Association in Rangoon, affiliated to FICCI. Since they extended short-term credit to agriculturists against the security of the latter's crop, it also led to their trading in rice and establishing mills. Many Chettiar firms were involved in the export of Burmese rice and timber logs into South India. A more important consequence of their moneylending operations, however, was that the community ended up acquiring huge swathes of fertile land from defaulting cultivators. By 1936 they held a mindboggling 23.93 lakh acres or a quarter of the farm land in Burma's thirteen principal rice-growing districts![16] Among them was Raja Sir Annamalai Chettiar – he was made knight as well as christened 'Raja of Chettinad' – who alone owned 86,000 acres.[17]

Having built such formidable marketing and credit networks spanning the whole subcontinent and even overseas spaces, the logical next step for the merchant communities was to channellize some of their surpluses accumulated from trade into manufacturing. This happened as the opportunities arose. The initial leap was taken by the Parsis. Cowasji Nanabhai Davar, in 1854, became the first Indian to float a textile mill. Over the next two decades, Maneckji Nusserwanji Petit (grandfather of Dinshaw Petit), Nowrosjee Nusserwanji Wadia, and Jamsetji Nusserwanji Tata, too, had set up mills. The next lot of industrialists were the Kutchi Bhatias: Morarjee Gokuldas, Damodar Thackersey Mulji, Khatau Makanji, and Dwarkadas Vasanji had mills by 1880. They were followed by the Gujarati Banias/Jains, who – led by the Sarabhais, Lalbhais, and Mangaldas Girdhardas – were running a parallel textile complex in Ahmedabad at the turn of the century. Marwari entry into industry on a significant scale happened only after World War I.

There are reasons why merchant communities in western India took to industrialization earlier compared to their counterparts elsewhere. The first had to do with belated British imperial expansion. Unlike in Bengal or Madras – where annexation was complete in all respects by the late eighteenth century – the motley princely regimes of the western and central regions continued to retain a semblance of administrative autonomy, giving that extra leeway for independent businesses to thrive. The most stark example of this was the export of Malwa opium to China through Rajasthan, Sindh and Gujarat before final shipment from

Karachi and Daman – a trade outside Company jurisdiction that could not be stopped despite all efforts.[18] The second reason was specific to cotton textiles. Eastern India's big industries – jute, tea, and coal – were British controlled, with the first two mainly geared towards exports. The Marwari advantage in upcountry raw jute procurement was, thus, more than offset by the fact that the markets for burlap, hessian, and gunnies lay in Europe, America, and Australia. It was not so for cotton textiles, where not only did India produce a fifth of the world's fibre, but also a sizeable home market for coarse fabrics and yarn existed amongst its general population and mass of handloom weavers. Further, the mills in Mumbai began producing low-count yarn for the Chinese and Far East markets, where the Parsis particularly had already developed extensive connections.

Things changed radically with the War and the Depression that followed, both of which tilted the balance decisively against foreign trade. For the first time, production (in opposition to imports) for the domestic market (as against exports) became not simply feasible but a desir ed option.[19] G.D. Birla established cotton textile units in Delhi and Gwalior, while a fellow Marwari and speculator in opium and cotton, Sarupchand Hukumchand, started three mills in Indore. Kamlapat Singhania similarly launched mills in Kanpur and Lala Shri Ram's DCM rose to be the Delhi–Punjab region's premier textile concern. This was also the period when the traditional Bania communities showed a marked inclination to come out of the shadow of British capital. Even before the War, the Marwaris had taken over the trade in raw jute through indigenous futures and hedging contracts known as fatka. Wartime speculative profits and demand for sandbags impelled the Marwaris towards jute manufacture. In 1917, G.D. Birla led the charge into direct exports by opening an office in London, though he was barred entry into the jute exchange on racial grounds and had to engage

English brokers to trade on his behalf. By the 1920s the Birlas, Hukumchand, the Singhanias, and Surajmull Nagarmull had all founded new jute mills; the likes of Badridas Goenka, Magniram Bangur, and Baldeodas Bajoria went on to buy out British mills (for whom they were banians and financiers) by acquiring shares as collateral against loans and from the secondary market.[20]

Growing assertiveness and awareness of their collective self-interest – in 1930, G.D. Birla declared that Kolkata's Marwari dealers in Manchester piece-goods were willing to discard the trade and henceforth purchase the 'whole production' of Mumbai and Ahmedabad mills[21] – enabled the pan-Indian business communities to wrest concessions from the colonial government, including a policy of 'discriminating protection' around 1925. That, in turn, triggered their investments in new areas, especially paper (Birlas, Bajorias, Singhanias), sugar (Birlas, Surajmull Nagarmull, DCM), and cement (Bangurs). Also, a new set of entrepreneurs emerged. Ramakrishna Dalmia, a Marwari from Rohtak (Haryana), created a conglomerate, Rohtas Industries, producing sugar, cement, paper, vanaspati (hydrogenated vegetable oil), and spun pipes. Between 1948 and 1952 he built controlling stake through deft market manoeuvring in British concerns such as Bennet, Coleman & Co. (owners of the newspaper *Times of India*) and Govan Brothers (Dhrangadhra Chemical Works, Indian National Airways), and also Punjab National Bank and Bharat Insurance. Two other industrialists who came via sugar were Jamnalal Bajaj, a Marwari from Wardha, near Nagpur; and Gujar Mal Modi, a Punjabi Bania whose great-grandfather arranged army rations for the nawab of Jhajjar and later for the British forces stationed at Patiala. Meanwhile, the Tatas had gone way beyond textiles. Their steel plant at Jamshedpur went operational in 1911 and by the end of the War the Tata hydroelectric companies too were in place. The 1930s saw the float of Tata Airlines, followed by

Tata Chemicals and Tata Locomotives in the 1940s. The other highly diversified group was that of Walchand Hirachand Doshi, a Gujarati Jain settled in Solapur (Maharashtra), who started as a railways contractor and forayed into coastal shipping through the Scindia Steam Navigation Company in 1919. In the 1930s, he also got into sugar (Ravalgaon Sugar Farm), reinforced concrete pipes (Indian Hume Pipe Company), and engineering (Cooper Engineering). But Walchand's most ambitious projects came during World War II in sectors such as shipbuilding (Hindustan Shipyard), aircraft-making (Hindustan Aircraft), and cars (Premier Automobiles). While the first two – and also Tata Airlines – were eventually nationalized, they nonetheless revealed growing maturity and self-confidence among Indian capitalists and their readiness to negotiate more complex industries. The Singhanias' Aluminium Corporation of India, the Birlas' Hindustan Motors, and the DCM group's Jay Engineering Works ('Usha' sewing machines) were again pre-Independence initiatives.

The Nattukottai Chettiars and Sindhis, on the other hand, practically abstained from industrial activity in the pre-1947 era. Chettiar capital, as we have seen, was overwhelmingly deployed in financing (and later acquiring) paddy fields in Burma, rubber plantations in Malaya, and coconut estates in Ceylon. The high returns on these offered no compelling reason for repatriating capital to India. If at all investments took place, it was mainly in banking. Raja Sir Annamalai Chettiar, for example, promoted the Indian Bank and the Rangoon-headquartered Bank of Chettinad. Likewise, the M.C.T. Chettiar family controlled Indian Overseas Bank, with branches at Karaikudi (in Chettinad), Madras, Rangoon, and Penang, and the United India Life Assurance Company. It also had an industrial venture – Travancore Rayons at Perumbavoor (Kerala) – incorporated in 1946. The only other pre-Independence industrialists worth mention were A.M. Murugappa Chettiar and Karumuttu Thiagaraja Chettiar. The former, with money-lending, rice milling, and trading interests centred in Moulmein (Burma), set up Ajax Products in 1939 to make office and steel security equipment at Thiruvottriyur near Chennai. This was forty years after a Parsi lawyer, Ardeshir Burjorji Godrej, began manufacturing security locks and safes, and laid the foundation for the House of Godrej. Karumuttu Chettiar started a clutch of textile units from the late 1920s, including the Meenakshi Mills and Loyal Textile Mills, and also the Bank of Madura. Like the Chettiars, the Shikarpuri Lohanas remained confined to indigenous banking, even as their Sindwork brethren evolved into a niche global trading community, with big multi-branch 'mother firms' such as Pohoomull Brothers, Wassiamall Assomull, Dhanamal Chellaram, J.T. Chanrai and M. Dialdas & Sons. Sindhi movement into industry per se did not happen till the sub-continent's partition in 1947, which forced the community's *en masse* migration from Shikarpur and Hyderabad.

Post-Independence Trends

The post-1947 period has witnessed a tremendous churning within the traditional business communities. Among Parsis, the Tatas continue to be India's No. 1 conglomerate, with interests in steel, auto, power, information technology (IT), telecom, chemicals, engineering, tea, watches, and hotels.[22] The Godrejs have also expanded from locks and safes to furniture, consumer durables, soaps and personal products, food, oleo-chemicals, home insecticides, and animal feeds. The Wadias, with their flagship Bombay Dyeing & Manufacturing Company, are still around, even if not half as influential as the Tatas and the Godrejs. In terms of power, there are few Parsis who wield it more today than Pallonji Shapoorji Mistry. A construction tycoon whose father financed the great

Hindi film *Mughal-e-Azam*, Pallonji Mistry's empire spans textiles (Gokak Mills), shipping, water purifiers, vacuum cleaners (Eureka Forbes), and light engineering. His real claim to fame, though, is in being the single largest shareholder in Tata Sons. Not being a Tata (even if his son-in-law is one) and yet having 18.5 per cent in the holding company has lent a certain mystique to this man, described as the Phantom of Bombay House. The other major post-Independence Parsi entrepreneur has been Rohinton Aga, who set up a boiler-making venture, Thermax Ltd, in the late 1960s. It is now a leading engineering firm, specializing in boilers, heaters, absorption coolers, wastewater plants, and co-generation systems. A less-known Pune-based boiler manufacturing and process engineering concern is Darius Forbes' privately held Forbes Marshall. Even more recent is Piruz Khambata's Pioma Industries, which owns the popular soft-drink concentrate brand 'Rasna'.[23] But notwithstanding the growth of individual groups, old and some new, the Parsis as a business community have diminished in importance. What may earlier have been advantageous factors – Anglicization and overwhelming concentration in Mumbai – lost potency with the thrust of economic activity shifting from foreign trade to producing for the domestic market. As industrialization spread to new areas, the inability to strike deeper roots and being Mumbai-centric, turned out if anything to be liabilities. Inbreeding and low fertility rates have only compounded matters: between 1941 and 2001 the Parsi population has shrunk in absolute terms from 114,890 to 69,601.

A similar tale of decline has characterized the other community that pioneered Mumbai's textile industry: the Kutchi Bhatias. The lands where the Khataus, Thackerseys, and Morarjees once had mills presently sport newly developed shopping malls and multiplexes. Save the Great Eastern Shipping Company (India's largest private shipping concern), Varun Shipping Company, and Marico Limited (owners of 'Parachute' hair oil, 'Saffola' and 'Sweekar' edible oils, 'Mediker' anti-lice treatment, 'Sil' jams and 'Revive' fabric starch), there are not too many Bhatia industrial houses left. Great Eastern's founders – Maneklal Ujamshi Mulji and his brother Jagjivan – were textile traders and importers of Java sugar before they launched into shipping in 1948. Varun Shipping was promoted in 1971 by Dilip Dharamsey Khatau, who is the great-grandson of Khatau Makanji. Marico's origins go back to Kanji Moorarji, who went from Kutch to Mumbai, where he started trading in spices in the late 1850s. In 1935 his nephew, Vallabhdas Vasanji, installed a spices processing plant at Alappuzha (Kerala) and became a prominent exporter of black pepper, leading to the title of Mariwala ('pepper man' in Gujarati). From spices, the Mariwalas diversified into copra trading and vegetable oil refining by setting up Bombay Oil Industries in 1948. It is this company's consumer products division that, in 1990, became Marico.

The Gujarati-speaking Lohanas are another community with a sound base in commodities trading. Some of the oldest names in cotton exports – Suresh Kotak's Kotak & Company, Chandrasinh Mirani's Khimji Visram & Sons, and the Mulani family's Khimji Poonja – are Gujarati Lohanas. So are Jagjivandas Jamnadas Tanna of Jamnadas Madhavji International (a major in oilseeds, spices, and grains), and Narsibhai Thakrar of Tilda Riceland Limited, the world's biggest basmati rice exporter. Again, the Lohanas have not particularly made a dent outside trading, barring maybe Kotak Mahindra and the Somaiya group. The former, promoted by Suresh Kotak's son, Uday, is a leading financial intermediary with stakes in banking, stock brokerage, asset management, and insurance. The family of Karamshibhai Jethabhai Somaiya controls the Godavari Sugar Mills at Bagalkot in Karnataka.[24]

Even more pronounced has been the marginalization of the Chettiars, a community that once commanded capital on a scale comparable to even the Marwaris. As we have seen, the bulk of it was invested in South East Asia, which, in retrospect, proved to be their bane. The Japanese invasion of Burma during World War II and the growth of nationalistic fervour across the region hit the community hard. With a substantial portion of their wealth locked up in land and other immovable assets, the Chettiars – who, as perceived exploiters of the peasantry, were easy targets for the nationalists – had to flee with precious little to salvage. Today's big Chettiar houses – they give a misleading impression of the community's diminished might – are basically the few that managed to retain a domestic presence or began strategically moving back assets foreseeing the disaster that was waiting to strike. These include the Raja Sir and A.M. Murugappa Chettiar groups. Raja Sir's younger son, M.A. Chidambaram, started in the 1950s with a scooter factory in Mumbai (Automobile Products of India) and the South India Corporation Agencies Limited (Sical), which is now primarily into movement of bulk and containerized cargo. The group later forayed into fertilizers and chemicals through the Southern Petrochemical Industries Corporation (SPIC) and associate companies such as Tamilnadu Petroproducts and Tuticorin Alkali Chemicals & Fertilisers Limited. The Murugappas are an equally diversified conglomerate, with companies like Tube Investments of India ('BSA' and 'Hercules' bicycles), Carborundum Universal (abrasives and ceramics), EID Parry (sugar and sanitaryware), Coromandel Fertilisers, Godavari Fertilisers and Chemicals, and Cholamandalam DBS Finance Limited.[25] Karumuttu Thiagaraja Chettiar's once-huge textile empire has been divided among his descendants through two wives. The Loyal Textile Mills is managed by Manikam Ramaswami (Karumuttu Chettiar's grandson through his first wife), while Thiagarajar Mills and Paramount Textiles are with the branch of the founder's second wife, Radha. The latter's grandson, M. Thiagarajan, is the promoter of the recently launched

Paramount Airways. The only other significant Chettiar business entity is the film and television serial production house AVM Productions, established in the 1930s by A.V. Meiyappan.

The most dynamic elements of the old business class in post-Independent India have been the Marwaris (including other Hindi-speaking Banias), Gujarati Banias/Jains, and Sindhis, in that order. Let us first take the Sindhis, a community originating from Shikarpur and Hyderabad but with a functioning pan-Indian and global merchant network even prior to 1947. The Partition severed the community's umbilical cord with Sindh and provided the impetus for their permanent relocation, in which pre-existing diasporic connections played a facilitating part. Parmanand Deepchand Hinduja, a Shikarpuri, went to Mumbai in 1914 to trade in cotton. Five years later, scouting for buyers, he reached Iran and ended up having a permanent commodities trading and merchant banking base there. The post-1947 happenings ensured no looking back, and the Hindujas remained headquartered in Iran till the 1979 Islamic Revolution forced them out. The founder's two eldest sons, Shrichand and Gopichand, settled in London. The third, Prakash, moved to Geneva, where he set up a finance company that evolved into the AMAS Bank (Switzerland) Limited, with subsidiaries in the tax havens of Mauritius and the British Virgin Islands. Alongside, the family started investing its surpluses in industry. In 1984 they bought Gulf Oil from the US oil giant Chevron, and in 1987 the UK-based Land Rover Leyland International Holdings. The latter acquisition gave them control over Ashok Leyland – India's No. 2 commercial vehicles maker after Tata Motors – and its associate, Ennore Foundries. The subsequent decade saw the Hindujas furthering their Indian involvement – under the youngest brother, Ashok – in varied fields from lubricants and explosives (Gulf Oil Corporation) to banking (IndusInd Bank) and cable television networks and IT (Hinduja TMT).[26] Another overseas Sindhi businessman to have built substantial stakes in India was Manohar Rajaram Chhabria. A petty radio parts dealer in Mumbai, Chhabria migrated to Dubai and, in 1974, established Jumbo Electronics Company, which became one of the world's biggest distributors for the Japanese multinational Sony. In the mid-1980s he stormed the Indian corporate world by taking over a string of British expatriate-owned companies, including Shaw Wallace, Dunlop India, Mather & Platt, and Hindustan Dorr Oliver. But unlike the Hindujas, Chhabria's reign did not last beyond the century, as most of the concerns went sick or were further acquired by others.

There are besides a number of Sindhi diasporic business families whose operations are predominantly outside India. In this category are the Harilelas (who run a sprawling hotel and real estate empire in Hong Kong), the Lebanon-born Micky Jagtiani's Landmark group (which operates a huge retail chain across the Persian Gulf), the Madhvanis (Uganda's leading conglomerate, with interests in sugar, breweries and television), and the Chellarams, Vaswanis (Stallion group), Shivdasanis (Inlaks), and Chanrais of Nigeria.

While the Sindhis come closest to being an 'international bourgeoisie', there has been no dearth of enterprise in the community back home either. Prahlad and Kishan Chhabria's Finolex group (a major manufacturer of polyvinyl chloride pipes, resins, and cables), Mohan Advani's Blue Star Limited (India's No. 1 central airconditioning and commercial refrigeration company), and J.B. Advani's Ador Group (formerly Advani-Oerlikon, a leader in welding equipment and electrodes) were all founded in the 1940s by men originally from Karachi. A sector in which migrant Sindhis have made a mark is real estate. The Mumbai-based property firm K. Raheja was started in 1956 by Lachmandas Raheja and has since been carved up into separate entities under his sons – Chandru, Gopal, and Suresh. The biggest of them is K. Raheja Corp owned by Chandru Raheja, who is also the promoter of the retail chain Shopper's Stop Limited. His cousin, Rajan Beharilal Raheja – whose family too started with real estate – controls Exide Industries ('Exide' and 'Standard Furukawa' batteries), H&R Johnson (the market leader in ceramic tiles), Prism Cement, Hathway Cable & Datacom (one of the country's top cable television and broadband networks provider), and *Outlook* magazine. This bouquet makes him the most pre-eminent domestic Sindhi industrialist today. More recent entrants into the realty business comprise people with highly educated backgrounds. The Hiranandanis – Niranjan and Surendra – of Hiranandani Developers are the sons of a well-known Mumbai surgeon, Lakhumal Hiranand Hiranandani. Ramesh Chandra of Unitech Limited, a big-time realtor in the national capital region, is similarly a civil engineer from the Indian Institute of Technology, Delhi. His firm started in 1971 as a civil technical consultancy firm and eventually expanded into turnkey construction and property. Other relatively new Sindhi entrepreneurs include Gulu Mirchandani of Mirc Electronics ('Onida' televisions), Ramesh Chandra Mansukhani of Man Industries India Limited (a prominent manufacturer of aluminium extrusions and welded steel pipes used for transmission of oil and gas), and the Bangalore-based Hindujas of Gokaldas Exports. The last company is India's biggest readymade garments exporter, promoted in 1979 by Jhamandas Hinduja and now with his three sons, Madanlal, Rajendra, and Dinesh. Another son, Jagdish – adopted by Jhamandas' brother, Narayandas – has a parallel concern, Gokaldas Images, which owns the 'Weekender' apparel brand.[27]

As far as the Gujarati Banias/Jains go, many of Ahmedabad's old textile combines like the Sarabhais and Mangaldas Parekhs have practically ceased to exist. The only ones to have hung on are the Lalbhais, whose rise truly began with the three brothers – Kasturbhai, Chimanbhai, and Narottambhai – promoting Arvind

Mills in 1931. The group also got into manufacture of starch and dyestuffs through incorporation of Anil Starch Products in 1939 and Atul Limited in 1947, respectively. Arvind is now among the world's top three producers of denim, just as Atul has expanded into a range of agrochemicals, aromatics, pharmaceutical intermediates, and colours. But the Lalbhais no longer have the iconic status that they commanded in Kasturbhai's time. More marked has been the fall of the house of Walchand Hirachand, an economic nationalist far ahead of his times who dabbled in sugar, construction, engineering, shipyards, aircraft, and automobiles. The only significant remains from the empire he bequeathed to his brothers – Gulabchand, Lalchand, and Ratanchand – are Hindustan Construction Company (HCC), Walchandnagar Industries, and Indian Hume Pipe Company. The others are barely surviving (Premier Automobiles, Ravalgaon Sugar) or sick (Scindia Steam).[28]

The big Gujarati Bania/Jain conglomerates today are Reliance, Torrent, and Adani: products of the 1970s, 1980s and 1990s, respectively. A Bania from Junagadh, Dhirajlal Hirachand Ambani or simply 'Dhirubhai', worked as a salesman for a French firm, A. Besse & Co, at Aden in the 1950s and as a synthetic yarn trader in Mumbai till the 1960s, before entering textile manufacturing. From churning out the 'Vimal' brand of polyester fabrics, Dhirubhai's Reliance Industries Limited (RIL) undertook an unprecedented vertical integration exercise to first produce yarn, then fibre intermediates (paraxylene, purified terephthalic acid, mono-ethylene glycol) and polymers, all the way to petroleum refining, and oil and gas production and exploration. The Reliance group's activities presently span petrochemicals, oil, power, and telecommunications.[29] Torrent Pharmaceuticals Limited was founded by the Palanpur-born Uttambhai Mehta, a medical representative with the Swiss multinational Sandoz, who started a tiny unit making tranquillizers for psychiatric disorders in the early 1970s. After setting up his first major plant in 1980, Mehta, eight years later, took over an insulated power cable company (now Torrent Cables). The group's major foray into power came in the mid-1990s with the acquisition of Surat Electricity Company (SEC) and Ahmedabad Electricity Company (AEC): previously these were government-managed distribution utilities operating in the two cities. Equally sensational has been the rise of the Adani brothers, Gautam and Rajesh, who, after a stint at their family's textile trading business, launched a partnership firm in 1988. This firm, incorporated as Adani Exports Limited in 1993, has grown to be India's most prolific trader in commodities from agro-produce to coal, fertilizers, steel scrap, textiles, and petrochemicals. The group is also the promoter of the country's largest private port at Mundra in Kutch, and Adani Wilmar, which sells refined edible oil under the 'Fortune' label.[30]

In addition, we can single out several others who are leaders in their respective industries. They include Asian Paints (an 'Indian multi-national', controlled by the Choksi, Dani and Vakil families, that has bested the likes of ICI and Goodlass Nerolac), Balvantray Kalyanji Parekh's Pidilite Industries (manufacturer of adhesive brands like 'Fevicol', 'FeviKwik', 'Dr. Fixit' and 'M-Seal'), and the two agrochemicals majors United Phosphorus of Rajju Shroff and Excel group of Kantisen Chaturbhuj Shroff (the last two are cousins). All these companies are of the 1940s to early 1970s vintage. So are Chimanlal Mehta's Deepak Group (Deepak Fertilisers & Petrochemicals Corporation, Deepak Nitrite), Praful Shah's Garden Silk Mills (of 'Garden Vareli' polyester-nylon sarees and dress material), and Mansukhbhai Mahadevbhai Kothari's Kothari Products Limited, whose 'Pan Parag' created a new consumer category of pan masala (betel nut-based mouth freshener) sold in sachets. Still more recent are the success stories of entities that were insignificant, if not non-existent, till the 1990s: the commodities trader Vishal Exports Overseas of Subhashchandra Mehta, and stainless steel producer Shah Alloys Limited of Rajendra Vijaykumar Shah.[31]

An industry that Gujarati Banias/Jains – especially the Jains from Palanpur, bordering Rajasthan – have come to monopolize on a global scale is diamond trading, cutting, and polishing. The community's hold over Mumbai's Zaveri Bazaar – much like what the Mulji Jetha wholesale textile market was to the Kutchi Bhatias – goes back to the famous gold jewellery firm of Tribhovandas Bhimji Zaveri setting up shop in 1864. From around the late 1940s, some jewellers, like Shantilal Lallubhai Shah, turned their attention to diamonds, buying low-end roughs from London and Antwerp and getting them cut and polished by local master-craftsmen into marketable gems. In 1956 Kirtilal Manilal Mehta became the first Indian to have a diamond-trading house at Antwerp. That was the time when the government introduced a 'replenishment licence' scheme allowing import of rough diamonds at concessional duty, subject to their being polished for re-export. It spawned a multi-billion dollar export industry concentrated in Surat and developed by Palanpuri Jains, who deployed their community and kinship resources worldwide to secure control over the entire diamond pipeline. The website of Kirtilal Mehta's Gembel group claims that its late founder 'helped 1800 other Jains to set up their own ... diamond business in Antwerp'.[32] In 1974 Shantilal Shah's son, Vijay, moved to Antwerp and started a firm, Vijaydimon, for supplying roughs to India and taking back the finished product to sell in Europe. Back home, B. Vijaykumar & Company under Vijay's brother, Bharat Shah, oversaw cutting and polishing operations at Surat, Palanpur, and Mumbai. By the 1980s the brothers had plants in Bangkok and Tel Aviv too, and were funnelling profits into Hindi films and real estate. Till his arrest in January 2001 for alleged underworld links, Bharat Shah was Bollywood's biggest financier. Arun Mehta's B. Arunkumar & Company, formed in 1960, has a similar tale. In 1973 Arun's brother, Dilip Mehta, established Rosy Blue NV at Antwerp as B. Arunkumar's first overseas office, and from there the group has expanded into fifteen countries.

Whether it is Gembel, Vijaydimon, Rosy Blue, or Pankaj Mehta's Eurostar Diamond Traders NV and Vasantlal Mehta's Blue Star group, the fact is the Palanpuri Jains have supplanted the Hasidic Jews as the world's foremost diamantaires. Except for the diamond mines that are still with the Oppenheimers – the South African Jewish family which owns De Beers – they rule the trade today, with nine out of every ten diamonds in the world processed in India.[33] But it is not the Palanpuris in Antwerp or Tel Aviv alone who have grown. There are a number of Gujarati Bania/Jain gold and diamond jewellery manufacturer-exporters headquartered within the country: Rajesh Shah's Rajesh Exports Limited, Jatin Mehta's Su-Raj Diamonds and Jewellery, Dinesh Shah's Asian Star Company, Chandrakant Bhansali's Classic Diamonds, Kirtilal Kalidas Doshi's Shrenuj & Company, and Mehul Choksi's Gitanjali Gems (which has brands like 'Asmi', 'Nakshatra', and 'D'damas').[34]

Coming to the Marwaris and other non-Gujarati Banias, most of the old business dynasties – the Birlas, Shri Rams, Singhanias, Goenkas, Bajajs, Bangurs, Modis, and Dalmias – have suffered divisions, while some, like Hukumchand and Surajmull Nagarmull, have plainly vanished. The major Birla groups now are of G.D. Birla's two sons, Basant Kumar (B.K.) and Krishna Kumar (K.K.). The B.K. Birla line (which includes the companies built by his son Aditya Vikram, and grandson Kumar Mangalam) has grown to be the most diversified industrial house after the Tatas. The companies under its fold include Grasim Industries (which produces a quarter of the world's viscose staple fibre), Hindalco (India's largest aluminium and copper manufacturer), UltraTech Cement (which, together with Grasim, controls a fifth of the country's production capacity), Aditya Birla Nuvo (which makes carbon black, insulators, and apparel under the 'Van Heusen', 'Peter England', 'Allen Solly', and 'Louis Philippe' labels), Indo Gulf Fertilisers, Century Textiles & Industries, Century Enka (polyester and nylon filament yarn), and Kesoram Industries (tyres and cement). The combine also has interests in telecom (Idea Cellular) and insurance (Birla Sun Life), besides owning the world's biggest single-location palm-oil refinery in Malaysia, copper mines in Australia, wood pulp ventures in Canada to feed its viscose plants, and yarn, chemicals, and carbon black units spread across Thailand, the Philippines, Indonesia, and Egypt.[35]

The K.K. Birla group's businesses encompass fertilizers (Chambal Fertilisers and Chemicals, Zuari Industries), sugar (Oudh Sugar Mills, Upper Ganges Sugar & Industries, Govind Sugar), media (the newspaper *Hindustan Times*), textiles (Sutlej Industries), and rail-wagon manufacturing (Texmaco Limited). The other relatively minor Birla factions descend from G.D. Birla's brothers, Braj Mohan (B.M.) and Rameshwar Das (R.D.). B.M. Birla's son Ganga Prasad, and grandson Chandra Kant, control Hindustan Motors ('Ambassador' cars), National Engineering Industries (which makes bearings), Orient Paper & Industries (paper and electric fans), and Hyderabad Industries Limited (asbestos sheets and other building materials). The main concerns of R.D. Birla's son Madhav Prasad (M.P.) are Birla Corporation (the Birla brothers' original Birla Jute Company, which is also into cement, vinyl floorings, and jute fibre-based auto interiors), and Universal Cables Limited.[36] The M.P. Birla group is an instructive case, where the childless founder's wife, Priyamvada, took charge on his demise in 2000. Priyamvada Birla's death in July 2004 sparked consternation: in her will the widow apparently 'gifted' the group's assets to the family's chartered accountant Rajendra Singh Lodha. More pertinently, the latter ended up with a 25 per cent share in Pilani Investments & Industries Corporation. Although the Birlas had carved up their empire in the 1980s, they retained an intricate structure of cross-holdings through various family investment arms. Lodha's gaining a significant stake in one such holding company led to the various Birla factions closing ranks against the 'outsider', albeit a Marwari on the lines of Pallonji Mistry *vis-à-vis* the Tatas. A legal battle between the family and Lodha is presently being fought in Kolkata.

The DCM group was split first between Lala Shri Ram's three sons – Murli Dhar, Bharat Ram, and Charat Ram. Murli Dhar's portion was further divided among his sons, Bansi Dhar (who got DCM Shriram Industries or DSIL) and Shri Dhar (DCM Shriram Consolidated or DSCL). Bharat Ram inherited the original flagship, DCM Limited and SRF, which were again apportioned between his sons, Vinay and Arun, respectively. The largest of these is DSCL, managed by Shri Dhar's sons (Ajay, Vikram, and Ajit) and active in fertilizers, seeds, sugar, chlorine-based chemicals, and alkalis. SRF produces nylon tyre cord, conveyor belting fabrics, and refrigerant gases, while DSIL's primary business is sugar, alcohol, and rayon tyre cord. Charat Ram's son Siddharth Shriram controls Usha International (which sells fans, sewing machines, home appliances, motors, and diesel engines), Siel Limited (chlor-alkalis, vanaspati, and refined oils), and Mawana Sugars. The JK organization (named after Kamlapat Singhania and his father Juggilal) has similarly been trifurcated between the branches of the former's sons: Padampat, Kailashpat, and Lakshmipat. The Lakshmipat line controls the tyre major J.K. Industries, J.K. Paper, J.K. Lakshmi Cement, Fenner India Limited (which makes industrial and auto belts, oil seals, and power transmission systems), JK Seeds, JK Sugar, and JK Dairy. Kailashpat Singhania's son Vijaypat heads the Raymond group, a leading player in worsted suiting fabric and menswear

('Park Avenue', 'Parx', 'Manzoni', and 'ColorPlus'), and is also into toiletries (J.K. Helene Curtis) and contraceptives ('Kamasutra' condoms). Padampat Singhania's son Gaur Hari's sole going concern is J.K. Cement. The Singhanias' banking, insurance (National Insurance Company), aluminium, and mining businesses were all nationalized by the early 1970s.[37]

The Goenkas' large-scale incursions into industry happened with Keshav Prasad (Badridas Goenka's son) buying out the British agency house Duncans Brothers in 1957, for which the family acted as banians. In 1960 Keshav Prasad promoted Phillips Carbon Black (PCB) and, over the next decade, enlarged his textile and jute mill interests. Then, in 1979, came the division. Keshav Prasad's youngest son Gouri Prasad (G.P.), was given the Duncans tea estates. The middle brother, Jagdish Prasad (J.P.) picked up the bulk of the textile and jute portfolio. Rama Prasad (R.P.) got PCB, India's largest producer of carbon black, a hardening chemical used in tyres. And it was he who carried forward his father's tradition to become corporate India's ultimate takeover specialist (along with Manohar Chhabria). Between 1981 and 1989 R.P. Goenka bought the tyre maker CEAT Limited; Kolkata's monopoly power utility CESC; the rubber and tea plantations company Harrisons Malayalam; the power transmission lines and towers supplier KEC International; the music recording company Saregama India ('HMV'); and the retailer Spencer's. The other brothers have not been as successful. Most of G.P. Goenka's firms – Duncan Industries (which added fertilisers to its tea interests), Andhra Cements, and Consolidated Fibres & Chemicals – are ailing. Only Star Paper Mills and NRC Limited (which makes industrial yarns and chemicals) are staying afloat.

The Bajajs, on the other hand, have so far just about averted a formal split. Rahul Kumar Bajaj – Jamnalal's grandson through Kamalnayan Bajaj – looks after the two-wheeler giant Bajaj Auto.

His brother Shishir runs Bajaj Hindusthan Limited, the group's maiden industrial venture that has, in recent times, emerged as India's No. 1 sugar producer. Bajaj Electricals is chaired by Shekhar Bajaj, the son of Jamnalal's other son Ramakrishna. Besides these there are two major outer-circle concerns. The first is Mukand Limited, a stainless, alloy, and special steels manufacturer. Originally a re-rolling mill-cum-foundry at Lahore, it passed in 1937 into the hands of Jamnalal Bajaj and his Gujarati Jain friend, Jeewanlal Motichand Shah, and continues to be jointly held by the two families. The second is Bajaj Tempo, since renamed Force Motors. It was co-promoted with Navalmal Kundanmal Firodia, a fellow Marwari and Gandhian industrialist (a bit of an oxymoron) who built ties with Jamnalal during the freedom struggle. Unlike in Mukand, the Bajajs have shared an uneasy equation with the Firodias from the late 1960s, but continue to hold a fifth of Force Motors' equity. The latter's forte is utility and light commercial vehicles ('Tempo' 3-wheeler, 'Matador', 'Minidor', and 'Trax'). The family of Navalmal Firodia's brother Hastimal Kundanmal controls Kinetic Motor Company, which makes scooters.[38]

In all the above cases, splits, howsoever deep, have not had the effect of causing grave long-term damage. The unshackling of familial bonds may have occasionally even been conducive for individuals to give full play to their entrepreneurial energies. The best instance of this is Aditya Birla who, on his own initiative, created a genuinely global corporation by the 1980s. One may well not have heard a lot about R.P. Goenka either, had he remained under the common family roof. But this cannot be said about the Bangurs and the Modis. Family divisions here have led to substantial dissipation of wealth over generations, and they do not seem to have produced individuals with the vision or enterprise of their founding patriarchs. The Bangurs – first Magniram and then the second generation brothers Govind Lal, Narayan Das, and Gokul

Chand – had made fortunes in property, shares, and jute speculation before setting up Maharaja Shree Umaid Mills at Pali (Rajasthan), and Shree Digvijay Cement at Sikka (Gujarat) in 1944. Soon after the War, they, in true Marwari style, acquired several jute mills from European managing agencies and during the initial decades after Independence were actually India's fourth largest industrial house behind the Tatas, Birlas, and Martin Burn. Today, they are fragmented beyond recognition. Narayan Das Bangur's son Benu Gopal controls Shree Cement Limited, while the original Digvijay Cement was sold to the B.K./Kumar Mangalam Birla – group in 1998. Gokul Chand Bangur's son Laxmi Narayan has Andhra Pradesh Paper Mills and Shree Umaid Mills. The other notable Bangur concerns are West Coast Paper Mills, Rama Newsprint & Papers, and Graphite India, of which the first two are with Shree Kumar Bangur, Govind Lal Bangur's grandson through his second son Ranganath. The last company, which makes graphite electrodes, is run by Krishna Kumar Bangur, great-grandson of Govind Lal via the Narsing Das–Balbhadra Das line.[39]

No less mind-boggling has been the division in Gujar Mal Modi's organization that had at one time undertakings for everything – from sugar, vanaspati, and vegetable oils to soaps, tin containers, biscuits, paints, electrodes, lanterns, textiles, carpets, threads, steel, alkalis, tyres, and tubes. The majority of these have folded up after being split among the founder's brother, Kedar Nath (K.N.), and five sons: Krishan Kumar (K.K.), Vinay Kumar (V.K.), Satish Kumar (S.K.), Bhupendra Kumar (B.K.) and Umesh Kumar (U.K.) Modi. The surviving companies include Modipon Limited (which K.K. Modi manages with K.N. Modi's son Mahendra Kumar), the B.K. Modi-owned mobile telecom operator Spice Communications Limited, and a couple of sugar mills controlled by U.K. Modi. In addition, there are two joint ventures – K.K. Modi's Godfrey Phillips India (for cigarettes), and V.K. Modi's Gujarat Guardian

Limited (for float glass) – where the respective American partners, Philip Morris and Guardian Industries, have made no secret of their intention to take over completely, in line with what Xerox Corporation did to B.K. Modi in Xerox Modicorp in 1999.

The break-up of Dalmia–Sahu Jain – as the combine of Ramakrishna Dalmia, his brother Jaidayal, and son-in-law Sahu Shanti Prasad Jain, was called – was the first, and the most bizarre, to have taken place after Independence. It saw Ramakrishna Dalmia not just losing everything, but also serving a two-year jail sentence after being charged of financial misappropriation by the Vivian Bose Inquiry Commission in 1962. The cement business – Dalmia Cement Bharat Limited and Orissa Cement (OCL India, which also manufactures refractory materials) – went to Jaidayal Dalmia and is now shared between four of his seven sons. The Sahu Jain faction got the prized possession, Rohtas Industries, and also Dhrangadhra Chemical Works (DCW), and Bennet, Coleman & Co. Rohtas Industries has since gone sick, while DCW, a chlor-alkali and polymer resins producer, is with the family of Shanti Prasad Jain's brother Shreyans Prasad Jain. The most valuable asset of the erstwhile Dalmia–Jain stable today – and an exclusive property of the Shanti Prasad Jain line – is Bennet, Coleman (the Times group), which is the country's *numero uno* media house. Another important industrialist is Sanjay Dalmia, the son of Jaidayal Dalmia's eldest son Vishnu Hari Dalmia (president of the right-wing Vishwa Hindu Parishad or World Hindu Council). His Gujarat Heavy Chemicals Limited (GHCL) is a leading domestic manufacturer of soda ash and home textiles.[40]

But what has been extraordinary about the Marwaris and other Hindi heartland Banias is their capacity for regeneration and throwing up fresh lots of businessmen generation after another. This seemingly hard-wired trait we saw among the Gujarati Banias/Jains and Sindhis too, though not so much in the Parsis and Chettiars.

Thus, there are many non-Gujarati Bania/Marwari houses whose rise occurred well after Independence, in the 1960s, and 1970s. Prominent in this are the Jindals, Ruias, Dhoots, and Shahras. Om Prakash (O.P.) Jindal started by fabricating steel buckets at Hissar in Haryana before commissioning a pipe unit in 1964 and six years later his first major concern, Jindal Strips. They were precursors to a domestic private steel conglomerate second only to the Tatas and now under his four sons: Prithvi Raj (Jindal Saw Limited), Sajjan (JSW Steel), Rattan (Jindal Stainless), and Naveen (Jindal Steel & Power). O.P. Jindal's brother Sita Ram owns Jindal Aluminium, a Bangalore-based aluminium extrusions manufacturer. Another brother, B.C. Jindal, manages Jindal Poly Films and Jindal Photo, while Maharashtra Seamless Limited, Jindal Drilling & Industries, and Jindal Pipes are with his son Dharam Pal Jindal. A partner in the early Jindal ventures was Basu Dev Agarwal who, in 1973, set up his own steel pipe company, which later diversified into bulbs, tubes, and other lighting products: Surya Roshni Limited. The family also promoted a steel project in Chhatisgarh, Prakash Industries.

The Ruias – Shashikant and Ravikant – are Marwaris whose father, Nand Kishore, made Chennai his base for commodities trading in 1956. After he died in 1969 the brothers shifted focus to contracts for construction of ports, jetties, and berths, and the related activities of pipe laying, dredging, and shipping. Their manufacturing debut happened only in 1987 with a sponge iron plant at Hazira in Gujarat, which further led to massive investments in steel (Essar Steel), power (Essar Power), petroleum (Essar Oil), shipping (Essar Shipping), and mobile telephony (Hutchison Essar Limited).

A Marwari from Maharashtra, Nandlal Madhavlal Dhoot's first industrial project was Gangapur Sakhar Karkhana, a sugar mill at Aurangabad in 1955. Given the stranglehold of co-operatives in

Maharashtra's sugar economy, it was doomed to failure. In the early 1980s Nandlal and his three sons – Venugopal, Rajkumar, and Pradeep – entered into a technical tie-up with Japan's Toshiba Corporation to launch televisions under the 'Videocon' brand. The group has since become India's leading consumer electronics and home appliances player, and also joined the global league in manufacture of picture tubes and glass shells.

The Shahras of Indore are the country's largest edible oil refiner, having pioneered its thriving soybean processing and de-oiled cake export industry in the early 1970s. Their house, founded by Mahadev Prasad Shahra, today has interests spanning not just the oilseed complex and assorted agro-produce (Ruchi Soya Industries Limited, Madhya Pradesh Glychem), but even steel (National Steel and Agro Industries, Ruchi Strips & Alloys) and port storage terminals (Ruchi Infrastructure).

Narotam Satyanarayan Sekhsaria's Gujarat Ambuja Cements Limited (GACL) and the Kalpataru group of Mofatraj Pukhraj Munot are two other relatively recent entitities. Promoted in 1981 by Sekhsaria, a cotton trader, and the Neotias (Suresh and Vinod), GACL snapped up the Tatas' stake in Associated Cement Companies Limited (ACC) in 2000 to emerge as India's top cement combine. The anticlimax came five years later, when the two families divested control to the Swiss cement giant Holcim. The Kalpataru group started with construction, executing big civil contracts in the Middle East during the 1970s. During the 1980s it diversified into fabrication and the erection of power transmission lines and substation structures, while strengthening its presence in construction and real estate.[41]

The man bigger than all the above put together, however, is the global steel czar and presently the third richest man on earth as per *Forbes* magazine's 2005 list: Lakshmi Niwas (L.N.) Mittal. In 1952 his father Mohan Lal (M.L.), bought a rolling mill at

Howrah, near Kolkata, and followed it with half-a-dozen mini steel units. In 1974 M.L. Mittal set up a full-fledged steel plant and, sensing opportunities abroad and licensing problems at home, chose Indonesia as the site. His son was deputed to run this undertaking, PT Ispat Indo. From the late 1980s L.N. Mittal went on a worldwide buying binge, acquiring and turning around sick, mainly state-owned steel mills in Trinidad & Tobago, Mexico, the former Soviet Bloc, Canada, Germany, Ireland, and other locations. Meanwhile at home M.L. Mittal and his other two sons, Pramod and Vinod, invested some of the profits from overseas operations to take over a sick cast and forged rolls unit, Gontermann-Peipers India, in 1981, and then established an integrated steel complex, Ispat Industries Limited, in Maharashtra. In 1994 the Ispat group's foreign and domestic interests were demarcated. L.N. Mittal went on to preside over the world's largest steel empire from London, even as his father and brothers manage a more modest business in India.

Mittal's counterpart in non-ferrous metals, though not as accomplished, is Anil Agarwal. Originally a scrap trader in Mumbai, Agarwal started Sterlite Cables (later Sterlite Industries) in 1976 to produce cables, conductors, and copper wires. His first big bucks were through supplying cables to the Department of Telecommunications (DoT) from the late 1980s. It led to Sterlite commissioning a continuous cast copper rods facility in 1989, followed by a smelter and refinery. In 1995 he acquired Madras Aluminium Company (Malco) and, seven years later, the state-owned Bharat Aluminium (Balco) and Hindustan Zinc under the then government's privatization programme. All these – not to mention copper mines in Zambia and Australia – are part of Agarwal's London-headquartered Vedanta Resources plc.[42]

If the telecom boom, privatizations, and the New Economy were integral to Anil Agarwal's success, so too were they to Sunil Bharti

Mittal, Naresh Goyal, Subhash Chandra, and Kishore Biyani. By origin a Punjabi Bania who manufactured bicycle parts in Ludhiana and later telephone handsets for the DoT, Sunil Mittal was just 28 when he promoted Bharti Telecom in 1985. Today, it is India's leading cellular mobile services operator ('Airtel').

The Patiala-born Naresh Goyal worked with his uncle as a sales agent for Lebanon International Airlines in Delhi before founding his own agency in 1974, Jetair Private Limited, representing Air France and Cathay Pacific. When the government opened up the domestic aviation sector to private players, he started Jet Airways (India) Limited with four leased aircraft in 1993. For this, a holding company, Tail Winds, was registered at the Isle of Man, in which Goyal got Gulf Air and Kuwait Airways to subscribe 40 per cent of the equity before buying them out in 1996. Since then, Jet has ousted even the public sector Indian Airlines to emerge as the country's No.1 air carrier.

Subhash Chandra (his family name is Goenka) was a grain trader at Hissar who made pots of money exporting rice to Russia from the late 1970s. But it is his satellite broadcasting and cable distribution venture, Zee Telefilms Limited, which propelled him into the elite corporate club during the 1990s.

Kishore Biyani – often described as India's answer to Walmart's Sam Walton – is again a product of the last decade. His Pantaloon Retail (India) Limited initially marketed trousers and shirts under the 'Pantaloons' and 'John Miller' brands through exclusive small franchisee stores. In 1997 Biyani opened his first large-format Pantaloons family store at Kolkata, which subsequently grew to a nation-wide retail chain stocking apparel, food, groceries, and consumer electronic goods.

IT is another area that has produced a new crop of Bania–Marwari businessmen: Narendra Kumar Patni of Patni Computer Systems, and Arun Jain of Polaris Software Lab Limited are names that immediately come to mind.

It would be erroneous, nevertheless, to conclude that the post-liberalisation period has been only for the New Economy and services. Even Old Economy sectors like textiles have attracted fresh faces. Take Ashok Bhagirathmal Jiwrajka's Alok Industries Limited, and Rajinder Gupta's Ludhiana-based Abhishek Industries. Or Gopiram Goenka, yet another Marwari from Hissar distantly related to the Jindals, who has two major companies: Welspun India, specialising in terry towels and bedsheets, and Welspun-Gujarat Stahl Rohren Limited which fabricates welded steel pipes. Even Subhash Chandra's journey from rice trader to media mogul was via manufacturing. His Essel Propack, founded in 1982 and now with factories in thirteen countries, supplies a third of the world's laminated plastic tubes used to package toothpastes, ointments, cosmetics, and other consumer products.[43]

Besides these very recent entrants, a few older (but post-1947) Marwari textile entrepreneurs are worth mentioning. Among them are Lakshmi Niwas Jhunjhunwala's LNJ Bhilwara group (Rajasthan Spinning & Weaving Mills, HEG Limited, Maral Overseas, and BSL), and the Kasliwal brothers' (Abhayakumar and Shambukumar) S. Kumars Nationwide Limited. We also have the Oswals of Ludhiana. The original house founded by Vidya Sagar Oswal today comprises three major factions: Jangi Lal Oswal's Malwa group (Malwa Cotton Spinning Mills, Malwa Industries Limited), Shri Paul Oswal's Vardhman group (Mahavir Spinning Mills, Vardhman Acrylics Limited), and Jawahar Lal Oswal's Nahar group (Nahar Industrial Enterprises, Nahar Spinning Mills Limited, Nahar Exports). Unrelated to the Ludhiana Oswals are the Oswals of the Indo Rama group: Mohan Lal (M.L.) and his sons, Om Prakash (O.P.) and Sri Prakash (S.P.). In 1974 M.L. Lohia, previously a piece goods trader in Burma and Nepal, bought a sick mill up for sale in Indonesia. This mill, PT Indorama Synthetics

Terbuka, rose to be Indonesia's largest producer and exporter of polyester. In 1989 the group entered India by commissioning an integrated polyester staple fibre and filament yarn complex at Nagpur, Indo Rama Synthetics (India) Limited. This company is now managed by O.P. Lohia, while S.P. Lohia heads the Indorama SPL group which has petrochemicals and downstream product operations in Indonesia, Thailand, Sri Lanka, Egypt, and Nigeria. If that resembles the trajectory followed by the Mittals, it is all the more so because L.N. Mittal's elder sister, Seema, is married to S.P. Lohia.[44]

Then, there are other significant Bania–Marwari groups in diverse industries – in pharma (Ajay Gopikrishna Piramal's Nicholas Piramal India, Dilip Shanghvi's Sun Pharmaceutical Industries, Shyam and Hari Bhartia's Jubilant Organosys, Desh Bandhu Gupta's Lupin Limited, and Soshil Kumar Jain's Panacea Biotec); sugar (Kamal Nayan Saraogi's Balrampur Chini Mills and Vijay Kumar Goel's Dhampur Sugar Mills Limited); steel (Brij Bhushan Singal's Bhushan Steel & Strips, Basant Kumar Jhawar's Usha Martin Limited, G.R. Surana's Surana Corporation and Surana Industries, Mukesh Gupta's Lloyds Steel Industries, and Chhotalal Ajmera's Shree Precoated Steels); plastic products (Bajranglal Taparia's Supreme Industries and Supreme Petrochem Limited); commercial vehicles (Vikram Lal's Eicher group); electrical equipment (Qimat Rai Gupta's Havell's India); construction (Bithal Das Mundhra's Simplex Infrastructures Limited); cargo transport (Prabhu Dayal Agarwal's Transport Corporation of India Limited); and shipping (Harish Kumar Mittal's Mercator Lines). Further, Ajay Piramal's brother Dilip owns one of the world's largest luggage manufacturing companies, VIP Industries, and its marketing arm Blow Plast Limited. Shyam Bhartia's youngest brother Uma Shankar, and father Mohan Lal, run India Glycols Limited, a leading producer of alcohol-based chemicals using cane molasses.[45]

Over and above these we have a whole assortment of Ansals, Bansals, Bindals, Bajorias, Bhorukas, Bhuwalkas, Dhanukas, Gargs, Himatsingkas, Jajodias, Jalans, Jaipurias, Kabras, Kajarias, Kedias, Khaitans, Khemkas, Maheshwaris, Manaksias, Mohnots, Morarkas, Parasrampurias, Patodias, Pitties, Poddars, Rankas, Rungtas, Sanganerias, Sanghis, Sethias, Somanys, Tayals. . . . Bania-Marwari industrial entrepreneurs are no more those purely bred and reared in Kolkata. In the post-Independence period they have sprouted in new centres such as Hissar (Jindals, Subhash Chandra), Ludhiana (Oswals, Sunil Mittal), Indore (Shahras), Aurangabad (Dhoots), and Chennai (Suranas).

3

Brahmins, Khatris, and Babus

In Premchand's classic, *Godaan*, the sugar mill owner, who also runs a bank and speculates in stocks, silver, cotton, and wheat, is called Mr Khanna.[1] Like all great writers, Premchand had a tactile sense of the ground beneath his feet as well as a capacity to transcend the immediate and the obvious. Khanna happens to be a Khatri surname; in 1936, when *Godaan* was published, there were hardly any big industrialists from this community. The only two famous Khatri names then were Karamchand Thapar (who had just about floated his first colliery and a couple of paper mills) and the sugar baron Gokul Chand Narang. The fact that Premchand consciously chose Mr Khanna as his mill owner, rather than a Mr Jhunjhunwala, a Mr Dalmia or a Mr Kanoria, only shows that the Khatris were an emergent force in Indian industry by the 1930s.

In this chapter, we shall focus on Khatris, Brahmins, Kayasthas, the Bengali bhadralok, and other such urbanized, upper-caste communities with a distinct middle-class orientation and cultural values. It is these communities that, by taking to education early, historically dominated the ranks of officialdom and white-collar professions, from law and accountancy to teaching, engineering, medicine, management, media, and publishing. Many of these so-called scribal castes have since medieval times also had an intermittent engagement with business, despite not being formally part of the Vaishya order. The moneylenders and financiers to the eighteenth-century Maratha state under the Peshwas were predominantly composed of Chitpavan and Deshastha Brahmins. The East India Company's first official bankers at Surat – the house of Arjunji Nathji Travedi (1680–1760) – were Nagar Brahmins, originally from Varanasi.[2] Yet another Nagar, Ranchhodlal Chhotalal, went on to found Ahmedabad's first textile mill in 1861. The association of Khatris and Aroras with business is even more deep, notwithstanding their uncertain, if not doubtful, claim to Kshatriya status.[3] In Jalandhar, Amritsar, and the big towns now part of Pakistan (Lahore, Rawalpindi, Multan, and Peshawar) the Khatris occupied the commanding heights of business, ahead of the Banias, who 'were practically unknown to the west of Lahore'.[4] They controlled much of the region's business in shawls and woollens and, along with the Shikarpuri Lohanas, also the overland transAsian trade in dry fruits, carpets, and furs across the Khyber Pass. In addition, there were migrant Khatri trading families who, from the late eighteenth century, had established themselves in the cities of the Gangetic valley as bankers (Lala Kashmiri Mull of Varanasi) and military contractors for the Raj (Joti Prasad of Agra and Sheo Prasad Tunti Mull of Kanpur).[5]

But the fact remains that neither the Khatris nor the Brahmins were comparable to the various Bania communities in terms of their sheer scale and spread of operations. The great Marwari firms moved goods and discounted hundis through long-distance networks enveloping virtually the entire subcontinent, while the Nattukottai Chettiars' financial arm extended to Ceylon, Burma, and South East Asia. In contrast, the Khatris and Brahmins were, at best, regional players. The majority were petty merchants, moneylenders, and shopkeepers, if not employed as lawyers, teachers, munshis (clerks), or kanungos (revenue officials and land record keepers). Moreover, the land to which the Khatris belonged had very little industry or rail infrastructure till well into the twentieth century. Barring the odd Egerton Woollen Mills set up in 1882 at Dhariwal (Gurdaspur) by an English missionary, industry in Punjab was nothing more than an assortment of flour mills, iron foundries, cotton ginneries, and shawl-making and carpet-weaving units. The scope for emergence of big indigenous capital in a primarily agriculture-based, landlocked province was limited. Even Khatri capital, which moved from the Punjab towns to Delhi, Agra, Lucknow, and Patna, was essentially supplementary to the omnipresent and fluid Marwari bazaar capital.[6]

The entry of Khatris and Brahmins into corporate industry in phenomenal proportions, as against sporadic or isolated ingressions, is largely a post-Independence feature. Even the 1965 Monopolies Inquiry Commission's list of India's 75 premier industrial houses had only two Khatris (Thapar and Mahindras) and five Brahmins (Sir Biren Mukherjee of Martin Burn, the Seshasayees, T.V. Sundaram Iyengar, S. Anantharamakrishnan of Amalgamations, and the Kirloskars).[7] Since then the two communities have made huge strides, to a position where they today account for the country's leading entities in pharmaceuticals (Ranbaxy of Parvinder Singh), bicycles and two-wheelers (Hero group of the Munjals), tractors (Mahindra), beer and spirits (UB Group of Vijay Mallya), and paper (Ballarpur Industries of L.M. Thapar), besides its No. 2 software exporter (Infosys of N.R. Narayana Murthy), well-known tyre maker (Apollo Tyres of Raunaq Singh), and internationally established hotelier (the Oberoi chain). Their relatively recent ascendancy owes in no small way to their early access to education and dominance in the bureaucracy and service professions, which have helped them leverage 'connections' to overcome initial handicaps of inadequate capital, both financial and cultural (in terms of inherited commercial acumen).[8] Interestingly, in *Godaan* too, Mr Khanna is someone who 'just ten years back' was a mere bank clerk whom the local zamindar, Rai Saheb Amarpal Singh, had seen transforming himself into a magnate 'in front of his eyes'!

Business Brahmins

When in 1713 the beleaguered Maratha king Shahu appointed Balaji Vishwanath Bhat as his peshwa (prime minister), it not only led to the family of this Chitpavan Bhat Brahmin from the Konkan becoming *de facto* rulers of the confederacy; it also created a new class of savakars (moneylenders) and traders who accumulated capital by financing the empire and supplying stores and munitions for its war machine. By 1740 Pune, which emerged as the financial metropolis of the Maratha state, had more than 150 big and petty savakars with names like Anagal, Bhave, Bhide, Bhokare, Bivalkar, Chiplonkar, Damle, Datar, Dikshit-Patwardhan, Gadgil, Gadre, Gosavi, Gujar, Gune, Joshi, Karje, Lele, Madhave, Moghe, Oak, Omkar, Pathak, Patwardhan, Raste, Sane, Shrotri, Tambavekar, Thatte, Tulsi-Bagwale, and Vaidya. They were all Chitpavan or Deshastha Brahmins. There were also some ingenious personages such as Brahmendraswami Dhavadshikar, a Deshastha Rig-vedi Brahmin, who became a leading moneylender by saving the dakshina (alms) received in the course of his religious advocacy. Another worthy, Babuji Naik, who was related to the Peshwa Baji Rao I, even made a spirited bid for the throne after the latter's death in 1740 on the basis of loans he had given to the late ruler! However, the reign of these state-assisted entrepreneurs was transitory and effectively sealed by the last peshwa Baji Rao II's defeat in the third Anglo-Maratha War of 1818. This was logical, given that the new Brahmin moneybags belonged basically to a class of crony proto-capitalists dependent on peshwa largesse; most savakars were rendered insolvent when the East India Company refused to honour their outstanding claims to the previous regime.[9]

The decline of the peshwas was a setback for Brahmin enterprise in western India: the old bankers and merchants of Pune were nowhere on the scene when Mumbai, from the second half of the nineteenth century, developed into the country's commercial capital. Nevertheless, the community retained its grip over education and the bureaucracy. Ranchhodlal Chhotalal (1823–98) was a Gujarati Nagar Brahmin from Ahmedabad whose ancestors (father included) had served various ruling groups from the time of the Mughals. He too was programmed towards a career in government and, not surprisingly, acquired proficiency in English, Persian (still a language of administration), Sanskrit (a must for any self-respecting Brahmin), and Gujarati. By 1853 the young Nagar had risen to be an assistant superintendent of customs – among the highest posts an Indian could aspire to at that time – before being suspended on charges of taking a bribe of Rs 8,000 from a native prince, allegedly to forward the latter's case in a succession battle. But his stint in government had brought Ranchhodlal in close contact with highly placed officials and businessmen of all hues. It was during these interactions that he conceived the idea of starting a textile mill. The real encouragement came from two Englishmen: Captain George Fulljames (who had connections with textile machinery suppliers back home) and James Landon (a cotton planter and ginner actively involved in promoting the crop in Bharuch and adjoining areas of southern Gujarat). However, it took Ranchhodlal a decade or more to realize his dream. The problem, as expected, lay in tying up finances. The only source of capital then were the Gujarati Vaishnav Bania and Jain bankers, for whom modern manufacturing was an alien concept entailing heavy opportunity costs in terms of income foregone by lending money elsewhere at 15–20 per cent. After years of persuasion, the Ahmedabad Spinning and Weaving Company was finally registered in August 1858 – just four years after a Parsi, Cowasji Nanabhai Davar, floated the first Indian-owned mill at Mumbai. Out of its initial 20 shares worth Rs 100,000 Ranchhodlal could only subscribe to 2; the rest were taken by the city's preeminent mercantile firms of Maganbhai Karamchand, Nagarsheth Premabhai Himabhai, and Jesingbhai Hutheesingh. Three years later, when the mill began distributing dividends, the same vacillating banking interests got into the act themselves. By the end of the century, Ahmedabad was a 'rival Manchester' to Mumbai with 25 mills, 21 of them controlled by Banias and Jains.[10]

While Ahmedabad's textile industry was fathered by a Nagar – Ranchhodlal may very well have preceded Cowasji Davar but for teething resource-raising issues – the early part of the twentieth century saw Brahmin entrepreneurs pioneering other new manufacturing activities. The brain behind the country's first glass-making venture in 1905 – Paisa Fund Glass Works at Talegaon, near Pune – was a Chitpavan, Antaji D. Kale. This was a remarkable experiment in economic nationalism inspired by Bal Gangadhar Tilak. The entire start-up capital of Rs 10,000 was mobilized through public contributions as low as 1 paisa so as to free it from debt servicing obligations from day one. Its underlying goal, moreover, was to provide a training ground for people seeking to set up similar indigenous glass production facilities elsewhere.[11] One such person to have gained experience at Paisa Fund Glass Works was Gurunath Prabhakar Ogale, also a Chitpavan, who started Ogale Glass Works Limited at Satara in 1919. None of these initial Brahmin-promoted concerns proved durable. When he passed away in October 1898 Ranchhodlal Chhotalal's two mills still made up a fifth of Ahmedabad's spindleage and a quarter of its looms.

But his successors were seemingly drawn more towards Sanskrit literature and Vedantic philosophy: Ranchhodlal's grandson, Chinubhai Madhowlal, who had a fine eye for thoroughbreds, was the first in Ahmedabad to own a car and also the first ever Hindu to be conferred the title of Baronet. By 1934 both the mills were liquidated and the plant and machinery sold as scrap. Ogale Glass Works somehow carried on till around 1981.

The sole early pioneer whose industrial house outlived him was Laxmanrao Kirloskar. He was born in 1869 at Gurlhosur in Belgaum district (now in Karnataka). His father, Kashinath, retired as a land surveyor with the Bombay Presidency government. Laxmanrao was initially schooled at Belgaum, before Kashinath, spotting the lad's penchant for drawing and mechanical craft, sent him to Mumbai's JJ School of Art. After two years Laxmanrao secured a job as a mechanical drawing instructor at the Victoria Jubilee Technical Institute (VJTI) on a monthly salary of Rs 35. Most of his spare time there was spent in the workshop, learning the intricacies of metal smelting and forging and gleaning information from *American Machinist*, *Scientific American*, and other technical journals. In 1890 Laxmanrao resigned, apparently hurt at being denied a promotion purely on racial grounds. He then embarked upon several unsuccessful ventures at Belgaum, from button-making to the sale and repair of bicycles, before settling down to manufacturing iron ploughs. By 1911 he had a small factory at the princely state of Aundh in Satara, whose heir apparent, Balasaheb Pant Pratinidhi, was a contact from his VJTI days. The thirty-two acres that the Brahmin princeling donated was the precursor to the industrial township of Kirloskarwadi. Starting with ploughs – for which the World War I textile boom and increased cotton demand provided a good market – the factory added other farm machinery: chaff-cutters, windlasses, pulleys to lift water from wells, sugarcane crushers, and groundnut decorticators. By 1926, six years after Kirloskar Brothers was incorporated, a diesel engine and centrifugal pump for irrigation purposes had been developed. The initiative now was coming mainly from Laxmanrao's eldest son, the Massachusetts Institute of Technology (MIT)-returned Shantanurao. The second generation – Laxmanrao died in 1956 – steered the group's diversification from farm equipment. In 1941 Mysore Kirloskar Limited was established to produce lathes and machine tools at Harihar (Davangere), this time on land gifted by the illustrious dewan of Mysore, Mokshagundam Visvesvaraya. In 1946 the Kirloskar Electric Company, for making electric motors, generators, and transformers, and Kirloskar Oil Engines, dedicated to diesel engines and generating sets, were started. Then came Kirloskar Pneumatic Company for compressors and transmission systems in 1958, and Kirloskar Ferrous Industries in 1994 for pig iron and castings. Today, this Rs 4,000 crore plus engineering conglomerate spans four generations of the family.[12]

The Garwares are the other significant Maharashtrian Brahmin group, where the succeeding generations have somewhat consolidated on the base built by the founder. Bhalchandra Digambar Garware was a dealer in imported second-hand automobiles at Mumbai who took up production of plastic buttons for the Indian navy during the 1940s. In 1946 he acquired a controlling stake in a British concern, Blundel Fomite Paints, later renamed Garware Paints. Bhalchandra's pioneering role, however, was in the indigenous manufacture of extruded thermoplastics like nylon bristles (used in toothbrushes, shaving brushes, and paint brushes, etc.), fishing and sports nets, twines and polyester films for X-Ray and sun-control (anti-glare) applications. Besides Garware Synthetics and Garware Polyester, promoted in the early 1960s, the group companies comprise Garware-Wall Ropes and Garware Offshore Services (formerly Garware Shipping Corporation). They have been split among Bhalchandra's sons, of which Garware Polyester and Garware Wall-Ropes – belonging to Shashikant and Ramesh Garwale, respectively – are doing well.[13]

In addition to the Kirloskars and the Garwares, western India has quite a few privately held big Brahmin businesses. Prominent among them are the Goa-based iron ore mining-cum-export and shipping families of Vasantrao S. Dempo and Vasudev M. Salgaonkar. Both were trading firms to start with. They also undertook stevedoring and related shipping agency services. In the late 1940s they took advantage of the mining concessions offered by the then Portuguese authorities – Goa was liberated only in 1962 – to enter iron ore exports, followed by the acquisition of barge vessels and bulk carriers, and later ship-building. Vasantrao Dempo's brother, Vaikunthrao, even had the distinction of being a member of parliament of Portugal, representing Goa. The two companies today contribute a major share of the Rs 1,500 crore annual export of iron ore from Goa, mostly to Japan and now to China.[14] They have also diversified, as is common, and evident from the examples of many other such entrepreneurs, into a variety of other industries. Dempo has interests in paints, pig iron and steel, and an English daily, *The Navhind Times*. Then, we have Chitpavan Brahmins behind some of the most popular homegrown brands of the pre-liberalization era: D.P. Dandekar of Camlin Limited ('Camlin' geometry boxes, pencils, crayons, inks, etc.), K.V. Pendharkar of Vicco Laboratories ('Vicco Vajradanti' toothpowder and paste), and G.D. Gokhale of Bombay Chemicals Private Limited (whose once-supreme 'Tortoise' mosquito repellant coil initially confirmed proverbial wisdom but lost out to parvenu hares of the repellant world like 'All Out' and 'Good Knight').

Karnataka's largest sugar plant, the Ugar Sugar Works Limited at Belgaum, and Sangli's well-known Chitale Dairy – started in the early 1940s by V.S. Shirgaokar and Bhaskar Ganesh Chitale, respectively – are also Brahmin-owned businesses. So is the Pune-based building firm, D.S. Kulkarni Developers Limited of Deepak Sakharam Kulkarni.[15]

Tamil Brahmins (Tambrams), Gowd Saraswat Brahmins (GSBs), and Others

In the south, just as in the west, the Tamil Brahmins or 'Tambrams' had a head start in education – particularly English education, the master key for opening the doors to the professions and service appointments. Brahmins represented 67 per cent of the university graduates in Madras Presidency in 1890; the proportion remained unchanged even around thirty years later.[16] There were also moneylenders among them: notably the Iyers of Kallidaikuruchi (Tirunelveli) and Monkombu in Alappuzha district of Travancore (Kerala).[17] The Kallidaikuruchi Iyers – named after a revenue-free inam village bestowed to them in the Tambraparni river valley – were, from the early nineteenth century, actively involved in financing trade in agricultural produce. By the close of the century, the number of Kallidaikuruchi Brahmin banking firms was variously estimated at between 100 and 175, and their personal capital from Rs 5.5 to Rs 7 crore. Their business of financing commission agents, who farmed out into the villages, was carried out from the large southern Tamil Nadu towns of Tiruchirapalli (Trichy), Madurai, Tirunelveli, and Thoothukudi. They mostly lent short on the security of crops held in the market, relying on very fast turnover and – rather more than the Chettiars – taking deposits from the public and modern-style banks to inflate their own fund base.[18]

The Tambram entry into industry dates from the 1920s and the lead, once again, was taken not by wealthy bankers but by men of obscure middle-class background. The trailblazers here were the Seshasayee Brothers, whose founders, R. Seshasayee and V.

Seshasayee, were in real life not even distantly related (though, as it invariably happens, they did become relatives when the former married the latter's sister). Starting with a mofussil road transport service in Trichy during World War I, the two friends – who, like Laxmanrao Kirloskar, shared an engineering bent from school days – branched off into the servicing of buses, cars, and motorcycles. This became the nucleus for Seshasayee Brothers Engineering Works, which undertook auto repair, electric wiring, and the installation of oil engines and generator sets in rice and oil mills. The first big jobs they executed included lighting up the palace of the raja of Ramnad (Ramanathapuram) and temples across Madurai and Rameswaram. From there the two went into genset-based power supply and distribution in interior towns of the Chettiar heartland, for which three companies were floated between 1923 and 1925: the Sree Meenakshi Electric Corporation at Devakottai, the Sree Meenakshi Sundareswara Electric Power Corporation at Karaikudi, and the Trichy Srirangam Electric Supply Corporation. These concerns – principally funded by Chettiar capital, with the Seshasayees as managing agents – were merged in 1940 to form the South Madras Electric Supply Corporation. Before that, the elder 'brother', R. Seshasayee, died in 1934, crashing the plane he was piloting on the tarmac at Trichy. Moments earlier, he had flown over the National College campus to drop flowers at the venue where Mahatma Gandhi was speaking.[19]

In 1940 the Seshasayee group diversified into production of caustic soda, bleaching powder, and chlorine through Mettur Chemical and Industrial Corporation in Salem. At the invitation of the Travancore dewan, Sir C.P. Ramaswamy Aiyar, the group also set up Fertilizers and Chemicals Travancore (FACT) and Forest Industries Travancore Limited (both near Kochi), and Aluminium Industry Limited (ALIND) at Kollam. FACT produced ammonium sulphate and superphosphate fertilizers (an extension of the heavy chemicals business at Mettur), whereas the other two were backward integration projects of sorts: Forest Industries was meant to supply FACT's firewood feedstock, while ALIND manufactured aluminium conductors and accessories to complement the electric transmission business.[20] In the 1965 Monopolies Inquiry Commission report, the Seshasayees were ranked India's No. 2 Brahmin industrial house, behind Martin Burn.[21] After V. Seshasayee passed away in 1958, the group's affairs passed on to S. Viswanathan, who was ironically a lawyer for Mettur Chemical's labour union and also a colleague of R. Venkataraman (Industries Minister of Madras and later President of India). The rechristened Esvin group forayed into new areas like paper (Seshasayee Paper and Boards), nickel-cadmium batteries (High Energy Batteries India), and sugar (Ponni Sugars Erode). The old Seshasayee entities were either nationalized (FACT, Forest Industries, and the electric utilities), sold (Mettur Chemical), or turned sick (ALIND).[22]

T.V. Sundaram Iyengar (1877–1955), whose group has come to be a veritable metaphor for Tambram capital, had middle-class roots similar to the Seshasayees. Sometime around 1908 he is said to have invested Rs 25,000 – inherited as share in ancestral property – in timber trading. The profits from it were deployed four years later to launch a bus service in Madurai: this was in partnership with a Muslim merchant.[23] In 1923 T.V. Sundaram Iyengar & Sons Limited was incorporated, with its business centred around the sale and servicing of automobiles. By 1925 it had acquired a subdealership for Chevrolet cars in the Madurai region, followed by a sole selling agency for General Motors' products. At the time of Independence, TVS & Sons had three subsidiaries: the Madras Auto Service for distribution of imported auto spare parts, Sundaram Motors for vehicle dealership, and Southern Roadways which ran a road transport and parcel service. The group's manufacturing activity was limited to a sole tyre re-treading facility. This changed with the government's policy to clamp down on the import of components and stimulate indigenous production. The result was a series of auto-parts-making companies, starting with Wheels India (1960), Lucas-TVS (1961), and Sundaram-Clayton and Brakes India (1962), to Sundram Fasteners (1966), Sundaram Brake Linings (1976), and India Nippon Electricals (1985). All these were collaborations with foreign auto engineering majors like Lucas, Dunlop, and Suzuki. Today, the Rs 10,000 crore, thirty-odd companies strong TVS group is a leading player in auto ancillaries, two-wheelers (TVS Motor Company, a subsidiary of Sundaram-Clayton), two-wheeler tyres (TVS Srichakra), automotive dealership, and logistics. In addition, there is Sundaram Finance, incorporated in 1954 as an auto hire and purchase finance company to complement the group's vehicle dealership business. It is now controlled by the branch of T.V. Sundaram Iyengar's youngest son, T.S. Santhanam, and also has stakes in mutual funds (Sundaram Asset Management Company) and insurance (Royal Sundaram Alliance Insurance).[24]

An equally important auto magnate of this period was S. Anantha-ramakrishnan, an accountant with an audit firm, Fraser and Ross, who, for some strange reason, was called 'J'. In 1930 he joined one of his clients, Simpson & Co., as its company secretary. A British expatriate firm established in 1840 as a coach-and-carriage builder, Simpson had expanded into diverse areas from harnesses, saddlery, and billiard tables to the distribution and servicing of imported automobiles. In 1938 the company promoted the Sri Ram Vilas Service, which, together with TVS, was soon plying a number of bus routes in south-eastern Tamil Nadu.[25] The same year, Simpson's chairman, Sir Alexander MacDougall, formed a holding company, Amalgamations Limited, and 'J' was inducted into its board. This company took over not just Simpson and Sri Ram Vilas, but a bunch of other mid-sized British trading entities, including Addison & Co, Higginbothams, George Oakes, and T.

Stanes & Co. By the late 1950s the original owners had lost interest and the management of Amalgamations was firmly vested with 'J'. Anantharamakrishnan steered the group into the manufacture of automotive paints (Addisons Paints & Chemicals) and pistons (India Pistons) in 1949, followed by transport diesel engines (through Simpson) and two-wheeler batteries (Amco Batteries) in 1955. In 1961 he established Tractors and Farm Equipment Limited (TAFE) as a tie-up with Massey Ferguson of the UK to produce its tractors locally. With its purchase of Eicher Motors' tractor division in June 2005, TAFE has become India's second largest tractor maker after the Mahindras. Amalgamations is today a highly diversified Rs 3,000-crore combine with some 43 companies (none of them listed), straddling industries ranging from tractors and auto-component manufacture to bookselling (Higginbothams) and plantations (Stanes Amalgamated Estates). There is, further, a TVS link: the granddaughter of 'J', Mallika Srinivasan, is married to T.V. Sundaram Iyengar's grandson, Venu Srinivasan.

Kasturi and Sons, publishers of the largest circulated English daily in the south – *The Hindu* – is an Iyengar concern founded in September 1878 by an Iyer schoolteacher. A social reformer by conviction – he advocated widow remarriage and lamented the 'degraded condition' of Dalits – G. Subramania Aiyer's views went against the grain of the paper's orthodox readership and did not help shore up its finances. In October 1898 Aiyer relinquished charge to his partner M. Veeraraghavachariar. The latter could not stem its declining sales either. On 1 April 1905 *The Hindu* was acquired for Rs 75,000 by S. Kasturi Ranga Iyengar, a lawyer from Kumbakonam (Thanjavur), who had been the paper's legal adviser since 1895.[26]

The other old Iyengar business family is that of T.T. Krishnamachari (TTK), whose father was a district judge. TTK was an apprentice with an indenting firm representing Unilever.

When its owner, A.R. Doraisami Iyengar, died in 1928, TTK was given a distributorship by the Anglo-Dutch multinational. In 1936, under C. Rajagopalachari's influence, he joined the Congress and drifted into politics, ending up as union finance minister in the late 1950s. By then TTK & Company was an established trading agency being managed by his sons. Post-Independence it began manufacturing consumer goods, with a wide portfolio covering 'Prestige' pressure cookers, 'Woodward's Gripe Water', 'Tantex' hosiery products, 'Kiwi' shoe polish, 'Brylcreem' hair cream, and 'Kohinoor' condoms. But the Rs 600-crore group has not really succeeded in leveraging the brand equity of its products into cutting edge business.[27]

The Kallidaikuruchi Iyers' move to industry is comparatively late, which tallies with our earlier observation on the Brahmins of Maharashtra: there, too, it was not bankers but educated middle-class folk who essayed the breakthrough. S.N.N. Sankaralinga Iyer belonged to a family of moneylenders from Kallidaikuruchi who graduated to organized banking through the Indo-Commercial Bank Limited in 1932 and the Prudential Investment Trust in 1936. By 1945 the bank's paid-up capital had touched Rs 18.7 lakh and its rolling capital Rs 3.2 crore.[28] In the late 1930s Sankaralinga Iyer and his son, K.S. Narayanan, moved into small-scale manufacturing, taking over a printing ink facility at Chennai (1939), the South India Rubber Factory (1940), and a carbide-making unit, Industrial Chemicals Limited (1943). The post-War construction boom prompted them to invest in a 100,000 tonne per annum cement project at Tirunelveli which had ample limestone deposits. In 1946 Sankaralinga Iyer and T.S. Narayanaswami, who was an agent with Indo-Commercial Bank, promoted India Cements Limited. Alongside, they started Travancore Cements at Kottayam, in which the princely state under C.P. Ramaswamy Aiyar held 32 per cent equity. While Travancore Cements was beset with problems from the start and taken over by the Kerala government, India Cements has grown to be the southern region's biggest cement producer, with an installed capacity of 9 million tonnes. India Cements is now controlled by Narayanaswami's son, N. Srinivasan. In 1962 K.S. Narayanan floated a separate polyvinyl chloride resin and chloro-chemicals concern in collaboration with B.F. Goodrich of the US. This company, Chemplast Sanmar Limited, is the flagship of the Sanmar group, named after his two sons, N. Sankar and N. Kumar. Besides chemicals, the Rs 1,400 crore group has interests in shipping and engineering (Sanmar Engineering Corporation, which has a number of foreign joint ventures to manufacture process control equipment like valves, flow meters, mechanical seals, and electronic weighing systems). Till as recently as 2005, the Sanmar group also had a 25 per cent stake in India Cements, which has been whittled down significantly.[29]

Yet another Kallidaikuruchi entrepreneur of the early 1950s was K.R. Sundaram Iyer, who, in partnership with his nephew K. Eswaran formed Madras Motors Private Limited to import British motorcycles into India. In 1953 they got an order from the Indian army to supply 800 Royal Enfield 'Bullet' motorcycles produced by the Enfield Cycle Company at Redditch in England. Two years later Sundaram established Enfield India Limited to manufacture 5,000 'Bullets' annually under licence from the Redditch company. At first the machines were assembled from components shipped out of England, but by 1962 production was fully localized. In 1967 the original British firm collapsed, but the 350 cc 'Bullet' continued to be made in India, riding high on its tough macho bike image. The arrival of fuel-efficient, easy-to-maintain, 100 cc bikes through Indo-Japanese joint ventures in the 1980s – Hero Honda, TVS Suzuki, Escorts Yamaha, and Kawasaki Bajaj – hit 'Bullet' sales hard. Barely managing to survive, Enfield India was in the early 1990s acquired by the Eicher group. K. Eswaran went on to found the Easun group, a low-profile player in transformers, switchgears, tap changers, relays, and other electric products. W.S. Industries India Limited, a leading Chennai-based power insulator maker, is also an Iyer concern promoted by N.S. Sethuraman and V. Srinivasan.[30]

K.V. Gopalakrishnan's Standard Motors Products of India Limited (SMPIL) has a tale similar to Enfield India's. It was a tie-up with the British Standard Motor Company to produce 'Standard Herald' and 'Gazel' cars for the Indian market and this it continued to do even after the Coventry-based company was taken over in 1960 by Leyland Motors. Till Suzuki's entry via 'Maruti' in the 1980s, SMPIL was the only domestic car maker besides Hindustan Motors and Premier Automobiles. 'Standard 2000', modelled on the Rover SD1 and powered by a gas-guzzling two-litre engine, was the company's last launch in 1985 – it failed in the market. Within the next few years the factory shut down and eventually went into liquidation. In October 2005 its 57.9 acres of property at Perungalathur in Chennai's suburbs was auctioned by the Madras High Court, fetching Rs 154 crore. The buyer, Shriram Properties, is part of the Shriram group of R. Thyagarajan. A former officer with the public sector New India Assurance Company, this first-generation Tambram businessman started an indigenous mutual savings and credit company ('chit') in 1974. Since then, Shriram Chits has risen to be India's No. 1 chit fund, with 465 branches handling a yearly auction turnover of Rs 3,500 crore. The group is also its biggest truck financier.[31]

The Gowd Saraswat Brahmins (GSBs) of coastal Karnataka, like their associates in Maharashtra and Tamil Nadu, are a community with an entrenched banking tradition. Canara Bank was established in 1906 by a GSB lawyer from Mangalore, Ammembal Subba Rao Pai. So were the promoters of the Manipal-based Syndicate Bank in 1925: Tonse Madhava Anantha (T.M.A.) Pai and his brother,

Upendra Anantha (U.A.) Pai, along with Vaman Srinivas Kudva. Both these banks were nationalized in 1969. The two privately held southern bidi (indigenous cheroot) majors – Mangalore Ganesh Beedi Works ('501' brand) and Bharath Beedi Works ('30') – were started in the 1930s by Bantwal Madhava Shenoy and B. Manjunath Pai, respectively. They too were from the same community.

The most prominent of all GSB industrialists, however, are T.M.A. Pai and Vittal Mallya. Around eight years after he co-founded the Syndicate Bank, T.M.A. Pai, a practising surgeon, bought 107 acres of land on a barren hilltop near Udupi for a song. On this rocky terrain, called Manipal, the Pai brothers started a tile factory and a few other small-scale ventures. When these did not click, the family tried out something totally alien to the country: self-financing colleges. In 1953 they set up the Kasturba Medical College. It became the embryo for a huge private educational empire – the Manipal Academy of Higher Education (MAHE) – comprising twenty-three colleges offering medical, dental, nursing, pharmacy, engineering, management, and other professional courses, with affiliates at Sikkim, Nepal, Malaysia, and Dubai. MAHE, which set the trend for other private universities, is presently headed by T.M.A. Pai's son, Ramdas Madhava Pai. U.A. Pai's son T. Ramesh Pai led the group into manufacturing rubberized coir mattresses and pillows (Kurlon Limited) and also built up now-failed financial services firms like Industrial Credit and Development Syndicate (ICDS) and Maha Rashtra Apex Corporation.[32] The Dhaka-born Vittal Mallya's father, Bantwal Ganapathi Mallya, was an army doctor. Educated at the Doon School in Dehradun and Kolkata's Presidency College, Vittal Mallya joined a stockbroking firm, Chunilal T. Mehta & Company, in 1944. Two years on, the 22-year-old Mallya started picking up shares in United Breweries Limited: a company formed in 1915 by a Scotsman, Thomas Leishman, through amalgamation of five small breweries in the south. In August 1947 he became the first Indian director on its board and soon replaced R.G.N. Price as its chairman. In 1951 Mallya bought McDowell & Co, a Chennai-based British trading firm that dealt in imported wines and spirits. Eight years later it began manufacturing Indian substitutes to foreign liquor from a distillery in Cherthala (Kerala), adding a new term, Indian Made Foreign Liquor (IMFL), to the business lexicon. Since then the UB group has been the undisputed domestic leader in beer ('Kingfisher' and 'Kalyani') and spirits ('McDowell's No. 1'). With its acquisition of Shaw Wallace ('Royal Challenge', 'Director's Special', 'Haywards', and 'Antiquity') and Herbertsons Limited ('Bagpiper') in 2005, the group is now the world's third largest spirits marketer.[33] In the same year the present group chairman, Vijay Mallya (who took over from his father in 1983), also launched Kingfisher Airlines.

The northern Brahmins have not particularly distinguished themselves in business and we can identify just a couple of notable names: Jaiprakash Gaur and Narendra Nath Mohan. The former, belonging to Bulandshahr in Uttar Pradesh, did a civil engineering diploma from Roorkee University in 1950. He then worked with the state irrigation department for seven years before turning into a government contractor undertaking petty works. By 1972, when Jaiprakash Associates was registered as a partnership firm, the business had grown. From contracting, Jaiprakash Gaur integrated backwards into cement, commissioning his first plant in Rewa district of Madhya Pradesh in 1986. Today, the Rs 3,000 crore plus Jaypee group has stakes in cement (three plants at Rewa, with aggregate capacity of 7 million tonnes), power (a 300 megawatt hydel station at Baspa in Himachal Pradesh), turnkey construction (especially for the state-owned National Hydroelectric Power Corporation), and hotels (Jaypee Hotels, which manages two 5-Star properties in Delhi, and one each in Agra and Mussoorie).

Narendra Nath Mohan's story has some resemblance to that of

S. Anantharamakrishnan or, for that matter, Vittal Mallya. Mohan was an employee of Dyer Meakin Breweries Limited, traceable to Edward Dyer, father of the notorious Brigadier-General Reginald Dyer – the man behind the shooting of hundreds at Amritsar's Jallianwala Bagh on 13 April 1919. In 1855 Edward Dyer set up a brewery at Kasauli in Himachal Pradesh and launched Asia's first beer, 'Lion'. Subsequently, he added breweries at Solan and Shimla (Himachal), Mandalay (Burma), Murree, and Rawalpindi (now in Pakistan). Around 1887 the Solan and Shimla breweries were sold to a rival Englishman, H.G. Meakin. By the 1920s the two firms had merged their businesses completely to form Dyer Meakin. After Independence, the British promoters decided to exit and, in 1949, sold their shares to Narendra Nath Mohan. The company became Mohan Meakin Limited in 1967. Despite owning brands such as 'Old Monk' rum, 'Golden Eagle' beer, and 'Solan No. 1' whisky, Mohan Meakin hasn't consolidated itself the way the UB Group has done after starting almost at the same time. The Mohans are Mohyals, a Brahmin sect from West Punjab with claims to a martial past, and with surnames like Bali, Chibber, Dutt, and Mohan. The Balis of Mount Shivalik group – the Chandigarh-headquartered brewers of high alcohol content beers, including 'Thunderbolt', 'Punjab Extra Strong', and 'Golden Peacock' – are also Mohyals and related to the Mohans. The only other northern Brahmin industrialist worth mentioning is Ashok Chaturvedi of Flex Industries Limited, a major manufacturer of flexible plastic packaging materials.[34]

Why have Brahmins in the north not replicated the success of the Maharashtrian Brahmins, Tambrams, and GSBs? There are intertwined cultural, historical, as well as economic factors behind this that we can only roughly outline. Culturally speaking, the western and southern Brahmins have demonstrated greater flexibility and moral neutrality in pursuing a variety of callings in addition to priesthood: agriculturist, cook, messenger, banker, clerk, soldier, doctor, trader, and so on.[35] They also took to modern education early, which was an invaluable asset in their pioneering activities: be it Ranchhodlal Chhotalal's textile mills, Laxmanrao Kirloskar's diesel engines, the Seshasayees' electric utilities, or the automotive industries of T.V. Sundaram Iyengar and S. Anantharamakrishnan. The majority of them, we have seen, were not born to shopkeepers or merchants but to schoolteachers, bureaucrats, judges, colonels, and doctors. What they lacked in capital they made up in with their knowledge of English and technical education – important ingredients for establishing contacts and starting complex industries, often through foreign collaborations and licensing arrangements. Their location – closer to the ports – was also probably conducive to imbibing commercial influences. All these received added impetus through government job reservations for non-Brahmins, which became a feature of public life all over South India and the Bombay Presidency by the early twentieth century. The Brahmins of the hinterland, by contrast, were relatively insulated from the winds of change blowing right through the late colonial era. As one perceptive writer noted: 'Our Brahmins were rarely erudite; in fact many of them were barely literate, possessing only a perfunctory knowledge of ritual and knowing just the necessary mantras by heart.'[36] With limited exposure to the secular disciplines and being ensconced in feudal settings, there was neither stimulus nor pressure to be enterprising. And, needless to say, this generality applies even to landed Brahmin communities of the south, such as the Namboothiris in Kerala.

During the last two decades there has been a further ingress of Brahmin entrepreneurs – again predominantly from the south and the west – into new sectors. These include IT (Nagawara

Ramarao Narayana Murthy of Infosys Technologies Limited);[37] drugs (Kailasam Raghavendra Rao of Orchid Chemicals & Pharmaceuticals and Rajnikant Thakorlal Vyas of Dishman Pharmaceuticals & Chemicals Limited); biotech (Kiran Mazumdar-Shaw of Biocon Limited); airlines (G.R. Gopinath of Deccan Aviation, which ushered in low-cost air travel in the country); and private courier services (Tushar Jani, a Gujarati Nagar who co-promoted Blue Dart Express Limited in 1983, before selling out to the German multinational, DHL, in 2005). As before, all of them are first-generation businessmen. Narayana Murthy and Gopinath were sons of schoolteachers from Karnataka's Kolar and Hassan districts, respectively, while Raghavendra Rao's father was a railway clerk at Tenali in Andhra Pradesh. Kiran Mazumdar's father, a Gujarati Brahmin, was the Managing Director of UB (again that strange Brahmin liquor connection). They are also well educated. Narayana Murthy was an electrical engineer and postgraduate from the Indian Institute of Technology (IIT), Kanpur. Raghavendra Rao did business administration from the Indian Institute of Management, Ahmedabad. Kiran Mazumdar, a zoology graduate of Bangalore University and a qualified master brewer from Australia's Ballarat University, used her knowledge of fermentation science to start a company that manufactures enzymes. Gopinath was an Indian army captain and Tushar Jani a Mumbai University science graduate. Suresh Kalmadi (the Congress parliamentarian from Pune and promoter of Sai Service Station Limited, one of India's largest dealers of 'Maruti' cars and 'Bajaj' two-wheelers) and Anurag Dikshit (an IIT-Delhi product and 30 per cent owner of the Gibraltar-based online casino company, PartyGaming, and the 10th richest Indian according to the *Forbes* magazine's rankings for 2005) are also Brahmin businessmen of quite recent origin.[38]

Khatri Capital

As already pointed out, pre-Partition India had only two great Khatri houses, namely Karamchand Thapar and Gokul Chand Narang. The Ludhiana-born Thapar had relatives who were wholesale merchants and coal dealers in Kolkata. After a short spell in college he joined them and, in 1929, floated Karamchand Thapar & Brothers. This was mainly a coal agency, with its head office in Kolkata and branches at Lahore, Ludhiana, and Jharia in Jharkhand. From this base in coal trade Thapar snapped up six collieries between 1933 and 1939, including Oriental Coal and Eastern Syndicate Limited. Simultaneously, he entered sugar, encouraged by the levy of 185 per cent duty on imports in 1932. After purchasing a tottering mill at Baitalpur in Deoria district of Uttar Pradesh (Shree Sitaram Sugar), Thapar promoted two more concerns: Deoria Sugar Mills and New Savan Sugar & Gur Refining Company. In 1936 he set up Shree Gopal Paper Mills at Yamunanagar in present-day Haryana by taking over Punjab Pulp and Paper Mills, then under liquidation. During this decade Thapar also forayed into insurance, starch (Bharat Starch and Chemicals), and dry ice (Dry Ice and Refrigeration Limited). From this diversified beginning, Thapar went on to acquire Greaves Cotton in 1947.[39] A British agency house with seven spinning mills in Mumbai under its belt before World War I, Greaves Cotton's focus had subsequently shifted to diesel engines and electrical equipment through an affiliate, Crompton Parkinson Works (later Crompton Greaves Limited). The other major late 1940s project of Karamchand Thapar was Jagatjit Cotton Textile Mills (JCT) at Phagwara in Kapurthala, Punjab.

Sir Gokul Chand Narang, a staunch Arya Samaji from Lahore and a lawyer by training, was the uncrowned sugar king of pre-Independent India. On the eve of World War II, Narang – he also served as Local Self-Government Minister in undivided Punjab – controlled eight factories with a combined crushing capacity of 6,900 tonnes of cane daily (tcd). That made him ahead of even Begg Sutherland (nine mills of 6,251 tcd), the Birlas (five mills of 5,400 tcd), and the Dalmia-Jains (two mills of 3,300 tcd).[40] The first of Narang's factories – the Basti Sugar Mills – came up as early as in 1927 and the others (including a unit at Phagwara near Thapar's JCT) after the grant of protective duty. However, the Narang citadel suffered an irreversible decline post Independence, losing out not only to the likes of Bajaj Hindusthan, Balrampur Chini, and K.K. Birla, but even to two other Khatri sugar combines born during the investment boom of the early 1930s: Triveni Engineering & Industries and The Saraswati Industrial Syndicate Limited. The former, founded by Ishwar Das Sawhney, is India's largest sugar producer after the three Marwari entities mentioned above, and also manufactures steam turbines, transmission gears, and wastewater plants. Dev Dutt Puri's Saraswati Industrial Syndicate operates one of the country's biggest single-location sugar mills (13,000 tcd) at Yamunanagar, apart from supplying sugar machinery, boilers, pressure vessels, and heat exchangers.[41] The Thapars' sugar mills have met the same fate as those of the Narangs, just as their colliery business was done in by the nationalization of coal mines in 1973. But, in paper, Ballarpur Industries Limited (Bilt) – formed after the acquisition of Ballarpur Paper and Straw Board Mills in 1946 and the merger of Shree Gopal Paper with it – is the industry leader. Similarly, Crompton Greaves is India's No. 1 private player in electrical engineering, producing a range of transformers, switchgears, motors, pumps, railway equipment, fans, and other home appliances, while Greaves Cotton has maintained its niche in diesel engines. The 100-odd Thapar companies were apportioned among the founder's four sons: Lalit Mohan, Brij Mohan, Man Mohan, and Inder Mohan.[42]

Karamchand Thapar and Gokul Chand Narang were originally from Punjab, but both made their fortunes in the Gangetic plain. This is significant in the context of our earlier allusion about how, despite their overwhelming control over the trade and money markets of west Punjab, there were limits to growth of Khatri capital in a primarily agro-based, landlocked, and industrially underdeveloped province. The community's full-fledged emergence on the national business map had to wait for a cataclysmic event like Partition, which literally pushed them in droves towards Delhi and its neighbourhoods. This massive exodus marked a human tragedy unparalleled in history, even as it opened up new avenues for a middle class with sound moorings in education and trade that had been driven to the wall. Proximity to the seat of power provided a platform from where they could be heard and also a vantage position to influence policy. A combination of enterprise, articulation, and strategic closeness to the national capital – which, in itself, was becoming a major growth hub and stimulating industrial activity in towns straddling the Sutlej–Beas and Yamuna basins – created conditions for Khatri capital to flourish in the post-Partition period. As Delhi grew in importance, so did the economic, social, and political profile of its Punjabi refugee community.[43]

The Mahindra brothers of Ludhiana, Jagdish Chandra (J.C.) and Kailash Chandra (K.C.), were educated at Cambridge and Oxford respectively, following which the former worked with the Tatas and the latter with Martin Burn. Having gained this early exposure to the steel industry, they joined government service towards the late 1930s. J.C. Mahindra became the first Indian to hold the post of Iron & Steel Controller, which was the canalizing agency through which all steel imports were undertaken and distributed through handling agents. K.C. Mahindra headed the Indian Supply Mission, Washington, the official body that issued tenders for steel imports against American aid. After the War, the two started their own private steel import business in partnership with Malik Ghulam Muhammad, who had been controller of general supplies and purchase. Mahindra & Muhammad, formed in October 1946, was a short-lived affair: after Partition, Ghulam Muhammad opted for Pakistan and became its first finance minister and later governor general. The original M&M was reborn as Mahindra & Mahindra in January 1948: the new name ensured that the already printed stationery displaying the M&M logo did not have to be changed!

Before this the brothers had secured a franchise from the Willys Overland Corporation of US to sell its 'Jeep' utility vehicles in India. In October 1947 the first batch of 75 Willys Jeeps was imported into India in completely knocked down (CKD) form. From their initial assembly of imported CKD Jeep kits the Mahindras took to licenced production by installing a plant in April 1955 at Bhandup near Mumbai. In 1963 – by which time over 10,000 Jeeps were being made annually with mostly locally sourced components – M&M tied up with the Virginia-based International Harvester to produce tractors. This joint venture – International Tractor Company of India – was, in 1977, merged with M&M, becoming its tractor division. Meanwhile, the group expanded its steel business through incorporation of Mahindra Ugine Steel Company in December 1962 for manufacturing alloy and special steels. The Rs 11,000-crore-plus Mahindra group – now managed by K.C. Mahindra's son, Keshub, and J.C. Mahindra's grandson Anand – is today the market leader in tractors, as well as in utility vehicles such as the indigenously designed 'Scorpio', 'Armada', 'Bolero', and 'Commander'. It also has stakes in real estate (Mahindra Gesco Developers) and IT (Tech Mahindra Limited).[44]

The Mahindras were not the only Punjabis to prosper from steel imports during the Iron & Steel Controller era. Before them there was one Pyare Lal who, in 1910, established a tiny foundry in his backyard at Jalandhar to make steel buckets, trunks, and farm implements. During World War II Amin Chand Pyare Lal – the firm prefixed the entrepreneur's father's name – became a major dealer in imported steel. The business grew substantially in the 1950s, when the Apeejay group – short for Amin Chand Pyare Lal Jalandhar and now under the founder's son Surrendra Paul (derived from Pyare Lal) – began sourcing steel and rails from the Soviet Bloc, against the traditional US–West European route. Steel imports led Apeejay into shipping through purchase of a 2,000 tonne vessel in 1948, and the group has since expanded to become India's largest privately held shipping company with subsidiaries in Singapore and Panama. The group further diversified into hotels ('The Park' in Delhi, Kolkata, Chennai, and Bangalore), tea (17 estates covering 30,000 acres in Assam), financial services (Apeejay Finance), retail (Oxford Bookstores), and education (Apeejay Schools). Surrendra Paul was killed by insurgents of the United Liberation Front of Assam (ULFA) in 1990, during a visit to his tea gardens. His brother, Swraj Paul, an MIT alumnus, migrated to England in 1968. There he created a parallel steel empire – the one billion euro Caparo Group – and, as Lord Paul of Marylebone, emerged as the most visible non-resident Indian industrialist till upstaged by Lakshmi Mittal and Anil Agarwal.

But neither the Mahindras nor the Pauls represent the typical refugees who made it big after arriving in India from the other side of the border. To that category belong Hari Prasad Nanda, the three cycle majors – Munjals of Hero, Kapurs of Atlas, and Pahwas of Avon – and Khatri Sikhs like Bhai Mohan Singh, Raunaq Singh and, to some extent, Mohan Singh Oberoi. Hari Prasad Nanda and his brother Yudhister had in 1944 set up Escorts Agents Limited at Lahore for distributing electrical appliances of the US multinational Westinghouse. With Partition, the venture (in which one of the partners was interestingly Vittal Mallya!) went bust. Nanda had to start anew in Delhi, using a bank loan for a transport business and trading in second-hand cars disposed of by exiting British officials. In 1948 he established Escorts Agricultural Machines Limited as a franchisee for the American farm equipment maker Minneapolis-Moline, and later for Massey Ferguson. In 1961 – the same year that TAFE tied up with Massey Ferguson – Escorts began assembling tractors at Faridabad, near Delhi, with technical knowhow from Ursus of Poland. Eight years later, the company was producing 'Ford' tractors under licence from the Michigan-based auto giant. Then came joint ventures with JC Bamford Excavators of the UK for earthmoving and construction equipment in 1979 (Escorts JCB Limited); with Yamaha of Japan to produce its motorcycles in 1985 (Escorts Yamaha Motors was formed in 1995); and with Claas of Germany for harvester combines in 1990 (Escorts Class Limited). The group's problems surfaced from the 1980s, with Swraj Paul mounting a hostile takeover in 1983: a bid foiled by the Indira Gandhi government after its initial covert support for a change in management. The subsequent decade saw break-ups with overseas partners. In 1996 the contract to produce 'Ford' tractors was dissolved, forcing Escorts to introduce its own 'Famtrac' and 'Powertrac' brands. By 2003 the group had also divested from its joint ventures with Yamaha, JC Bamford, and Claas. Adding to these were internal problems between Hari Prasad Nanda's sons, Rajan and Anil, which came into the open after the founder's death in 2000. Escorts, under Rajan Nanda, is still India's No. 3 tractor concern after Mahindra and TAFE, but has definitely seen better days. Anil Nanda has sold his majority stake in Goetze India Limited to the American partner, Federal Mogul Corporation (formerly Goetze-Werke of Germany). A major producer of pistons and piston rings, it was started in 1954 and, in fact, marked the group's first foray into manufacturing.[45]

The Munjals – Dayanand, Satyanand, Brij Mohan Lall, and Om

Prakash – were the sons of a grain commission agent at Kamalia in Lyallpur (Faisalabad). In 1944 they started a cycle parts trading business in Amritsar. Partition forced the brothers to completely sever links with their home town and move permanently to Ludhiana, where they began manufacturing handlebars, front forks, and chains. In 1956 Hero Cycles Limited was registered for assembling full bicycles. By 1975 'Hero' was India's leading brand and, in 1986, entered the *Guinness Book* as the globe's No. 1. From a mere 25 bicycles per day, Hero Cycles today churns out around 18,000 units.

Ludhiana's other big bicycle maker, Avon Cycles, was established earlier in 1952 by a refugee from Sialkot, Hansraj Pahwa. Even prior to them was Atlas Cycles, whose Lahore-born founder, Jankidas Kapur, started at Sonepat (Haryana) in 1950. By the end 1970s, the Khatri trio produced almost 65 per cent of the country's bicycles, displacing the Birlas' Hind Cycles (Mumbai), the Murugappa Group's TI Cycles (Chennai) and Sen Raleigh (Kolkata). In 1978 the Munjals diversified into mopeds (Hero Majestic) and, in 1984, launched motorbikes through Hero Honda Motors Limited. The formula employed was the same: an equity-cum-technical tie-up with Japan's Honda Motor Company. Within ten years over a million bikes had been manufactured; by 2004–5 yearly sales alone crossed 2.5 million, something unprecedented in the world. The Rs 12,000 crore Hero group is today to bicycles and two-wheelers what the Mahindras are to tractors and utility vehicles.[46] A crucial element of their success – the same applies to TVS and others – has been the state's role in guaranteeing protection against imports, and, equally important, against potential 'jettisoning' by the foreign collaborator. Till as late as January 2005 there was this innocuous sounding yet diabolically designed 'Press Note 18', mandating any foreign company wanting to set up shop independently to first get a no-objection from its local partner in an existing venture. Such provisions enabled the likes of Hero, Mahindra, TVS, and Bajaj to build up marketing networks and technological capabilities over time, enough to prepare them for the competition ahead.

Raunaq Singh hailed from Daska in Sialkot and his corporate journey began as a salesman for a steel pipes merchant in Lahore. Soon, he had opened a modest trading outlet, making the most of an acute water pipes shortage in villages around Lahore. Partition rendered the 25-year-old penniless and he had to restart from a cycle shop in Delhi's Chandni Chowk before going back to steel pipe distribution. By the early 1960s, Raunaq Singh had graduated to manufacturing through Bharat Steel Tubes Limited (BSTL) at Ganaur (Sonepat) and taking on entrenched companies, including Tata Tubes, and Kalinga Steel of Orissa's chief minister Biju Patnaik. His next venture was Bharat Gears in 1974, which became the country's largest supplier of gears for buses, trucks, tractors, and utility vehicles. The flagship, Apollo Tyres, was registered in 1976. The original licence for its plant at Perambra, near Kochi in Kerala, belonged incidentally to two Malayali Christians, Mathew T. Marattukalam and Jacob Thomas, before being bought over by Raunaq Singh. The latter had by now cultivated strong links with Indira Gandhi and her son, Sanjay, and was made the first chairman of the then state-owned car maker Maruti Udyog. Apollo Tyres evolved into one of India's leading tyre companies, though Raunaq Singh had to suffer the ignominy of being unseated by his eldest son, Onkar Singh Kanwar, born of his first wife. After ceding control in 1993 he was formally ejected as chairman just a week before passing away in September 2002. BSTL has gone sick, while Bharat Gears is headed by Raunaq Singh's other son Surinder Kanwar.[47]

Bhai Mohan Singh's theme is a slight variant of the Apollo patriarch's. Born in Rawalpindi to a Hindu father and a Sikh mother, he amassed wealth during World War II building roads in the North East for the British Army, then anxious to check the rapid Japanese advance through Burma. Relocating to Delhi after Partition, he turned to moneylending, only to take control of a defaulting firm, Ranbaxy, for Rs 2.5 lakh in 1952. Established in 1937 at Amritsar, it was named after Ranjit Singh and Gurbax Singh, who were distributors for A. Shionogi, a Japanese pharma producer. In 1961, in collaboration with Lapetit of Italy – whose distributorship Ranbaxy had taken in 1951 – Bhai Mohan set up his first plant at Okhla in Delhi. Within five years the relationship soured. Lapetit's pullout meant that Ranbaxy had to develop its own products and brands. In 1969 the company successfully launched the sleeping pill 'Calmpose', a copy of Roche's Valium, which the Swiss multinational had not bothered to patent in India. When the country shifted to a process patent regime in 1970 – it is rumoured that the Hathi Committee report of 1975, which gave a huge boost to the domestic pharma industry, was drafted in Bhai Mohan's office – Ranbaxy was the first to exploit reverse engineering possibilities and come out with blockbusters such as 'Roscillin', 'Cifran', and 'Revital'. But Bhai Mohan, too, fell victim to an ugly boardroom brawl with his eldest son, Parvinder Singh, who had joined the company in 1967 after doing a doctorate in pharmacology from Michigan. By 1989 the family business was partitioned, with Parvinder being given Ranbaxy and the other two brothers, Manjit and Analjit, getting Montari Industries and Max India, respectively. Bhai Mohan was compelled to resign from the Ranbaxy board in 1993, coincidentally around the time Raunaq Singh lost out at Apollo. While Ranbaxy prospered further under Parvinder (who died in July 1999, seven years before his father), occupying the top slot in the Indian pharma industry, Montari went sick: Manjit Singh and Bhai Mohan were even convicted in a cheque-bouncing case in 2004 that nearly denied the latter the Padma Vibhushan, the country's second highest civilian honour.

Analjit Singh co-promoted Hutchison Max Telecom (the 'Hutch' cellular mobile operator) in 1992, only to sell his 41 per cent stake six years later to the Hong Kong-based Hutchison Whampoa for Rs 561 crore. Max India's main interests are now in healthcare (Max Hospitals) and life insurance (a joint venture with New York Life).

Mohan Singh Oberoi's move from Pakistan pre-dates its creation. After spending his early years in Chakwal, a town close to Rawalpindi, and enrolling for a typing-cum-shorthand course after matriculation, Mohan Singh got a job at a shoe factory in Lahore through his paternal uncle. Its closure drove the 22-year-old Sikh, who no longer kept a beard and long hair, to Shimla, where he flunked an exam for a junior clerk post in the Public Works Department. With no place to go, he decided to stay put in Shimla and joined the Cecil Hotel as a billing clerk in 1922. Its manager, Ernest Clarke, took a shine to him: when the Carlton Hotel at the neighbouring Mall was put on sale, he bought it and made the hardworking Mohan Singh its manager. After running it for a few years Clarke had to return to England and he offered the hotel to Mohan Singh for Rs 20,000. The latter raised the whole sum from his uncle, Khanchand Kapur, a retired bureaucrat who had been dewan to assorted petty kingdoms. Thus, in August 1934, Mohan Singh became proprietor of Clarke's Hotel. Five years later, he took on lease Kolkata's Grand Hotel, which had been lying closed since a cholera epidemic in 1933. With his usual diligence and a great deal of luck – wartime ensured that the hotel was fully booked by British troops – Mohan Singh not only turned it around but made enough profits to acquire the Associated Hotels of India in 1943. Besides hotels at Lahore, Murree, Peshawar, and Delhi, this combine also owned Shimla's Cecil, where Mohan Singh had first slogged it out as a clerk! In 1949 he incorporated East India Hotels Limited (EIH), which operates some thirty-five properties across six countries, making it the country's largest chain after the Tatas' Indian Hotels.[48]

There are numerous other first-generation post-Partition Khatri entrepreneurs. A prominent name is Harbans Lal Malhotra who, in 1949, established a family-owned razor blade empire. With brands like 'Topaz', 'Laser', 'Galant', 'Silver Prince', and 'Bharat', the House of Malhotras – inclusive of the breakaway Vidyut Metallics ('Super Max') of the founder's youngest son – is India's top and the world's No. 2 shaving blade manufacturer after the US consumer products giant Gillette. Then there is the sports goods industry, whose foundations were laid in Sialkot by two Khatri Sikh brothers, Ganda Singh and Jhanda Singh. In 1903 Ganda Singh visited England and his Uberoi Limited began making cricket bats using imported English willows and power machines; he even brought in overseas experts to train local craftsmen. One of his protégés was F.C. Sondhi, who set up branches at Rangoon and London in the 1930s. The London office was bombed down during the War and, with no transport available to return to India, the young manager started a small toy dealership by the name of F.C. Sondhi and Company Limited in 1944. After Partition, many of Sialkot's skilled workers settled in Jalandhar. Soon, Sondhi was importing small sports goods consignments into England, before putting up a manufacturing facility at Jalandhar in 1967. The company's 20-acre factory outside Jalandhar is today a major producer and exporter of cricket and hockey gear. The other big industry centre is Meerut. Here again the main players are Khatris such as Kedar Nath Anand's genteel-sounding Sanspareils Greenlands Limited (makers of 'SG' cricket bats) and N.K. Sareen's Sareen Sports Industries ('SS Sunridges').

The community also has an established presence in assorted other sectors, from rice milling to media, including films. Jugal Kishore Arora's Satnam Overseas (makers of 'Kohinoor' basmati rice), Raghunath Arora's L.T. Overseas ('Daawat' brand), Kartar Singh's Amar Singh Chawal Wala ('Lal Qilla') and Balbir Singh Uppal's Lakshmi Energy and Foods Limited are all Khatri outfits.[49] So are the India Today group (*India Today* and *Aaj Tak*) of Aroon Purie and the Jalandhar-based Hind Samachar Limited, publisher of the Hindi daily *Punjab Kesri*, founded in 1948 by Lala Jagat Narain. They represent two generations of Khatri businessmen: the Lala, a refugee from Gujranwala who headed the Lahore City Congress Committee during pre-Independence, and Purie, a London-trained chartered accountant before he launched *India Today* in 1975. More recent is Raghav Bahl, who worked as an anchor person and production consultant for the India Today group's video newsmagazine *Newstrack* in the late 1980s. In 1993 he started Television Eighteen India Limited, which broadcasts the CNBC-TV18 and CNN-IBN news channels.[50] In entertainment there are a dime a dozen Khatri production houses, from Raj Kapoor's RK Films and Dev Anand's Navketan to Baldev Raj Chopra's B.R. Films, his brother Yash Chopra's Yash Raj Films, Subhash Ghai's Mukta Arts, and Ekta Kapoor's Balaji Telefilms, not to mention outfits owned by Prakash Mehra, Shekhar Kapur, and Vidhu Vinod Chopra.[51]

Aroon Purie and Raghav Bahl are not exceptional Khatri magnates of the second-generation phase after Partition. Since the 1970s, a whole new crop of industrialists has come up, especially in areas such as auto components and IT. Sona Koyo Steering Systems of Surinder Kapur, Subros Limited of Ramesh Suri, Rico Auto Industries of Arvind Kapur, Omax Autos of the Mehta brothers (Jatender and Ravinder), and Amtek Auto of Arvind Dham were all set up in the 1980s as ancillary suppliers to Maruti Udyog, Hero Honda, and Escorts. Indeed, in Sona Koyo and Subros, Maruti was not just a captive buyer of their steering gears and airconditioning systems, but even an equity investor. And here, community linkages did work. Surinder Kapur – whose father owned the capital's well-known jewellery chain Kapur Di Hatti – is married to the daughter of Raunaq Singh, who, we have seen, was Maruti's first chairman. His son Sanjay is incidentally married to Raj Kapoor's granddaughter, the actress Karisma Kapoor. Ramesh Suri is the brother of the late Lalit Suri, at one time a close friend of Sanjay Gandhi and promoter of Bharat Hotels Limited, which runs luxury hotels in major cities under 'The Grand' banner.[52]

Prominent Khatri figures in electronics and IT include Satish Kaura of the Samtel group (a prominent television picture tube manufacturer) and Deepak Puri of Moser Baer India Limited (a global leader in optical storage media, covering floppy disks, compact discs, and digital versatile discs or DVDs), and, of course, the Silicon Valley entrepreneurs Sabeer Bhatia (the creator of Hotmail, which he sold in 1997 to Microsoft for $400 million), Vinod Khosla (co-founder of Sun Microsystems), and the venture capitalist Kanwal Rekhi. In addition, there some important recent industrialists like Rajinder Miglani of Uttam Galva Steels, Ashok Punj of PSL Limited (a leading steel pipes supplier), Sudhir Dhingra of Orient Craft (one of the country's top garment exporters), Ponty Chadha (North India's most powerful liquor baron, who also dabbles in real estate, films, and sugar), Kuldip Singh Dhingra of Berger Paints India, and the two engineering-cum-construction firms Punj Lloyd Limited of Atul Punj and D.S. Constructions of Darshan Singh Narula.[53]

Bhadralok and Babus

Few educationally enlightened communities harbour a more deep-seated aversion towards trade and industry than do the Bengalis. The bhadralok – an urbanized, upper-caste cluster of Brahmins, Kayasthas, and Vaidyas which dominates West Bengal's political and cultural, but not economic, life – are considered intellectually imperious and devoid of entrepreneurial drive; more comfortable in adda (informal group) discourse about Rabindranath Tagore, Satyajit Ray, Karl Marx, and football rather than the murky world of business.

Like all received notions, this has its element of exaggeration. Nevertheless, there are historical reasons for this perceived elite Bengali indifference towards business. Bengal was the first province to have been comprehensively annexed and brought under direct colonial administration after the Battle of Plassey in 1757. While in other parts of India continuing nominal control exercised by native states and a not-so-neat imperial division of economic space gave opportunities for Indians to gain a toehold in modern industry, this was not so in Bengal. Eastern India was a classic British enclave. At the onset of World War I, all its fifty jute mills were controlled by European managing agencies, while 86 per cent of tea plantations and 47 per cent of coal firms were in British hands. The numbers were even higher – 96 per cent and 89 per cent – for the tea concerns and collieries organized on joint-stock, as against proprietary or partnership, lines.[54] These three key industries – and, prior to them, opium and indigo – were essentially export-oriented, where the Europeans, with their monopoly over shipping lines and superior knowledge of overseas markets, had a clear advantage. The situation changed somewhat with the War and more so the Depression, which led to a drastic contraction of foreign trade and heralded the era of tariff protection favouring entrepreneurs geared to supplying the domestic market. But the beneficiaries here were the Marwaris, who, apart from investing in sugar, paper, and cement – industries with comparatively low foreign presence – also challenged European dominance in jute and coal by acquiring blocks of shares in existing companies from the secondary market along with establishing new mills and collieries.

The Marwaris, we saw in the last chapter, were well placed to exploit the declining power of the expatriate agencies, many of whom had to sell off their indebted, cash-strapped companies to their erstwhile brokers and financiers. The Bengalis, by contrast, lacked the upcountry trading and money market networks to sustain commodity businesses, where skill in buying raw material and selling the finished product, and ability to finance the holding of stocks counted far more than acquaintance with the technical processes of manufacture.[55] An oft-quoted case is of the bhadralok N.C. Sircar, who, at the end of the War, managed seven collieries with an aggregate paid-up capital of over Rs 30 lakh. During the slump that set in from 1925, he borrowed heavily from a Marwari trader, Sukhlall Karnani, and ran into repayment problems. The latter then tightened the screws and forced Sircar to transfer his mines to H.V. Low and Company, which, too, could not discharge its debts and eventually sold its assets to the Marwari. N.C. Sircar spent his last years as a repentant mendicant on the banks of the Ganga in Varanasi.[56] The Bengalis were nowhere to be found when the last European bastion, tea, also started crumbling from the 1950s, culminating in Keshav Prasad Goenka's buyout of Duncan Brothers, Brij Mohan Khaitan's of Williamson Magor and McLeod Russel, and Surrendra Paul's of the estates of Gillanders Arbuthnot.

But even in this overall unfriendly environment, there were some remarkable bhadralok business figures. The Nobel laureate Rabindranath Tagore's grandfather, Dwarkanath (1794–1846), came from a landed Brahmin family whose members held high offices under the Raj and worked for agency houses like Mackintosh & Co. The suave Dwarkanath was himself appointed dewan to the Board of Customs, Salt and Opium in 1829. In October 1834 he floated Carr, Tagore and Company as an equal partnership with a British indigo trader, William Carr. Initially, it exported indigo, sugar, and silk, sourced mainly out of the Tagore family's estates. In January 1836 Dwarkanath purchased the Raniganj colliery at Burdwan for Rs 70,000. From there Carr and Tagore went on to promote a spate of joint stock enterprises: the Calcutta Steam Tug Association (to operate tugboats between Kolkata and the mouth of the Hooghly river), the India General Steam Navigation Company (to run a steamboat service between Kolkata and Allahabad), the Calcutta Steam Ferry Bridge Company (a floating ferry across the Hooghly powered by a steam engine fixed to the shore), the Bengal Tea Association, and the Bengal Salt Company. They were all mainly forward integration ventures that consumed the coal from Dwarkanath's Raniganj fields. By 1844 he had also set up the Bengal Coal Company by taking over a rival colliery at Naraincoory and merging it with the Raniganj property. The management of all these companies was vested with Carr, Tagore & Co. In the process, Dwarkanath had innovated a totally new concept of joint-stock companies in which the 'firm' took the place of the 'individual' as manager.[57] This was the prototype for the managing agency firm that corporate India later institutionalized, before it was abolished in 1970 and board-managed, shareholder-controlled companies became the norm.

But howsoever original these schemes may have been, the visible hand of colonialism could not be wished away. After Dwarkanath died in 1846, not only did Carr, Tagore & Co. go under, but also its ventures were either scrapped or reorganized sans Indian partnership. The Bengal Coal Company – the biggest in the province – passed into the hands of Andrew Yule, while India General Steam Navigation went to Schoene, Kilburn and Company. Even while alive, Dwarkanath saw his most ambitious project – a 160 km rail line connecting the Raniganj coalfields to Kolkata – being derailed by the authorities. His Great Western Ben-gal Railway was viewed as rivalling the East Indian Railway

Company of Rowland McDonald Stephenson, who obviously enjoyed greater clout with the authorities. Similar Indo-European partnerships involving Motilal Seal (with George Oswald), Raja Barada Kanta Ray (with one Henry Fuller King), and other bhadralok also ended up as disasters. Their descendants showed no inclination to carry on and a general loss of faith in modern business gripped the Bengali psyche. The affluent chose to invest their surpluses in land and zamindari rights, which were considered safe, prestigious, and moreover profitable under the Permanent Settlement regime that gave landlords extensive powers to collect rent and other payments from tenants.[58]

One partnership that endured even well after Independence, though, was Martin Burn. The person behind it, Rajendra Nath Mookerjee (1854–1936), was an engineer who started a firm, T.C. Mookerjee and Company, specialising in the construction of waterworks. In spite of executing some big pipe-laying contracts for the Calcutta municipality, Rajendra Nath found the absence of pedigree an operational impediment. In 1892 he joined hands with an Englishman, Acquin Martin, and adopted the name Martin & Company in order to make things easier.[59] At the turn of the century, the company had developed into a giant engineering entity commissioning several water-work stations, feeder railways, and building projects (including Kolkata's magnificent Victoria Memorial) all over India. In 1924 Martin & Co. – the name was retained despite the Mookerjee family assuming firm control after Acquin Martin's death – took over Burn & Company which, six years earlier, had promoted the Indian Iron & Steel Company (IISCO). This was basically a pig iron concern that commenced steel production only from 1939 at Burnpur in Burdwan district. Well up to the mid-1960s Martin Burn – as the group, now under the founder's son Biren Mookerjee, was known – was the country's largest industrial house after the Tatas and the Birlas, with interests in steel, engineering, wagon building, power, refractories, etc. Its flagship, IISCO, was the only Indian scrip quoted on the London Stock Exchange. Till 1966 it used to declare dividends higher than Tata Steel and manufacture around 1 million tonnes annually. That also made it a prized target for many a Marwari, from Haridas Mundhra to Ramnath Goenka of the *Indian Express*. The group's sudden fall – starting with wild speculation in its stocks and labour unrest from mid 1967 – is shrouded in mystery. By 1972 IISCO's output had nosedived to 4.3 lakh tonnes, leading to its nationalization alongside other group companies. Were the strikes instigated, did they have anything to do with those mounting hostile bids for IISCO, what role did the government and its individual ministers play? – these are still grey areas. At the end of it all, Bengal's perhaps most distinguished business family faded into oblivion.

Partnerships aside, there was a wave of purely indigenous Bengali entrepreneurship in the early decades of the twentieth century. Inspired by nationalistic renaissance personalities such as Prafulla Chandra Ray and Jagadis Chandra Bose, it gained traction with the swadeshi agitation following the partition of Bengal in 1905 by the viceroy, Lord Curzon. The Banga Luxmi Cotton Mills and Mohini Mills were started during this time and their products widely advertised as 'Bengali cloth woven in Bengali mills by Bengali weavers and sold through Bengali retail stores'.[60] Very many swadeshi ventures, moreover, were in new areas where neither British firms nor Marwaris were present: Bengal Chemicals & Pharmaceuticals (drugs), Calcutta Chemical Company (soaps, toothpaste, and herbal cosmetics), Bengal Immunity (vaccines), Bengal Lamps (electric bulbs), Bengal Waterproof (raincoats and footwear), the Bande Match Factory and Oriental Match Company (safety matches), Bengal Potteries, etc. The two newspaper groups, Ananda Bazar Patrika (ABP) of the Sarkars and Amrit Bazar Patrika-Jugantar of the Ghosh family were also protagonists of the swadeshi cause. The promoters in these were often men of outstanding technical calibre: for example, Bengal Chemicals' founder, Prafulla Chandra Ray, who had a chemistry doctorate from the University of Edinburgh; and the Oxford-educated Kiran Shankar Roy of Bengal Lamps.

The above concerns, barring some like ABP and Bengal Waterproof, did not survive beyond their initial idealist phase. The ABP group, headed by Aveek Sarkar, publishes the largest circulated Bengali daily, *Ananda Bazar Patrika*, and also Kolkata's leading English newspaper, *The Telegraph*.[61] Debabrata Bose's Bengal Waterproof is a barely Rs 100 crore company after over eighty-five years, known more for its 'Duckback' brand of rainwear, gumboots, and school bags. The rest couldn't survive the competition. This time, it came from the new European and American multinationals – Unilever, General Electric, Philips, and Swedish Match Company, among others – who had started Indian subsidiaries during the 1920s and 1930s in order to jump the tariff walls erected by the authorities. The swadeshi companies were typically closely held, under-capitalized and not technologically equipped or market savvy as the multinational consumer goods giants. They either fell by the wayside (the match firms), were bought over (Calcutta Chemical by Henkel), or nationalized (Bengal Chemicals). A genuine bhadralok capitalist class could thereby never emerge, which meant that, even as the British managing agencies were packing up, their space was occupied by the ever-alert Marwaris. Matters worsened after Independence, as Kolkata lost its pre-eminence in finance and politics to Mumbai and Delhi. Even the big Marwari houses that had accumulated their capital in the trading floors of the Calcutta Stock Exchange and the bylanes of Burrabazar, gradually shifted base. By the time the Left Front was permanently ensconced in Writers' Building from 1977, the process of capital flight and deindustrialization had attained a life of its own.

The Bengali tycoons of the last three or four decades are mostly qualified professionals who have made it big outside their region of origin. This is true of the economist-turned-media baron Prannoy Roy of New Delhi Television Limited (NDTV). It holds even truer of Amar Gopal Bose and Bicky Chakraborty. The former was an electrical engineering professor at MIT before founding, in 1964, what became a byword for audio speaker and sound reproduction technology: the Massachusetts-headquartered Bose Corporation. Bicky Chakraborty is regarded as the richest Indian in Scandinavia, having gone from Kolkata to study at Stockholm's Royal Institute of Technology in the 1960s and started the Elite Hotels chain at Sweden. He is also the main investor in Westbank Hospital near Kolkata, promoted in 1998 by a group of overseas Bengali doctors. But the non-resident Indian to have sunk deeper roots in his home state is Purnendu Chatterjee. An engineer from IIT Kharagpur who did a doctorate at the University of Berkeley in California, Chatterjee worked for ten years at McKinsey & Company. After becoming a principal there, he quit in 1986 to launch The Chatterjee Group (TCJ), affiliated to Soros Fund Management of the global hedge fund investor George Soros. TCJ is the majority shareholder in Haldia Petrochemicals Limited, an integrated naphtha-based petro-chemicals complex commissioned in April 2000. With an investment of over Rs 5,000 crore this project – a joint venture with the state government – has been a turning point for the Left Front regime which has been desperately aiming to cultivate an industry-friendly image in recent times.

The two most prominent national-level 'Bengali' business groups today are Sahara India Pariwar of Subrata Roy and Dabur of the Burmans. Their operations are concentrated outside Bengal. Subrata Roy's story has shades of Winston Churchill's description of Russia: a riddle wrapped in a mystery inside an enigma. Starting as a small para-banking business with three workers in 1978 at Gorakhpur (eastern Uttar Pradesh), his Sahara India claims an asset base of over Rs 50,000 crore, with interests in public deposit mobilization, real estate, media, and aviation. None of Roy's businesses are listed; his lavish lifestyle and flaunting of connections with the world's rich and famous have further added to the conspiratorial aura.

Dabur's beginnings date back to a corner store Ayurveda pharmacy that a Kolkata-based physician, S.K. Burman, opened in 1884. The group – its name is short for 'Daktar (doctor) Burman' – moved its offices to Delhi in 1972 and is now a Rs 2,000 crore herbal products major, owning brands like 'Hajmola' digestives, 'Dabur Chyawanprash' health supplement, 'Dabur Amla' hair oil, 'Lal Dant Manjan' tooth-powder, and 'Real' fruit juices.[62] The Burmans are actually 'Bengalicized' Punjabis who were settled in Kolkata for generations.

It would be an exaggeration, however, to assert that homegrown bhadralok businessmen don't exist. We have mentioned ABP. There are similar other venerable names such as Peerless General Finance and Investment Company, G.D. Pharmaceuticals (makers of 'Boroline' antiseptic cream), Dey's Medical Stores Manufacturing Limited ('Keo Karpin' hair oil), and TIL Limited (formerly Tractors India). Peerless was started in 1932 by a schoolteacher, Radhashyam Roy, as a swadeshi insurance company which, after nationalization of this sector in 1956, shifted to small savings mobilization. With annual deposit collections of over Rs 1,000 crore, it is the country's leading residuary non-banking company along with Subrata Roy's Sahara India Financial Corporation. G.D. Pharma (named after its founder, Gourmohan Dutta) and Dey's Medical (after B.N. Dey) are also products of the 1930s.

Avijit Mazumdar's TIL began in 1944 as a dealer for the American construction equipment giant Caterpillar. It has since diversified into the manufacture of mobile cranes while continuing to represent Caterpillar and other global material handling and earth-moving equipment companies. More recent are Bijon Nag, Swapan Sadhan (Tutu) Bose, Suresh Chandra Dey, and Santanu Ghosh. Bijon Nag, a technocrat who worked in Germany and Switzerland, promoted Indian Fine Blanks Limited (now IFB Industries) with foreign collaboration in 1974 to manufacture precision (fine blanked) components and tools used for automotive applications. Subsequently, he tied up with the German white goods maker Bosch to launch washing machines. In the 1980s the group also ventured into country liquor and IMFL.

Tutu Bose wears many hats: owner of the Bengali daily *Sangbad Pratidin* (launched in 1992), President of Kolkata's football club Mohun Bagan, and a Trinamul Congress Member of Parliament. His family also owns E.C. Bose & Company, a prominent stevedoring and port handling services provider.

Suresh Dey founded Sreeleathers in 1957 which, over the last decade, has grown into a major footwear and leather accessories retailer, with outlets across eastern India and in the north. Santanu Ghosh is the completely new kid on the block. A computer science graduate from Portland State University in the US, Santanu and his childhood friend Tathagata Dutta started Xenitis Infotech in 1999. By 2004–5 the turnover of this company – which markets affordable range personal computers under the 'Aamar PC' brand – had touched Rs 180 crore. The group has further launched *Kolkata TV*, a 24-hour Bengali news channel. But all these men are medium-league industrialists at best. Whether they point to a resurgent indigenous Bengali capitalist class, only time will tell.[63]

What is not in doubt is that the post-Independence period has thrown up several business groups drawn from castes that traditionally straddled the various service professions and administration. Besides Brahmins, Khatris, and the bhadralok there have been successful houses from other non-commercial savarna communities like the Nairs, northern Kayasthas, and Rajputs as well. T.P.G. Nambiar of India's once biggest (and now sick) consumer electronics company BPL Limited is a Nair. In 1963 he incorporated British Physical Laboratories to produce instrumentation panel meters at Palakkad, Kerala. With the delicensing of the electronics industry in the 1980s he got into the manufacture of televisions and telecom equipment. In 1995 the group entered mobile telephony through BPL Communications, which Nambiar's estranged son-in-law, Rajeev Chandrasekhar, later took over before selling it to the Ruias of Essar in mid 2005. Chandrasekhar has since gone on to pick up a majority holding in the leading Malayalam television channel company Asianet Communications, whose original promoter was a Moscow-based Nair, Raji Menon.

The other famous Nair industrialists are the Kannur-born C.P. Krishnan Nair of Hotel Leelaventure Limited ('The Leela' hotels) and the late 'biscuit king' J.M. Rajan Pillai. The latter, hailing from a family of cashew tycoons at Kollam, had a controlling stake in Britannia Industries Limited from 1988 to 1993, before Nusli Wadia controversially edged him out. Rajan Pillai's uncle, K. Ravindranathan Nair, owns Vijayalaxmi Cashew Company, the country's No. 1 cashew products exporter. Subash Menon of Subex Systems Limited (a Bangalore-based telecom software products firm), P.N.C. Menon of Sobha Developers Limited (Bangalore's leading real estate company), and Ram Menon (who heads a chain of auto ancillaries at Kolhapur) also happen to be Nairs.[64]

Kayastha presence in industry is inversely proportional with the scores of Bhatnagars, Mathurs, Saxenas, Srivastavas, Sinhas, and Sahays dotting government and corporate bureaucracies. The 1965 Monopolies Inquiry Commission report did have J.P. Srivastava, a cotton millowner from Kanpur and supporter of the right-wing Hindu Mahasabha. His now-defunct textile house was ranked seventeenth in the list of seventy-five industrial groups. Another successful businessman at one time was S.P. Sinha who, in 1973, acquired Jenson & Nicholson India from its British parent. This once-premier paint concern is currently ailing.

The only Kayastha magnate with some standing today is Jagdish Saxena of Elder Pharmaceuticals Limited. Saxena, whose relatives (father included) were mainly government babus, served as chief executive of the Apeejay Group's pharma division prior to launching his own company in 1988.[65]

As for Rajputs, the one industrialist worthy of mention – if we ignore the artful politician and Subrata Roy's alter ego Amar Singh – probably is Ramesh Chauhan of Parle Bisleri Limited. His company owns 'Bisleri', the market leader in bottled water. Ramesh Chauhan is, however, remembered more for creating popular soft drink brands like 'Thums Up, 'Limca', and 'Mazaa' and then selling them to the Coca Cola Company in 1993. His brother, Prakash Chauhan, controls Parle Agro Limited ('Frooti' juices and 'Bailley' mineral water), while their cousin Vijay Chauhan owns Parle Products which makes 'ParleG', 'Krackjack', and 'Monaco' biscuits.

4

Kammas, Reddys, and Rajus

Within a nation that harbours bitter memories of colonial subjugation, it is rare to discover an Englishman revered by its people, least of all someone who was very much part of the imperial establishment. The irrigation engineer Sir Arthur Thomas Cotton (1803–99) is an exception. In the fertile coastal delta tracts of Andhra Pradesh (AP) he is nothing short of a deified icon. Unlike Annie Besant, C.F. Andrews, Verrier Elwin, Madeleine Slade, and others who denounced imperialism, Cotton was no renegade. And yet, amidst the endless expanse of paddy and sugarcane fields, it is not uncommon to spot busts of 'Cotton Dora' (the respected one) serving as valuable landmarks in remote hamlets. In West Godavari district there is a village – Cottonreddypalem – named after him. The main square of Tanuku town has an impressive bronze statue of Arthur Cotton riding a horse next to that of Nannayya Bhattaraka, the eleventh-century Aadi Kavi (the first poet) and author of *Andhra Mahabharatamu*, the oldest recorded Telugu literary work. Since the coming of Nandamuri Tarakarama Rao (NTR) and his Telugu Desam Party (TDP) in the 1980s, there has been an even more organized effort at veneration of the legendary

British engineer. At Dowleswaram, the site near Rajahmundry where he built the famous barrage across the Godavari more than 150 years ago, there is a Cotton Museum that was opened by NTR on 21 February 1988. Another lasting legacy of NTR's chief ministerial tenure is the array of statues of Andhra's historical luminaries erected on the eastern side of Hyderabad's Hussain Sagar lake (Tank Bund, in popular parlance). Here again, Arthur Cotton finds a place alongside the likes of Nannayya, the classical saint-composer Thyagaraja, the city's founder Muhammed Quli Qutb Shah, the thirteenth-century Kakatiya warrior queen Rudrama Devi, and the revolutionary Urdu poet Maqdoom Mohiuddin.

Until well into the 1850s the agricultural economy in the four coastal delta districts of East and West Godavari, Krishna, and Guntur was hostage to the random acts of nature.[1] In the absence of any mechanism to harness the waters of its mighty rivers – irrigation channels to spread them over the surface of the land on either side or embankments to secure the standing crop from destruction by floods – the region was ravaged alternately by drought and excessive rains. Between 1820–1 and 1853–4 Rajahmundry district experienced only seven 'favourable' years,[2] while nine were 'ordinary' and the rest 'either years of deficit rainfall or those of floods and famines'.[3] The scale of depredation can be gauged from the fact that over the twenty-one years ending 1842–3, Rajahmundry's population registered an absolute decline from 738,308 to 561,041.[4] During the Great Famine of 1833 Guntur likewise 'had five hundred thousand inhabitants when the famine began: there were but three hundred thousand when it had passed away'.[5] For the colonial authorities the concern was not just over loss of lives and livelihoods but also over the drying up of revenues. From about Rs 18.6 lakh in 1821, land revenue from Rajahmundry dipped to as low as Rs 13.7 lakh in 1838 and Rs 15.1 lakh in 1842.[6]

It was under these circumstances that Arthur Cotton, then a captain in the Madras Engineers Corps of the British army, was in August 1844 asked to furnish a report on the state of irrigation in the district and 'its capabilities of improvement'. The rest is history. At Dowleswaram – a village at the head of the delta, where the Godavari stands over six km wide – Cotton designed an anicut: a gigantic barrier thrown across the river to arrest its waters that could then be diverted through a network of channels to irrigate a million acres of rich alluvial soil. This barrage – which, in his words, aimed at 'converting the water of the Godavari into money instead of letting it run into the sea'[7] – was built between 1847 and 1852. Cotton projected a similar anicut on the Krishna at Bezwada (as Vijayawada was called), the work on which commenced in 1852 and was completed in 1855. The results were dramatic. Rajahmundry in the pre-anicut period was a net importer of rice; the average value for the triennium ending 1843–4 being Rs 4.42 lakh.[8] By 1875–6 it was officially producing 601,000 tonnes, against an estimated nutritional consumption and seed requirement of 337,000 tonnes, translating into a marketable surplus of 44 per cent![9] While the district's population shrank by almost a quarter between 1821–3 and 1842–3, in the subsequent fifty years to 1891 it nearly quadrupled from 561,041 to 2,078,782. Most heartening for the administration was a fourfold-plus jump in revenues – from Rs 17,25,841 in 1843–4 to Rs 70,95,481 in 1894–5.[10] A similar transformation was witnessed in the neighbouring Krishna district, which, in 1875, was generating a marketable surplus amounting to 57 per cent of its gross rice production.[11]

More than 150 years after Sir Arthur Cotton unveiled his grand anicut schemes, the coastal delta region continues to be the grain bowl of AP. The four districts together produce 49 per cent of the rice and chillies, 39 per cent of the sugarcane, and 33 per cent of the cotton grown in the state.[12] On the other hand they constitute only 14 per cent of its total geographical area and 23 per cent of the population, as per the 2001 Census. Areas that barely grew a single rain-fed crop of rice during monsoon now comfortably cultivate two crops: the normal kharif (transplanted in mid-July/early–August and harvested in end-October/November) and an extra rabi (transplanted in early-January and harvested by mid-April). And in between the rabi harvest and raising the nursery for the ensuing kharif paddy, the farmers take out a 90-day forage or pulse crop as well.

Beholden to Cotton

The biggest beneficiary of Arthur Cotton's irrigation works – which transformed a land once prone to frequent famines into one of intensive wet rice cultivation – was the predominantly Kamma peasantry of coastal Andhra. As one of their more articulate representatives told the governor of Madras, Sir M.E. Grant Duff, on his visit to Vijayawada in the early 1880s: 'Even in famine years the Kistna [Krishna] never fails to do its duty and the dire poverty that existed during the childhood of middle-aged men is almost forgotten in the general prosperity... we should express gratitude to the good Government that has done these great things for us.'[13] The Kammas make up less than 5 per cent of AP's population, but are sizeably concentrated in the coastal districts. The 1921 Census reckoned their share in population at 25.8 per cent in Krishna, 36 per cent in Guntur, 12.5 per cent in Nellore, and 6.4 per cent in the undivided Godavari district.[14] More important, they formed the largest cultivating and landowning caste in the region. Although communities like the Kapus may have been more numerous, especially in the Godavari delta, they did not control as much land as the Kammas.

Before the sudden arrival of irrigation there was little to distinguish the farmers in the delta from those in the dry zone of the Madras Presidency. In the dry districts, 70 per cent of all pattas (official document bestowing the right to hold land under the ryotwari system of revenue assessment) were for land revenue payment of less than Rs 10 per annum in 1900. The average payment in pattas of this class was Rs 4, roughly corresponding to the produce from a four-acre plot. But in the Godavari delta, only 4 per cent of wetland was held in revenue pattas below Rs 10. Over 62 per cent represented the middle payment range from Rs 30 to Rs 250. Under dry cultivation, 8 acres paid between Rs 2.25 and Rs 18 per annum in revenue and its cultivator languished 'somewhere between poverty and beggary'. The same holding in a wet area paid between Rs 36 and Rs 70 and its cultivator would have been 'a substantial, if not particularly rich, peasant'.[15] Cotton's anicuts had, simply put, produced an agrarian revolution embracing a large section of coastal Andhra's Kamma middle peasantry.

This was, furthermore, a peasantry with a pronounced commercial bent – a development fostered not just by its newfound ability to generate surpluses but also by the ryotwari form of revenue settlement. Under the earlier amarakam system, the government jointly rented out whole villages and assigned the job of mobilizing revenues to the prominent zamindars or land controllers in those villages. In the ryotwari system that took shape around the same time as canal irrigation was introduced, the government dealt directly with each landholder (ryot), who was issued a patta and the revenue settlement was based on a uniform money rate. Being a money rate, it compelled farmers to part with a share of their crop, thereby stimulating commodity production. And, being a uniform rate, there was the added incentive to grow high-value cash crops.[16] Thus, in the deltas, coarse cereals such as jowar and bajra were obliterated by rice and sugarcane, whereas in the drier up-lands, farmers opted for cotton, chilli, tobacco, and oilseeds. This, in turn, promoted the growth of new market towns like Rajahmundry, Eluru, Vijayawada, Masulipatnam (Machilipatnam), Guntur, and Tenali, as farmers sought to sell their produce across the region. The 420 km long Buckingham Canal along the Coromandel coast, connecting Peddaganjam on the Krishna down to the Marakkanam backwaters of South Arcot, came handy for delta cultivators to tap distant grain markets in Madras and other Tamil districts. Large quantities of rice were also exported via Kakinada port. As early as the late 1860s, 'the leading *ryots*, merchants and the Cocanada [Kakinada] Chamber of Commerce were pleading for a railway line in the coastal districts'.[17] These were eventually laid by the early 1890s.

The extent of market orientation among cultivators unleashed by Cotton's anicuts and the ryotwari tenure can be seen in a report of the Board of Revenue dated 17 December 1903:

> In Bezwada there is a regular corn exchange where the price of paddy is fixed daily by the *ryots* with their samples, and the buyers are either merchants who buy on commission for Madras or agents of Bombay and Poona companies. The Tenali prices are ruled by the prices fixed at Bezwada, Masulipatnam, Madras, Secunderabad, etc. The merchants who buy or else the rich cultivators *who are nearly all becoming traders* store their grain till prices have risen and bring it to Tenali. Paddy is exported wherever the highest prices is obtainable [italics added].[18]

The delta farmer's business acumen was also noted by the Royal Commission on Agriculture appointed in 1926: 'Once he (the *ryot*) has paid his land revenue (*kist*) he keeps a steady eye on the prices primarily for rice imports from Burma, and is in no haste to come to towns with the agent or buyer if the towns do not suit him.'[19] What is more, this savviness was not restricted to the delta peasantry; it extended to the progressive Kamma farmers of the uplands as well. As the peasant leader N.G. Ranga pointed out in his study on Guntur's tobacco trade:

> The bigger *ryots* have begun, from 1916, to buy up large quantities of tobacco at the time of harvest, at very low prices, from the other smaller *ryots* and store it up in anticipation of a rise in prices. As the competition between the merchants has increased, the cultivators of tobacco have almost given up their former practice of going in search of prospective buyers. It is now the merchants or their agents who have to go in search of the producers. These village dealers are thus able to dictate their own terms.[20]

It is the same commercial proclivity that led farmers in the drier talukas of Guntur to grow cigarette-grade flue-cured virginia (FCV) tobacco for British American Tobacco (BAT) from the 1920s: perhaps India's first ever 'contract farming' project in which a foreign company supplied seedlings and technology for cultivating a crop against buyback at predetermined rates. Unlike the desi (indigenous) leaf used in bidis (cheroots) or snuff, FCV tobacco was an alien crop embodying new techniques of cultivation and processing. Once harvested, the green leaf had to be cured in closed barns with heat from a coal furnace conveyed through flues (iron pipes) – a radical departure from the simple sun or rack curing employed for desi tobacco. So rapid was the diffusion of the new technology that between 1930 and 1940 alone the number of barns in Guntur increased from 200 to 6,000, most of them built by the more affluent agriculturists.[21] Towards the mid 1950s Guntur had over 50,000 hectares under FCV tobacco, which crossed one lakh hectares during 1971–5, accounting for 65 per cent of the country's total FCV area.[22] In recent times farmers here have replicated this success in cotton, where the district's yields are twice the national average.[23]

By the early decades of the twentieth century a stratum of agriculturists had emerged who were looking at new avenues for investing savings accumulated from intensive farming of paddy and high-value cash crops such as virginia tobacco, turmeric, and chilli.

Some went into the grain trade, buying paddy on commission and transporting it to rice mills. Many of the mills that sprang up during this period were 'often built with the capital of the local *ryots*'.[24] In Guntur, 'in every village there are a few enterprising Kammas who have ten to twenty acres of land and who are anxious to do some sort of business or other', wrote Ranga, himself a Kamma from Nidubrolu in the same district.[25] The Kammas were also among the early non-Brahmin rural communities to take to modern education. According to the 1931 Census report, the literacy rate in the deltas 'grew faster than anywhere else in the Presidency'. In 1925 'Rajahmundry had at least five newspapers with a combined circulation of 4700 and Masulipatnam also maintained five with a circulation of 8,000. No other *mofussil* towns possessed anything like this level of activity.'[26] The Madras Banking Enquiry of 1933 observed that in the deltas, 'substantial sums of money were found to have been expended on the education of children.'[27]

While education definitely played a part in honing entrepreneurial skills among the Kammas – by integrating the town and countryside and broadening their circle of acquaintances beyond the village community – there is a second aspect that needs highlighting. This is that the hold of traditional merchant communities in South Indian business was generally weaker compared to that in the rest of the country. True, there were specialist mercantile castes like the Komatis (Arya Vaishyas) and the delta region did have some big banking firms from this community: the Mothey family of Eluru, the Pydahs of Kakinada, and the Maddi and Majeti families of Guntur. But these groups were largely urban-based and not entrenched in villages in the way the ubiquitous Bania was in the North Indian countryside. From the available evidence it appears that the Komatis and even immigrant Marwari financiers flocked to the delta countryside only well after canal irrigation had begun to yield results. And, despite their entry, a post-Depression enquiry for Guntur revealed that 87 per cent of the moneylenders were agriculturists themselves.[28] Similarly, data on land transfers in Krishna district during 1893–6 – a rough indicator of whether merchant capital was making inroads into the farm economy – showed that in about three-fourths of the cases the transactions were happening within the agricultural community. The number of cases where traders purchased land did not exceed 10 per cent of the total.[29] In such a scenario it was not difficult for a farmer with sufficient capital and drive – which N.G. Ranga's 'enterprising Kammas' were not lacking in – to diversify into trade and industry. As we will see in Chapter 8, this was not the case in the North, where the overbearing presence of traditional Vaishya communities acted as a hindrance for even prosperous and politically powerful agrarian castes to make such a seamless transition. This basic difference in the socio-business template forms a recurrent theme in the chapters that follow.

The First Wave of Kamma Entrepreneurs

Till around the early 1930s the affluent Kamma peasantry's locus of diversification was restricted to rural moneylending and trade or erecting small rice and oil mills. The turning point was the Great Depression, as the collapse of the rural credit system and falling commodity prices rendered these hitherto safe activities unviable. The Depression, in a way, created an impetus for rural capital to examine investment options outside these traditional lines of business. The lead here came mainly from large zamindars and estate holders – people with resources and deep pockets – rather than ordinary well-to-do cultivators, as was the case later on.[30]

An early pioneer was Yarlagadda Sivaramaprasad, usually referred to as the raja of Challapalli in Krishna district. While Andhra Bank's founder may have been a Brahmin – the freedom fighter and Congressman Bhogaraju Pattabhi Sitaramayya – it was Sivaramaprasad who committed the financial resources for starting the institution in November 1923. The raja was also instrumental in setting up Sarathi Films in 1938 in association with Gudavalli Ramabrahmam, a journalist who authored a book on the history of the Kammas. The Sarathi banner produced a number of Telugu hits, including *Malapilla* (a 1938 classic rubbishing Brahminic rituals and caste discrimination) and *Raitu Bidda* (1939). The latter was a powerful critique of the zamindari system, though its producer was himself a member of the landed gentry. When the film was released, the rajas of Venkatagiri and Bobbili threatened to go to court and burnt some of its prints, even as Sivaramaprasad ensured it did not run in his own territory! Another venture that the raja of Challapalli floated was the Andhra Scientific Company for manufacturing precision measurement instruments, which went sick and was acquired by the state-owned Bharat Electronics in 1982. In addition he, along with other wealthy Kamma zamindars, financed a co-operative sugar factory in 1936 at Vuyyuru (Krishna district) that could crush 800 tonnes of cane daily (tcd). The same group of landlords put up a sugar mill at Rayagada, a district in Orissa bordering Vizianagaram. The promoters even acquired land in the area to induce experienced growers from the Godavari delta, mostly Kammas, to migrate and cultivate cane for the factory.[31] Both the Vuyyuru and Rayagada units ultimately became part of the KCP group.

KCP's founder Velagapudi Ramakrishna came from a prominent Kamma landowning family in Krishna. After doing engineering in England before World War I and stints at Oxford and the London School of Economics, he joined the Indian Civil Service. Having risen to be Industrial Adviser to the Madras government, Ramakrishna retired prematurely to take over the ailing Vuyyuru Co-operative Agricultural Industrial and Credit Society, which became a public limited company, KCP, in 1941. The Rayagada unit, Jeypore Sugar Company, expanded into the mining of manganese and chrome deposits in the region, before commissioning a facility in 1958 to manufacture ferro-alloys used in steel plants. KCP Limited also established a heavy engineering division near Chennai in 1955 to fabricate machinery for sugar, cement, steel, and power plants, followed by a cement unit at Macherla (Guntur) in 1958. A diversified conglomerate giant had come into being; the Monopolies Inquiry Commission of 1965 ranked it forty-fifth among India's top seventy-five business houses, with assets of Rs 13.61 crore and a turnover of Rs 10.52 crore.[32] Ranked two notches below was the V. Rangaswamy Naidu group belonging to the affiliated Kammavar Naidu community of Coimbatore.[33] The two groups had, in fact, already cultivated a link through the marriage of Ramakrishna's daughter Rajeswary to Rangaswamy Naidu's son, P.R. Ramakrishnan.

After Ramakrishna's departure the KCP empire was divided among his three children, though there are significant cross-holdings between the different factions. In 1996 the two sugar units of KCP Limited at Vuyyuru and Lakshmipuram (in Challapalli), with a combined crushing capacity of 12,000 tcd, were hived off into a separate company, KCP Sugar and Industries Corporation. The original KCP Limited – with interests in heavy engineering and cement, besides controlling two 2,500 tcd sugar plants at Chittoor district and Vietnam through separate subsidiaries (Sudalagunta Sugars and KCP Vietnam Industries) – is under V.L. Dutt, while KCP Sugar was placed under the management of Ramakrishna's other son V. Maaruthi Rao. The Jeypore Sugar Company, on the other hand, is with Rajeswary Ramakrishnan.[34] Although initially engaged in mining and sugar production in Orissa, the company's flagship today is an 8,000 tcd unit at Chagallu in West Godavari. This plant came up in 1961, after the experiment of running a factory in Rayagada by importing yeoman cane farmers from the delta failed. Jeypore Sugar has also practically exited from mining, after leasing out its ferro-alloys facility to the Hyderabad-based VBC group of M.S. Rama Rao (another Kamma) in June 2005.[35]

Two other major zamindar-promoted sugar ventures in this first wave of Kamma entrepreneurship were Andhra Sugars at Tanuku in West Godavari and Sri Sarvaraya Sugars at Chelluru in East Godavari district. Andhra Sugars, which commenced crushing in 1951, was an initiative of Mullapudi Harischandra Prasad and his brother-in-law P.S.R.V.K. Ranga Rao – both big landlords with individual holdings of over 1,000 acres in the most fertile zone of the Godavari delta. As we shall see in a later case study, Velagapudi Ramakrishna had a hand – financial and otherwise – in floating this company too, which became the nucleus of a Rs 1,000 crore plus combine with activities spanning sugar, chemicals, fertilizers, vegetable oils, and textiles. Sarvaraya Sugars, with a capacity of 4,000 tcd, was set up in 1959 by members of the Kapileswarapuram estate. The same family promoted a spinning mill at Kakinada, Sarvaraya Textiles, which is now sick.[36] A crucial factor that certainly influenced the flow of zamindari capital into industry during this period was the prospect of land reforms. Sustained anti-zamindari and 'land-to-the-tiller' agitations from the 1930s – leading to forcible occupation of estate lands, as happened to the raja of Challapalli – had already triggered a law abolishing zamindari estates in 1948. For the more discerning sections of the gentry the Madras Estate (Abolition and Conversion into Ryotwari) Act was the forerunner to the imposition of land ceilings, lending urgency to the need for converting fickle rural wealth into industrial capital. While the majority of early Kamma industrialists belonged to the landlord class, by virtue of being from a 'peasant' community they became at the same time role models for enterprising caste brethren of more humble stock.[37]

Apart from sugar or agro-processing, the typical businesses that first-generation rural Andhra entrepreneurs invested in were construction, government contracts, and transport. A 1940s list of leading Public Works Department (PWD) and Railways contractors in Madras Presidency contained many Kamma family names: Devineni, Yarlagadda, Yalamanchali, Kavuri, Surapaneni, Vallabhaneni, Gogineni, Chalasani, and Kakani.[38] The Kakinada-based Sri Ramadas Motor Transport Limited (SRMT) was started in 1944 by a group of predominantly Kamma cultivators. What began as a small-time passenger transport service plying buses in Kakinada expanded into a complete logistics concern with a fleet of 200 trucks connecting 350 branches across Andhra Pradesh, Karnataka, and Tamil Nadu. In 1953 SRMT branched into the manufacture of motor spare parts (piston pins, bushes, propeller shaft components, wheel bolts, road- and clutch-repair kits) supplying to state transport undertakings all over India. Two years later it acquired the dealership for 'Tata' commercial vehicles in East Godavari, Visakhapatnam, Vizianagaram, and Srikakulam. By 1989 the company had forayed into engine valves production through a subsidiary, Sri Vijaya Engine Valves. SRMT remains even now a privately held company controlled by the family of K.V.R. Choudary, a former TDP Member of Parliament from Rajahmundry.

Then, of course, we have the Telugu film industry which, from the Challapalli raja's days, has been a Kamma preserve. It is said of the prosperous Kamma farmer that after every paddy harvest he goes to Chennai with the proceeds and makes a 'picture' (as movies are called in regular Telugu lingo and pronounced 'pitcher'). When failing health prompted Gudavalli Ramabrahmam's exit from Sarathi Films, the man the raja turned to for directing his 1946 film, *Grihapravesham*, was Akkineni Lakshmi Vara Prasad Rao, who came to be known as L.V. Prasad. Born to a landed agricultural family in Somavarapadu village of Eluru taluka (West Godavari), Prasad was smitten early by the moving picture: his first exposure to wornout prints of imported silent-era films came during visits to Eluru town for mending pumpsets and farm tools. In 1930 the 22-year-old Prasad left home for Mumbai to try out his luck in tinsel town. By then the family's farming business had gone bust – his father had piled up huge debts, while embarking on a plan of clearing forest lands to bring additional area under cultivation. The move unfortunately coincided with the Depression, which had sent farm prices downhill. In Mumbai Prasad did odd jobs as a theatre watchman, light boy, camera assistant, and bit-role artist: he had the unique distinction of fleeting appearances in India's first 'talkies' made in Hindi (Ardeshir Irani's *Alam Ara*), Tamil (H.M. Reddy's *Kalidas*), and Telugu (Reddy's *Bhakta Prahalada*), all made in 1931! After a decade in Mumbai Prasad moved to Chennai, by which time he had also done stints as an assistant director. Once the raja of Challapalli gave him his first full directorial break in 1946, Prasad's career chart soared. Thereafter he directed several blockbusters, from *Mana Desam* and *Shavukar* (the films that launched NTR) in 1949–50 to *Pelli Chesi Choodu*, *Manohara*, and *Missamma* (remade as *Miss Mary* in Hindi) in the 1950s. In 1956 Prasad turned producer with *Ilavelpu* and churned out hits, including in Hindi (*Milan*, *Khilona*, *Bidai*, and *Ek Duje Ke Liye*). By 1965, he had opened Prasad Studios at Chennai, with facilities for recording, dubbing, and editing, followed nine years later by a film-processing unit, Prasad Film Laboratory. The latter is still the country's largest film lab, with branches at Hyderabad, Bangalore, Thiruvananthapuram, Mumbai, Bhubhaneswar and Delhi.[39]

The man who upstaged L.V. Prasad in movie production – even if not in the realm of post-production – is Daggubati Rama Naidu, a Kamma from Karamchedu in Prakasam district. Like Prasad, Rama Naidu wanted to be an actor – an ambition that took him to Chennai – and instead ended up producing films by the dozen. His Suresh Productions has, to date, made close to 150 movies – a *Guinness Book* record – starting from *Ramudu Bheemudu* in 1964 with NTR as lead to Hindi potboilers like *Tohfa* and *Maqsad*.[40] Yet another prolific Telugu producer to have tasted success in Hindi films – *Andha Kanoon*, *Aakhri Raasta* (both starring Amitabh Bachhan), and *Chaalbaaz* (starring Sridevi) – is Atluri Purnachandra Rao. He is again a Kamma from Chowtapalli near Gudivada in Krishna district.

But the list does not stop here. Among actors, besides NTR, Akkineni Nageswara Rao (ANR) and Krishna (his real name is Ghattamaneni Sivarama Krishna Murthy) are also Kammas, originally from Gudiwada and Tenali, respectively. So is Mohan Babu, a Rayalaseema Kamma from Chittoor. In recent years their kin have taken the star leap too: Balakrishna (NTR's son), Nagarjuna (ANR's son), Sumanth (ANR's grandson) and Venkatesh (Rama Naidu's son). As if this wasn't enough, some have their own production houses: ANR's Annapurna Studios and Krishna's Padmalaya Telefilms Limited.[41] The sole matinee idol to have challenged the Kamma monopoly in Telugu cinema is Chiranjeevi, a Kapu from Narasapur in West Godavari. The other is the action heroine Vijayashanti ('Lady Amitabh'), also a Kapu from Warangal.

Another industry associated with the first wave of Kamma entrepreneurship – pre-1980s – is tobacco. As mentioned, by the 1940s Guntur's farmers had fully mastered the technique of growing and curing FCV tobacco. Some had even constructed sizeable barn capacities, which could be used to cure the green leaf of smaller ryots. That opened up avenues for their becoming village-level dealers who stored large quantities of tobacco at harvest time and offered it on commission basis to big exporting firms. In a few cases the rural 'curer capitalist' would not just cure, but fine grade the katcha leaf bought from the growers and have it further processed, packed and baled ready for export. But the scope for these was somewhat limited because, right till the War years, BAT (through its Indian Leaf Tobacco Division or ILTD) controlled 80 per cent of tobacco output through contractual relationships with growers. This changed post-Independence, which saw new export markets for Indian FCV tobacco – especially the Soviet and Eastern Bloc – develop through state trading concerns. In the years preceding Independence, over 60 per cent of the virginia leaf grown was exported and, of that, 80 per cent went to the UK. By the 1960s UK's share had fallen to 35 per cent, while that of the former communist economies crossed 40 per cent.[42]

Diversification of the export market, coupled with the diffusion of FCV cultivation and processing technologies, led to the entry of a new set of exporters from the ranks of rich cultivators-turned-traders. Previously, there was a handful of exporters other than BAT, whereas by 1982 out of the Guntur region's ninety-two exporters registered with the Tobacco Board, over 60 per cent were Kammas and half of them established in the late 1950s and early 1960s. At an all-India level, out of nineteen companies with a turnover of Rs 1 crore or more, nine were owned by Kammas.[43] The most notable of the Kamma tobacco magnates is Rayapati Sambasiva Rao, a three-time Congress MP from Guntur. Prior to the disintegration of the Soviet Union his Jayalakshmi Group commanded 35 per cent of India's tobacco exports to Russia. The same channels were leveraged to also corner a quarter of the Russian market for Indian tea. The group further owns a 30,000-spindle textile mill at Chebrolu, near Guntur. Other leading Kamma tobacco exporters are Best India Tobacco of Yemparala Venkateswara Rao (who lost the Guntur Parliament seat to Sambasiva Rao in 2004, after defeating him in 1999), Transcontinental Tobacco India of Chebrolu Narendranath, Yaralagadda Exports of Y. Ankamma Chowdary, and Mittapalli

Audinarayana & Company of M. Rama Rao. To be fair, there are big exporters from other communities too, like the Bommidala, Maddi Lakshmaiah, and Polisetty Somasundaram groups (all Komatis), and Deccan Tobacco and Rahamankhan Tobacco Enterprises (Muslim). Together, they have brought down ILTD's share in FCV tobacco exports to 28–30 per cent.[44]

One more important Kamma industrialist in this phase is Devineni Subba Rao. Born near Machilipatnam, Subba Rao was a brilliant student who did his master's at Banaras Hindu University and a doctorate from New York University. After returning to India in 1949 he worked at the National Chemical Laboratory in Pune and joined Tata Steel in 1954. Two years later he went to V. Ramakrishna's KCP Group and helped set up its ferro-manganese plant at Rayagada. In 1972 Subba Rao and two of his colleagues formed their own company, Nava Bharat Ferro Alloys Limited. It is today's one of India's largest integrated producers of chromium and manganese alloys, with plants at Paloncha (Khammam) and Khadgaprasad (Dhenkanal) in Orissa. In 1980 Subba Rao forayed into sugar by taking over the Deccan Sugar and Abkari Company's unit at Samalkot (East Godavari) from EID Parry. The plant, a division within Nava Bharat Ferro Alloys, has a crushing capacity of 3,500 tcd.[45]

Telugu Desam Party (TDP) and After

At the beginning of the 1980s the Kammas had penetrated a range of industries from sugar, tobacco, and rice milling to government contracts, transport, textiles, ferro-alloys, and cinema. This transformation for a primarily agriculture-based community had come within a matter of fifty years. What it had not yet managed to do, however, was translate this newly gained corporate wealth into effective political power. The Kammas had not produced any chief minister (CM),[46] nor had they a party they could call their 'own'.

For a brief period before and after Independence they flirted with the Left, so much so that the Communist Party of India (CPI) in Andhra was once branded a 'Kammanist Party'. The CPI's anti-zamindari mobilization had attracted the Kamma peasantry, a big chunk of which comprised upwardly mobile tenant cultivators and ordinary ryots. Although this section was by no means poor – as we have noted earlier, access to assured irrigation made even 5–10 acre farms viable – there was an underlying conflict between them and the zamindars, who were revenue intermediaries between peasants and the state. Even as late as in 1940–1 a quarter of the agricultural land in the delta districts was held under zamindari tenure, while this percentage was three-fourths in the Visakhapatnam-Srikakulam belt. The privilege extended to collect revenues for the government made the zamindars a virtual 'state within the state', pitting them against both landless farm labourers as well as an aspiring rural middle-class peasantry. This combination of forces helped the CPI to emerge as a formidable opposition in the 1952 assembly elections.[47]

However, by the late 1950s, the Kammas had gravitated towards the Congress. The latter, to neutralize the Left's influence, had firstly enacted legislation abolishing all intermediary tenures and transferring the vast zamindari and jagirdari estates of Andhra and Telangana to their erstwhile tenant cultivators. This was followed by the inception of a new Panchayati Raj system in 1957 wherein government funds for development projects were channelled through local village, taluka, and district bodies. Since tenancy reforms had detached the old gentry from the countryside and made them relinquish lands to their former tenants, it gave an opportunity for the emergent peasant elite to capture these institutions and dominate the village political economy. This Kamma rural middle class – not to be confused with the old rajas of Challapalli or Kapileswarapuram – was, thus, successfully co-opted by the ruling

Congress dispensation.[48] But the honeymoon did not last. During the early 1970s the Congress central leadership under Indira Gandhi attempted to take its rural reforms agenda one step ahead through socio-economic programmes specifically targeting Dalits, tribals, and other backward classes. Also, in what was perceived as a bid to undermine the hold of the dominant peasant castes over these groups – who provided a captive 'vote bank' for exercising power in rural localities – the state government of P.V. Narasimha Rao introduced a land ceilings act prohibiting individual families from owning more than eighteen acres of irrigated land growing two crops. For the Kamma middle peasantry this foreclosed the potential to acquire cultivable land beyond a certain physical (and psychological) threshold. To add to their discomfiture, a Supreme Court ruling in October 1972 upheld a nizam-era firman (decree) reserving government jobs in Telangana (which included Hyderabad) for only mulkis (residents) of the region. The decision sparked off a 'Jai Andhra' movement, spearheaded by the rural middle class of the coastal districts, who cried foul over their treatment as 'second class' citizens in their own state. The Kamma alienation from the Congress was now complete.[49]

With land ceilings and job reservations blocking conventional routes of upward mobility and capital accumulation, doing business was now looked upon more as a compulsion than an option for the educated Kamma. It was basically they who sought a party that would accommodate this aspiration and break the hegemony of the predominantly Reddy-led Congress in Hyderabad. But that called for a charismatic leader to take on Indira Gandhi. NTR – the silver screen hero who had enthralled Telugu audiences by essaying the roles of many a Hindu mythological character – fitted the bill. The TDP was formed on 29 March 1982, just a year before the thespian turned 60. Fighting on a plank of 'Telugu self-respect and dignity', NTR capitalized on the educated electorate's disillusionment with the Congress, which seemed a tired, faction-ridden party of corrupt politicians who kowtowed to bosses at the Centre (AP was subjected to four CMs within two years from October 1980). In order to extend his party's appeal to the weaker sections, NTR promised a spate of populist measures, such as hiking the quantum of subsidized rice sold through ration shops. The campaign was a runaway success and on 9 January 1983 NTR took oath as the state's first Kamma CM.

Chief among those who contributed immensely to this entire brand-building exercise for NTR and the TDP was Cherukuri Ramoji Rao and his barely eight-year-old Telugu daily *Eenadu*. Ramoji Rao (born 16 November 1936) hailed from Pedaparupudi, near Gudivada, close to NTR's village, Nimmakuru. Like many Kamma youth of that time, he was drawn to communism and became a CPI cardholder while a student at Gudivada. The start of the 1960s took Ramoji Rao to Delhi, where he worked for an advertising firm, Ad Crafts. Although it was brief, the Delhi experience opened him to a new world and also gave him the idea of starting something of his own. In 1962 he floated a rotating savings and loan institution, Margadarsi Chits, in Hyderabad. To get it going Ramoji Rao disposed of all his family land and property and shifted to Hyderabad. In a few years he had opened a second branch at Visakhapatnam, where he also established the Dolphin Hotel in 1969. While Delhi had also familiarised him to the print media, it was the political ferment of the 1970s affecting his own community that propelled Ramoji Rao to start a daily. He had tested the waters before with a farmers' magazine, *Annadata*. The chit fund business – in which his company organized monthly auctions of 'chits' and pocketed a 'foreman commission' on the pooled surpluses distributed among subscribers – had already laid the financial foundations for the group and become a quasi-institution to mobilize community savings. On 10 August 1974 the first edition of *Eenadu* was launched at Visakhapatnam. By mid 1978 two more, at Hyderabad and Vijayawada, were added and the paper's circulation had crossed a lakh. At the time of TDP's birth it was well over two lakh and provided the ideal platform for disseminating NTR's message. Ramoji Rao, on his part, made no effort to conceal this liaison.

Today, the Ramoji group is unquestionably the No. 1 Kamma conglomerate, way ahead of the KCPs and the Andhra Sugars. Not only does *Eenadu* sell a million copies every day,[50] but the group has since 1995 branched into cable television, probably overstretching itself in the bargain. With eleven channels – in Telugu, Kannada, Bengali, Marathi, Urdu, Gujarati, and Oriya – Eenadu Television has one of India's largest satellite TV networks. Before that, in 1980, the 'Rupert Murdoch of the South' had diversified into food through Ushodaya Enterprises, which makes the 'Priya' brand of pickles.[51] By the mid 1980s the group was into films as well, producing Hindi hits like *Nache Mayuri* and *Pratighat* (both Telugu remakes) under the Ushakiron Movies banner. This was a precursor to the 2,000-acre Ramoji Film City that came up outside Hyderabad in 1997. Considered the world's biggest integrated film studio complex, it is a one-stop shop for everything from shooting to post-production work. The Film City has gardens, lakes, hills, and flexible façades of forts, airports, city streets, and apartment blocks – enough to 'walk in with your script and walk out with your print'. Meanwhile the original venture, Margadarsi Chits, has grown into a leading financial intermediary, doing an annual auction turnover of Rs 2,500 crore through ninety-odd branches spread across AP, Tamil Nadu, and Karnataka.

While the Ramoji group's origins may pre-date the TDP, there is no doubt that the party's coming into power has coincided with a resurgence of Kamma capital. And unlike the past, this has been powered not by the old landlord class but by educated folk of relatively humble farming background. A 1983 field survey of small-scale units in the industrial estate area of Visakhapatnam found 68 per cent of the owners to be from the dominant cultivating castes (mostly Kammas). Of these, 57 per cent had individual holdings of less than 20 acres and only 3 per cent possessed 50 acres or more. Also, 47 per cent had used agricultural profits as a source of start-up capital, with another 22 per cent employing the Ramoji Rao formula of selling land.[52] In other words there has been a trend towards 'democratization' of capital within the community. Further, in the new phase we see the rise of Kamma industrialists from not just the delta heartland but from the adjoining regions of Nellore and Khammam, and even the Rayalaseema districts.[53]

The 1980s were a time when some massive public sector projects were taken up for implementation in AP. These included the Visakhapatnam Steel Plant (for which a violent agitation was mounted way back in 1966), the mega power station of the National Thermal Power Corporation (NTPC) at Ramagundam, the Srisailam Right Branch Canal, and the Telugu Ganga Project. The last – a brainchild of NTR – involved laying a 400-km-long canal between the Srisailam reservoir across the Krishna in Kurnool district and the Poondi reservoir near Chennai. Along with supplying drinking water to Chennai, the project was conceived to irrigate some 5 lakh acres of parched territory in Rayalaseema. How much of the water has reached the farmer is a moot question; what is indisputable about projects of this scale is the opportunities they have thrown up for aspiring entrepreneurs. The fortunes of many Kamma construction magnates can be traced to this period and the subsequent decade that witnessed huge public investments in roads, highways, bridges, and flyovers under the aegis of the National Highways Authority of India (NHAI) and other state agencies. We can pinpoint at least three such big-time contractors. The first is Kavuru Sambasiva Rao, a Kamma from Dosapadu in

Krishna district who studied at the Regional Engineering College in Warangal before establishing Progressive Construction Limited in the 1970s. His firm has expanded into a Rs 500-crore-plus group which also controls the Medwin Hospitals at Hyderabad.[54] The second is Lagadapati Rajagopal, another engineer originally from Nellore. His Rs 1,000 crore Lanco group started off with irrigation contracts in the 1980s before venturing into pig iron manufacturing and power (see end-chapter case study).

An even more recent entrant is Nama Nageswar Rao, who is from Khammam – a rare Telangana Kamma industrialist. A former employee of the state-owned Singareni Collieries, Nageswar Rao floated Madhu Constructions as a partnership concern in 1983. In March 1990 it was incorporated as Madhu Continental Constructions before going public five years later as Madhucon Projects Limited.[55] The company's growth was in the 1990s, when it undertook excavation jobs in the Srisailam right branch and main canals and also earthwork, tunnel, and bridge building for the Konkan Railway Corporation. Madhucon also constructed a number of flyovers in Hyderabad as part of the city's beautification drive initiated by the government of Nara Chandrababu Naidu (NTR's son-in-law, who took over the TDP's leadership after its founder died in late 1995). The early years of this century saw Madhucon handling even bigger contracts for NHAI like four-laning the Vijayawada–Eluru national highway section. Besides construction, the group has a granite processing and export unit (Madhucon Granites) and a sugar mill (Madhucon Sugars), both in Khammam. The latter was originally a co-operative that was privatized during the Chandrababu Naidu regime. In the 2004 general elections Nageswar Rao contested as a TDP candidate but lost to Renuka Chowdhury, a fellow Kamma earlier with TDP and presently a Congress union minister. Lagadapati Rajagopal and Kavuru Sambasiva Rao were luckier, winning on Congress tickets from the Vijayawada and Eluru parliament constituencies, respectively.

Large-scale construction (as against executing petty PWD or panchayat-level contracts) apart, pharmaceuticals is a sector that has produced an avalanche of new-generation Kamma entrepreneurs from the 1980s. Prominent among them are Nimmagadda Prasad of Matrix Laboratories (see separate case study), Murali K. Divi of Divi's Laboratories, Venkaiah Chowdary Nannapaneni of Natco Pharma, and R.T. Ravi of Krebs Biochemicals & Industries Limited.[56] They are all people with impeccable educational backgrounds. Murali Divi, a pharmaceutical sciences doctorate, started as a trainee superintendent with the multinational Warner Lambert in Hyderabad, before moving to the US and working for a number of drug firms there. In 1984 he co-promoted Cheminor Drugs with Anji Reddy of Dr Reddy's Laboratories (DRL). Six years later he quit Cheminor (subsequently merged with DRL) to form Divi's Laboratories. Nannapaneni did a pharmacy master's at Andhra University in Visakhapatnam and worked in the US for fifteen years. On returning in 1981 he started Natco Pharma. Krebs Biochemicals' founder is similarly a trained biochemist. All these companies are mainly into manufacture and export of generic active pharmaceutical ingredients (API), i.e. bulk drugs not protected by patents.

Then there are smaller firms like Suven Life Sciences of Venkat Jasti (another pharmacy postgraduate from Andhra University) and Vimta Labs Limited of S.P. Vasireddi (he is actually a Kamma).[57] Both derive a large part of their revenues from doing contract research, clinical trials and related knowledge process outsourcing work for global drugs and life sciences majors. Krishna M. Ella, who did a doctorate in molecular biology from the University of Wisconsin-Madison and launched Bharat Biotech International Limited in 1996, is also a Kamma. His company specializes in the production of vaccines (Hepatitis-B and typhoid) and bio-therapeutics. Loosely linked to drugs are hospitals, and Hyderabad has quite a few of them owned by the community: Kamineni Hospitals of K. Suryanarayana (who also has a medical and dental college at Nalgonda), the Bollineni group of B. Krishnaiah (Krishna Institute of Medical Sciences at Hyderabad and hospitals at Nellore, Rajahmundry, and Kadapa), Medwin Hospitals of Kavuru Sambasiva Rao, the Usha Mullapudi Cardiac Centre of Ratnam V. Mullapudi (a US-returned cardio-thoracic surgeon), and the L.V. Prasad Eye Institute.

In addition to the above, there are assorted other big Kamma industrialists of recent vintage. The Chittoor-born Ramachandra Naidu Galla, an electrical engineer from Anantapur Engineering College and a postgraduate in applied electronics from Roorkee University, went to the US in the 1960s for higher studies at the Michigan State University. After fifteen years with the US Steel Corporation and the Chicago-based Sargent & Lundy, Galla came back and founded Amara Raja Batteries Limited in 1985. It was a venture to make valve-regulated lead acid batteries, which, unlike normal batteries, are free from electrolyte leakage and require no adding water. For sourcing the technology – completely new to India – Galla tied up with Johnson Controls, a world leader in automotive and building control systems from Wisconsin. Initially, Amara Raja supplied batteries for power plants, railways, telecom, defence and other industrial applications. Later, it expanded into automotive batteries under the 'Amaron' brand. The company, in which Johnson Controls holds an equal 26 per cent, is today India's No. 2 battery producer behind Exide Industries.

Then we have Nuziveedu Seeds and Heritage Foods India Limited. The former, started by M. Venkat Ramaiah at Guntur, is a leading domestic seed breeder, with its 'Bunny' cotton being a widely cultivated hybrid. Heritage Foods is the second biggest private dairy concern in the South (after Hatsun Agro) and its promoter, Bhuvaneshwari Devi, is none other than the wife of Nara Chandrababu Naidu. The latter, like Ramachandra Galla, hails from Rayalaseema. The country's two largest shrimp exporters – P. Brahmanandam of Devi Sea Foods and Sreeram Atluri of Nekkanti Sea Foods Limited – are also Kammas based in Visakhapatnam.[58]

The one thing standing out in these accounts is the premium attached to higher education by the community: a phenomenon which, we saw, has roots going back to the early twentieth century. And who better than the Kammas to make business out of this insatiable hunger! Across the state, one encounters hordes of 'teaching shops' that train students in taking entrance exams for engineering and medical colleges, besides other professional and even regular degree or school-level courses. Many of these are run by educational chains bearing exotic names like Vikas, Nalanda, Vignan, and Sri Chaitanya. Take Vikas Educational Institutions, which began in a rented space at Visakhapatnam with 200 students and 10 staff members in 1993. It was set up by Yarlagadda Rajasekhar Babu and Tummala Naga Prasad, one an engineering graduate and the other a postgraduate in mathematics. Originally from Nuzvid, near Vijayawada, the two youngsters set up shop in Visakhapatnam, knowing that the area had no coaching centre and students were going all the way to Guntur or Nellore. Today, their group has four centres in the city and branches at Rajahmundry, Hyderabad, and Tirupati, besides a Nalanda Talent School in Visakhapatnam and an Oakridge International School at Hyderabad to literally 'catch 'em young'. A. Vijaya Babu's Nalanda Educational Institutions, started from Vijayawada in 1988, likewise operates nearly fifty 'campuses' in every corner of AP, from Visakhapatnam, Kakinada, Bhimavaram, Guntur, Tenali, and Nellore to Hyderabad, Anantapur, Chittoor, and Kadapa. Not content with that, it has gone to Bhubhaneswar and even Patna, close to the 'real' Nalanda! Each of them – Vikas, Nalanda, Vignan of Lavu Rattaiah (who started with a tutorial centre at Guntur in 1982), and Sri Chaitanya (founded by a Kamma doctor couple, B.S. Rao and B. Jhansi Lakshmi Bai) – boast of 25,000 or more students on their rolls.

Reddys *et al.*

The Kammas are not the only landowning peasant caste in AP to have expanded into industry. There are also the Reddys, Rajus, Velamas, and others who have made the transition, albeit with varying degrees of success and not as spectacularly as the Kammas. In this section we shall highlight some aspects of their industrialization trajectory.

The Reddys constitute about 6.5 per cent of the state's population.[59] This is a bit higher than the Kammas' 4.8 per cent, but, as against the latter, they are spread out across the state. The community is present more in the Telangana and Rayalaseema regions, but even here they are not concentrated the way the Kammas are in Krishna, Guntur, and Prakasam. The dry tracts of Telangana and Rayalaseema, we have observed earlier, could never sustain dynamic farming systems based on a substantial middle peasantry. To be in a position to market his crop and preserve some economic independence, a ryot needed to hold a minimum 20 acres of good quality dry land. By that yardstick only 5–10 per cent of landowners were independent,[60] whereas in the canal-irrigated deltas the proportion was nearly 70 per cent. The majority of peasants in the dry zone were landholders in name: they had precious little capital to sink wells or maintain good bullocks and farm equipment, nor the wherewithal to hold on to their crop and choose the right buyer and time to sell. In any given village there were only one or two very large landowners with the capacity for this. These men had sufficient land which they could lease out to others to cultivate, sufficient surplus produce that they could dispose of in the market, sufficient cash that they could lend to the lesser ryots – and use these instruments to establish a patron–client relationship with their agrarian dependants and thus dominate the village economy. In the dry districts a sizeable number of them were Reddys; the very term denotes 'village headman'.

But these rural magnates were hardly enterprising commercial farmers of the delta genre. The latter were better attuned to the logic of producing for the market, experimenting with new crops (e.g. FCV tobacco), and migrating to other lands to pursue fertile cultivation opportunities. Indeed, there are several cases of Kamma yeomen agriculturists going to Khammam and Nizamabad or even the Bellary–Hospet–Raichur belt in the Tungabhadra basin of Karnataka, and acquiring land with latent irrigation potential. By contrast, with all their ability to command men and resources, the Telangana and Rayalaseema Reddy landlords were essentially bosses in their backyards. Small wonder that their initial diversification ventures were scant in industries like agro-processing and considerable in mining and public works contracts: businesses built mainly around muscle power rather than enterprise. Mining in the Rayalaseema region and Nellore was virtually the monopoly of rich Reddy landlords: a detailed study of 146 working mines in Nellore in 1944 revealed that they controlled 55 per cent of the mining leases.[61] Some went into film production. Bommireddy Nagi Reddy, who came from Kadapa, founded Vijaya-Vahini at Chennai in 1950, which became Asia's biggest film studio. He made mega-grossers from *Pathala Bhairavi* and *Maya Bazar* (Telugu) to *Ram Aur Shyam* and *Julie* (Hindi), while also starting the popular children's magazine *Chandamama* in twelve languages in 1947, and the Vijaya Hospitals at Chennai in 1972. Still, well up to the

1970s, there were no Reddy industrialists on par with a Velagapudi Ramakrishna or a Mullapudi Harischandra Prasad.

Today's big Reddy houses are all products of the last few decades. Gunapati Venkata Krishna (G.V.K.) Reddy and Tikkavarapu Subbarami Reddy were both contractors from Nellore who prospered from the commissioning of the Nagarjuna Sagar dam in the 1960s. Designed to irrigate a million acres mainly in the Telangana districts of Nalgonda and Khammam (besides the dry uplands of Guntur, Prakasam, and Nellore), it was the world's tallest masonry dam that Jawaharlal Nehru identified as one of his coveted 'temples of modern India'. What it and projects like Sriram Sagar and Somasila also did was produce a first generation of contractors, mainly Reddys, who were hitherto engaged in nickel-and-dime works (the Kammas' chance came later with Visakhapatnam Steel and Telugu Ganga). After profiting from Nagarjuna Sagar, G.V.K. Reddy set up Novopan Industries Limited in 1979 to manufacture pre-laminated particle boards. To meet its requirement of amino resins, he established Nova Resins and Chemicals, later renamed GVK Petrochemicals. In the mid 1980s Reddy built Krishna Oberoi, Hyderabad's first five-star hotel. It is now part of Taj GVK Hotels & Resorts, a joint venture with the Tatas formed in December 1999. This company, in which the Tatas hold 25.5 per cent, manages three luxury hotels in the city, apart from a property at Chandigarh. In the1990s, Reddy forayed into power through a 216-megawatt (MW) gas-fired plant at Jegurupadu (East Godavari), which was completed in July 1997. Simultaneously, his construction business has flourished: the group has executed a Rs 710 crore project awarded by the NHAI involving six-laning of a 93 km national highway stretch between Jaipur and Kishangarh in Rajasthan. That adds up to a highly diversified group with a Rs 2,000-crore-plus turnover.[62]

Tikkavarapu Subbarami Reddy has not been as successful in diversifying his business operations. His present identity is more as a high-profile Congress parliamentarian with the right connections in Delhi. Subbarami Reddy owns a sugar unit (Gayatri Sugars) at Nizamabad with a modest 3,500 tcd capacity, while his other two manufacturing concerns – Gayatri Starchkem Limited (which makes sorbitol, a chemical used in toothpastes and drugs) and Gayatri Tissue & Papers – are ailing. It is his construction company – Gayatri Projects – that has all through been a money-spinner. Subbarami Reddy's nephew T. Venkattram Reddy (son of his brother T. Chandrasekhar Reddy) heads Deccan Chronicle Holdings Limited, which runs the two English dailies *Deccan Chronicle* and *Asian Age*. Like his brother, Chandrasekhar Reddy was a Congressman involved in many activities, from making aluminium foils to soft drinks bottling and hotels, before Venkattram Reddy decided to focus on the family's core newspaper business.[63] Another prominent Congress businessman, who also started out in the 1960s, was Magunta Subbarami Reddy (no relation of his namesake). A liquor baron brutally murdered by left-wing militants in 1995, his Chennai-based Balaji group also had interests in steel (Balaji Industrial Corporation), shipping, hotels, and a Telugu daily, *Udayam*. These have all gone sick or shut down. Even its once thriving flagship, Balaji Distilleries Limited, is tottering. The Magunta family – Subbarami Reddy, Parvathamma (his wife), and Sreenivasulu Reddy (brother) – has represented the Ongole parliamentary seat in Prakasam almost continuously since 1991.

But it is again the 1980s that have thrown up many of the contemporary topnotch Reddy business groups. Dr Reddy's Laboratories (DRL) was promoted in 1984 by Kallam Anji Reddy, a chemical engineering doctorate from Pune's National Chemical Laboratory who worked with the public sector Indian Drugs and Pharmaceuticals Limited (IDPL) between 1969 and 1975 (the latter's role in making Hyderabad a pharmaceutical hub is pretty similar to what Bharat Electronics and Hindustan Aeronautics have done for Bangalore's infotech industry). After quitting IDPL, Anji Reddy became founder-managing director of Uniloids Limited and then in 1980, started Standard Organics Limited (SOL) with Chandrasekhar Reddy, a textile engineer who had made money working in Nigeria. Four years later Anji Reddy launched DRL, which is now the third largest domestic drug producer after Ranbaxy and Cipla.

Aurobindo Pharma Limited was founded in 1986 by Penaka Venkata Ramaprasad Reddy – he had been previously with SOL – and it has almost caught up in terms of sales. Even more recent is Bandi Parthasaradhi Reddy's Rs 700 crore Hetero Drugs Limited, which has become an established player in the anti-retroviral (HIV/AIDS) segment. A like example of an upstart in the construction sector is provided by Eragam Sudhir Reddy of IVRCL Infrastructures & Projects Limited (IVRCL). Originally incorporated as I. Venku Reddy Constructions Private Limited in 1987, IVRCL has, in a short span, become a Rs 1,000-crore-plus company, specializing in laying pipelines and other municipal water infrastructure projects.

The other famous Reddy industrialist is Pratap C. Reddy, who established his first Apollo Hospitals at Chennai in 1983. The Chittoor-born cardiologist's Apollo Hospitals Enterprise Limited now owns and manages thirty-eight hospitals, making it Asia's No. 1 and the world's fourth largest healthcare provider.[64]

Two Reddy entrepreneurs who are not as famous as the brands they have created are B. Venkatarama Reddy and L. Jaipal Reddy. The former promoted Nutrine Confectionery Company in 1952. A premier producer of confectionery and toffees ('Maha Lacto' and 'Kokanaka' brands), this family-run concern was sold to the Godrej group in 2006 for Rs 270 crore. Jaipal Reddy was an engineer with the Maharashtra State Electricity Board (MSEB), who, along with a colleague, Jaikumar Pathare, chucked his job in 1971 to start a rather unusual business: manufacturing men's underwear. In the process they converted a previously also-worn commodity into a visibly advertised brand called 'VIP'. The Rs 400 crore VIP group – through its flagship, Maxwell Industries Limited – is the market leader in branded undergarments. Another industrialist worth mentioning is K. Bhasker Reddy of Creamline Dairy Products Limited, which sells liquid milk under the 'Jersey' brand in AP, Tamil Nadu and Karnataka.

The Rajus, who are considered the Kshatriyas of AP, account for a minuscule 1.2 per cent of the state's population.[65] The community shares certain features with the Kammas, being concentrated in coastal Andhra, particularly Bhimavaram (West Godavari) and Vizianagaram. Secondly, like the Kammavar Naidus of Coimbatore, it was the migrant Rajus in Tamil Nadu (especially those at Rajapalayam in Virudhunagar district) who took the initial plunge into industry. An early bird was Poosapati Ramasamy Raja, who promoted the Rajapalayam Mills in 1936. It is now part of a Rs 1,500 crore empire with interests in cement (Madras Cements Limited), asbestos products (Ramco Industries), software (Ramco Systems), and textiles (Rajapalayam Mills, Ramaraju Surgical Cotton Mills).[66] The coastal Andhra Rajus' entry is more recent, beginning with Gokaraju Subbaraju (G.S.) Raju. A postgraduate from the University of California, he set up a pharmaceutical formulations concern in 1950 at Vijayawada by the name of South India Research Institute Private Limited (SIRIS). The SIRIS group went on to be a leading producer and exporter of bulk raw materials, intermediates, and formulations (particularly sulphamethoxazole and ciprofloxacin), apart from pesticides, vegetable oils, and herbal extracts.

The community's two biggest business icons, however, are Kanumuri Venkata Krishna (K.V.K.) Raju and Byrraju Ramalinga

Raju. The former, a mechanical engineer who studied at Michigan State University and the University of Minnesota, worked at Union Carbide in India for about fifteen years. In 1974 K.V.K. Raju started a cold rolled steel strips facility near Hyderabad (Nagarjuna Steels), for which he apparently travelled extensively across the state to raise deposits from peasant families belonging to his community. His group's flagship was a massive urea plant commissioned at Kakinada in the early 1990s (Nagarjuna Fertilizers & Chemicals Limited). In 1994 it expanded into pesticides through Nagarjuna Agrichem Limited. Ramalinga Raju hailed from a family of rich agriculturists in Bhimavaram. The profits from farming were enough to enable his grandfather to buy a small sugar mill, which did not do well. His father Satyanarayana Raju then moved to Hyderabad in 1962. He, along with other migrant community members, pioneered the commercial cultivation of grapes in the city's outskirts. In no time the family had more than recouped its losses. Ramalinga Raju, a commerce graduate from Vijayawada's Loyola College, was sent to the US in 1975 to do a master's in business administration at Ohio. On returning he invested in a textile unit (Sri Satyam Spinning and Weaving Mill) and real estate (Satyam Constructions). Nearly a decade later Raju launched Satyam Computer Services Limited in 1987, which has emerged as one of India's top five infotech firms (after HCL, TCS, Wipro and Infosys). Two men who helped Ramalinga Raju found Satyam were his brother-in-law, Dandu Venkata Satyanarayana (D.V.S.) Raju, and Chintalapati Srinivas (Srini) Raju – both US-educated engineers. In late 1995 after serving as Managing Director of Satyam, D.V.S. Raju left to set up his own VisualSoft Technologies Limited. He quit VisualSoft as well in 2005 to concentrate on another project: this time for developing a Rs 2,000 crore port at Gangavaram catering to the Visakhapatnam hinterland. Srini Raju remained as Chief Operating Officer of Satyam till 2000, before becoming a venture capitalist.

His firm, iLabs Capital, has invested in assorted software companies (including Megasoft Limited, which has acquired VisualSoft) and also *TV9*, a 24-hour Telugu news channel beaming to audiences both within India and the US.[67]

Construction and cement are two other industries with some major Andhra Raju names. Nagarjuna Construction Company Limited (NCC) was floated as a partnership firm in 1978 by Alluri Venkata Satyanarayana (A.V.S.) Raju, who belonged to a family in East Godavari already into construction. In the late 1950s he shifted to Hyderabad and was actually one of the co-promoters of K.V.K. Raju's Nagarjuna Steels before starting NCC. NCC is now a Rs 1,000 crore construction giant in the league of Madhucon, IVRCL, Progressive Construction, and Gayatri Projects. K.V.K. Raju and A.V.S. Raju were also involved in establishing the country's first mini-cement plant, Deccan Cements Limited (DCL), at Nalgonda in 1980. DCL's chief promoter, Manthena Bangar Raju, also ventured into the manufacture of polyester filament yarn in 1990. The company, DCL Polyesters Limited, ran into losses and its plant at Nagpur was bought by the Reliance group in 2001.[68] But the real Raju cement titan at one time was B.V. Raju, who controlled about 3 million tonnes capacity through Raasi Cement Limited and Sri Vishnu Cement. In one of Indian corporate history's landmark hostile takeovers, the Chennai-based India Cements Limited, in February 1998, made an open offer to acquire 20 per cent stake in Raasi Cement, having earlier accumulated 18 per cent from the market as well as from a disgruntled son-in-law of B.V. Raju. The bid caused consternation amongst Andhra's industry stalwarts, from Anji Reddy to Ramalinga Raju, who held a press meet in support of B.V. Raju, invoking the familiar 'Telugu pride' slogan. The resistance was transitory: by April, Raju had himself negotiated a good sell-out price and, the following year, he exited from Sri Vishnu Cement as well. Thus, for every resurgent Nagarajuna and

Satyam, there are also once-formidable Raju groups (SIRIS, Raasi, and DCL) that have been marginalized over a period.

The Velamas, Kapus, and other dominant peasant castes of AP have not succeeded in following in the footsteps of the Kammas, Reddys, and Rajus. The rajas of Bobbili, Pithapuram, Narasaraopet, Nuzvid, Venkatagiri, and Mirzapuram along coastal Andhra were all Velama feudatories lording over vast estates. Virtually none of them foresaw the changing times and so did not foray into entrepreneurship. The raja of Mirzapuram, Venkataramaiah Appa Rao, put money in films; he built Chennai's Shobanachala studios after World War II and his daughter, N.R. Anuradha Devi, holds the record for being the world's most prolific woman film producer. The Bobbili raja floated a couple of sugar mills in Vizianagaram, but they did not prove durable ventures. The only Velama industrialist of note has been J. Nrupender Rao of the Pennar group. An engineer from the Indian Institute of Technology, Kharagpur, and Purdue University in the US, Nrupender Rao was an employee of Nagarjuna Steels at its plant near Hyderabad. In the mid 1980s he left K.V.K. Raju's company (apparently with the latter's blessings) to start his own cold rolled steel outfit, Pennar Steels. In November 1997 he took over Nagarjuna Steels and merged it to form Pennar Industries Limited. During the same decade he also set up Pennar Profiles and Pennar Aluminium Company Limited. The last two have gone sick, while Pennar Industries has turned around. Another recent Velama entrant is G. Devender Rao of Yashoda Hospitals, which is one of the many corporate hospital chains to have sprouted in Hyderabad.

While the prosperous coastal Andhra Kapus are conspicuously absent in industry, there are interestingly a couple of entrepreneurs from the officially 'backward' Munnuru Kapu community of Telangana. One of them is B. Vasudev Rao, who is acknowledged as the 'Verghese Kurien of Indian poultry'. The Hyderabad-born

Rao began his career tending birds at the Osmania University's farms after doing a basic poultry-training course. As it was a temporary job he moved to work in poultry farms at Delhi and Khopoli (near Mumbai), before starting a hatchery on a seven-acre plot outside Hyderabad which was incorporated in 1971 as Venkateshwara Hatcheries (VH). The turning point was in 1972 when an American, Bill Todd – whom he had met at Khopoli – offered Rao the franchise to propagate a pure line developed by the Ithaca-based Babcock Poultry Farms. The imported strain proved hugely popular and Rao was hawking day-old chicks out of hatcheries established all over India. In course of time he indigenized the imported grandparent lines to evolve broiler and layer breeds adapted to local conditions. The VH group is today a Rs 1,300 crore fully integrated poultry conglomerate – Asia's largest – with operations spanning hatcheries, poultry processing and manufacture of feed, vaccines, and equipment.[69]

The other big, though not so reputed, Munnuru Kapu industrialist is M. Kishan Rao. His company, Bambino Agro Industries, makes vermicelli and pasta products under the 'Bambino' brand. Kishan Rao was also one of the promoters of a 210 MW power plant at Kakinada (Spectrum Power Generation Limited) in the early 1990s. It ran into trouble amidst wrangles between the various stakeholders and lenders. Kishan Rao was further accused of having awarded engineering contracts to the English firm Rolls Royce in return for kickbacks paid to a fictitious company account at the British Virgin Islands.

The Telangana Dimension

From our discussion, two things clearly emerge. The first relates to the sheer magnitude of Andhra peasant caste incursion into industry, embracing a wide spectrum of sectors. As a consequence they have virtually edged out traditional mercantile communities: in this case, the Komatis and immigrant Marwaris. Indeed, the only worthwhile Komati industrialist today – besides tobacco exporters like Bommidala, Polisetty, or Maddi Lakshmaiah – is Grandhi Mallikarjuna Rao. A mechanical engineer whose family was in the business of trading jute yarn at Rajam, a small town in Srikakulam, Rao has interests in ferro alloys, sugar, power (three plants at Chennai, Mangalore, and Rajahmundry with an aggregate capacity of 800 MW), and roads. His group is also building Hyderabad's new international airport, slated to come up by 2008. But it is their successful bids for privatization and modernisation of the existing airports at Delhi and Mumbai, respectively, that have brought the GMR and GVK groups visibility on a national scale.[70]

The second aspect has to do with the fact that our list of industrial houses contains only a handful from the Telangana region. The premier Kamma and Raju groups are all from coastal Andhra, save the odd Madhucon (Telangana) or Amara Raja Batteries and Heritage Foods (both Rayalaseema). The Reddy tycoons, too, are mostly of coastal Andhra (Nellore-Prakasam-Guntur) or Rayalaseema stock. Initially, much of their capital floated within Vijayawada or Guntur. Some part, especially the Reddy capital of Nellore and Rayalaseema, flowed to Chennai, given its proximity to these areas. The Telugu film industry, for one, was mainly based out of Chennai. Things have changed since the 1980s, which has seen a lot of coastal Andhra capital gush into Hyderabad – the TDP storming into power being its most potent symbol, and NTR installing Arthur Cotton's statue in Tank Bund conveying a subtler message. It is this wealth that has transformed a once-laid-back seat of the nizams into a happening metropolis. Needless to say, it has contributed in no small measure to a revivification of the separate-Telangana State movement, whose leaders have tapped an undercurrent of resentment against the 'takeover by coastal people'. And that has sent property prices skyrocketing in the entire Guntur–Vijayawada stretch – on the expectation that Telangana's formation will necessitate the development of a new capital city for the Andhra region.

We shall now take up a few illustrative micro-studies of business groups from the Kamma community.

Case Studies from the Kamma Community

1. Andhra Sugars

Tanuku was till the 1940s practically a village in West Godavari. Around 35 km from the Arthur Cotton barrage, it was one of those delta hinterlands that substantially benefited from canal irrigation. Being its richest zamindar, owning 1,200 acres of prime paddy-sugarcane fields, Mullapudi Harischandra Prasad was the munsif (hereditary revenue official) of Tanuku. When Panchayati Raj was introduced he served as its first village panchayat president from 1959 to 1964. After Tanuku was upgraded to a municipality in 1981, Harischandra Prasad became its chairman. To top it all, he was its elected Member of Legislative Assembly (MLA) between 1955 and 1967. In short, here was the archetypical rural-local boss,[71] who was just 26 when Andhra Sugars Limited was incorporated on 11 August 1947. Harischandra Prasad's partner is this project was Pendyala Sri Ramachandra Venkata Krishna (P.S.R.V.K.) Ranga Rao. The latter, married to his sister Atchayamma, was a 1,600-acre zamindar of Dommeru, a village 40 km from Tanuku towards Rajahmundry.

But the real inspiration for Andhra Sugars was Velagapudi Ramakrishna, who six years earlier had founded the KCP group by taking over a sick co-operative sugar mill at Vuyyuru, near Vijayawada. 'He was my mentor and encouraged me to start a sugar mill. He accompanied me when I went to Europe to procure machinery for the factory', recalls Harischandra Prasad.[72] Andhra Sugars was once upon a time even part of the 'outer circle' of the KCP group, by virtue of the latter holding a minority interest.[73] The Tanuku mill opened in 1952 with a capacity of 600 tcd, which was gradually raised to 1,000 tcd in 1957, 2,000 tcd in 1969, and 5,000 tcd in 1981. In 1997, the company commissioned its second 2,500 tcd mill at Taduvai and then, in 2003, acquired a co-operative factory at Bhimadole, whose capacity is being enhanced from 2,000 tcd to 6,000 tcd. Both are in West Godavari district, within 50 km of Tanuku.

However, Andhra Sugars' story is not simply about sugar. In 1962 it set up a distillery at Tanuku to utilize molasses, obtained as a byproduct from crushing cane, to make industrial alcohol. This, in turn, went into manufacturing alcohol-based chemicals, namely acetic acid, acetic anhydride, and ethyl acetate. In 1978 the company went a step further by installing a plant for recovering and purifying carbon dioxide from the distillery and using it, along with the acetic anhydride, to produce salicylic acid, the intermediate for aspirin. Andhra Sugars' aspirin facility is, in fact, India's largest, meeting the bulk requirements of companies like Reckitt Benckiser ('Crocin') and also exporting to the US and Europe. Parallel to this integrated sugar and alcohol-based chemicals operations at Tanuku, the company, in 1960, established an inorganic chemicals complex at Kovvur, again in West Godavari. It started as a sulphuric acid plant to produce super phosphate fertilizers for farmers in the area. In 1966 a second stream was added to make caustic soda and chlorine for the paper industry and also use the chlorine and hydrogen byproduct to produce hydrochloric acid and chloro-sulphonic acid, a raw material for bulk drugs. In 1997 a bigger caustic soda-sulphuric acid complex was commissioned at Saggonda, also in West Godavari. Apart from sugar and chemicals, a third line was taken up in 1974 – this time at Perecherla in Guntur – for the processing of cottonseed and rice bran to make refined vegetable oils, vanaspati, and cattle feed.

The end-result of these diversifications is that sugar *per se* now contributes less than 46 per cent to Andhra Sugars' revenues, while 48 per cent comes from inorganic chemicals. The latter includes unsymmetrical di-methyl hydrazine (UDMH), a rocket propellant used in the country's space programme, for which it obtained knowhow from the Vikram Sarabhai Space Centre, Thiruvananthapuram. The Andhra Sugars group is today a Rs 1,000 crore conglomerate, which, besides the main company, comprises Andhra Petrochemicals Limited (APL), Jocil Limited, and Andhra Farm Chemicals Corporation Limited (AFC).[74] The Visakhapatnam-based APL was promoted in 1984 to make oxo-alcohols (for plastics, adhesives, paints, surfactants, etc.) using naphtha from the adjacent refinery of Hindustan Petroleum Corporation. Jocil's unit at Medikondur (Guntur) mainly produces fatty acids, glycerine, and soap products derived from vegetable oils. It was acquired by the group in 1988 as a complement to its oilseeds processing complex. AFC, established at Kovvur in 1968, manufactures hydrazine hydrate – an ingredient in pesticides – for which the technology was sourced from the Indian Institute of Chemical Technology, Hyderabad. The group also controls four spinning mills: Sree Akkamamba Textiles, Sree Satyanarayana Spinning Mills, Sree Venkataraya Cotton Mills, and Sree Ananthalakshmi Textiles. All four units, with a combined capacity of over 1.2 lakh spindles, are located at Tanuku.

What is fascinating about Andhra Sugars is that its growth has taken place around a village locality, which has *pari passu* graduated to a bustling town. In 2001 Tanuku became the first town in AP to achieve total literacy. 'We are the only industrial group in India to have its headquarters and management in a rural area', declares Harischandra Prasad. True, what Andhra Sugars has done to Tanuku is pretty much in line with what the Tatas have contributed to Jamshedpur or Nestle to Moga (Punjab). But the difference is that the transformation in the latter two was brought about by outsiders, whereas Andhra Sugars represents endogenous capital accumulation. It is a phenomenon of a rooted landlord strata skilfully deploying its local dominance to convert itself into an industrial capitalist class. The factories and other institutions – a polytechnic and a 300-bed hospital at Tanuku and also the Rangaraya Medical College at Kakinada (named after P.S.R.V.K. Ranga Rao, who died in 1958) – have further reinforced the family's hegemony in the region. The most emphatic expression of this is Harischandra Prasad's claim that Andhra Sugars has not faced a single strike in its history. It has also been reflected in the political sphere. While Harischandra Prasad is an old-time Congressman, his heir apparent, Bolla Bulli Ramaiah (son-in-law of P.S.R.V.K. Ranga Rao), is a four-time TDP MP from Eluru and former union commerce minister. A chemical engineer who studied at Wisconsin and Harvard, Ramaiah has been the technical brain behind the group's diversification drive.

2. The Lanco Group

Unlike Andhra Sugars' founders, Lagadapati Rajagopal does not boast of any zamindari background. His grandfather, Lagadapati Venkatasubba Naidu, owned twenty acres of irrigated land in Amarappa Naidu Kandrika village (named after the latter's father) of Atmakur taluka in Nellore. That made him a prosperous, though not a terribly rich, paddy farmer. Venkatasubba Naidu had three sons: Amarappa Naidu, Venkata Rama Naidu (Rajagopal's father) and Venkata Ratnam Naidu. In the early 1950s Venkatasubba Naidu invested in a small business – plying buses with his brothers at Nellore. Due to differences, the partnership broke up and Venkatasubba Naidu was left with a single bus, which he gave to his sons and they converted it into a truck. 'Over a 20-year period, they had built a fleet of trucks, along with excavators and other construction equipment. These were hired out to big contractors like Tikkavarapu Subbarami Reddy', notes Rajagopal, who was born on 16 February 1964 in Nellore town.[75]

By 1978 the brothers had formed their own contracting firm, Uma Maheshwari Constructions. The first contract they undertook was a site-levelling job for the Visakhapatnam Steel Plant. From there they took up irrigation works at the Nagarjunasagar right canal, Pochampadu (Sriram Sagar), and Telugu Ganga projects, and also the Hidkal dam in Belgaum (Karnataka). By the mid-1980s, they had grown sizeably, owning 150 trucks, 8 excavators, 10 bulldozers, and 15 drilling machines. However, around 1986, disaster struck. The firm was involved in the excavation of a 2-km canal near Nandyala in Kurnool, as part of the Telugu Ganga project. It was a Rs 7 crore order that had been sub-contracted to them by one Yettury Ramachandra Reddy. Rajagopal, who was educated at Guntur's Loyola Public School and graduated in mechanical engineering from the Siddhartha Engineering College at Vijayawada in 1985, had just joined the family business. 'We were cheated and did not get the full money. It went into litigation and our business went bust. In the process, my uncle, Amarappa Naidu, had a massive heart attack that claimed him in 1987', he adds.

In end-1986 Rajagopal acquired S.V. Contractors. It was owned by L. Rama Naidu, a cousin of his father, who, despite being a licensed government contractor, was not keen on the business. In the first year the concern did a small Rs 10 lakh road contract at Visakhapatnam. The big order came a year later and it was for laying a water supply canal to the Visakhapatnam Steel Plant from the Yeleru reservoir. While the contract was supposedly worth Rs 6 crore, Rajagopal bagged it by quoting Rs 2.8 crore. 'The contract was structured in such a way that the payments were to come in equal instalments through the project period. My calculation was simple. Since it was a 100 feet deep canal and the cost of excavating the top layer was much lower than the bottom portions, we could make a killing in the first year. Although this would be offset by losses in subsequent years, I could make a neat profit of Rs 1 crore in the first year and use this cash flow to bid for other projects', explains Rajagopal. His firm bid for a number of irrigation projects: the Rs 10 crore Banakacharla regulator at the Srisailam Right Bank Canal, the Rs 5 crore Velugodu reservoir (part of Telugu Ganga), and the Rs 30 crore Indi Branch Canal near Gulbarga in Karnataka. In March 1993 Rajagopal and his brother-in-law Garlapati Bhaskara Rao (married to his only sister, Padma) incorporated Lanco Constructions to take over the business of S.V. Contractors, which was a partnership. 'We had by then reached an annual turnover of Rs 25 crore. Lanco was an acronym for Lagadapati Amarappa Naidu Company in the memory of my uncle, who was like a father to me', states Rajagopal.

Even before this Rajagopal had embarked on a mini-blast furnace project to manufacture 100,000 tonnes of pig iron annually, against the standard one million tonne capacity for a large blast furnace. The job was assigned to his brother, L. Madhusudhan Rao, also an engineer, who had done his master's at Wayne State University, Detroit, and was working for a Ford auto ancillary. Madhusudhan returned in end-1991 and, in September 1993, work began on a Rs 54 crore plant near Tirupati in Chittoor. It was financed by institutional loans of Rs 32 crore and a public issue of Rs 9 crore. The promoters put in Rs 13 crore, including 'funding by some of our US-based doctor friends belonging to Guntur-Vijayawada'. The plant came up by August 1994 'in a record eleven months'. In 1995 a Rs 13 crore facility was added to use the slag from the plant to make cement. Initially, the company – Lanco Industries Limited – supplied its entire pig iron to foundries in Coimbatore.

In 1997 another concern, Lanco Kalahasthi Castings Limited, was formed in the same complex to produce ductile iron spun pipes and castings from the pig iron.

But Rajagopal's biggest project was a 368-MW gas-based power plant at Kondapalli, near Vijayawada. In 1995 NTR's government had unveiled a policy inviting competitive bids for private players to set up generation stations against power purchase agreements (PPAs) signed with the state-owned transmission company. Rajagopal went for it and recruited a young Kamma mechanical engineer, Yarlagadda Harish Chandra Prasad, who had studied at the City University of New York and been with the Japanese power equipment giant Toshiba. 'We signed the PPA on 31 March 1997 and commissioned the plant on 25 October 2000. It was the largest private power project in South India', he observes. The Rs 1,100 crore plant of Lanco Kondapalli Power Private Limited had a Rs 340 crore equity component, in which Lanco's share was 34 per cent. The rest was mobilized from foreign investors: Genting group, Malaysia (30 per cent), the UK government-owned equity investor CDC plc (25 per cent), and Doosan Heavy Industries & Construction Company, Korea (11 per cent). Then came a 120-MW gas-based station at Thanjavur in Tamil Nadu (TN), which went operational in August 2005. Its original promoter was the Chennai-based Aban group, with interests in offshore oil drilling and windmills. In September 2002 Lanco took over this concern – Aban Power Company – that had been selected by the TN government to implement the project. Lanco holds 51 per cent in the company, in which Genting again has a 36 per cent stake.[76]

The Lanco group now has a turnover of around Rs 1,200 crore, much of which is from power. Having set up stations in AP and TN, the group is next working on an imported coal-based 1,015 MW unit at Mangalore, an indigenous coal-fired 1,200 MW plant at Korba (Chhatisgarh), a 500-MW hydro project across the Teesta river in Sikkim, and a series of small hydel and run-off-the-river schemes in Himachal Pradesh. As regards Rajagopal's maiden venture, Lanco Industries, in 2002 the group sold its controlling stake in the company to Electrosteel Castings Limited, Kolkata. 'We wanted to concentrate on our main business, which is energy and construction', avers Rajagopal. Lanco Constructions, renamed Lanco Infratech Limited in 1993, does an annual business of over Rs 200 crore. Among the large contracts executed are a cofferdam at the Tehri hydro project site in Uttaranchal and a Rs 300 crore Veeranam pipeline work (yet another scheme for bringing water to Chennai). It is also developing an IT park ('Lanco Hills') over 100 acres of land at Manikonda on the outskirts of Hyderabad.[77]

In February 2003 Rajagopal announced his 'retirement' from business to enter politics full time. His father-in-law, Parvathaneni Upendra, a close confidant of NTR, had been the TDP's leader in parliament and Union Minister of Information & Broadcasting during the National Front government in 1989–90 (coincidentally, the period when Rajagopal's career was taking off). After NTR's death Upendra switched to the Congress, successfully contesting from the Vijayawada seat in 1996 and 1998. Rajagopal followed his father-in-law and joined the Congress right when the TDP's (more accurately, Chandrababu Naidu's) popularity was on the wane. He fought the 2004 elections from Vijayawada and won by over 1.1 lakh votes. While the Lanco group is now formally headed by Madhusudhan Rao, Rajagopal's youngest brother Lagadapati Sridhar has plumped for the favourite Kamma passion of making films. His first movie, a Telugu slapstick *Evadi Gola Vaadidi*, ran for 175 days and was declared the biggest hit of 2005.

3. Matrix Laboratories

If Rajagopal's meteoric rise can raise quite a few conspiratorial eyebrows, the story of Nimmagadda Prasad is probably no less sensational. His father Nimmagadda Vijaya Saradhi was an ordinary soldier in the Indian army who joined as a havaldar and retired as subedar-major in the rank of an honorary captain. Since the job entailed postings in remote areas, Prasad (born on 11 October 1961) spent his early childhood at his maternal village Edulamaddali, some 10 km from Gudivada in Krishna district. 'My mother's father was a progressive farmer. He had a knack for identifying barren lands in distant places that could be turned around for cultivation. He farmed about 100 acres, of which 30 were his own and the rest taken on lease. My father's side is from Majeru, a village close to Machilipatnam. My paternal grandfather died when my father was just five', says Prasad.[78]

Prasad studied till the fifth standard at the village school and from there up to class nine at the Andhra Nalanda High School in Gudivada. Subsequently, he moved to Hyderabad and did his tenth class at the St Thomas SPG School, eleventh and twelfth at the Wesley Boys Junior College, and Bachelor of Science at the Babu Jagjivan Ram Degree College. After graduating in 1981 Prasad went to Delhi University and mastered in physics. 'I was not a very good student and usually got second division marks', he admits. Prasad had enrolled for a Master of Philosophy programme in 1983, when he landed a job at the Indian Molasses Company, an associate of the UK-based United Molasses. 'They were into procuring molasses from sugar mills and exporting it. My work was to report the sugar content in the samples. It involved no great science and towards the end I could simply taste and predict within a reasonable margin how much sugar there was. I even told my boss that it was a waste spending so much money on testing facilities and equipment', he states. The company nevertheless sponsored Prasad for pursuing a master's in business administration at the Institute of Management Technology in Ghaziabad, near Delhi.

'I used to attend classes after work in the evening. For a change, I did well academically and specialized in business strategy and marketing', he adds.

After finishing a three-year part-time course in 1989 Prasad went back to Hyderabad, where his father had got his last posting. In April 1989 he joined the French multinational Rhone-Poulenc Chemicals (now Aventis) as an area sales officer looking after AP. The company supplied fine chemical intermediates to Hyderabad's major bulk drug manufacturers, including Dr Reddy's, SOL, and SIRIS. 'I was there till June 1993 and was actually selected for an Asia-Pacific region posting at Singapore. But somehow I lost interest in working with such a huge organization. We had an intermediate compound, guaiacol (used in cough remedies) that was sold to clients like Synthokem Labs. During a sales presentation I said that we could easily market 50 tonnes a month, whereas my own manager pegged the target at 15 tonnes. The whole approach seemed to be to under-budget and over-achieve', he remarks. Prasad's decision to leave was also prompted by V. Ramakrishna Rao, the owner of Vorin Laboratories. It was a loss-making Rs 4-crore-turnover company that produced ibuprofen, norfloxacin and ciprofloxacin bulk drugs. 'Vorin was my buyer and during one of our meetings, Ramakrishna Rao suggested that I join as general manager, marketing. It was a struggling concern and I felt it would be worth a challenge. For about six months, there was no money to even pay salaries, but in a year's time, we were making profits', he observes. However, by end-1994 Ramakrishna Rao had sold his controlling interest to a group of US-based Andhra doctors who entrusted the company's running to Prasad.

In September 1996 the shares changed hands again, with Ranbaxy picking up 30 per cent in Vorin which, by then, had a turnover of over Rs 20 crore. Three years later, when Ranbaxy had hiked its stake to 51 per cent, the company was doing annual sales of Rs 70 crore and meeting the former's bulk ciprofloxacin requirements. Prasad remained as managing director though his own holding was hardly 1 per cent. In April 2000 Prasad quit Vorin, this time to set up something of his own. 'There was this company, Herren Drugs and Pharmaceuticals, belonging to one B. Sarat Gopal, manufacturing ibuprofen and sulpha-methoxazole. Despite recording losses of Rs 9 crore on a turnover of Rs 45 crore, I felt it would be a good buy for Vorin. But the Ranbaxy people were not keen to increase their exposure in Hyderabad. So I decided to purchase it', he notes. In May 2000 Prasad, along with a pharma trader M. Ravinder (related to the state's then home minister T. Devender Goud), bought Herren Drugs for about Rs 7 crore. In June 2001 it was renamed Matrix Laboratories Limited (MLL).

The company's growth since then has been simply astounding. From a loss of Rs 9 crore on a turnover of Rs 45 crore in 1999–2000, MLL has reported a PAT of Rs 130.27 crore on net sales of Rs 636.76 crore during the year ended 31 March 2005. Part of this has to do with mergers. When Prasad left Vorin he had taken with him some of its best men, including C. Satyanarayana, a doctorate in organic chemistry with fifteen years of industrial research experience. Their departure had an impact on Vorin's performance and Ranbaxy, too, found it difficult to manage the company from Delhi. In April 2002 Vorin was formally merged with Matrix, alongside Medicorp Technologies (a subsidiary of the Chennai-based Shriram group), with combined revenues exceeding Rs 150 crore. Being all-stock deals – the shareholders of Vorin and Medicorp were issued two shares of Matrix for every thirteen shares held – the mergers entailed no cash outflows. This was followed by similar takeovers of a slew of mostly Hyderabad-based companies, including Vera Laboratories and Fine Drugs and Chemicals. The second reason for Matrix's success is the new strategy it employed of moving away from commodity bulk drugs like ibuprofen and sulphamethoxazole to producing low-volume, high-value APIs for regulated premium markets in the US and Europe. The focus was on generic drugs, which had or were slated to go off-patent. The companies acquired by Matrix may not have been doing all that well financially, but they all had manufacturing facilities approved by the US Food & Drug Administration and other overseas regulatory agencies.

In February 2002 Matrix filed a 'non-infringing' process patent for citalopram, an anti-depressant molecule developed by a Danish company, Lundbeck. The product turned out to be a huge money-spinner for Matrix, contributing 50 per cent of its income in 2002–3, 35 per cent in 2003–4 and 24 per cent in 2004–5. It led to Lundbeck first offering Matrix Rs 200-odd crore to buy out its new process and, when the latter declined, filing patent infringement suits against its generic buyers in Europe. But it was eventually forced to withdraw these cases. Matrix is today Hyderabad's largest drug company after Dr Reddy's and Aurobindo Pharma, deriving two-thirds of its revenues from regulated international markets. Since 2005 it has expanded its acquistion arena beyond national borders: a $ 263 million (Rs 1,200 crore) buy-out of the Belgian generics player Docpharma, a 60 per cent stake in the Chinese anti-retroviral maker Mchem, and joint ventures with South African drug major Aspen. Prasad and Lagadapati Rajagopal personify a new lot of middle-class Kamma entrepreneurs that is aggressive, quick to grab opportunities, and globally oriented, and whose parents had already undertaken the initial journey from village to town.

Postscript: In August 2006 Matrix Laboratories announced that Mylan Laboratories Inc., US, was acquiring 71.5 per cent controlling interest in it for approximately $ 736 million. N. Prasad's holding in Matrix was to come down to 5 per cent, after he had pocketed for himself some Rs 570 crore from the deal: this on an original investment of Rs 7 crore that Prasad and his friends had made in a loss-making concern!

5

Kongunad Naidus and Gounders

'Manchester of the South; Light Engineering Powerhouse of India' – these are the usual catchphrases used for Coimbatore, a district in Tamil Nadu (TN) that produces roughly 15 per cent of the country's cotton yarn, generates 45 per cent of its knitwear exports, and meets half of the domestic pumpsets requirement.[1]

At one level the basis for these appellations defies conventional explanation. Coimbatore possesses none of the classic attributes associated with mainstream industrial centres. It has no abundance of mineral wealth to speak of. The Kongunad region of western TN – mainly Coimbatore and Erode districts – is landlocked, surrounded by the Western Ghats and hills on almost all sides. Being far removed from the major ports – Chennai is over 500 km by road, while it is 450 km to Thoothukudi and 190 km to Kochi – Coimbatore enjoys none of the location advantages accruing to Mumbai, Surat, Jamnagar, Kolkata, or Visakhapatnam. Neither has it been strategically positioned like Ahmedabad on major commercial routes connecting the ports with the principal towns of the hinterland. Historically, the Kongu upland plains may have served as an important gateway for troops and commodity movement over the Ghats through the Palakkad gap. Being in the middle of the southern peninsula also made it a buffer of sorts between the rulers of the great Tamil valley centres and those in the Mysore Deccan and west coast kingdoms. Even these functions were undermined by the thick forest cover and lack of good roads, which meant that the region was sparsely populated right till the early part of the nineteenth century.[2] Also, never in its history has Coimbatore reaped the concomitant economic benefits of being a political or administrative headquarters like Delhi, Kolkata, and Chennai, a financial capital on the scale of Mumbai or, for that matter, an ancient temple town *a la* Madurai, Thanjavur, Ramanathapuram, and Kanchipuram.

Last, but not least, Coimbatore's emergence as one of India's pre-eminent manufacturing hubs has been brought about not by Nattukottai Chettiars or other traditional mercantile interests but by industrialists of two communities – the Kammavar Naidus and Kongu Vellalas (Gounders) – whose primary vocation is farming. That would convey an impression of a region with a well-endowed agro-climatic regime, buttressed by perennial rivers and munificent monsoons. Again, the facts point otherwise. The western zone districts of Coimbatore, Erode, Karur, and Dindigul receive an average annual rainfall of 714 mm, which is not only below the all-India level of 1,190 mm, but even the overall 925 mm figure for TN. Indeed Kongunad lies in a veritable rain-shadow, rendering it the driest region of the state.[3] It has also not been blessed by extensive irrigation works of the kind seen in the Cauvery delta or the Vaigai and Tambraparni rivers in the southern Tamil districts. Unlike the relatively dry and newly settled Kongu country, these systems have been the backbone of a fecund rice-based valley civilization stretching back to their early Chola and Pandya builders,[4] and capable of sustaining two, or even three, crops a year.

The present chapter looks at how Coimbatore has risen to what it is today, in spite of all its perceived inherent infirmities. More specifically, it examines the two main communities that have contributed to its 'Manchesterization' and transformation into a land of foundries, machine shops, and engineering units fabricating a whole range of goods from castings, motors, and compressors to pumpsets and wet grinders. If the evolution of Chennai and its neighbourhoods into a major engineering and automotive hub owes a lot to Tamil Brahmin groups like TVS and Amalgamations, the same can be said about the Naidus and Gounders *vis-à-vis* Coimbatore.

Antecedents of Commerce in the Region

Kongunad might not have been bestowed with the magnificent irrigation networks of the great Tamil valleys, nor with fine alluvial soils rendered fertile by the silt washed down by rivers. What it did have though was large tracts of black cotton soil and significant reserves of underground water. These soils were heavy in texture, prone to water-logging, and tended to develop deep cracks under dry conditions. At the same time they contained sufficient clay and organic matter which, in conjunction with exploitation of the subsoil aquifer, could yield a decent if not bumper harvest. This, however, called for cultivation of an intensive nature centred around well-irrigation, as opposed to the surface tank or riverine flush irrigation resorted to by delta farmers. It further entailed considerable investment in boring wells through the hard local gneissic rocks, additional provision for drainage, and deploying stronger ploughs and bullocks to till the heavy soil and extract water tucked several feet below. A facilitating factor here was that Kongunad had been settled comparatively late, because of which its soils were less overworked and retained a lot of natural fertility.

In the process, its agricultural economy evolved on different lines from that in the river valleys. While the secure paddy agriculture of the deltas spawned a landed aristocracy of Brahmin and Mudaliar mirasidars and kaniyatchikarans (literally, controllers of land) who distanced themselves from cultivation, the land in Kongunad could not support such a regime. Since field preparation alone was a rigorous exercise, often necessitating secondary tillage, the characteristic production unit was the independent thottam or open well irrigated, compact garden plot. The soil texture demanded a style of capital-intensive farming that was adequately remunerative, but not conducive for absentee landlordism or a detached approach. Most holdings clustered around an optimum size of 5–10 acres that could be watered by a single well and intensively cultivated by a family and team of hardy cattle (the local Kangayam breed). The counterpart to the Brahmin-Vellala deltaic kaniyatchikaran in Kongunad was the 'sturdy' Gounder and 'enterprising' Naidu agriculturist. Not that there were no mirasidars, but rarely were they absentees living in big towns or cities.[5] The Kongunad mirasidar was typically a hands-on manager, who took a close interest in the tenanted holdings. Operating at higher levels of capitalization also made him more commercially oriented and involved in marketing the crop to ensure returns commensurate with the investment in his land. Further, he was more receptive to new productivity-enhancing techniques such as installing engines to draw water from wells in place of the conventional bullock-powered lifts. Indeed, among the valuable dowry items that P.S.G. Naidu – a prominent mirasidar and one of Coimbatore's industry doyens whom we shall encounter in the next section – is said to have presented to his daughter Rangammal when she married in 1911 was an oil engine to irrigate her in-laws' lands![6] Another indicator of the region's commercialized agriculture was land prices: a tenancy survey in 1946 recorded the average rental value of Coimbatore's thottams to be virtually the highest for TN and to have risen the most in the preceding thirty-odd years. This reflected the huge capital investments in land improvement, including building and maintenance of wells and subsidiary channels.[7]

Initially, Kongunad peasants produced coarse grains like cumbu (pearl millet), cholam (sorghum), and ragi. The main cash crops were castor, horse-gram, cotton, groundnut, tobacco, gingelly, and chilli. The decisive change was the introduction in 1904–5 of 'Cambodia' – an exotic long-staple variety of cotton from Indo-China (Cambodia). Till then, Indian farmers were growing only short-staple local cultivars, *Gossypium herbaceum* and *Gossypium arboreum*. These desi cottons were suited for coarse handspun and woven cloth but had limited demand in overseas markets or even among domestic spinning mills. The colonial authorities' attempts to develop long-staple American upland cotton – *Gossypium hirsutum* – acclimatized to Indian conditions, had also come to naught. 'Cambodia', on the other hand, yielded good quality fibre, even as it had long roots (unlike normal *hirsutum* varieties) that reached down to the deep water table. It was, therefore, ideal for the black soils of Kongunad. With mills willing to fork out a premium, farmers took up large-scale cultivation of the new variety, which was termed Marvadi Paruthi or 'moneylending cotton' in view of its profitability. When the century began, Kongunad had no organized market for cotton. By World War I, Tirupur – hitherto a nondescript ginning centre 40 km from Coimbatore – became a leading cotton market of the Madras Presidency, even attracting thirty-odd traders from Mumbai in 1916 who went around villages offering loans to farmers to produce 'Cambodia'. At the end of the War, cotton occupied a third of the region's sown area and had roughly doubled its coverage in a quarter of a century.[8]

But Kongunad peasants did not stop at cultivation. Given their commercial predisposition, they were less inclined to leave the marketing of their crop to merchants. As G.K. Sundaram, the nonagenarian chairman of Lakshmi Mills Company Limited, puts it: 'Our growers even then knew what was happening in Bombay, about daily price movements and when to sell.'[9] A sample survey in 1919 showed that a third of the cotton sold in Tirupur was brought into the market yard by the cultivators themselves.[10] Some of them sold the kapas (raw cotton) directly to ginners, realizing much more than what they would have done by marketing it to local merchants. Soon, a section – especially the bigger mirasidars – became commission agents, handling the crop from not only their own but even the neighbouring farmers' fields. From there they went on to be traders, then ginners, and eventually millowners.

The Naidu Entry

While the Gounders made up the bulk of Kongunad's peasantry, the foray into industry was led by large landowning mirasidars from the Kammavar Naidu community: originally migrants affiliated to the Kammas of Andhra Pradesh (whom we saw in the previous chapter). Among them was G.K. Sundaram's father Govindaswamy Kuppuswamy Naidu. Belonging to Pappanaickenpalayam on the outskirts of Coimbatore, Kuppuswamy Naidu was 22 when he set up a small ginning unit in 1905 that used a pair of oxen to pull the rollers in the gins. Coimbatore then had only one mill owned by Robert Stanes.[11] The Stanes were basically coffee planters in the Nilgiris who had established a curing facility in Coimbatore in 1861, before starting the Coimbatore Spinning and Weaving Mills Company in 1888. To cater to this mill Robert Stanes encouraged locals to put up gins and it was ostensibly at his prodding that Kuppuswamy Naidu installed oil engines to replace oxen power. In 1910, Kuppuswamy Naidu promoted Lakshmi Mills. Although only a ginning factory, it was intended to become a full mill in due course. The plan was derailed due to heavy losses incurred by him during the War in forward trading and speculation in kapas. When the War ended Kuppuswamy Naidu was saddled with huge margin-financed stocks which he had to dispose of at throwaway prices in Mumbai.[12]

As a result, the credit for floating the first ever Naidu-owned textile mill went to the family of Peelamedu Samanaidu Govindaswamy (P.S.G.) Naidu – referred to in the previous section – which founded the Sri Ranga Vilas Ginning, Spinning & Weaving Mills in 1922. Close on its heels was the Radhakrishna Mills, promoted in 1923 by yet another mirasidar-turned-ginner and trader, V. Rangaswamy Naidu. Kuppuswamy Naidu had to wait till 1929 to commission his first Coimbatore Cotton Mills. Lakshmi Mills remained a ginning factory until 1933, before becoming a regular mill. All these concerns were largely funded by capital mobilised through community and kinship networks. The Ranga Vilas mill was incorporated with a share capital of Rs 3.3 lakhs. Of its 45 shareholders, 38 were Naidus, with the PSG family owning a 55 per cent controlling stake.[13] Similarly, when Lakshmi Mills was registered in 1910 with a capital of Rs 100,000, Kuppuswamy Naidu's chief associates were P.R. Narayanaswamy Naidu, S.N. Nain Naidu, P.R. Rangaswamy Naidu, and R. Krishnaswamy Naidu.[14]

Someone who appears to have played a significant part in this period is K. Krishnaswamy (K.K.) Naidu, son-in-law of P.S.G. Naidu and beneficiary of the earlier-mentioned oil engine gifted by the latter for his daughter's marriage. A mirasidar from Karadivavipudur village in Palladam taluka, K.K. Naidu not only supplied cotton to the ginning units of PSG & Sons but supposedly bailed the family out once by extending a personal guarantee, following financial difficulties arising from a contract entered into by them with Volkart Brothers, a Swiss trading firm. The PSG family reciprocated this assistance by contributing to the share capital of Sri Balasubramania

Mills that K.K. Naidu himself floated in 1934.[15] K.K. Naidu and his maternal cousin C.N. Venkatapathy Naidu were also initially partners in Kuppuswamy Naidu's Coimbatore Cotton Mills. But differences of opinion between the directors caused a split, with K.K. Naidu and Venkatapathy Naidu deciding to have their own separate Balasubramania and Kasthuri mills, respectively.[16] K.K. Naidu was instrumental in providing venture capital and related support to a number of other mills in Coimbatore. These include Sri Ramakrishna Mills Coimbatore Ltd of S.N. Rangaswamy Naidu (SNR group) and Sri Ramnarayan Mills of N. Velappan.

At the start of the century Kongunad had a solitary mill belonging, as we saw, to the Stanes. By 1947 there were 32 in the Coimbatore-Salem belt, accounting for 48 per cent of the Tamil region's total spindle capacity. Of the 32, 16 were owned by Naidus, with 10 of them being controlled by the PSG, Kuppuswamy Naidu, and V. Rangaswamy Naidu groups. The three families exercised marginal control even in some of the remaining Naidu undertakings. Interestingly, most of these came up after the onset of the Depression, by which time the textile industry in Mumbai had gone into long-term decline.[17] 'The Depression actually helped us because the textile machinery manufacturers in Manchester were willing to supply their equipment cheaply, which we could install', says G.K. Sundaram.[18] Moreover, the new mills were consciously located nearer the villages, helping them to further prune capital and labour costs. Also, the crisis in the Mumbai industry may have proved a blessing by way of restricting competition – something that got an added boost through the clamping of duties on imported yarn in 1927 and 1931, besides the Civil Disobedience movement and the swadeshi (indigenous production) drive during this period.[19]

But a more important reason for Coimbatore emerging as a mini-Manchester, even as the mills in western India were floundering, had to do with structural factors. Unlike the composite spinning-cum-weaving mills in Mumbai, the Coimbatore textile units were primarily spinning concerns, selling yarn to the numerous handloom weavers concentrated in the region. 'We never faced a serious problem of marketing, since Coimbatore was itself a big handloom centre', notes G.K. Sundaram. The substitution of mill yarn for handspun yarn actually stimulated the cottage weaving industry by enhancing raw material availability and contributing to the latter's productive capacity. This physical proximity and symbiotic link with the handloom sector[20] – in later years this extended to the knitwear and powerloom clusters in adjoining areas like Tirupur, Erode, Karur, and Salem – conferred the region's mills with a tremendous advantage over the Mumbai industry and also explains its continued resilience today.

An issue worth addressing here is: why couldn't the successful industrial transition achieved by the Kammavar Naidus of Coimbatore be replicated by the same community in the southern Tamil districts, where, too, it took to the cultivation of 'Cambodia' in a big way. A plausible explanation may have been the entrenched European presence in the cotton markets of the far South.[21] Being close to the Tuticorin port, the cotton-growing areas of Tirunelveli and other southern districts were basically geared towards production for the export market. The big European expatriate firms were, hence, active there right from the beginning. Volkarts built its first gin in Tuticorin in 1876. A. & F. Harvey followed suit two years later. Elsewhere, Rallis had gins in Sattur, Virudhunagar, and Tirumangalam. Before the century ended the Harveys also had spinning mills at Papanasam, Tuticorin, and Madurai. Kongunad, by contrast, was relatively virgin territory. The Stanes there had 46,434 spindles in 1941, whereas the corresponding spindleage with the Harveys and Binnys (who had the Buckingham and Carnatic mills near Chennai) was 465,424 and 119,108, respectively. All the mills of the Lakshmi, PSG, and V. Rangaswamy Naidu families put together had a spinning capacity of 205,724 or less than half that of the Harveys.[22] The dominance of the Harveys can be gauged from the fact that its yarn prices set the market benchmark and other mills had to sell for 'round about 2 annas less'.[23] These would well have deterred the southern Naidus from taking a leaf out of the books of their Kongunad brethren, who ironically may have benefited by being distant from the ports.

But not all the pioneering Naidu entities have built on the lead given by their founders. The V. Rangaswamy Naidu group was ranked forty-seventh out of the country's top seventy-five industrial houses listed by the Monopolies Inquiry Commission in 1965. The Industrial Licensing Policy Inquiry Committee of 1969, too, rated it fifty-third among seventy-three premier groups.[24] Apart from owning a clutch of textile units (Radhakrishna Mills, Jayalakshmi Mills, Tirumurti Mills, VR Textiles), the group had forayed into sugar (Kamala Sugar Mills) and aluminium (Madras Aluminium Company Limited or Malco). Most of these are now either closed (including Radhakrishna Mills) or have been sold (Malco, which was acquired by Anil Agarwal's Sterlite Industries in 1995).[25]

The PSG family is known today mainly for the trust set up by the founder's four sons – P.S.G. Venkataswamy Naidu, P.S.G. Rangaswami Naidu, P.S.G. Ganga Naidu, and P.S.G. Narayanaswamy Naidu – in 1926, running several educational institutions in Coimbatore.[26] It also has an 'industrial institute' that manufactures motors, pumps, machine tools, and castings, even while PSG has ceased to exist as a business group *per se*. The original Sri Ranga Vilas Mill has been taken over by the state-owned National Textiles Corporation (NTC). Sri Kumaran Mills, established by the group in 1936, is now under D. Krishnamurthy, whose father G.V. Doraiswamy is the son of P.S.G. Venkataswamy Naidu. Another mill, Sri Varadaraja Textiles, is with Krishnamurthy's brother D. Varadarajan. Then we have Sri Karthikeya Spinning & Weaving

Mills of G.R. Karthikeyan, the grandson of P.S.G. Ganga Naidu through G. Ramaswamy. G.R. Karthikeyan is incidentally also the father of Narain Karthikeyan, 'the fastest Indian on wheels'.[27] All these are mills not big by modern-day standards or even in relation to some of the newer and more dynamic textile conglomerates we shall study later.[28] The only entrepreneur of note from the PSG stock today is probably Rajshree Pathy, the granddaughter of P.S.G. Ganga Naidu through another son, G. Varadaraj. She heads Rajshree Sugars & Chemicals, which has two sugar mills at Theni and Villupuram districts with a crushing capacity of 7,500 tcd. Rajshree is married to G.K. Sundaram's son S. Pathy, although she insists that her business, set up in 1990, is distinct from that of Lakshmi Mills.[29]

Among the old mirasidari Naidu business families, it is only Lakshmi that has survived. Beginning with mills, the group diversified into textile machinery by investing in Textool Company (started in 1946 by a Sheffield-trained engineer, D. Balasundaram) and Lakshmi Machine Works (LMW) in 1962. It also went into making artificial fibre through South India Viscose (SIV) – a joint venture with the V. Rangaswamy Naidu family – in 1957, besides promoting a fabric processing company, United Bleachers, in collaboration with some other mills in Coimbatore. SIV was taken over by the Shapoorji Pallonji Mistry group in 1983, before being wound up in 2003. In the same year Textool was merged with LMW. United Bleachers was sold in 1996 and eventually declared sick. While Lakshmi Mills (with over 200,000 spindles) and LMW are still there, it is the latter that is now the real cash cow.[30] With a 60 per cent share in the domestic spinning equipment market, LMW is seen as being one of the few global manufacturers of the entire textile machinery range.

The waning influence of the Naidu textile gentry does not, however, mean that the community is a spent force. On the contrary

Naidu capital has moved on to other areas. Even in textiles, they continue to wield significant power, though the new magnates are no longer drawn from traditional mirasidar ranks, as we will find out in the following section.

New Vistas

Like textiles, the origins of Coimbatore's fabled engineering industry lie in the commercialization of its agriculture. The progenitor of its first foundry – today, the region has some 600 of them – was Narayanaswamy Naidu. Hailing from Pappanaickenpalayam, the village from where Kuppuswamy Naidu came, he initially worked in Robert Stanes' workshop (the latter, besides popularizing cotton ginning using oil engines, also introduced the lathe and the drilling machine to Coimbatore). In 1922 Narayanaswamy Naidu opened a small unit to repair gins and sugarcane crushers. Since procuring castings was not easy then, he is believed to have gone all the way to Kochi to study the operations of the crucible furnace at the Cochin Shipyard.[31] Two years later the Dhandayuthapani Foundry (DPF) was born. By 1928 it had produced Coimbatore's first belt-driven pump. The PSG Industrial Institute similarly started off as a workshop – to service and manufacture ploughs and other farm equipment – followed by a foundry that came up almost the same time as DPF.

But if there is one enduring symbol of Coimbatore's engineering ethos it is G. Doraisamy (G.D.) Naidu. Indeed, so pervasive is the legend of this 'Thomas Alva Edison of India' that parables detailing his exploits abound to this day. Originally from Kalangal village where his father, Gopal Naidu, farmed about forty acres, G.D. Naidu (1893–1974) studied for barely three years in the local school. He left the village as a 20-year-old, the apparent trigger being an auto-cycle belonging to an English settlement officer. The

Englishman, one Mr Lancashire, had visited the village on survey work in this strange-looking vehicle that became an object worthy of possession for the young Kalangal resident. The story goes that G.D. Naidu went to Coimbatore and worked as a hotel boy for a couple of years to save enough to approach the same Mr Lancashire and convince him to part with the bike. Once got, the machine was ripped apart; the parts were dismantled and reassembled a sufficient number of times to permit a thorough scrutiny of its structure and working.

How true the above tale is in all its minute details cannot be ascertained. What definitely exists is a photograph of G.D. Naidu seated on the said auto-cycle. And what cannot be denied is the man's creative genius and self-experimentation capacity, proof of which is the range of things he designed and made on his own: valve radios, slide rules, clocks, a 16 mm projector and movie camera with a distance adjuster, a model two-seater car, a vote-recording machine, and an electric razor-cum-blade that he got patented in Germany. The 'Rasant' razor, incorporating a small motor and operated by dry cells fitted inside, was made by G.D. Naidu at a factory in a German town called Heilbronn.[32] Many of these inventions can be seen at a museum in Coimbatore bearing his name, which also displays the famous auto-cycle and numerous gadgets accumulated from his travels round the world.

G.D. Naidu's signal achievement though was in developing the country's first indigenous electric motor in 1937 along with D. Balasundaram, even before the Kirloskar Brothers. It was the motor's success that fuelled the foundation of Textool by Balasundaram and later on LMW. How the two went about it is a story in itself, best told by G.D. Naidu's son G.D. Gopal: 'First, they made the castings and then the windings, the shaft and the stamping. In the beginning, the bearings and enamelled wires were being imported, which stopped when War War II intruded. So, they fabricated a machine to make and draw the wire, followed by an enamelling plant to produce the enamel for the copper wire. They also tried to manufacture the bearings by making the steel balls and rings. By then, the War had ended.'[33]

As a businessman G.D. Naidu's career was no less spectacular. After the stint at the hotel he worked in a ginning factory, before managing to mobilize capital to establish his own gin. But like many others he was bitten by the trading bug and went to Mumbai, where his associate in cotton speculation and blowing-up savings was none other than Kuppuswamy Naidu. With little money in hand, G.D. Naidu offered his services as a mechanic to Robert Stanes who, instead, advanced him a loan to buy a bus. This coach, operating between Pollachi and Palani in 1920 with G.D. Naidu himself behind the wheel, was the precursor to the United Motor Service (UMS). By the 1930s UMS was running a fleet of 600 buses across Coimbatore, the Nilgiris, and the Cochin-Malabar districts. G.D. Naidu left his distinct imprint here as well. Among his innovations were an automatic ticketing machine (a variant of his vote-recording machine), a vibrator-testing device, and auto-radiators requiring little water. UMS further diversified into manufacturing radios, fans, pumps, motors, valves, sanitary ware, wet grinders, and assorted goods like electronic voltage stabilizers and mosquito terminators. Some of G.D. Naidu's ambitious plans to undertake commercial production of the 'Rasant' electric razor and even putting up an automobile factory in Coimbatore failed to take off. The locally available steel did not meet the specifications of the Norwegian steel that he had originally used to fabricate the blade.

The UMS group still remains, though its activities are somewhat low profile, focusing mainly on tool and die making, plastic injection moulding, prototype design, and the manufacture of precision lathes and CNC (computer numerically-controlled) machines. Likewise, DPF continues to manufacture pumps, motors, monoblocks, diesel engines, and machinery spares, while not being the force it was in the pioneering days of Narayanaswamy Naidu. Balasundaram's inventive zeal has been carried forward to an extent by his son B. Jayachandran, whose Jaya Automotives has the distinction of developing the first indigenous diesel engines for the 'Ambassador', 'Premier Padmini', and 'Standard 2000' cars, besides rolling out India's first 'own car' by the name of 'Mayura' in 1986. The contribution of G.D. Naidu, D. Balasundaram, and Narayanaswamy Naidu (one should perhaps include Robert Stanes as well here) etc. has been to foster a culture of industrial research and shopfloor innovation that has become a hallmark of Coimbatore. From producing its first pump in 1928 and India's first motor in 1937, the organized pumpset industry in Coimbatore is alone today worth Rs 1,200 crore, out of an all-India market of Rs 2,500 crore.[34] And this is a sector dominated by Naidus: CRI Pumps of G. Rajendran (see case study below), Fisher Pumps (part of the Sharp Tools group of K.K. Ramaswamy), Mahendra Pumps of Mahendra Ramdas, Suguna Industries of V. Lakshminarayanaswamy, Ellen Industries of V. Dhamodaraswamy, and Perfect Engineers of R.R. Ranganathan. Much of the region's strength is derived from its foundries and skilled human resource base.[35] These have made it a manufacturing haven for castings, auto components, and light engineering goods of all hues.

When G.D. Naidu bought the first bus that he drove in 1920, the man on the conductor's seat was a cousin of his, L.R. Govindarajulu (L.R.G.) Naidu. By the time the second bus arrived, they had split the business. While UMS operated the Coimbatore–Kerala belt, L.R.G. Naidu's Varadaraj Motor Service (VMS) plied eastern districts like Madurai and Tiruchirapalli. Over time VMS also grew into a fleet of 250 buses. From a fleet operator L.R.G. Naidu went into bus bodybuilding and in 1937 founded L.G. Balakrishnan & Brothers (LGB). From producing chains for two-wheelers and four-wheelers LGB has become India's largest supplier of automotive and industrial chains ('Rolon' brand). Another company, Elgi Equipments, was set up in 1960 to make garage service station equipment. It is the market leader in this segment – covering vehicle hoists, wheel balancers, crash repair systems, paint booths, and airconditioning recovery units – and also a major player in air compressors and diesel engines. The Elgi group is today a premier light engineering conglomerate. Other concerns in its fold include Pricol Limited (the biggest domestic manufacturer of automotive dashboard instruments and accessories), Elgitread India (a specialist in tyre retreading machinery and raw materials), Elgi Electric & Industries (motors, alternators and diesel generator sets), and Elgi Ultra Industries (which produces 'Ultra' wet grinders, among other things).

Even though automotive engineering has been the Elgi group's forte, like all mainstream Naidu industrial houses it has a stake in textiles, through Precot Limited and Super Spinning. 'Our entry into spinning was mainly due to V.N. Ramachandran, who was married to my sister, Vijayalakshmi', says L.G. Varadaraj, son of L.R.G. Naidu.[36] Premier Cotton Spinning Mills Limited was incorporated in 1962 by V.N. Ramachandran and his brother N. Damodaran, along with L.G. Balakrishnan (Varadaraj's brother). Precot is an offshoot of this company and, together with Super Spinning, controls over 300,000 spindles. While Precot and Super Spinning are part of the Rs 2,000 crore Elgi empire,[37] V.N. Ramachandran's son, R. Jagadish Chandran has his own Premier Mills Group with 200,000-plus spindles. Both these groups are currently as big, if not bigger, names in the textile industry than the old Naidu mill magnates, the Lakshmi Group included.[38]

Another important 'new' Naidu textile combine is the KG Group. Its founder, K. Govindaswamy Naidu, was born in 1909 at Peelamedu, the village of P.S.G. Naidu. However, unlike the latter's 1,200 acres-plus landholding, Govindaswamy Naidu's father, Kondasamy, cultivated a mere twelve acres. Govindaswamy was not enamoured of agriculture and migrated to Annur, which is an hour's drive from Coimbatore. There he first took up road construction, before starting a raw cotton-trading venture in 1932. By 1942 he had built his first gin to separate lint from the raw kapas and was supplying to the scores of mills that had come up in and around Coimbatore. Over the next couple of decades he added three more ginning factories. The next stage was to enter milling, which his group did by not establishing new, but buying existing, units. In 1970 it took over Sri Kannapiran Mills, followed by the Kadri Mills Coimbatore Limited in 1975, both of which were incorporated in 1946 and had changed hands several times.

Since then the KG group has become a fully-integrated textile major with operations straddling ginning, milling, weaving, knitting, the manufacture of terry-towels (Sharadha Terry Products Limited), denim fabric (K.G. Denim Limited) and jeans-wear ('Trigger' jeans). The Rs 700 crore group also has interests in the production and export of gray iron castings through CPC Limited, formerly Coimbatore Premier Corporation. Further, there is the K. Govindaswamy Naidu Medical Trust which runs the 350-bed 'super-speciality' KG Hospital in Coimbatore and an Eye Hospital that claims to have conducted 65,000 free cataract surgeries with intra-ocular lens implant. Heading the trust is G. Bakthavathsalam, the group founder's son, who is a cancer surgeon from the Madras Medical College. 'I was doing a postdoctoral fellowship at Mount Sinai, Chicago, in the early 1970s, when my father called me over to start the hospital. He had studied only till the fifth standard, but was keen that I become a doctor. We began with 25 beds in 1974 and today it is a Rs 40 crore business on its own', he notes.[39]

An even more remarkable medical venture is the Aravind Eye Care System (AECS) of Govindappa Venkataswamy, who initiated it as an eleven-bed private clinic in 1976 after retiring from Madurai's Government Medical College as head of its ophthalmology department. Today, it is a case study in the world's top business schools, forming part of every other management guru's evangelical armory.[40] In 2004 the five Arvind Eye Hospitals at Madurai, Coimbatore, Tirunelveli, Theni, and Pondicherry, with a 3,600-bed combined strength, performed a mindboggling 228,894 surgeries and handled 1,635,500 outpatient visits. Cumulatively, from 1976, AECS has conducted more than 2.2 million eye surgeries and attended to nearly 18 million outpatients. Three-fourths of surgeries and two-thirds of outpatient visits are serviced free of cost; yet it has proved to be a financially self-supporting venture with an estimated annual turnover of Rs 60 crore. The system also has a manufacturing division, Aurolab, to produce intra-ocular lenses and suture needles, which have considerably brought down the cost of cataract surgeries.

Besides textiles, engineering, and hospitals, the Naidus have a presence in industries such as paper and poultry. The Venkatesa group – whose founder G.V. Govindaswamy Naidu established the Sri Venkatesa Mills in 1934 – owns a number of paper mills in Udumalpet taluka, even as its original textile business has grown to roughly 85,000 spindles. The group, now under the founder's son-in-law V. Genguswamy Naidu, also runs a chain of schools all over Tamil Nadu and a women's college at Udumalpet.

Equally well known in paper is R. Ramaswamy who, in fact, pioneered the design and manufacture of paper plants in India. Formerly employed with LMW, he set up Servall Engineering in the early 1970s, which is a leading integrated paper and pulp machinery maker. Ramaswamy's company also had a coated duplex paperboard facility that he sold in 2000 to L.M. Thapar's Ballarpur Industries, before the latter disposed of the same to ITC in 2003. B. Soundararajan's Suguna Poultry group is another Naidu concern to have come up only in the last two decades or so. It is now a Rs 1,000 crore enterprise – next to Venkateshwara Hatcheries – with operations extending from the breeding of grandparent and parent stock to contract broiler farming, poultry feed manufacture, and processing meat for exports and the domestic market.

The Gounders

We have so far fleetingly referred to the Gounders. Partly, this has to do with their comparatively late entry into industry. The Gounders, no doubt, formed the numerically dominant section of Kongunad's peasantry. Like the Naidus they were progressive agriculturists, drawn pretty early into marketing their own crop. A souvenir released on 28 October 1938 to mark the 'silver jubilee' of the Kaleeswarar Mills, founded in 1906, gives information on its first board of directors. Among them is V.C. Vellingiri Gounder, described as a 'landlord' from Vellakinar village. The same souvenir carries the copy of a glowing 'address' to the company's managing agent, P. Somasundaram Chetty, by prominent 'cotton and yarn merchants of Coimbatore' on 8 March 1926. Two names in this list of merchants are E.R. Kandasamy Gounder and P. Rathinasabapathi Gounder.[41]

Notwithstanding this involvement in the cotton trade, the first Gounder-promoted mill did not come up till 1935, by which time the initial Naidu industrial trickle had turned into a veritable flood. And even after the establishment of Gnanambikai Mills by V.C. Vellingiri Gounder – who almost three decades back was in the first board of Kaleeswarar Mills – no new Gounder mill was floated in the next twenty years. Then, between 1955 and 1957, two mills were started: the Sri Karunambikai Mills of A.V. Ramana Gounder at Somanur and Sri Sakthi Textiles of N. Mahalingam at Pollachi (both in Coimbatore district). The latter mill happened to be the maiden industrial venture of what is today the Rs 1,600 crore Sakthi group, whose foundations were laid in the early 1930s by Mahalingam's father P. Nachimuthu Gounder. We will study this conglomerate – with interests in sugar, transport, finance, auto components, textiles, education, edible oils, etc. – in greater detail later.

But the arrival of Gounder capital, in the true sense – in contrast with isolated cases of industrialists from the community – is a phenomenon mainly of the 1980s, coinciding with Tirupur's emergence as a pre-eminent cotton knitwear export hub. Between 1984 and 2004 the export of cotton knitwear from Tirupur soared from 10.42 million pieces (valued at Rs 9.69 crore) to 400.47 million pieces, worth Rs 4,553.77 crore or more than a billion dollars. That translates into an annual compounded growth of 31 per cent in rupee terms. Further, these only represent direct exports and exclude indirect shipments routed through agents in Mumbai, Delhi, and other centres. Of India's total export earnings of Rs 9,948.90 crore from knitted garments in 2004, Tirupur's share was 46 per cent.[42] In the process Tirupur has displaced traditional knitwear export clusters such as Mumbai, Ludhiana and Delhi to storm into the *numero uno* position.

To understand the relevance of all this to us one needs only to examine the profile of Tirupur's exporters. Of the top fifty firms – which accounted for Rs 2,200 crore or slightly under half of exports from the region in 2004 – as many as thirty-three are Gounder-owned. The community's dominance becomes all the more stark when we look at the composition of the office bearers of the Tirupur Exporters' Association (TEA). In this case, six out of seven – A. Sakthivel of Poppys Knitwear (president), N. Chandran of Eastman Exports Global Clothing (vice-president), S. Duraiswamy of Prem Knitwear (vice-president), K. Manthrachalam of Jaihind Mills (joint secretary), P. Vidhyaprakash of Styleman, and K.A.S.

Thierumurthi of Stallion Garments – are Gounders. The odd man out is the secretary, G. Karthikeyan of General Textile Industries, who is from the Kaikola Mudaliar weaving community. Viewed against this background, we ought to explore Tirupur somewhat closer.

Tirupur, as already noted, shot into prominence as a cotton market in the early part of the twentieth century. This was facilitated by its location in the middle of a cotton-growing belt and also a railhead built in 1862 linking it to both the east and west coast ports of Madras and Beypore. In 1931 Tirupur had six cotton presses and eighteen ginning factories; by decade-end it also had three mills, two of them owned by Devanga Chettiars (a weaving caste) and one by a Muslim trader (Asher Textiles).[43] The early knitting units, too, were set up primarily by the two communities. They included M. Abdul Raguman Sahib's Azad Knitting Company (started in 1926), Rajendra Knitting of Pethi Chetty, and Khadar Knitting of S.A. Khadar, who founded the South India Hosiery Manufacturers' Association (SIHMA) in 1956. Easy access to yarn, the availability of cheap land and labour (relative to Coimbatore), and hard water from the Noyyal river conducive to bleaching were key drivers behind the mushrooming of knitwear units in Tirupur. The 1961 Census put their number at 230.[44]

There were two basic characteristics of these units. Firstly, they pre-dominantly produced banians (vests) for the domestic market. For the same reason, Tirupur is still called India's 'banian capital', a tag it has not been able to shrug off to this day. Secondly, they were composite units, wherein all operations were under one roof. The yarn sourced from mills was knitted into fabric, which was then calendared (for shrinkage control) and bleached to produce the 'white' cloth ready for garmenting. The processed fabric was cut to the required dimensions before stitching, labelling, ironing, packing, and dispatch of the finished product.[45] All these were carried out in-house, with only bleaching being occasionally contracted out. This system was in vogue till roughly the late 1960s. The impetus to change came from labour militancy. Kolkata, at that point, was still the country's most important centre for cotton knitwear in terms of output. A series of strikes and lay-offs there prompted North Indian merchant capital to look at Tirupur as an alternative sourcing base. They began by supplying fabric from Ludhiana, to be cut and stitched by workers at their homes. In due course this became standard practice even among local factory owners, who encouraged employees to put up their own finishing units with offers of regular orders. Soon, there were individual households with not just a power table bearing 6–7 stitching machines, but even second-hand circular knitting machines bought from Ludhiana that converted yarn into fabric. Towards the end 1970s the erstwhile workers were producing whole garments on contract and subcontracting portions of their work to further layers of job-workers. The old order of vertically integrated knitwear companies had crumbled, as manifest in official data recording a decline in the number of workers per unit in Tirupur from 74 in 1965 to 21 by 1984.[46]

What this fragmentation of the production process simultaneously did was provide an entry point for Gounders into knitwear manufacture. While the traditional Kamma or Naidu transition to industry may have taken place through investment of accumulated agricultural surpluses, in this case certain push factors appear to have been more at work. Many of the first-generation Gounder knitwear entrepreneurs were farmers from villages surrounding Tirupur who had been pushed into employment in hosiery units because of consecutive monsoon failures, declining water tables, and rising cultivation costs.[47] At the same time the demise of composite manufacturing had vastly reduced the outlays required for starting a unit, enabling the Gounders to gain a foothold in the industry. And once that happened it was only a matter of time before they had taken over; a study in 1984 provided the following community-wise break-up of Tirupur's knitwear units: Gounders 62 per cent, Chettiars 14.4 per cent, other Hindus 18.8 per cent, and non-Hindus 5.5 per cent.[48] The basis for Gounder dominance lay not in access to capital as much as in their exercising control over the entire subcontracting network. One estimate showed 72 per cent of indirect exporters (units supplying to the ultimate exporters) and 74 per cent of job-workers in Tirupur to be Gounders.[49] That in itself created formidable entry barriers for 'outsiders', including direct exporters who, ergo, had to confine themselves to sourcing rather than manufacturing.

Like their predecessors the new Gounder firms began by producing banians for the local market. While Tirupur was exporting small inner-wear consignments even in the 1970s – mainly through traders in Mumbai and Kolkata – the real boom began in the ensuing decade. The man who is said to have triggered it by making the first high-volume export purchases from Tirupur was Antonio Verona, an Italian agent who came in 1979 through exporters based in Kolkata. Sensing Tirupur's potential, Verona stayed on to expose local knitwear units to the intricacies of producing for the world market and even invested heavily in a Gounder-owned concern, City Knitting.[50] Although it folded up eventually after the rejection of a major order, the process of export-led manufacture was well in place. Also, a second generation of Gounder businessmen had then come onto the scene. These were either educated siblings of existing ex-worker-owners or a new lot of professionals on whose initiative TEA was formed in 1990 (as a parallel to the more domestic market-oriented SIHMA). Alongside, Tirupur's product profile expanded to 'basic' T-shirts, and then to more fashion-intensive sportswear, jackets, sweatshirts, Bermudas, children's wear, skirts, and lingerie, largely catering to global buyers like C&A, Wal-Mart, JC Penney,

Sara Lee, Marks & Spencer, Tommy Hilfiger, and GAP.

A typical case of a Gounder ex-worker from a rural background making the switchover to local banian maker, indirect exporter, and, finally, direct exporter is provided by S. Ramasamy of Best International. 'Best' Ramasamy, as he prefers to be known, belonged to a farming family in Velayuthampalayam, which is 25 km from Tirupur. Being a dry area, where accessing water meant digging a bore-well 1,200 feet deep, life wasn't easy. At the age of 16, Ramasamy, who had failed to make it even to high school, went to Tirupur as a labourer in a bleaching unit. 'That was in 1962 and I worked there [Murugan Bleaching, owned by a relative] for five years', he recounts.[51] In 1967 Ramasamy set up a banian unit in which he invested Rs 10,000. Half of this came from his savings while working and the rest by mortgaging his twenty-acre agricultural land. Ramasamy also managed to raise Rs 15,000 from the State Bank of India (SBI), which went towards procuring 'Sieko overlock' sewing machines from Ludhiana. Initially, the fabric was purchased from outside and his unit, employing eight workers, did the bleaching, manual cutting, stitching, ironing, and packag ing. In 1975 he installed four knitting machines – sourced from Raj Mechanical Works, again of Ludhiana – to undertake direct fabrication from yarn.

For the first ten years Ramasamy restricted himself to making banians and marketing them under 'Simla' brand in the four southern states. In 1977 he fulfilled an export order through a Mumbai-based Gujarati trader ('one Mehta of KT Corporation'). But the big order came four years later from Uganda. That was the time when that country's military dictator, Idi Amin, had been deposed and been succeeded by Milton Obote. 'It was part of a 40 lakh T-shirts order timed for their elections. Basically these were banians on which Milton Obote's photo had to be printed on the front and the name of his party, Uganda People's Congress, on the back. I had to deliver 40,000 pieces valued at Rs 30 lakh, which was more than my company's net worth. But the problem was that banks refused to open a letter of credit (LC). A Uganda LC is worse than toilet paper, they told me. Thankfully the payment came in a year's time', Ramasamy states. After that there was no looking back. In 1985 Ramasamy ventured into direct exports and today his group has an annual turnover of over Rs 200 crore. This includes exports of Rs 125 crore, mainly undergarments and kidswear supplied to American and European retail giants, such as Sara Lee, Mothercare, C&A, Tesco Stores, and Wal-Mart.

While Gounder entry into knitwear was originally facilitated by the breakup of the old composite units, the last ten years or so have witnessed a renewed trend towards vertical integration. Best International, for instance, now has five garmenting factories with facilities for not just knitting, cutting, and stitching, but even for fabric compacting, rotary printing, computerized embroidery, and steam ironing. It also has a unit that makes elastic tapes for undergarments. The only operation being outsourced is bleaching and dyeing, even as the company is putting up a dyeing plant at Perundurai in adjoining Erode district. As if these were not enough, the company has two spinning mills at Dharapuram with a capacity of 60,000 spindles. This case of the wheel turning full circle is not specific to Ramasamy. As the TEA president, A. Sakthivel, points out, all major exporters are aiming at vertical integration and the pressure for it is coming from the buyers. 'They want us to install state-of-the-art fabrication and processing machinery within our own unit that makes it more amenable to quality control and meeting their stringent norms', he notes.[52] Thus, the old Ludhiana-make second-hand circular knitting machines capable of making only 'fine' fabric have been substituted by imported German or Italian equipment that can knit a wider range of 'Jacquard', 'Inter-lock', 'Single Jersey', 'Honeycombed', and 'Waffle' structures. Similarly, traditional steam calendaring and open winch bleaching have given way to compacting, tumble-drying, and 'soft flow' dyeing, while rotary printing and steam ironing have replaced screen-printing and electric irons. And, like Best International, all the big direct exporters, from Eastman to Poppys, Centwin, KPR Knits, Prem Knitwear, and the Royal Classic group (which owns the 'Classic Polo' and 'Smash' brands), have established their own spinning mills of 20,000 to 30,000 spindles each, so as to secure supplies of yarn. This, to a great extent, was spurred by the spiralling of yarn prices during the mid 1990s, in the wake of the government liberalizing exports. 'We were then at the mercy of the Naidu mill-owners of Coimbatore, which is no longer so', says a leading knit-wear exporter.

In fact the massive Gounder foray into spinning since the 1980s is something not as well documented as their overwhelming domination in cotton knitwear. One of TN's biggest textile barons today is P.S. Velusamy, whose Sri Shanmugavel group controls nine mills in Dindigul district with aggregate spindleage of 3.5 lakhs. Other major Gounder spinning concerns are the KPR group of K.P. Ramasamy (which also owns KPR Knits), Sangeeth Textiles of E.N. Ramasamy, the Chola Textiles group of A.P. Appukutti, and Eveready Spinning Mills of A.R. Subramaniam. All have capacities in excess of one lakh spindles each, making them bigger than even the 'old' Gounder textile entities like Gnanambikai, Karunambikai, and Sri Sakthi. What is further interesting is that these mills have come up in Dindigul, Erode, and satellite towns around Coimbatore such as Annur and Tirupur. Thus, the Naidu textile bastion of Coimbatore has been subjected to aggressive Gounder encroachment from the fringes.

Textiles apart, the Gounders have a substantial presence in engineering and agri-business. The Rs 200-crore-plus Texmo Industries, promoted in 1956 by Ramaswamy Gounder, is a market leader in agricultural pumpsets. His son R. Kumaravelu runs a separate company, Aquasub Engineering, that also markets pumps under the 'Texmo' and 'Aquatex' brands. P. Subramanian's Shanthi Gears – listed among the hundred best small-sized companies of Asia-Pacific and Europe by *Forbes* magazine in its 1 November 2004 issue – is a major manufacturer of industrial gearboxes, gear wheels, motors and assemblies. K. Ramaswamy's Roots Industries is India's leading and the world's eleventh biggest supplier of electric and air horns for automobiles and commercial vehicles. In sugar there is – besides N. Mahalingam's Sakthi Sugars – Bannari Amman Sugars of S.V. Balasubramaniam and Dharani Sugars and Chemicals of Palani G. Periasamy. Bannari Amman, as we shall later see, is an off-shoot of the Sakthi group and, like the latter, a diversified Rs 1,200 crore conglomerate. Dharani Sugars' founder previously taught economics and business management at the University of Baltimore in the US. Palani G. Periasamy also owns the Hotel Le Royal Meridien at Chennai and runs various educational institutions, including the PGP College of Engineering & Technology at Namakkal. Another US-returned entrepreneurial venture is the Coimbatore-based Kovai Medical Center and Hospital Limited (KMCH) of Nalla G. Palaniswami, an endocrinologist from Wayne State University at Michigan. His group, too, operates colleges offering paramedical courses in nursing, pharmacy, physiotherapy, and occupational therapy.[53]

One Gounder businessman of recent vintage who deserves mention is M. Ramasami. Hailing from Rasipuram village in Salem, Ramasami graduated from the Tamil Nadu Agricultural University, Coimbatore, in 1966, after which he worked with the state agriculture department as an extension officer. In 1973 he went into the seed business by organizing production for big domestic companies like Mahyco and Mahendra Seeds. The companies would supply Ramasami the foundation seeds, which he then multiplied. 'I did this by contracting with other farmers. Though my father had 50 acres, I chose not to use it because the land was joint family property. Also, seed production was a new concept for them', he discloses.[54] In 1986 Ramasami established his own research farm of 140 acres at Attur in Salem. By 1992 his company had released its first cotton research hybrid, RCH-1, which was followed by RCH-2 in 1994. The latter hybrid created a record by covering an estimated 22 lakh acres in 1998–9, which was a tenth of India's total cotton area. Today, Ramasami's Rasi Seeds is engaged in contract seed farming over 10,000 acres. In 2004 it became India's second company after Mahyco to commercially launch a genetically modified version of its cotton hybrid, incorporating the controversial 'Bollgard' (Bt) gene of the US life sciences major, Monsanto. The Rs 200 crore Rasi group has further put up a 20,000-spindle spinning mill at Attur and a garmenting unit at Tirupur, so as to cover the whole chain from basic seeds research to final knitwear products.

But the ultimate embodiment of Gounder capital is Tirupur and specifically TEA: arguably one of the country's most effective industry associations. Part of its success derives from the dominance of one community in ownership networks. An equally important factor relates to the size of the individual exporters. Collectively, Tirupur's direct knitwear exports are well over Rs 4,500 crore; however, its single largest exporter, Eastman Exports, did just Rs 350 crore in 2004. 'Our strength is our smallness that is conducive to co-operative effort. You don't find this in a place like Ludhiana, where there are big individual companies who are not as keen to develop the export cluster', says R.M. Subramaniam, adviser to

TEA.[55] The result: Ludhiana, which used to be a pre-eminent exporter of woollen knitwear in the Soviet era, hardly exports any now. Its annual knitwear exports of about Rs 630 crore comprise only cotton.

The most visible sign of TEA's collective lobbying strength has been a scheme to bring 185 million litres per day (LPD) of water to Tirupur from the confluence of the Bhavani and Cauvery rivers in Erode through a 55 km pipeline. Out of the 185 million LPD, 125 million LPD is to meet the requirements of Tirupur's dyeing and bleaching units, with 25 million LPD being earmarked for the local municipality and the remaining water for villages along the route. Billed as the first ever 'public-private partnership' project in India's water sector, the implementation authority for the Rs 1,000 crore project is the New Tirupur Area Development Corporation, in which the main stakeholders are the TN government, TEA, and Infrastructure Leasing & Financial Services Limited. 'Our own current requirement is around 100 million LPD, whereas we have been getting only 85 million LPD. The project is designed to serve not just our present-day, but future growth needs as well', Subramaniam adds. The industry has also demonstrated its clout by repeatedly stalling official moves to impose stringent effluent discharge norms on bleaching and dyeing units, which are seen to be primarily responsible for polluting the Noyyal river. Although there was a setback in the form of a High Court judgment in July 2005, requiring compulsory installation of reverse osmosis plants for secondary treatment of effluents, the units have managed to rally political opinion seeking financial assistance from the state and union governments to enable them to conform to the 'unfair' order.[56]

We shall end this chapter by examining case studies of some industrial groups from the two communities surveyed.

Case Studies[57]

1. Sakthi Group

The Sakthi group's roots are in Pollachi, an overgrown village 40 km south of Coimbatore towards the Annamalai hills, where P. Nachimuthu Gounder was born on 11 November 1902. His father Palani Gounder was a modest landowner who mainly farmed groundnuts on about 10 acres. Nachimuthu Gounder broke away from the family vocation early in life (he managed to study up to the seventh standard) by plying 6–7 bullock-carts from Pollachi to the Valparai tea estates up the hills. In the early 1920s he moved from hiring out carts to operating taxis and then lorries, before launching the Anamallais Bus Transport (ABT) Limited in 1931 with fourteen buses. By 1940 this had grown to forty. Simultaneously, the scope of his business expanded to servicing and repair of buses and trucks. At the time of nationalization of public transport services by the state government in 1972, ABT boasted a fleet strength of 150 buses. In short, yet another industrial family from South India – we already noted this in the case of T.V. Sundaram Iyengar, the Seshasayees, G.D. Naidu, and L.R.G. Naidu – that started off as mofussil transport operators.

N. Mahalingam was 23 when he joined his father in 1946, after doing a bachelor's in physics at Chennai's Loyola College and mechanical engineering at the Guindy Engineering College. During Nachimuthu Gounder's time – he passed away on 7 February 1954 – the group confined itself to transport. Besides ABT, which ran buses and serviced heavy vehicles, the other big group concern was Gounder & Company, formed in 1950 as a distributor for 'Tata' vehicles and seller of spare parts. The activities of Anamallais Retreading Company and Sakthi Finance – incorporated in 1954 and 1955, respectively – were again transport-related. Sakthi Finance was essentially into hire-purchase financing of trucks to complement the vehicle dealership business. By then Mahalingam had also entered politics, winning the 1952 state assembly elections from Pollachi. He remained a Congress legislator for a further two five-year terms. But Mahalingam's career in politics ended with the 1967 general elections, when he unsuccessfully contested the Coimbatore parliament seat.[58]

The group's first manufacturing project was Sri Sakthi Textiles, started in 1957 at Pollachi with 12,000 spindles. The following year, the Indo-Swiss Synthetic Gem Manufacturing Company (now Sakthi Synthetic Gems) was set up at Mettupalayam, north of Coimbatore, to produce rough synthetic diamonds and gem crystals used in jewellery. The group's flagship, Sakthi Sugars, commissioned its first plant in 1964 on the Bhavani riverside at Erode. Mahalingam had conceived of it in the late 1950s while being a director of the Amaravathi Cooperative Sugar Factory at Udumalpet. There were also some disastrous promotions like Sakthi Pipes to fabricate cast iron spun pipes for water projects. The unit at Elavur, near Chennai, was doomed right from the time orders were placed for the plant and machinery from Germany. The rupee's steep devaluation in 1966 pushed up the foreign-exchange component to Rs 1 crore, against the anticipated Rs 60 lakhs. The slashing of budgetary allocations on infrastructure accompanying the deflationary policies of this period made matters worse, especially for a project dependent on government contracts. The company's management was taken over by the TN government in 1972, before it was sold to Electrosteel Castings Limited of the Kejriwals in 1982 (the same Kolkata Marwari group that acquired a dominant stake in Lanco Industries, whom we saw earlier).

How much did community networks help in the group's industrial forays? 'Well, quite a bit, particularly in the initial stages of raising monies. Since we were pioneers in the community, there was lot of backing for our initiatives', admits M. Manickam, Mahalingam's eldest son, who is vice chairman and managing director of Sakthi Sugars. Take Sakthi Sugars, in which the promoters subscribed to only 5.45 per cent of the initial share capital. Between 1961 and 1989 the promoters' (family members and group concerns) stake ranged between 1.43 per cent and 5.45 per cent. The largest block of shareholders comprised community people (mostly farmers) and public financial institutions, who held 40 per cent each, the rest being with the public. 'My father had full faith in the farmers and he believed that they will never sell their shares to outsiders. But I insisted that if the company had to be effectively managed, we must increase our stake to at least 26 per cent. So in 1990 the company came out with a rights issue to increase its share capital from Rs 3.6 crore to Rs 5 crore and we picked up Rs 1.25 crore of the additional equity, while the other shareholders renounced their rights. Thus, we raised our holding to 23 per cent and over a period it has gone up to 40 per cent', says Manickam.

The other route for mobilizing funds was Sakthi Finance, which once used to be the Pollachi Credit Society and has an asset base of nearly Rs 250 crore now. Community connections also proved useful in the not-too-distant period, when sugar prices had nosedived and Sakthi Sugars accumulated cane payment arrears of Rs 70–80 crore. 'It was a harrowing time from 2001 up to mid 2004. Given the low realizations from sugar, we wanted to put up a 32 MW cogeneration plant, which banks, however, refused to finance. We held back cane payments for 14–18 months and practically took the growers' money on credit to fund it. But for our community links, all this would not have been possible. We somehow convinced them that the company will pay later and ultimately the cogeneration plant is in everyone's interest', reveals Manickam.

Today, the Sakthi group is a Rs 1,600-crore-plus combine, out of which more than Rs 700 crore comes out of sugar and associated products, including alcohol and power. Apart from its Bhavani plant that has a capacity of 7,500 tcd, Sakthi Sugars operates a 4,000 tcd unit in Sivaganga district and a 2,000 tcd facility at Dhenkanal in Orissa.[59] The group additionally owns Sri Chamundeswari Sugars, which has a 4,000 tcd plant at Mandya in Karnataka. The transport-related businesses have also grown, notwithstanding nationalization of its bus services. The parent company, ABT Limited, with a turnover of Rs 275 crore, is the largest dealer for Maruti Udyog in TN and runs a network of auto service stations and workshops. Besides, it is involved in cargo transport and courier services. Another company, the Rs 370 crore ABT Industries, is a leading distributor of 'Tata' vehicles and operates a one lakh litre per day dairy plant.

The group also has interests in manufacture of castings and auto components (which contribute about Rs 130 crore), soybean and related products (Rs 50 crore), and education (the Kumaraguru College of Technology in Coimbatore and Dr Mahalingam College of Engineering and Technology at Pollachi). Then, there are family-owned firms like Anamallais Retreading Company, Anamallais Engineering (engaged in automobile body-building and fabrication), N. Mahalingam & Company (dealership of home appliances and 'Tempo' and 'Kinetic' vehicles), and Sakthi Estates (coffee, tea, and cardamom plantations), which together generate roughly Rs 120 crore. The group's original manufacturing ventures – textiles and synthetic gems – have, more or less, been relegated to the background. Its two spinning units – Sri Sakthi and ABT Textiles – have an aggregate capacity of just 75,000 spindles, after nearly fifty years.

2. The Bannari Amman Group

The Bannari Amman group's founder, S.V. Balasubramaniam, is technically N. Mahalingam's cousin: his father, Sangampalayam Vedanayagam Gounder, was the brother of Mahalingam's mother

Rukmani Ammal. However, given the age gap of seventeen years between them, Mahalingam was more of a father figure to Balasubramaniam, who was the eldest of four brothers and a sister. Born on 4 February 1940 in Sangampalayam village of Pollachi, Balasubramaniam's father cultivated groundnuts in 45 acres of dry land, and tobacco, chilly and vegetables in another 10 acres of thottam or irrigated land. After studying till the seventh standard in a local private school, Balasubramaniam joined the Udumalpet high school before going to Chennai's Vivekananda College to do an intermediate in physics, chemistry, and natural sciences. 'I wanted to pursue medicine. But in 1956, my father died. Since my sister was not married and the family needed to be looked after, I had to return. Moreover, my father happened to be the village munsif [headman]. As this was a hereditary post, my aunt [Mahalingam's mother] did not want the family to abdicate it and I got back to the village', he recalls.

It was here that Mahalingam, sensing Balasubramaniam's keenness to study, took over the responsibility of financing the education of the four brothers. Balsubramaniam decided to give up medicine and, instead, graduated in commerce at the Government Arts College in 1959 and qualified to be a chartered accountant in 1964 (later, in 1981, he passed the company secretary examination as well). On Mahalingam's direction he joined Sakthi Sugars as its internal auditor and rose to be chief accounts officer in 1966, deputy general manager in 1967, general manager in 1974 and finally vice chairman in September 1983. Around this period Mahalingam's son Manickam returned from the US, after doing a master's in business management at Ann Arbor, Michigan. 'I felt that the time had come to start something on my own. Mr Mahalingam had also suggested this to me a couple of times before. I resigned on 8 September 1985, having been with the company for twenty-one years from 1 September 1964', notes Balasubramaniam.

He did not have to begin from scratch, though. Much before Balasubramaniam laid down office, his brothers and brother-in-law, P.K. Doraiswamy, had their businesses going: Annamallai Retreading Company (different from the Sakthi group's Anamallais Retreading Company) and Anamallais Agencies for dealership of 'Escorts' tractors and Hindustan Motors vehicles. 'Mr. Mahalingam gave us these firms in 1974. My father and he were originally partners in them', says Balasubramaniam. Further, they had developed a cargo parcel concern, ARC Parcel Service. In 1980 there was a split wherein Doraiswamy took the parcel service company and the brothers retained the retreading and agency concerns. In the same year they established Sakthi Murugan Transports, followed by Vedanayagam Hospital at Coimbatore in 1981 under a brother, S.V. Kandasami, who is a professional urologist.

Even prior to all this Balasubramaniam was a 'silent partner' with V.M. Kailasam (formerly commercial director of Sakthi Sugars) in Kamadhenu Drinks, which was set up at Erode in 1972 to make arrack (country liquor). 'This was an independent venture of Kailasam [who managed to get the licence] and myself. Mr Mahalingam did not want Sakthi Sugars to be involved in liquor as a matter of principle and they have stuck to this. After Kailasam died in 1976, I took charge while continuing to be in Sakthi Sugars', observes Balasubramaniam. In 1978, he floated Coimbatore Alcohol and Chemicals Private Limited (CAC) to produce industrial alcohol and extra neutral spirit. In 1983, during the chief ministerial tenure of M.G. Ramachandran, Balasubramaniam got a licence to manufacture Indian-Made Foreign Liquor (IMFL) using the extra neutral spirit from CAC. The new company, Shiva Distilleries, started making liquor under various names like 'Monitor' whisky and dry gin, 'Brisnoff' vodka, and 'Shivas' brandy and rum. The last two labels ran into some trouble because of their phonetic similarity with the illustrious 'Smirnoff' and 'Chivas Regal' brands. The liquor business did well to generate adequate investable surpluses for Balasubramaniam.

His first venture after leaving the Sakthi group was Bannari Amman Sugars. But here, too, Sakthi Sugars subscribed to 300,000 shares of its initial equity capital in 1985, which was more than the 250,000 shares held by Balasubramaniam himself. After a rights issue in 1992, Balasubramaniam's stake in Bannari Amman Sugars increased to 970,000 shares, against the 600,000 shares owned by Sakthi Sugars. It was only in 1994 that Sakthi Sugars' entire holding was bought up by Balasubramaniam, a pointer to the nurturing role played by Mahalingam. As Balasubramaniam emphasizes, 'it was he who even gave the name Bannari Amman to my company'. Its first unit was commissioned in early 1986 at Sathyamangalam in Erode. Beginning with a capacity of 1,250 tonnes, it was expanded in phases to 4,000 tcd along with a 28 MW cogeneration plant. A second unit at Nanjangud near Mysore in Karnataka came up in 1992, which now can crush 5,000 tcd and produce 36 MW of power. CAC was merged with Bannari Amman Sugars in 1995, while Shiva Distilleries and Kerala Alcoholic Products (another IMFL unit at Palakkad incorporated in 1992) remained independent entities.

Today, the Bannari Amman group has a turnover surpassing Rs 1,200 crore. Sugar and derived products aside, it has interests in textiles (Bannari Amman Spinning Mills and Shiva Texyarn, with combined spindleage of 100,000), wheat milling (two flour mills that can process nearly 300 tonnes of wheat per day), education (Bannari Amman Institute of Technology at Erode) and the manufacture of granite slabs and tiles. Like the Sakthi group, it is also involved in transport (Sakthi Murugan Transports and Shiva Cargo Movers), auto dealership (for Hindustan Motors and Mahindra & Mahindra), and tyre retreading.[60]

3. CRI Pumps

In our case study of a Naidu-owned business, we will profile a family with no mirasidari trappings which is yet a product of Coimbatore's unique industrial environment bequeathed by the early pioneers from the community. Krishnaswamy was by no means a big landowner; even the ten acres that he farmed in Palladam was taken on lease. His son, K. Gopal, studied till the sixth standard and was 18 years old when he began working as an apprentice in the foundries of the PSG Industrial Institute and Textool Company. That was in the late 1940s, when a host of engineering establishments had sprung up in Coimbatore. Like many others employed with these units, he learnt on the job and became a skilled moulder.

In 1957 Gopal branched out to set up a small non-ferrous foundry at Ganapathy, which is today one of Coimbatore's main engineering hubs. In 1961 he used the in-house foundry to start a unit, Rajendra Industries, to fabricate valves for pump priming systems. By the middle of the decade he was selling these valves – basically spares for agricultural and domestic pumps – under the 'CRI' brand, with 'RI' being short for Rajendra Industries and 'C' denoting that the product was from Coimbatore. A strike in 1970 led to Rajendra Industries closing shutters for about six months. On being reopened it was rechristened CRI Industrials. In 1972 Gopal established one more valve-making concern. This was in another industrial area, Avarampalayam, and was called Coimbatore Rajendra Industries, to distinguish it from the earlier Rajendra Industries.

In 1978 Gopal took the next step of producing agricultural pumps at Coimbatore Rajendra Industries. These were ordinary belt-driven pumps, in which the engine is separately installed on the well mouth and power is transmitted to the pump near the water level through a belt drive. But within the next couple of years he was also manufacturing motors and 'monoblocks' (in which the motor is fused with the pump, making it a more efficient system) under the 'CRI' brand. Simultaneously, another facility, Chola Raja Industries, came up at Saravanampatti to supply machined castings and other pump parts to Coimbatore Rajendra Industries. 'My father had this fascination for the ancient Chola emperor, Rajendra. I was also named after him', remarks G. Rajendran, Gopal's third son. Shortly after that, in April 1980, Gopal passed away; he was barely 50 years old. His eldest son Velumani was already helping out with sales then. After Gopal's death, the two other sons, Sounderarajan and Rajendran, joined the business. 'But it was our mother, Ranganayaki, who was the guiding force. She used to visit the factories every day, before she passed away in 1996', adds G. Rajendran, who has a diploma in electrical engineering from PSG College of Technology.

By the end 1980s the family's business had grown. In 1988 Chola Raja Industries became Chola Pumps Private Limited, which manufactured jet pumps, monoblocks, and single-phase motors for domestic household use. Coimbatore Rajendra Industries was likewise converted into CRI Pumps Private Limited in 1996, focusing on agricultural pumps and motors. Another company, Ransar Industries was set up in 2000 to produce submersible pumps for both domestic and agricultural applications. In addition a modern mechanised foundry, Meltech Castings, was established at Chinnavedampatti in 1992 to cater to all the pump-making concerns, even as the original CRI Industrials (now called CRI Industries Private Limited) continued to produce valves and pump spares. 'We were the first in South India to get the Bureau of Industrial Standards' ISI certification for our valves. Also, we are one of the few fully-integrated pump concerns in India, with our own foundry and in-house facilities to manufacture valves, spares and motors', claims Rajendran.

The privately-held CRI Pumps group today has a turnover of Rs 250 crore, with an annual production capacity of 750,000 pumps and motors, and exports to over forty countries. It is one of the three top players in Coimbatore's Rs 1,200 crore organized pump-sets industry, along with Texmo Industries (a leader in agricultural pumps) and Fisher Pumps (a specialist in mini-monoblocks or regenerative pumps for garden-use). 'Our strength is big centrifugal pumps of 0.5 to 20 horsepower', explains Rajendran, who looks after production and research at CRI Pumps, while Velumani (the chairman) and Sounderarajan are in charge of financial management and marketing, respectively.

6

Nadars and Ezhavas

Our survey of business communities till now has focused on castes within the ambit of the classical Hindu chaturvarna social hierarchy comprising Brahmins, Kshatriyas, Vaishyas, and Shudras. We started with the traditional mercantile communities clubbed under the Vaishya order (Banias, Marwaris, Jains, Parsis, Chettiars, etc.), followed by Brahmins and other 'white collar' professional classes. The latter included Kayasthas, Khatris, and the Bengali bhadralok – communities whose entry into business was predicated upon their strong educational base and a secure presence in the civilian and political establishment. From these we moved to the intermediate castes, covering landowning peasant communities such as Kammas, Reddys, Naidus, and Gounders who have made a successful transition from the field to the boardroom over the last century. In the conventional varna scheme these communities, along with other 'dominant castes' like Patidars, Marathas, and Jats (whom we shall examine in later chapters), were categorized as Shudras.[1]

Needless to say, the above classification is nebulous and not amenable to cast iron straitjacketing. As the eminent sociologist M.N. Srinivas has noted, the varna system, far from being rigid, permitted fair bit of movement, especially for castes in the middle rung of the hierarchy. Indeed, many erstwhile Shudra castes, after acquiring economic and political power, laid claim to more exalted pedigree by offering military service, adopting vegetarianism and teetotalism, abjuring widow remarriage, and 'sanskritizing' their rituals and pantheons.[2] Thus, there have been conscious attempts by Marathas, Jats, and other dominant rural communities to reinvent a Kshatriya identity for themselves, just as in post-Industrial Revolution England 'Dick Arkwright, the barber's apprentice, made his fortune in the spinning jenny (and) metamorphosed into Sir Richard'.[3] But the point is that this upward social mobility for parvenus in the Indian context was an option mostly restricted to the upper landowning crust among the Shudras. It was less so for castes occupying the lowest ritual ranks within the Shudras, let alone for those outside the purview of the varna system: the avarnas or 'untouchables'.

In this chapter we will look at two remarkable business communities, who were traditionally condemned to a social limbo somewhere between the Shudras and the outcaste untouchables. Given their ritually impure calling as toddy-tappers, the Nadars and Ezhavas were seen 'as belonging to the highest division of the lowest classes or the lowest of the middle classes; poor, but not paupers; rude and unlettered, but by many degrees removed from a savage state.'[4] Association with alcohol and a profession almost as debased as butchery or tanning meant that till the early part of the twentieth century these two communities were barred from entering Hindu temples and using public wells, and their women were obliged to leave their upper torso uncovered. Their rise from near-untouchable status to becoming business communities formidable enough to produce, among others, the owners of India's biggest infotech enterprise and one of its most read newspapers is a story that is profound testimony to the tenacity of the human spirit.

Degraded Pasts

At the start of the nineteenth century, the Nadars – or 'Shanars' as they were pejoratively called – were concentrated in present-day Kanya-kumari, Tirunelveli, and Thoothukudi districts of southern Tamil Nadu (TN). The bulk of them inhabited tracts south of the Tambraparni river: particularly Nanguneri (in Tirunelveli), Srivaikuntam, and Tiruchendur (in Thoothukudi), besides the whole of Kanyakumari. Compared to the paddy-rich fertile soils bordering either side of the river, this belt – save Kanyakumari, which was part of the old Travancore state and shared its tropical vegetation – was dry and desolate. The only things growing in these stretches of loose, red and sandy lands were the palmyra and the thorny udai scrub bush used as firewood. The majority of Nadars eked out a living by cultivating the palmyra and tapping the sap from its flowering shoots. The saccharine sap collected early morning was allowed to ferment during the day for sale as toddy or further distilled into arrack. Alternatively, the sap was preserved in its original sweet neera form (by adding an anti-fermenting agent, usually lime) and boiled over slow fire in earthen pots to produce a thick syrup that, on cooling, crystallized into hard, black jaggery cakes. The resultant palm gur was marketed as coarse sugar.[5]

In the palmyra forests of Tiruchendur, Nanguneri, and Srivaikuntam the Nadars formed the overwhelming majority. As there were no other dominant castes, the community on the whole enjoyed a semblance of autonomy and did not suffer serious social disabilities. Instead, there was a divide within the Nadars: between the 'Nadans' who owned the palmyras and the land on which they stood, and ordinary 'Shanars' who climbed and tapped the trees. This was in contrast to the Nadars elsewhere. In northern Tirunelveli and Ramanathapuram (Ramnad), they were a landless minority and subjected to severe discrimination by the dominant landowning castes – Maravars (Thevars), Naickers (Naidus), and Vellalas. The number of trees in this region, too, were limited and sufficed only to yield juice for fermented toddy and not for making palm gur. Economically dependent on the owners of the trees, the Nadars climbed the palmyra during the tapping season from March to September and worked as farm labourers in the remaining months.[6] It was no different for the Nadars in the Kanyakumari–Thiruvananthapuram area of the former Travancore state where they, despite their numbers, worked as toddy-tappers and subtenants of Nair landlords. Like their Malayali Ezhava counterparts, they were not permitted to carry umbrellas, use footwear, milk cows, or build houses higher than one storey. Above all, their women could not wear gold ornaments and cover their bosoms.[7] There was little to separate the Nadars from the Ezhavas, except that the latter belonged to Kerala and tended the coconut palm instead of the palmyra.[8] Both were almost at par with the untouchable castes, namely the Pulayas and Parayans. Though nominally not bonded agricultural labourers like the latter, they were required to perform oolium, i.e. corvee labour demanded by the state.

The striking feature of these social disabilities is their durability: how they survived well into the twentieth century, by which time the two communities had, in fact, made considerable progress in economic terms and a nascent bourgeoisie had emerged within their ranks. Alummoottil Kuttakkakaran Sekharan Channar, a major Ezhava abkari (liquor contractor) in Travancore, is known to have employed Nair pappans (mahouts) for his twelve elephants. Although extremely rich, strictly enforced 'pollution' rules meant that Channar, on approaching temples, had to dismount, even while his Nair pappan could ride past on elephant back.[9] The same rules denied Ezhavas admission to state-run schools until as late as 1910. Even if they studied in missionary schools, it did not qualify them for government service. The legendary community reformer

P. Palpu came second in the all-Travancore medical entrance exam but was refused admission and had to go to the Madras Medical College. Even after this he was not granted recognition by the Travancore Medical Council and had to take up employment with the Mysore government in 1891.[10]

The most stark symbol of the disconnect between their newly acquired economic power and defiled ritual position was the ban on admission to temples, which the Nadars and Ezhavas sought to defy through concerted action from the late nineteenth century. This inevitably brought them into confrontation with dominant castes, taking umbrage at their growing wealth and assertion to higher social status. Occasionally it assumed violent forms, as in the infamous Sivakasi riots of 1899 between the Nadars and Maravars, following attempts by the former to gain access to the local Viswanadhaswamy (Shiva) temple. Another high-profile instance was the 'Kamudi case', arising from the forced entry into the Meenakshi Sundareswara temple at Kamudi (Ramnad) by a group of fifteen Nadars in May 1897. It provoked a suit filed by the raja of Ramnad (a Maravar), seeking a permanent injunction restraining the Nadars from entering the temple. The subordinate judge of Madurai not only ruled against the community, but also ordered it to fork out Rs 500 to carry out 'purification' ceremonies in the temple. The Nadars contested the injunction and took the case all the way to the Privy Council in London, which, too, in 1908, affirmed the decree of the subordinate judge.[11] Efforts by Ezhavas at temple access found expression in the 'Vaikom satyagraha' of 1924–5, a campaign focusing on the right of low castes to use public roads around the main temple in Vaikom town of central Travancore. Engineered by T.K. Madhavan – a nephew of the earlier-mentioned Kuttakkakaran Sekharan Channar – it was supported by Mahatma Gandhi. All these eventually culminated in the Congress government in Madras under C. Rajagopalachari legislating the historic Temple Entry Authorization and Indemnity Act of 1939, which was preceded by a royal proclamation by the maharaja of Travancore in November 1936, opening temples there to all castes.

Economic ascendancy manifested itself in other kinds of social mobility actions as well. To start with, the Nadars tried to establish a Kshatriya identity by claiming they were descendants of the ancient Tamil Pandyan rulers who, after being defeated by the Telugu Nayaks in the sixteenth century, were stripped of their titles and forced into the degraded occupation of toddy-drawing. To buttress the theory the Nadar Mahajana Sangam (NMS) demanded that the government stop referring to the community in its records as 'Shanars', which had 'acquired an offensive and contemptuous significance' in view of its association with toddy-drawing. In January 1921 the Sangam passed a resolution calling upon Nadars to return their caste as 'Kshatriya' in the forthcoming census. But as 'Kshatriya' was 'too general and too vague' a description, the authorities narrowed in on the simple term 'Nadar' to substitute the deprecatory 'Shanar'. During this period the NMS also urged community members to abandon toddy-tapping for liquor-making purposes which, it felt, was 'held in low estimation by the people' and was not conducive 'for the social and moral advancement of the Nadars'.[12] Interestingly, a similar campaign was mounted by the spiritual leader of the Ezhavas, Sree Narayana Guru (1855–1928), who in 1921 likened liquor to 'poison' and exhorted his followers not to tap, sell, or drink toddy. This came alongside his initiatives to replace the traditional religious practices of Ezhavas, such as blood sacrifice, hook-swinging, and mantravadam (sorcery), with more sankritized forms of worship.[13] While the latter reforms found widespread acceptance amongst the community, the same cannot be said of the directive against toddy-drawing. As we will see, it was too lucrative a trade to be given up, particularly for a section that had enriched itself not by engaging in actual climbing as much as in becoming influential abkaris and owners of licensed bars and vends.

The Nadars: How They Rose

Three factors played a prominent part in unshackling the Nadars from the narrow confines of their palmyra groves and bringing them into the mainstream of society and commerce. The first of these was to do with Anglican missionaries, who began proselytization work in Tirunelveli in the closing decades of the eighteenth century. 'Christianity and the palmyra have appeared to flourish together. Where the palmyra abounds, there Christian congregations and schools abound also; and where the palmyra disappears, there the signs of Christian progress are rarely seen', wrote Robert Caldwell, consecrated as the first Bishop of Tirunelveli in 1877.[14] When the century ended Tirunelveli had the greatest number of Christians in the Madras Presidency and, among the Protestants, 95 per cent were Nadars. Christianity had provided access to a resource hitherto denied to the community – education – apart from investing them with a sense of superior identity and belief in the capacity for advancement. And it is not just the Christian Nadars who benefited; nearly one-third of the boys enrolled in mission schools were non-Christians.[15]

The above development coincided with a second factor, which was the movement of European plantation capital into Sri Lanka and South East Asia from the 1830s, simultaneous with the opening of coffee and tea estates in the hills of the South Indian peninsula. The employment avenues created by these led to unprecedented migration, touching 4,000–6,000 per annum to Malaysia alone and 40,000 a year to Ceylon in the second half of the century.[16] A substantial number of the emigrant labourers were Tamilians, including Nadars from Tirunelveli and Kanyakumari. The more educated lot, especially Christians, found work as clerks, supervisors and kanganis (labour contractors). On returning, most of them abandoned toddy-tapping and took to more 'respectable' vocations such as petty shopkeeping or cultivation. This was reflected in a notable rise in the number of land titles held by Nadars, who intensively farmed garden crops such as chilli, onion, and betel-vine in these often small plots.[17] Some invested in plantations themselves, with active support from missionaries keen to build up self-sufficient congregations.[18] Among the successful kangani-turned-planters were P.D. Devasahayam and Alfred Vedam Thomas. The latter's Rs 600 crore AVT group, founded in 1925, today has 4,500-odd hectares under tea, cardamom, rubber, coffee, and spices, in addition to interests in leather, agro-chemicals, plant biotechnology, shipping, and warehousing.

But the majority of Nadar businessmen were neither Christians nor migrants to overseas lands and the Western Ghat plantations. They were simply small-time traders, to begin with, who wandered among the palmyra topes south of the Tambraparni, aggregating the products of the trees and dealing in palm gur, dried fish, salt, and assorted agro produce. Their area of operations was limited by the lack of good roads and general lawlessness, and made worse by the multiple duties levied on goods over short distances by local poligar chieftains. For these petty Nadar merchants, it was a third factor – the benign impact of British rule on transport infrastructure and law and order – that proved crucial. By the early nineteenth century the poligar rebellion had been ruthlessly snuffed out.[19] Roads and bridges were being laid to enable the colonial state to secure effective control over its conquered territories. These, in turn, helped the Nadars expand the locus of their business beyond the Tambraparni. Many of them moved northwards, settling down mainly in the six towns of Sivakasi, Virudhunagar, Aruppukottai,

Palayampatti, Tirumangalam, and Sattankudi. It is from the 'Six Town Ramnad Nadars' that the embryo of a business community emerged by the middle of the century. Initially, they accumulated capital by trading in palm gur, for which there was growing demand especially from the newly opened sugar factories and distilleries. These units – the first of which was set up by the English agency house of Parry's in 1845 at Nellikuppam (Cuddalore) – refined the gur, which was the basic raw material used to make sugar before cane cultivation came into vogue.

From palm jaggery, the Nadars diversified their commodity basket to cotton, groundnut, and tobacco. Even prior to the export boom following the 1861 American Civil War, they had acquired a foothold in the kapas trade as intermediaries between the growers and European export firms – the Harveys, Volkarts, and Rallis. Just as they meticulously collected gur from the palm groves in the interior, the merchants handled the primary sourcing of kapas from the fields and supplied it to the export houses against forward contracts. It was no surprise that, when the boom began, European firms built their gins precisely in towns occupied by the community. Towards the end of the century, four Nadar families monopolized kapas supplies in Tuticorin, while there were ten such groups in Virudhunagar. These families, and others in Sattur and Tirumangalam, were related through marriage ties and caste institutions. The opening of the railways in 1876 made Virudhunagar the premier cotton market of the Presidency – a position it held till Tirupur's arrival with the onset of World War I. Between 1871 and 1911 its population quadrupled, while tripling and nearly doubling in Sattur and Tirumangalam, respectively.[20]

How did the Ramnad Nadars establish themselves as a strong trading class, and this in a matter of less than a century? One reason was that they entered a niche business area – that of village-level procurement and aggregation of farm produce, mostly on behalf of large European exporting firms – at a time of expanding global trade in commodities. This was a segment where there was no significant presence of traditional mercantile communities like the Chettiars, whose operations were mainly focused on moneylending and financing trade rather than on trading *per se*. Moreover, from the 1830s – a phenomenon that accelerated after the 1870s – there was an exodus of Chettiar capital away from Madras to Sri Lanka and South East Asia, in response to higher returns from moneylending in these new frontiers for colonial exploitation. Ergo, there existed in the South, unlike elsewhere in the country, a considerable 'Vaishya vacuum' that could be filled by enterprising communities such as the Nadars.

While the Nadars took advantage of the new opportunities arising from India's assimilation into the colonial economy, hand in hand with the easing of internal trade barriers and relative peace conferred by Pax Britannica, their ascendancy was no less an outcome of purposive community organization. Wherever they settled, the Nadars built pettais (fortified enclosures) for conducting business, financed through mahamai, a communal tax that traders had to pay to use the commercial infrastructure. Control over the mahamai funds was vested with a council, the uravinmurai, composed of members from the concerned pettai. These institutions – commanding a degree of authority extending beyond the sphere of business – were a response to the ground situation in Ramnad, where the Nadars were a minority *vis-à-vis* the Maravars and Naickers in the countryside. Being middlemen with rising economic power made them natural targets for reprisal, thereby forging a sense of cohesion and tight organization manifested in the uravinmurais based in various trading centres.[21] As the community made forays northwards into Madurai and Chennai by the late nine-teenth century, the need for a more comprehensive association to promote its corporate interests and social aspirations led to the formation of the NMS in 1910.

From Bazaar to Factory

At the start of the twentieth century the Nadars were a business community in the true sense: moneyed, confident, and increasingly assertive in the economic and social arena. A process, ignited by missionaries and the stabilizing effects of British rule, had assumed a self-propelling dynamic through the Sangam and its associated uravinmurais. The community had, in May 1921, even registered a bank of its own: The Nadar Bank Limited, renamed Tamilnad Mercantile Bank in 1962. With their well-organized networks for procurement, warehousing, and distribution of agricultural products like palm jaggery, salt, cotton, tobacco, oilseeds, foodgrains, and pulses, the Nadars were perhaps the pre-eminent trading community of Madras Presidency. In becoming so they had virtually repudiated a stigmatized past. The flip side was that the community's domain was still restricted to trade, though one of the stated objectives of the NMS was 'to promote commercial and industrial enterprise among the members'. In spite of their strong presence in cotton wholesaling, the Nadars, in contrast to the Naidus of Coimbatore for instance, had not promoted a single textile mill. This feeling of inadequacy was conveyed even as late as in the Sangam's conference of 1965, whose theme was the role of the community in India's industrialization. With endemic food shortages creating popular discontent against the merchant class, a speaker warned of the government's resolve to bypass middlemen through the establishment of a state-owned food corporation.[22] Industrialization was, thus, posed as the panacea for stasis.

The initiative in this direction came not from the Nadars of

Virudhunagar – which, with the rise of Coimbatore's textile mills, had ceded its primacy in cotton trading to Tirupur – but from Sivakasi. In 1922 two men in their late teens – P. Ayya Nadar and a cousin, A. Shanmuga Nadar – set off for Kolkata, after reading about its safety match industry. The city had quite a few units – notably the Oriental Match Manufacturing Company and the Bande Match Factory – that had sprung up during the first swadeshi flush of 1905–6. The year the youngsters went to Kolkata, the fledgling industry had also got a shot in the arm with the revenue-starved colonial government imposing duties varying from 100 to 200 per cent on imported matches.[23] At that time the major domestic manufacturers operated on factory lines, employing imported semi-automatic machines. After a six-month stay in Kolkata, where they acquainted themselves with the production process, the two men returned to Sivakasi with machines procured from Germany. But in no time they found machine-based production to be unviable, as these could use only certain kinds of wood from foreign poplar and aspen species. So, they opted for hand-made production of matches under the 'Bengal Lights' banner.

The decision turned out eminently sensible. Sivakasi lay in a zone that received hardly 800 mm of rain annually – a third lower than the national average. Nor had it groundwater reserves to sustain agricultural employment beyond three months of the year. As a result a culture of seeking non-farm work was pervasive, involving the whole family unit and reflected in high workforce participation rates. Even in the 1991 Census, while the overall ratio for Tamil Nadu was 44 per cent of the population, it hovered around 60 per cent in Sivakasi and adjoining blocks, pointing to the sizeable deployment of women and child labour to supplement family income. A state government survey in 1994 showed that female adults made up 55–62 per cent of the area's match industry workforce, with child workers accounting for another 27–32 per cent. Given this sort of labour profile, wages in the industry tended to be marked down relative even to the agricultural wage for adult males (already low in an arid zone). Adult male presence was limited to 'dipping' splints and side-painting outer boxes, which entailed the handling of chemicals. Other operations, from box assembly to filling, affixing labels, and packing, were done by women and children.[24]

To cut the point short, the ability to tap large volumes of cheap incremental family wage labour and a dry climate made Sivakasi conducive for manual match manufacture. It also had access to soft woods from indigenous tree species like semul (*Bombax ceiba*) and white mutty (*Ailanthus malabarica*). There were a number of units in Kerala that processed the timber logs from these trees into box-size veneers and splints. To add to these was the union government's policy in 1973 to 'reserve' match production for the small-scale sector and simultaneously freeze the capacity of the Western India Match Company Limited (Wimco) to 13.7 million boxes per day. The latter, a subsidiary of the Stockholm-based Swedish Match AB,[25] is India's sole large-scale mechanised match-maker, with factories at Ambarnath (near Mumbai), Chennai, Kolkata, Dhubri (Assam), and Bareilly (Uttar Pradesh). Although Wimco's Indian operations go back to 1923 – when higher tariffs on imported matches forced the Swedish parent to go in for local manufacturing – there was tacit agreement even prior to 1973 that it would not supply more than 50 per cent of the domestic demand.

The net result of all this is a Rs 1,000 crore match industry in Sivakasi and the neighbouring areas of Sattur and Kovilpatti that now produces 80 million-odd matchboxes per day, representing four out of every five boxes made in the country. On the other hand the cap on its capacity – coupled with the savings accruing to the non-mechanized sector from access to cheaper labour, lower overheads, the non-applicability of factory regulations, and differential excise duties – has led to Wimco's share dwindling to just 12 per cent. Furthermore, shortages of high-quality lumber have prevented the company's plants from running to even their full licensed capacity of 13.7 million boxes a day. The gainer has been the Sivakasi-Sattur-Kovilpatti match belt, dominated by some twenty Nadar groups linked by familial and other connections. Each of them own up to twenty-five match units and control many more through decentralized subcontracting systems outside the purview of factory legislations. They include the Rs 400 crore Pioneer Asia group, founded by K.A.A. Shankaralingam and K.A.A. Arunachalam (see case study), and Hind Matches Limited of N.R.K. Rajaratnam. The former produces 7–8 million boxes a day under the 'Chavi' (key), 'Bell', and 'Rhino' brands, while the latter makes about 5 million ('Train' and 'Sunflower'). Others include the Ayya Nadar group ('Camel'), Sundaravel Match Industries of S.S. Sankaralingam ('27'), and Arasan group of A.M.S. Ganesan ('Double Tiger' and 'Geyes'), who all sell in the region of 3 million boxes each.

Safety match production, in turn, has spawned an equally large fireworks and pyrotechnic chemicals industry in Sivakasi. The pioneers here again were P. Ayya Nadar and A. Shanmuga Nadar, who, by 1926, had parted ways to form their separate match businesses.[26] Having tasted success there, the two men set up National Fireworks (now Ayyan Fireworks) and Sri Kaliswari Fire Works, respectively. But the industry's growth happened after import controls on explosives were imposed during World War II. This led to the establishment of Standard Fireworks Private Limited in 1942, followed by the Metal Powder Company Limited (Mepco) in 1961. Standard Fireworks was a collaboration of three equal partners: Pioneer Asia, Hind Matches, and the Bell group of A. Chelladurai. It is today India's premier pyrotechnic firm, with factories in China as well. Mepco is a joint venture of Standard Fireworks and Ayyan Fireworks for making aluminium powder (the main explosive substance in fireworks) and red phosphorous (used in the friction surface of match boxes). Further, there is Pandian Chemicals, a Mepco subsidiary incorporated in 1975 to produce potassium chlorate, another safety match raw material used in the head chemical composition.

It is a combination of Nadar enterprise, cheap labour and organised backward integration into production of raw materials that has really made Sivakasi's safety match and fireworks industry what it is today. The leading names in Sivakasi's Rs 700 crore fireworks business, catering to 90 per cent of the national market, are all Nadars: Standard Fireworks (which sells under the 'Peacock' label), Sri Kaliswari ('Cock'), Ayyan Fireworks ('Bunny'), Arasan group ('We Two'), Anil group of Pabanasa Nadar ('Anil'), Coronation Fireworks of P. Kanagavel ('Coronation'), and Ravindra Fireworks of Annamalai Nadar ('Conch'). Many of them, including Standard Fireworks-Mepco, Sri Kaliswari, and Arasan have facilities to produce aluminium powder, the basic raw material used in sparklers, flower-pots, twinkling stars, and spinning chakrams (catherine wheels). 'Both powder and saltpetre (potassium nitrate, which provides the oxygen for burning) are available locally. It is only sulphur (the igniting substance) that is not produced here', notes S. Rathinagiri, secretary of the Tamilnadu Fireworks and Amorces Manufacturers' Association.[27] A company like Mepco has further expanded its product profile from aluminium powder to a range of non-ferrous metal powders for pyrotechnic and other varied industrial applications.

Another byproduct of Sivakasi's match revolution is its offset printing industry. The mushrooming of match and firework units created a growing requirement for trademark labels and posters. Although Nadar Press Limited came into being as early as in end 1922, the bulk of the material had to be sourced from Mumbai – a situation that did not change until litho printing was introduced into Sivakasi. In 1930 K.S.A. Arunagiri Nadar, who was an agent with Nadar Press from its inception, imported a litho machine from England and set up the National Litho Press. By 1947 there were nearly a dozen litho printers. But the development of an industry with an independent identity had to wait for the diffusion of offset printing technology. The foundation for this was laid by S. Kaliappa Nadar in 1937 through his Sivakasi Industrial Printing Works.[28] An industry that began by making match and fireworks labels has since then evolved into a Rs 1,000 crore business performing more sophisticated jobs, from printing notebooks, calendars, diaries, greeting cards, and brochures to flight tickets and bank cheque books. And predictably, it is the Nadars who call the shots, whether it is Coronation Litho Works Limited of K.C.A.D Gnanagiri Nadar, Lovely Offset Printers of C. Kadakarai, or the Chennai-based Eagle Press of M.J. Prathapsingh (the last name is a misnomer).

The biggest of them all, however, is the Rs 250 crore Srinivas Fine Arts (SFA) group, best known for having launched the world's most expensive 'Silver Oak Diary' priced at Rs 57,000.[29] Its founder, R. Chockalingam, was an assistant manager in Hind Matches during 1955–6, after which he also worked with A. Chelladurai's Bell Pins – India's largest producer of wire-based stationery goods like drawing pins, safety pins, paper and pad clips, staples and stapler machines. In 1964 he started SFA, which initially supplied labels in art paper for sari manufacturers in Rajkot. In 1967, around the period when Indian standards of measurement shifted to the metric system, the company ventured into the design and printing of graph sheets and notebooks incorporating the newly adopted standards. 'I used to buy paper from traders and give the printing work on contract. In 1969 I purchased a second-hand, single-colour, Solna offset machine from Gnanagiri Nadar's Coronation Litho Works', recalls the 68-year-old Chockalingam.[30] SFA has since grown into a Rs 80 crore company, producing premium diaries, note-books, and other paper products under its own 'Nightingale' brand. Roughly half of its turnover comes from the export of technical books, religious texts (from the Holy Bible to the Koran and Bhagvad Gita), and other high-value literary material to Europe, US, and the Middle East countries. During the 1980s Chockalingam also become a paper distributor for leading mills through three new outfits: Roseflower, Speciality Paper, and Glory Papers. The group is now not only one of the country's largest paper traders but also a major dealer of inks and pigments for companies like BASF and Colour-Chem.[31]

An important consequence of the growth of printing and other industries in Sivakasi has been that the labour equation has undergone a perceptible change. The old process of capital accumulation based on employing female and child labour at bare subsistence wages has run its course. 'The era of abundant cheap labour is over. Earlier, 100 per cent of our match production was hand-made, whereas that would now be just half. Operations like frame-filling and dipping are largely being performed by machines', notes S. Ashok, director, Pioneer Asia group.[32] Nadar industrialists are increasingly laying emphasis on consolidation and mechanization. 'Small-scale reservation helped us initially. But now it is time to modify the policy and raise investment limits in plant and machinery', adds Ashok. A related trend has been to move up the value chain, similar to the transition made by Tirupur's knitwear units from plain banian-making to producing fashion garments for global retail chains. Sivakasi's premier match concerns have diversified their product profile from conventional hand-made wooden box matches to manufacturing wax and other fancy matches for exports, using high quality cardboard with multi-colour printing and lamination. Also, with large companies like ITC sourcing matches from units in Sivakasi, there has been further stimulus for technology and quality upgradation.[33]

In the printing industry this process has advanced a great deal from ordinary litho to offset and, in the last few years, to state-of-the-art digital printing. The latter has made pre-press operations like image-setting, painting, retouching, and plate-making – highly skilled jobs that were a closely guarded town secret – almost redundant, replacing them with universal digital colour scanning and proofing on computers. The new technologies have, to an extent, dented the specialized 'artistic' edge that once gave Sivakasi an estimated 60 per cent share of India's offset printing market. That figure has now fallen by half. 'We are looking more at the export market. Sivakasi can become a major global printing outsourcing hub, if only we get the kind of support that the Tirupur exporters have received', asserts Chockalingam. The Sivakasi Master Printers' Association has successfully lobbied for a Tirupur-style special purpose vehicle which would receive 75 per cent federal funding under the Industrial Infrastructure Upgradation Scheme. 'Through this, we will establish world-class infrastructure and common facilities for members, facilitating the development of a genuine printing cluster in Sivakasi', he hopes.

If Sivakasi is to the Nadars what Tirupur has been to the Gounders, it is not that the other traditional Nadar commercial centres have faced complete marginalization. The Virudhunagar Nadars retain an active presence in agro-business. One commodity over which they exercise an absolute grip is sesame oil, to which palm gur is, incidentally, added as a flavouring agent and preservative. The production of sesame oil in Virudhunagar was taken up from the late 1930s by four brothers – V.V. Shunmuga Nadar, V.V. Vanniaperumal, V.V. Dhanushkodi Nadar, and V.V. Ramasami – who branched out to establish separate businesses. While Shunmuga Nadar's VVS & Sons had its 'VVS' brand, Vanniaperumal's concern, VVV & Sons, was further split between his sons. One of them markets sesame oil under his own name, 'V.V.V. Anandham', with another son, V.V.V.

Rajendran, producing it under the 'Idhayam' label since 1986. The latter – whose literal translation is 'heart', an endorsement of the product's putative health benefits – is today India's top sesame oil brand worth over Rs 100 crore. Dhanushkodi Nadar's VVD group is based at Thoothukudi where, in addition to selling coconut and sesame oil under the 'VVD Gold' and 'Piriyam' brands, it has interests in the manufacture of corrugated boxes and containers, warehousing, stevedoring, shipping, and related services.

A more recent Nadar entrant in edible oils is G. Munusamy. Starting with a small grocery store in the 1970s, he went into bulk trading in vegetable oils. In the mid-1990s, Munusamy acquired and turned around a sick refinery (Kaleesuwari Refinery Private Limited) near Chennai, which makes 'Gold Winner', a popular sunflower and ground-nut oil brand in the South. Another relatively new businessman is R.G. Chandramogan. Hailing from Sivakasi, he set up Hatsun Foods in 1986, which is the country's biggest private sector dairy, handling 12 lakh litres of milk per day. Chandramogan's company markets 'Arun' ice-cream and liquid milk under the 'Arokya' and 'Komatha' labels.[34] The man who introduced the sale of shampoos in small sachets in the early 1980s before Hindustan Lever and others latched on to the idea – Chinni Krishnan Rajkumar of 'Velvette' fame – happens to be a Nadar too. His brother, C.K. Ranganathan, runs the even more successful Rs 500 crore CavinKare group which owns brands like 'Chik' and 'Nyle' shampoo and 'Fairever' fairness cream.

The Nadars also have significant stake in plantations (we have talked about A.V. Thomas) and commodities like salt, seafood, and pulses. Ramesh Exports, promoted by M.S.P. Rajah, is one of India's leading coffee planters and curers, with annual exports of Rs 100 crore and ownership of over 1,000 acres of estates in the Annamalai and Shevaroy hills. It has an interesting history, starting with M.S.P. Rajah's grandfather Senthikumara Nadar.

The latter, who was awarded the title 'Rao Bahadur' and became the first chairman of the Virudhunagar municipality in 1910, owned a textile shop before venturing into trading of cardamom and coffee by sourcing from British planters. In 1932 the family started exports in a small way and around this time bought a 300 acre estate in the Shevaroy hills. By 1940 it had established Hill and Tiller, a firm whose name was deliberately chosen to appeal to European buyers. Hill and Tiller became Ramesh Exports after a family division in 1974 between M.S.P. Rajah and his brother M.S.P. Rajesh.[35] Thoothukudi's major salt manufacturers, including K.S.P.S. Natarajan & Company, and its big seafood exporters, such as Diamond Seafood Exports of S. Devanesam and Nila Sea Foods of D. Chandran, are also Nadars.

A segment that the community has managed to penetrate in a big way is organized retailing, an extension of its traditional activity of buying and selling a range of commodities. Chennai is often described as the Retail Capital of India. Among its large retail chains, quite a few are owned by Nadars, each grossing yearly sales of a couple of hundred crores or more, and being mainly partnership firms. Prominent here are S. Yogarathinam's Saravana Stores Enterprises and P.S. Rathnam Nadar's Rathna Stores – who hawk everything from stainless steel utensils to jewellery, provisions, eateries, textiles, and consumer durables – and Vasanth & Co, a big-time dealer of home appliances and consumer electronics goods. Its proprietor, H. Vasanth Kumar, is a Kanyakumari Nadar who learnt the ropes of retailing while working in a showroom of the VGP group during the 1970s. The latter, founded by V.G. Panneerdas, a Christian Nadar belonging to the same district, is also involved in real estate, hotels, and amusement parks, including the VGP Golden Beach Resort outside Chennai. Then there is P. Rajagopal Nadar, a village school dropout from Tirunelveli who went to Chennai in the early 1960s and did odd jobs before opening a provision store in the K.K.

Nagar suburb. In 1981 he started a restaurant in the area which was the precursor to the Saravana Bhavan chain of South Indian vegetarian restaurants. Currently, it operates over 30 outlets not just in Chennai and other southern cities but even in Delhi and overseas locations like Dubai, Muscat, Singapore, Kuala Lumpur, London, New York, California, and Ontario.[36]

But the two highest-profile Nadar names in the world of industry are Shiv Nadar and B. Sivanthi Adityan. Unlike most Nadar business groups, both are originally from Tiruchendur, and belong to the community's elite 'Nadan' crust. The former's ancestral village, Moolaipozhi, is about 10 km from Tiruchendur town, while the Adityans are pannaiyars (landlords) of Kayamozhi. They are, further, related: Shiv Nadar's mother Vamasundari Devi, and Sivanthi Adityan's father S.P. Adithanar, were siblings. Shiv Nadar's father Sivasubramaniya Nadar was a district and sessions judge who had been posted all over TN. After doing his pre-university at Madurai's American College and electrical engineering at the PSG College of Technology in Coimbatore, Shiv Nadar joined the Walchand group's Cooper Engineering at Pune in end 1967. A year later he went to Delhi as a management trainee with DCM Data Products. After becoming national sales manager Shiv Nadar, along with five of his colleagues, quit in 1975 to form Microcomp, a concern to make calculators. In August 1976 the same ex-DCM men led by Nadar created Hindustan Computers Limited (HCL). India, at that point, had a total of 250 computers. In 1977 the new Janata government at the centre ordered the American multinationals, Coke and IBM, to dilute their stake in their subsidiaries to 40 per cent, failing which they had to wind up. They chose the latter. IBM's exit, in a sense, paved the way for HCL to lay the seeds of domestic computer hardware manufacturing. The HCL group – HCL Infosystems (which makes computers, workstations, servers, and other hardware products) and HCL Technologies Limited (which does software development and business process outsourcing services) – is today the country's No. 1 IT conglomerate, with net sales of Rs 11,500 crore.[37]

Sivanthi Adityan heads *Daily Thanthi*, the largest circulated Tamil daily. His father S.P. Adithanar was a lawyer who took his degree from London's Middle Temple and practised in Singapore for eight years, starting in 1933. On returning in 1942 he launched the first edition of *Thanthi* from Madurai. Modelling it on the British tabloid *Daily Mirror*, which he admired for its mass reach, Adithanar is considered to have pioneered the simultaneous publication of an Indian-language newspaper from a number of centres.[38] Apart from *Thanthi*, Adithanar promoted the Sun Paper Mills at Tirunelveli. After he died in 1981 the businesses passed on to Sivanthi Adityan. Earlier, Adithanar's estranged son-in-law K.P. Kandasamy had launched his own *Dinakaran* in 1977, which became the third largest Tamil daily behind *Thanthi* and *Dinamalar* (started in 1951 by a Brahmin, T.V. Ramasubbaiyer).[39] The *Dinakaran* stable also has two evening papers, *Tamizh Murasu* and *Malai Murasu*, competing with the *Thanthi* group's *Malai Malar*. In June 2005 *Dinakaran* was acquired by Kalanithi Maran's Sun Network.[40]

Emerging Fissures in the Nadar Community

Sitting in the rundown office of NMS at Madurai's crowded South Chitrai Street overlooking the majestic Meenakshi Temple complex, its general secretary G. Karikolraj minces no words when asked about the key ingredients of the community's success story: 'The Sangam, the uravinmurais and the missionaries. It is they who infused a spirit of co-operation and unity among our people, but for which we would have remained forever backward'.[41]

Purposive community organization has, indeed, been

fundamental to the economic and social life of the Nadars, right since they built pettais along their trading routes and areas of settlement. In later years this was manifested in companies like Standard Fireworks, Mepco, and Pandian Chemicals: essentially joint ventures between Sivakasi's major match-cum-fireworks makers to undertake more complex and capital-intensive manufacture of raw materials. The Sree Ayyanar Spinning and Weaving Mills was similarly incorporated in 1962 by a group of Virudhunagar Nadars led by M.S.P. Rajah. At its inception the company had some fifty directors on its board! The same co-operative effort led the Sivakasi Master Printers' Association to create an Institute of Printing Technology in 1977 for meeting its requirement of trained plate makers, scanner operators, and offset printers. The Mepco Schlenk Engineering College at Sivakasi, the Kamaraj College of Engineering and Technology at Virudhunagar – not to speak of numerous other schools and colleges run by the Sangam and its 1,500-odd uravinmurai affiliates – were again products of concerted community action. All these were buttressed by its political clout, symbolized best by Kumaraswami Kamaraj Nadar (1903–75), chief minister of TN from 1954 to 1963 who later became president of the Indian National Congress.[42] Many prominent Nadar businessmen have been politicians themselves – V.V. Ramasami, Ayya Nadar, A.V. Thomas, S.P. Adithanar, K.P. Kandasamy, H. Vasanth Kumar, to name a few – which has further enhanced the community's capacity to wrest concessions, e.g. reserving match production for small-scale units.

The last couple of decades have, however, witnessed an undermining of collective Nadar business enterprise. The fortunes of individual business groups have grown along with those of the community. This has engendered a tendency for the interests of co-operative capital to be subsumed by the overriding ambitions of particular capitalists. Take the case of Sree Ayyanar Mills, whose shares were widely dispersed among a number of Nadar businessmen from Virudhunagar, making it virtually a co-operative entity. By 1989, though, its ownership was vested with the Pioneer Asia Group which, over time, bought blocks of shares from individual investors and acquired a controlling stake.

But a more stark example of community capital facing subversion from within is provided by the Tamilnad Mercantile Bank (TMB), a bank that, as at March 2005, had deposits of 4,826.88 crore, net owned funds of Rs 558.84 crore, and advances of Rs 2,626.24 crore. The idea of a community-owned bank was mooted during the Sangam's annual conference held in 1920 at Thoothukudi. The Nadar Bank Limited was accordingly registered on 11 May 1921. Even after a change of name to TMB on 26 November 1962, the bank's basic character did not change and it continued to cater to the community's financial needs. The initiative for starting it came mainly from the Nadars of Thoothukudi, especially A.M.M. Sinnamani Nadar, whose family owned 30 per cent of the shares. The latter also floated Tuticorin Spinning Mills Limited (TSM) in 1948, marking the maiden Nadar foray into textiles. The other major shareholder in TMB was the M.S.P. family of Virudhunagar (13 per cent). In 1984 a misunderstanding between G. Kathiresan and G. Vettivel – the grandsons of Sinnamani Nadar – resulted in the TSM group offloading a 12 per cent stake to Pioneer Asia. Although a rights issue in 1990 helped the family restore its original share, the Pioneer Asia group, which had hitherto held a mere one per cent, managed to garner 15 per cent in the bank.

The real drama began in October 1994, when Pioneer Asia sold its 15 per cent stake to the Essar group of Shashi and Ravi Ruia. The move was prompted by its apparent frustration over not being able to assert management control over the bank, in contrast to the group's successful buyout of Sree Ayyanar Mills. 'For us, a 15 per cent share was just a piece of paper. So when the Ruias made a good offer, we opted to exit', says S. Ashok, director of Pioneer Asia. Within a few days the M.S.P. family had also disposed of 10 per cent, citing the same reason. Once the Sivakasi and Virudhanagar Nadars had sold out, it was a matter of time before the original Thoothukudi promoters, too, followed suit. The only issue was the price. Before the Ruias entered the scene, TMB shares were being informally traded at Rs 800. When Pioneer Asia and the M.S.P. family decided to sell, they received Rs 3,000 per share. For the TSM group's 30 per cent share, Essar upped its bid to Rs 3,500, a price that the former willingly accepted. The inconceivable had happened. A bank once considered the pride of the Nadars was overnight a 67 per cent owned property of a Marwari concern!

Once the news spread, retribution was swift. Irate Nadar mobs took to the streets. At the bank's annual general meeting in January 1995 at Thoothukudi – the first after the takeover – Essar's representatives had to literally retreat and the venue for the next assembly was shifted to the safer environs of Tirupur.[43] The Sangam stepped in and a Nadar Mahajana Bank Share Investors' Forum was constituted under B. Ramachandra Adityan (Sivanthi Adityan's brother) to 'retrieve' the shares from Essar. But the drama had not ended. Even before negotiations could make headway, it was discovered that the Ruias had, in October 1997, offloaded their entire 67 per cent holding in TMB to C. Sivasankaran, a non-resident Indian (NRI) businessman who happened to be a Mudaliar. The sale was made by a cash-strapped Essar as part payment for a licence owned by Sivasankaran to operate mobile telephony services in Delhi.

Since then it has been an unceasing tale of bargaining between the Nadar Forum and the Sterling group of Sivasankaran. In 2001 the latter transferred 34 per cent of its holding in TMB to the Forum for Rs 81 crore and fresh share certificates were issued in the name of the 25,000-odd investors who had contributed towards 'retrieving' the community's pride and ownership of the bank. Then in February 2004, just before the national elections, an agreement was inked at New Delhi in the presence of the then deputy prime minister, L.K. Advani, to transfer the Sterling group's balance 33 per cent stake. This time it was to be made to seven Nadar investors including Ramachandra Adityan (and not to the Forum) for a consideration of Rs 130 crore. In all, the salvage mission was to cost Rs 211 crore, translating into an average price of Rs 12,000 a share. Compare this to the Rs 28 crore that Essar had invested in its original acquisition and the Rs 65 crore value at which it had reportedly offloaded to Sivasankaran! The 'true' value of TMB shares had been unlocked, even if the ultimate gainer from this turned out to be no one from the community, but a Mudaliar NRI. Even after the deal for retrieving the shares was struck, it did not mend fissures in the community. TMB's original promoters, whose commercial decisions triggered the crisis in the first place, challenged the transfer of Sivasankaran's stake to the Forum. Their contention was that as per the 1994 sale agreement with the Essar group, the latter, in the event of choosing to offload its stake, was obliged to first make an offer to the promoters. In this case the Ruias had unilaterally transferred the shares to Sivasankaran, who had independently negotiated with the Forum. Moreover, divisions surfaced within the ranks of the retrieval warriors, with the Sangam's secretary Karikolraj accusing 'some' Forum members (read Ramachandra Adityan) of cutting private deals with Sivasankaran to enable him to retain control over the bank.[44]

The above episode illustrates, in some ways, the limits of community capital. The very process of capital accumulation – aided by caste associations and other avenues of community assertion and integration – generates and widens internal differentiation over a period of time. Collective business enterprise or what is perceived as representing the 'community's interest' then gets steadily undermined by the vaulting ambitions of individual capitalists. That this has happened within the Nadars only signifies how much Nadar capital has matured.

The Ezhava Route

The founder of NMS, T. Rattinasami Nadar, belonged to a wealthy family of abkari contractors in Poraiyar (Nagapattinam). He was an exception, though. The overwhelming majority of Nadar businessmen, we have seen, had little to do with the liquor trade and this, if nothing else, was corroboration of the community having snapped its links with a past it considered degraded. But the same does not hold for the Ezhavas, whose rise as a business community is, in no small measure, attributable to the coconut palm and products derived from it.

The Ezhavas, along with the Syrian Christians, were beneficiaries of land reforms initiated by the Travancore state during the nineteenth century, which, in fact, preceded the more radical legislations enacted by the elected Communist governments of Kerala in 1957 and 1969. Having supplanted many of its big landlords and brought four-fifths of the arable area under state control at the start of the nineteenth century, the Travancore government followed it up in the 1860s with measures conferring tenants farming its paddy lands full ownership and protecting those cultivating private lands against arbitrary eviction. These moves – compared by the economist K.N. Raj to Japan's post-Meiji Restoration land reforms of the same period[45] – led to 75 per cent of Travancore's cultivators owning land by the turn of the century. By contrast, proprietary cultivators constituted only 8 per cent of the landholdings in British Malabar. Also, tax and rent payments aggregated 15 per cent of Travancore's net agriculture income in the early 1930s; these were as high as 60 per cent in Malabar.[46]

Access to land and overall favourable agrarian conditions encouraged many Ezhava cultivators to farm cash crops, especially the coconut palm. Unlike tea or coffee, it was an ideal smallholder's crop that grew luxuriantly along the coast, requiring no plantation-scale working capital or overheads. Moreover, in 1859 an Irish-born American, James Darragh, had put up a coir manufactory at Alappuzha. It was the harbinger of an organized industry for weaving and processing of coir – a natural fibre extracted from the husk of the coconut fruit. But while weaving could be done in factories, extraction and spinning of the fibre were inherently decentralized and spread-out affairs. After manually separating it from the nut, the husk had to first be 'retted' (soaked) in brackish water for 9–10 months – the Travancore lagoons were highly conducive for this operation – to soften and loosen the fibre. The fibre was then extracted by pounding the retted husk with mallets, after which it was handspun into coir yarn. Thus the development of an organized coir fabric and matting industry spawned village dealers and middlemen who transported boatloads of husk, fibre, and yarn along the backwaters to the Alappuzha manufactories.

Till the first two decades of the twentieth century the manufactories were predominantly European-owned. There was a good market for coir floor coverings in ordinary European and American homes, where the fibre gained acceptance for its cheapness and durability. Exports of mats and matting rose from an average 30,000 quintals during the War years (1913–14 to 1917–18) to 100,000 quintals for the five years ending 1925–6, while export unit values more than doubled.[47] The boom attracted Indian entrepreneurs to the industry, including some Ezhava farmers-turned-coir yarn dealers and commission agents. The first of them was K.C. Karunakaran, who promoted S.K.V. Industrial Works in 1919 and the Alleppey Company in 1927. Married to a German – their wedding was celebrated at Sree Narayana Guru's Sivagiri ashram (retreat) near Kollam – Karunakaran was seemingly insulated from discrimination by foreign shipping lines that native exporters were regularly subjected to: he allegedly 'enjoyed privileges at the hands of the European Steamer Agents, which (were) denied to all other Indians.'[48]

Besides the larger Alappuzha-centred coir manufactories set up by the likes of K.C. Karunakaran, a number of small-scale units came up in the adjoining countryside of Cherthala and Muhamma from the 1930s. They were, to begin with, feeder firms supplying coarser mat varieties and semi-finished products to shippers who finished, graded, and packed them for export. Some of them soon developed market contacts to become regular shippers and even formed their Associated Cottage Industrialists and Shippers Union (ACISU) in 1938 at Cherthala. Most of these rural manufacturer-shippers were Ezhavas: out of ACISU's 45 members in 1941, 34 were from the community.[49] Since then the Ezhavas have consolidated their position further. The Karan group founded by K.C. Karunakaran is India's premier coir exporter, with its three concerns – The Alleppey Company, Kerala Balers Limited, and William Goodacre & Sons – claiming to control Asia's largest integrated capacity for weaving natural fibre floor coverings (the last named company was originally floated by a Britisher, who was even portrayed in a popular Malayalam historical genre film of the 1990s, *Rakthasakshikal Zindabad*). Other prominent Ezhava coir manufacturers include Travancore Mats and Matting Company of V.R. Prasad (his father was an overseer in a European coir firm) and Charankattu Coir Manufacturing Company of C.R. Devaraj.[50]

The other coconut-derived product that begot the new Ezhava bourgeoisie – even before coir – was toddy. Although tending the coconut tree and tapping its inflorescence for toddy was an old Ezhava vocation, it was the Travancore state's new abkari regulations of 1834 that drew the community into the trading mainstream.

In the earlier amani system revenues from toddy and arrack were collected by government officials directly from cultivators and tree owners.[51] Under the new regime that evolved, mobilization was done through contractors (abkaris), who were given exclusive monopoly to market liquor in an area, in return for which they paid a certain fee. The fee was determined by public auction of individual vends or all licensed shops within a defined 'range'.[52] By creating an intermediary layer between toddy producers and the excise department, the abkari system essentially helped a section of tappers to become toddy-shop owners and further graduate to contractors who bid for a whole range or a cluster of ranges. In the process a substantial avenue for capital accumulation was opened up, which the rising Ezhava business class later sought to convert into cultural capital through support for social uplift movements under the aegis of organizations like the Sree Narayana Dharma Paripalana Yogam (SNDP).

It is another thing that over time toddy itself got marginalized, as the shops found it more profitable to sell arrack distilled from sugarcane molasses produced in Karnataka and Tamil Nadu. Very often the contractors simply brought in rectified spirit which was blended, diluted, and bottled in local 'distilleries'. And not infrequently the spirit was smuggled from the border with official collusion. Combined with the compulsion for abkaris to over-bid in auctions to pre-empt competition, it resulted in massive under-reporting of sales,[53] simultaneous with a widespread proclivity to compromise on quality. Occasionally these degenerated into hooch tragedies, sparking off a public outcry and crackdowns on the 'liquor mafia'. In 1996, just before assembly elections were due, the Congress government under A.K. Antony banned the sale of arrack. The 4,300-odd country liquor shops were to henceforth dispense only toddy. However, given that toddy-drawing as an activity has conspicuously declined in Kerala, a large mystery surrounds what precisely gets sold in these vends.

But toddy or no toddy, the Ezhava stranglehold over Kerala's liquor trade is an undisputed fact. The general secretary of SNDP, Vellapalli Natesan, reckons that the community makes up 75 per cent of the state's toddy shop licensees and contractors.[54] A former abkari himself, Natesan used his surpluses from liquor to execute road contracts awarded by the state public works department. During the mid 1980s he undertook earth-filling works for the Southern Railways in the newly laid Ernakulam–Alappuzha line and also in Trichy, Virudhunagar, and Salem. Before taking over as general secretary in late 1996 he was doing lucrative jobs for the Konkan Railway Corporation as well. 'I gave it all up to concentrate full time on serving the community', claims Natesan, sipping tender coconut juice in his fortress-like home-cum-office at Kanichukulangara, near Cherthala. That has not deterred him from establishing the 'Prince' hotels in Alappuzha and Kottayam, and the 'Travancore Palace' at Cherthala.

Hotels and bars have been a logical diversification for Ezhavas who made their initial bucks from the country liquor business. G. Mohandas, who owns the five-star 'South Park' property in Thiruvananthapuram and runs the Mohandas College of Engineering and Technology there, started as an abkari. So did Rameshan Contractor, another liquor baron from Thiruvananthapuram, who is now heavily into hotels and real estate. An even more successful case is the Thrissur-based Elite group founded by K.S. Chathunny and his nephew T.R. Raghavan. During the 1950s, the family moved from liquor to investing in hotels, textile showrooms, tile units, and real estate. The group also owns the 350-bed Elite Mission Hospital in Thrissur. One family branch under T.R. Ragulal (Raghavan's son) is a leading manufacturer of bread and cakes in the South ('Elite' brand). 'The abkari business has facilitated many in our community to go into new areas. The ban on arrack is a setback', opines Natesan. Not only has arrack been banned, but the Communist-led government that rode into power in 1996 (despite Antony's pre-poll gambit) went a step ahead by nationalizing both wholesaling and retailing of IMFL through the Kerala State Beverages Corporation. Further, it handed over toddy retailing to workers' co-operatives and put an end to licensing shops to individuals – a decision that the subsequent Congress administration rolled back in 2002. 'It is all part of an organized conspiracy to economically crush us. Today, to sell IMFL, you need a hotel or bar licence and most of these are in the hands of Christians. Nobody wants our businessmen to come up', alleges Natesan.

Another field where the Ezhavas have had a long-established tradition is Ayurvedic medicine, a link again ascribed by some to alcohol: many of the traditional kashayam and arishtam formulations are alcohol-based.[55] The primary source for Hortus Indicus Malabaricus – a treatise on the plant wealth of Malabar compiled in 1678 by its then Dutch governor, Hendrik Adriaan van Rheede – was the palm leaf inscriptions of Itty Achuthan, an Ezhava vaidyan (physician) of Cherthala. In modern times some of the community's practitioners have tried to channellize this tradition to the mass consumer products segment. 'Chandrika', a popular Ayurvedic soap commanding a good overseas market as well, was contrived in 1940 by C.R. Kesavan Vaidyar, a small-time physician from Irinjalakuda near Thrissur. The same goes for 'Medimix', created in 1969 by V.P. Sidhan, who was from a well-known Ayurvedic family of Valapad in Thrissur. Today his Rs 250-crore Cholayil group owns 'Medimix' herbal soap and 'Cuticura', a talcum powder brand that it bought in 2001 from Muller and Phipps, an American multinational.

The interesting bit about groups like Elite, Chandrika, and

Cholayil is that they all hail from northern Kerala and not the traditional Ezhava–SNDP heartland of Travancore.[56] This is also the case with the Kozhikode-based KTC group of P.V. Sami (see case profile later), the Empee group of M.P. Purushothaman (originally from Kannur), the Gokulam group of A.M. Gopalan (from Vadakara, near Kozhikode), and Jyothy Laboratories Limited of M.P. Ramachandran (from Guruvayur near Thrissur). The Rs 500 crore Empee group has interests in hotels (the three-star 'Grand Orient' and 'New Victoria' in Chennai, besides a new five-star property to be managed by the British hospitality major Hilton International), liquor (Empee Distilleries), sugar (Empee Sugars and Chemicals, which operates a 2,500 tcd mill at Nellore, Andhra Pradesh), and aquaculture (Empee Marine Products). The Gokulam group's flagship, Sree Gokulam Chit & Finance Company, handles annual chit auctions of about Rs 1,000 crore through over 100 branches mainly in Tamil Nadu and Kerala. In addition, it runs hotels (Gokulam Park at Kochi and Chennai), a sprawling residential school at Vadakara, and the Sree Gokulam Medical College at Thiruvananthapuram. Jyothy Laboratories makes 'Ujala', the country's top fabric whitener brand that has dislodged the British multinational Reckitt-Benckiser's once-supreme 'Robin Blue'. The company also owns brands like 'Jeeva' herbal soap, 'Maxo' liquid mosquito repellent, 'Exo' dishwashing bar, and 'Speed' detergent powder.[57]

Some features are common to these northern Kerala Ezhava groups. Firstly, many of them operate outside Kerala, being headquartered at Chennai (Empee, Cholayil, and Gokulam) and Mumbai (Jyothy). Secondly, barring Empee and Elite, their businesses are far removed from liquor, making them distinct from Travancore's abkari barons. Thirdly, their promoters are mostly new-generation, well-educated entrepreneurs. V.P. Sidhan was a doctor from Chennai's Kilpauk Medical College and worked with the railways before launching 'Medimix'. M.P. Ramachandran, who promoted Jyothy Laboratories in 1983, is a postgraduate in financial management. As against the old Ezhava gentry that prospered around coir or the abkari trade, the entry of these men into business owes primarily to the 'secular' processes of education and modernity: routes historically denied to the community. Nobody exemplifies this better than E.D. Shibulal and Ajit Balakrishnan. Shibulal, a postgraduate in physics from Kerala University and master's in computer science from Boston, is one of the co-founders of a 'Brahmin' institution called Infosys Technologies! Ajit Balakrishnan shot into fame first through Rediffusion, the ad agency he started in 1973, and then, twenty-two years later, the Internet portal Rediff.com.

The Telugu-speaking Idigas from Karnataka represent yet another traditional toddy-tapping community to have made significant economic, social, and political progress over the previous century. Like the Ezhavas, quite a few Idigas became excise contractors and distillers. Some accumulated surpluses during the World War II period, which they invested in other businesses. One example is Moola Laxmi Narayana (M.L.N.) Swamy, who set up Vahini Pictures in the 1940s. He also owned cotton ginning and handspinning-cum-weaving units at Tadpatri in Anantapur district of Andhra Pradesh, apart from co-floating a number of industrial ventures: Cuddapah Ceramics, Cuddapah Electric Supply Company, Rayalaseema Bank, and Rayalaseema Mills, Bellary. But these diversifications did not pay off as M.L.N. Swamy got embroiled in income tax problems that accompanied him to his death. The Vahini Studios was given on lease to B. Nagi Reddy around 1949 and the latter subsequently bought and revamped it as Vijaya-Vahini Studios.[58] The other major liquor contractor to have gone into a new area was K.N. Guruswamy, who established the newspaper *Deccan Herald* in 1948 (see case study).

However, the Idigas have not been as successful as the Ezhavas (let alone the Nadars) in developing an extended business profile. Karnataka's big-time excise contractors continue to be Idigas: the families of J.P. Narayana Swamy, H. Dasappa, H.R. Basavaraj, and H.G. Ramulu, among others. The community has, moreover, produced important politicians, from the former chief minister S. Bangarappa, to union ministers like Janardhan Poojari and R.L. Jalappa. Both H.G. Ramulu and H.R. Basavaraj have also been parliamentarians, while Narayana Swamy is the president of the Arya-Idiga Association. Yet, all this clout has not translated into businesses substantially transcending liquor. H.G. Ramulu's interests outside liquor are limited to owning some iron ore mining leases in Bellary and a resort (Kishkinda Heritage) at Koppal. Others have built cinema halls or forayed into film-making and distribution, taking a cue from M.L.N. Swamy and the Kannada matinee idol Rajkumar (also an Idiga). None of them can still be remotely called movie moguls. Even in liquor, Idiga abkaris are not in the league of the UBs, the Shaw Wallaces, or the Khodays. They have, at best, been contract brewers and distillers for these bigger branded liquor players. Some, like H.R. Basavaraj's Gemini Distilleries, have even sold off their plants (in this case, to the Kishore Chhabria group). In other words, this is a community that has made an incomplete transition to industry.

We will now proceed to study a few prominent industrial groups from the communities surveyed in this chapter.

Case Studies

1. Pioneer Asia Group

The founders of the Pioneer Asia group, K.A.A. Sankaralingam and K.A.A. Arunachalam, were wholesale traders in rice, largely imported from Burma. The entry of the two brothers into safety matches was the result of a family connection: the owner of Hind Matches, N.R.K. Rajaratnam, happened to be their maternal uncle. Earlier, they had taken over an agency business – Nataraj Stores – from Rajaratnam's brother for distributing products of consumer good giants like Hindustan Lever, Nestle, and Parrys. By the time Pioneer Match Works was set up in 1940, 'the match revolution in Sivakasi was well under way', notes S. Ashok, the youngest of K.A.A. Sankaralingam's three sons.[59]

The relatively late foray has, however, not prevented Pioneer Match Works – which became Asia Match Company Private Limited in 1954 – from emerging as Sivakasi's premier match-maker, with a daily output of 7–8 million boxes. That makes it India's second largest producer after Wimco, which does about 13 million boxes a day. The difference though is that while Wimco's entire production is through four fully-mechanized factories in the country's different corners, Pioneer Asia's operations are scattered over twenty-five units within Sivakasi and half of the output is hand-made. At the same time, economies of scale in the supply of raw materials have been attained through backward integration joint ventures with other leading Nadar business groups. The first of these – Standard Fireworks – was formed in 1942, in partnership with Rajaratnam's Hind Matches and A. Chelladurai's Bell group. Mepco, a collaboration of Standard Fireworks and the Ayya Nadar group, followed in 1961.

The profits from the match business have fuelled the group's expansion both vertically as well as horizontally into other areas. In 1978 it set up Asia Glues and Chemicals Private Limited for producing gelatin from animal bones as a natural binding material for matches. This company was, in August 1991, converted into Pioneer Miyagi Chemicals Private Limited, in which Jellice (formerly Miyagi) of Japan has a 25 per cent stake. The joint venture manufactures alkali ossein (a raw material for photographic-grade gelatin used by the likes of Kodak) and di-calcium phosphate (a poultry feed ingredient). The bulk of the produce from its plant near Cuddalore is exported. In a bid to extend its reach beyond Sivakasi, Pioneer Asia has also taken its safety match business to Sri Lanka and Africa. The Sun Match Company in Sri Lanka, floated in 1979, where the group holds 25 per cent, produces 'Soorya' wax matches and has a 70 per cent share in the island's market. In late 1990 it promoted a separate outfit, Pioneer Overseas Private Limited, for supplying match machinery and technical know-how and exporting chemicals to other countries. 'Through this, we have entered into technical tie-ups with companies such as Afoma in Madagascar, Alfa Match Industries in Tanzania and Match Masters in Kenya. Today, out of the 7–8 million boxes per day produced, we export 2 million boxes', adds Ashok. Some of the overseas projects have led to totally new businesses. In 1998 the group invested 75 per cent in Pioneer Pine Lanka Private Limited, which acquired 3,000 hectares of pine plantations in Sri Lanka on long lease. The venture taps pine trees for oleo pine resin, which is packed in barrels and sold to distillers, who then extract turpentine oil from it for perfumery and related applications.

As if these diversifications were not enough – indicative of the surpluses generated from its main match business – Pioneer Asia has, since the mid 1980s, fanned out into further unrelated territories, from finance and textiles to wind energy and auto components. It made a bid for Tamilnad Mercantile Bank by picking up a 15 per cent stake (only to offload it to the Essars, after failing to garner more shares) and took over the 50,000-spindle Sree Ayyanar Spinning and Weaving Mills at Virudhunagar by buying out existing shareholders (see section titled 'Emerging Fissures in the Nadar Community' in this chapter). All this has contributed to the group's image of a 'corporate raider' among sections of the

Nadar business community. The foray into wind power, explains Ashok, was primarily guided by tax considerations. 'We saw scope for installing mills in the Kanyakumari belt, where there is plenty of wind activity through the Western Ghat passes. We could sell power from the wind farms to the grid and draw equivalent power for our Virudhunagar mill by paying a nominal wheeling charge to the state electricity board. Besides, the government was offering a ten-year tax-free income and accelerated depreciation benefits on renewable energy investments', he points out. From wind mills the group went into manufacture of wind turbines through Pioneer Wincon Limited. This Pondicherry-based venture is a collaboration with Wincon Westwind of Denmark for production of 250 kilowatt (KW) wind turbines. For larger 850 KW turbines it entered into a separate tie-up with Gamesa Eolica of Spain.

In between there were some failed projects too. Pioneer Overseas Finance Limited – established in 1989 with equity participation from the Indian Overseas Bank – ran into rough weather after the Reserve Bank of India tightened norms on deposit taking. This came in the wake of several non-banking financial companies going bust during the late 1990s. Pioneer Asia had to sell its majority stake in the company to the Shriram group of Chennai. Similarly, attempts to produce matches in Sikkim and sourcing veneers and splints through a timber-processing unit at Little Andamans have borne little fruit. For all its aggressive efforts at diversification, safety matches still contribute about Rs 120 crore out of the group's revenues of Rs 400 crore. The rest is mainly from its textile mill (Rs 80 crore), wind turbines (Rs 100 crore), and chemicals (Rs 50 crore). The group also has interests in printing and transport.

2. The KTC Group

Parayarukandy Vettath Sami was an atypical old-generation Ezhava businessman, purely because he had no link whatsoever with the liquor trade. Born in 1913 to an ordinary farming family in Peruvanna near Kozhikode – where his father Chathu grew tapioca and coconut on a tiny two-acre plot – Sami studied up to the fifth class in a local school. Financial problems at home meant he had to discontinue education and look for ways to supplement family income. Sami's first commercial undertaking was a small shop, for which his mother Unichira advanced a sum of Rs 25. 'It was a tiny corner store that hawked charatta (coconut shells), chakiri (dried husk), chootu (native torch made from coconut leaf bundles), and assorted coir items. The shop ran for a year, when it was ransacked by a thief. He was not even 13', mentions P.V. Chandran, Sami's eldest son.[60]

The shop's closure forced Sami to leave the village and go to Kozhikode, where his maternal uncle had a coir products shop in the main Palayam market. After working for two years as an assistant, Sami managed (with his uncle's support) to buy space in the same market, from where he began a petty vegetable business. 'The vegetable trade in our area was always controlled by Tiyyas (as Ezhavas are called in northern Kerala). Our people owned 75 per cent of the vegetable shops there. So, it was not difficult to start something', observes Chandran. Sami used to procure vegetables from Mavoor, Mukkam, Kondotty, Chathamangalam, and other areas near Kozhikode, load them in carts, and bring to the Palayam market. In course of time he had progressed from retail to wholesale trade, specializing in commodities like chena (yam, which earned him the sobriquet 'Chena Sami'), tapioca, and ginger, which he used to send to places as far as Salem, Chennai, and Mumbai.

By 1945 Sami's business had grown sufficiently to enable him to add a furniture shop to his vegetable establishment and also invest in a lorry. He bought five more in the next couple of years, all financed by loans taken at 24–36 per cent from Multani (Sindhi) and Iyer Brahmin moneylenders. In 1949 disaster struck after Sami bagged a contract from the forest department to transport timber from a reserve in Wyanad to its depot at Beypore, near Kozhikode. 'In his over-enthusiasm, my father quoted very low rates. Also, he had only six trucks as against the larger fleets commanded by established contractors of that time. It was a miscalculation that cost us Rs 1 lakh and we almost defaulted on our truck loans. Fortunately, Kaloor Krishnan, a tile dealer close to my father, took over the responsibility to repay the loans', says Chandran. With his business in tatters, Sami had to go back to vegetable trading. Towards 1952–3 he had recouped the losses and also reclaimed the trucks that he had pledged with Kaloor Krishnan in return for the latter's bailout operation. There was no looking back after that.

On 1 April 1958 Sami and Chandran – who was slightly over 18 and had just finished pre-university at Kozhikode's Guruvayurappan College – incorporated the Kerala Transport Company (KTC). 'We began a parcel service with 8 trucks and went on adding 2–3 of them every year. We transported all kinds of stationeries, home appliances, fast moving consumer goods, and food items, save perishables like fruits and vegetables. By then my father had also transferred the vegetable business to his nephews, Velayudhan and Raghavan, so that we could concentrate on transport. My father would travel all over India, while my brother P.V. Gangadharan (who joined the concern in 1962) and I managed affairs at Kozhikode', says Chandran. By 1980 KTC was operating 800 trucks – 300 of its own and 500 hired – making it one of India's premier road freight carrier along with Transport Corporation of India, Patel Roadways, and the TVS and ABT (Sakthi) groups.

From the 1970s the family entered new businesses, starting with petroleum products marketing (7 petrol pumps at Kozhikode, Kochi, and Mahe) and plantations (a 500 acre rubber estate at Thiruvambadi). In 1977 it constructed the PVS Hospital at Kozhikode, followed by another 'super-speciality' PVS Memorial

Hospital at Kochi, which came up in 1992 after the founder's death in September 1990. The group also ventured into film distribution and production through Grihalakshmi Productions. But its biggest coup was acquiring a 28 per cent stake in the second-largest circulated Malayalam daily *Mathrubhumi* – something that had a more than symbolic significance.[61] Started in 1923 in response to Mahatma Gandhi's Non-Cooperation Movement, *Mathrubhumi* was a product of enlightened caste Hindu nationalism: the 350-odd founder-shareholders, led by K.P. Kesava Menon, were overwhelmingly Nairs. Its ownership being widely dispersed, with nobody holding more than 250 out of its 3,500 paid-up shares, the newspaper was a soft target for creeping acquisition by outsiders. 'There were many wanting to sell their shares, as it was yielding them no return. I bought my first 10 shares in 1978. By 1990 we had purchased 1,000 shares from various people, including the families of P. Govindan Nair, Padmanabhan Nair, Kuttikrishnan Nair, and V.K. Eradi', reveals Chandran. KTC is the second biggest shareholder in *Mathrubhumi* – by virtue of which Chandran is its managing editor – after the former union minister M.P. Veerendra Kumar, a Jain originally from Karnataka, who controls 1,350 shares. 'We did not invest in *Mathrubhumi* to make money. For us, it was more an issue of prestige and social service', claims Chandran.[62]

But the KTC group has not really consolidated on the solid foundations laid by P.V. Sami. The 1990s saw its core transport business flounder. Labour problems – a pet management grouse in Kerala – have reduced its truck fleet to about 200. 'Though it still generates revenues of over Rs 100 crore, we are not keen to expand this line any more', declares Chandran. KTC Tyres, set up in 1985 to produce two- and three-wheeler tyres, turned sick in no time. The group's sole manufacturing concern today is a wheat roller flour mill near Kozhikode. A hotel venture at Kozhikode was sold to the Tatas even before it got fully built (the present Taj Residency).

Grihalakshmi Productions' heyday was in the 1980s, when several hits from *Naayattu* to *Angadi* were made under its banner. The mainstay of the Rs 400 crore group is its automobile dealership for Hyundai Motors, Ford, Mitsubishi, Honda, Mahindra & Mahindra, and Tata commercial vehicles: a business that has developed over the last 10–15 years and contributes about Rs 150 crore. The other 'fast growing' division is its real estate arm PVS Apartments, which is engaged in the construction of residential flats and commercial buildings in Kozhikode, Thrissur and Ernakulam. KTC – as opposed to the more dynamic newer generation Ezhava businessmen – has failed to seize growth opportunities outside the state and remains a fundamentally Kozhikode-centric business group.

3. The Deccan Herald Group

K. Nettakallappa was an Idiga, a Telugu-speaking traditional toddy-tapping caste, from Kanekal village of Raidurg taluka in Bellary district. The latter, although now in Karnataka, shares a historical affinity with the Rayalaseema region of present-day Andhra Pradesh, being one of its four districts – Kurnool, Anantapur, and Kadapa apart – to have been 'ceded' to the British by the nizam of Hyderabad in 1800.

Nettakallappa entered the liquor trade in the 1890s and at the turn of the century had shifted to Bangalore, even while extending his operations to the Bombay Presidency and the nizam's dominion. 'He had seven sons. All, except me, had interests in toddy contracting and handled separate territories, from Bellary to Gadag, Hubli and Solapur. Only I became a doctor, fulfilling my father's ambition that at least one of us should graduate', recalls Nettakallappa's youngest son K.N. Chandrasekharswamy, who was only 7 when his father passed away in 1928, aged 60.[63] By then Nettakallappa had carved out a formidable abkari empire, a pointer to which was the

'Rao Saheb' title conferred on him on 4 June 1928, three months before he died. Nettakallappa was also a municipal councillor and district board member of Bellary and nominated to the Mysore Representative Assembly as a 'special interests' category member, while being actively involved in promoting education within the Idiga community.

After Nettakallappa's death the mantle of running the business fell on his eldest son K.N. Guruswamy, who was born on 1 October 1901. World War II was a boom time for the trade. Guruswamy had 10–15 partners and together they formed a cartel in the Mysore region. They were all Idigas, though there were a couple of outsiders, including one Dr Kapadia (a Parsi) and a certain Mr Dhondusa (from the Marathi-speaking Savji community, to which the well-known distillers, Khodays, belong). In 1948, at the suggestion of the dewan of Mysore, Arcot Ramaswamy Mudaliar, Guruswamy and his associates decided to start an English newspaper. Mysore, unlike Madras or Bombay Presidency, did not have an English daily and it was ostensibly to fill this vacuum that Ramaswamy Mudaliar approached the liquor barons who were perceived loyalists of the state. The non-official explanation that did the rounds then, though, was that Mudaliar, given his Justice Party affiliation, wanted a publication espousing the anti-Brahmin cause in Mysore. Another version – again in the realm of speculation – was that the proposed daily was blessed by the beleaguered nizam, who had additionally lured the promoters with the promise of awarding mono-poly of excise contracts in his state. Adding grist to the rumour mill was the very name of the paper that was launched on 16 June 1948: *Deccan Herald*. Guruswamy had earlier experimented with the Kannada paper *Mathrubhumi*, in which he had sunk more than half a lakh of rupees.[64]

The Printers (Mysore) Private Limited, under whose aegis the paper was started, was set up with a capital of Rs 5 lakhs. Out of its initial twenty shares of Rs 25,000 face value each, Guruswamy subscribed to eight, while his two old mates right from their Government High School days at Bellary – K. Venkataswamy and Moola Rangappa (a cousin of M.L.N. Swamy) – bought two each. Of the remaining eight, one was issued to M.K. Swamy, a fellow Idiga, while Dr Kapadia and Mr Dhondusa took four and three shares, respectively. Within no time it was realized that the capital had to be raised to Rs 10 lakh, which was also easily subscribed by the cash-rich abkaris. Simultaneously, the management felt the need for a sister Kannada daily and that resulted in *Prajavani* coming out in October 1948. But soon the venture was bleeding. The promoters had no experience in running a business quite different from managing excise auctions and the company slipped into the red. A combination of factors – from a cantankerous editor (Pothan Joseph) to a hostile chief minister (Kengal Hanumanthaiah), who put the clamps on government advertisements to the paper – led to its losing money. A sustained economy drive and streamlining of operations heralded a turnaround and the company, for the first time in 1958–9, returned a book profit of Rs 80,000. From there on it was steady progress and *Deccan Herald* and *Prajavani* emerged as the No. 1 English and Kannada newspapers in the state – slots that they held well into the 1990s. Also, Guruswamy's family had consolidated its hold on the company.

But things changed notably after Guruswamy's time: he passed away on 17 June 1990. By then complacency seemed to have crept into the organisation, even as the social profile of Bangalore was itself changing with the coming of the IT revolution. There was a new type of reader looking for 'something different' from the standard fare dished out by a seemingly tired old rag. The first blow came with the *Times of India* arriving in Bangalore and unleashing a price war that *Deccan Herald* was unprepared for. Worse was in store. In October 1999 Vijay Sankeshwar – a Lingayat from

Gadag and owner of a 2,000-truck fleet company (Vijayanand Roadlines) – launched *Vijay Karnataka.* It was published from nine centres in Karnataka (against *Prajavani's* five editions) and priced 50 paise lower. Sankeshwar also leveraged his vast transport network to ensure that his paper reached every nook and corner of the state. The sheer level of aggressive marketing and innovations in editorial content by rivals has pushed both *Deccan Herald* and *Prajavani* to distant No. 2 positions in terms of circulation.[65]

The above problems have been compounded by tussles within the management, which, since the early 1980s, had passed on to Guruswamy's three grandsons.[66] In August 2001 the eldest of them, K.N. Hari Kumar, quit as editor and also resigned from the company's board, supposedly over differences with his brothers on the way the paper was to be run. Despite the tremendous brand recall that *Deccan Herald* and *Prajavani* still command in Karnataka, the Rs 120 crore group is today a pale shadow of what it used to be till the 1980s. No longer has it a direct stake in the liquor trade either. 'It was getting too corrupt and dirty a business. There was much uncertainty, as the contracts were renewable on a year-to-year basis. The younger generation, my father included, had lost interest in it. Even by the 1970s we were just sleeping partners and it was my grandfather's associates who were running the show', confesses K.N. Shanth Kumar, the current editor and the youngest of the three brothers.[67] The group has no other large business interests. K.N. Guruswamy Oil Mills, a solvent extraction unit at Dharwad established by K.N. Tilak Kumar (the middle brother, who is incidentally married to the former chief minister S. Bangarappa's daughter, Sujatha), has stopped functioning.

7

Patidars and Marathas

There is in Gujarat a dairy conglomerate belonging to some 2.5 million farmers. Like any other business undertaking, it operates on strictly commercial principles. With an annual turnover of Rs 4,000 crore, the Gujarat Cooperative Milk Marketing Federation Limited (GCMMF), along with its affiliated district unions, is India's largest food company and owns one of its most adored consumer brands: Amul.[1] But its way of doing business and servicing share-holders does not conform to the regular schoolboy rules of companies. To start with, its shareholders are not based in Mumbai or Delhi, let alone Geneva or New York. Most of them live in Gujarat's hinterlands, owning one or two, sometimes more, milch animals. Secondly, they are not bothered about the value of their shares; since these are not traded in the first place, the issue of capital appreciation or booking losses does not arise. For them, earnings per share, dividend yields, and price-earning ratios are of no consequence. What matters is how much money the company is able to pay for every litre of milk that it procures from them. The company's job is not to maximize the return on capital invested by its shareholders (which is only incidental), but to maximize the return on the raw material they supply to its dairies. And that is in turn a function of how efficiently the milk is processed and marketed.

During 2004–5 (April–March), the twelve district unions of GCMMF procured, on an average, 6 million litres of milk every day. Effectively, it means every third litre of milk flowing from the udders of a cow or a buffalo in Gujarat is processed in one of the federation's affiliate dairies.[2] Of the remaining two-thirds, the bulk is consumed within the village and its neighbourhoods or sold to the odd private processor (that there are hardly any such large organized dairies in Gujarat is perhaps a measure of the GCMMF system's value to its shareholders). A farmer pouring buffalo milk with 6 per cent fat content to a Gujarat co-operative in 2004–5 would have received Rs 13–14 per litre, which is 25–30 per cent more than the corresponding farmgate prices paid by dairies elsewhere in the country. Moreover, the procurement price is linked to fat content, which is tested each time the farmer brings his milk to the society. If the electronic tester displayed in front were to show the fat content for a particular lot of milk at 8 per cent, the milkman would be entitled to a proportionately higher price of Rs 17–18 per litre.[3] Taking an average rate of Rs 13, the GCMMF dairies would in 2004–5 have pumped in around Rs 2,800 crore to their farmer members, constituting 70 per cent of their aggregate turnover of Rs 4,000 crore.[4] By contrast, milk purchase costs are less than half the value of product sales for a company like Nestle India,[5] marking the essential difference between a farmer-controlled co-operative and an investor-owned concern.

To be sure, a co-operative is not unique to Gujarat. Even in the most diehard Western free market economies, the dairy business is predominantly organized on co-operative lines. The biggest milk products company in the US, the $8.4 billion Dairy Farmers of America (DFA), is a co-operative. So is New Zealand's Fonterra Co-operative Group Limited. There is an enormous difference in scales, though. The GCMMF unions procure 6 million litres per day from 2.5 million farmers, whereas Fonterra handles the equivalent of 36 million litres from less than 12,000 of its supplier-shareholders. DFA similarly markets about 69 million litres of milk daily, sourced from 22,000 farmer-members.[6] Thus, while a typical DFA or Fonterra farmer supplies over 3,000 litres of milk every day, his counterpart in Gujarat pours a mere 2.5–3 litres. That may not add up to even a dollar; nevertheless, it makes the GCMMF system arguably the country's most efficient and transparent rural employment scheme.

What Gujarat has in milk, Maharashtra has in its sugar co-operatives. This is a state that cultivates only 15 per cent of India's sugarcane and yet produces a third of its white sugar – almost the whole of which is accounted for by co-operative factories.[7] Again, one indicator of their relative efficiency is the fact that these mills utilize about 90 per cent of the cane grown in Maharashtra, with the rest going for seed, feed, and chewing purposes. Compare this to the leading cane producing state – Uttar Pradesh (UP) – where factories crush only 45–50 per cent of the crop and a significant portion is diverted towards making alternative sweeteners like gur and khandsari. The average recovery of sugar from cane in Maharashtra mills is also a couple of percentage points more than that in UP.[8] As a result, growers in Maharashtra receive 20–30 per cent higher prices for their sugarcane. Much of it has to do with the manner in which mills manage their cane supplies. In Maharashtra it is the factory that decides when and how much area each member is to plant during a given season. Harvesting and transport are also centralized affairs, with the factory undertaking these operations through contract labour teams to dovetail them to a pre-planned crushing schedule. No such system exists in UP, where the farmers have to harvest and take the cane to the mills themselves. There is usually a 24- to 36-hour gap between the time the cane is harvested in the fields and gets crushed in the factory, during which period the sucrose content suffers depletion, leading to overall lower sugar recoveries.

The co-operatives in Maharashtra are also more complex creatures relative to those in Gujarat. Virtually every sugar mill is the leaven for a host of other co-operative enterprises: from dairies, consumer and lift irrigation societies, to banks, schools, and medical and engineering colleges. Each of these constitutes a giant empire, associated with a particular co-operative baron nominally elected by the farmer-members of that area. Unlike Gujarat, Maharashtra's co-operatives have no federal marketing organization like GCMMF. They are more akin to autonomous, self-governing republics headed by powerful chieftains whose collective interests at state and national level are usually mediated through a supreme commander enjoying their confidence. Initially, it was Yashwantrao Balwantrao Chavan who performed this role and after him the baton passed on to Vasantdada Patil and then to Sharad Pawar. All the three Maratha strongmen have been powerful chief ministers (CMs).[9]

In this chapter our focus is not on co-operatives as much as on the two dominant peasant castes – Patidars and Marathas – who have provided much of their leadership in western India. The question of interest to us is: what is it that has made co-operatives attractive to these communities, who have effectively used them as vehicles for upward economic mobility? Why has the co-operative route for making the transition from agriculture to industry not been employed by the Kammas, Gounders, and other equivalent intermediate castes outside Maharashtra and Gujarat?

The Backdrop

When reference is made to co-operatives in Maharashtra and Gujarat, we need first of all to be clear which parts of the two states are being talked about. If one looks at Gujarat, the region where co-operatives flourish is the mainland, running from Valsad, Surat, and Bharuch in the south through Vadodara, Kheda, and Ahmedabad in central and right up to the northern districts of Mehsana, Sabarkantha, and Banaskantha. In contrast to this, peninsular Gujarat – comprising Kutch and the whole of Saurashtra, which together cover over 56 per cent of the state's area and 30 per cent of its population[10] – has very little co-operative enterprise. The GCMMF has no milk union in Kutch, while the Saurashtra region has a sole district union at Rajkot, contributing a paltry 2.4 per cent of the total procurement by co-operative dairies in Gujarat.[11] The state's co-operative sugar mills – which produce its entire sugar[12] – are also concentrated in the Valsad-Navsari-Surat-Bharuch-Vadodara stretch. The same skewed pattern holds for Maharashtra. Well over three-fourths of its sugar output comes from co-operative factories in the seven western, non-coastal districts of Nasik, Ahmednagar, Pune, Solapur, Satara, Sangli, and Kolhapur, occupying 29 per cent of the state's geographical area. The mills in the Khandesh, Marathwada, and Vidarbha regions – which encompass 60 per cent of Maharashtra – produce less than 25 per cent of its sugar.[13]

The above picture should not surprise anyone. Gujarat's major rivers – the Narmada, Tapti, Mahi, and Sabarmati – all flow through its mainland before emptying into the Gulf of Khambat (Cambay) in the Arabian Sea. There are, thus, large areas of the mainland, particularly in the southern and central parts, with fertile soil-beds formed by the silt deposits of these rivers. These areas have historically sustained robust agricultural economies built around a substantial middle peasantry and, as we shall see, most of the successful co-operative ventures are products of their initiative. The black soil plains of south Gujarat have traditionally been known for cotton (the famous Broach cotton), while Kheda's farmers were among the first to grow tobacco when the crop was introduced in the country in the seventeenth century. The Charotar tract of Kheda (covering the four talukas of Anand, Nadiad, Petlad, and Borsad) under the British was 'one of the most highly assessed areas in India, with a revenue fixed at five times the amount paid on the best black-soiled lands of the Deccan.'[14] Besides their rivers, the southern and central Gujarat mainland housed the ports of Surat, Broach (Bharuch), and Cambay. These maritime centres – Surat was the East India Company's oldest base in India – were also instrumental in shaping the commercial attitudes of the region's farmers. The laying of the railways – the Ahmedabad–Mumbai line was operational in 1863 – gave further fillip to this process. By 1918, even before Amul was born, 'dairy exports from Anand town were worth twenty-four lakhs of rupees a year . . . a sum greater than the total land revenue of the district (Kheda)'.[15]

Peninsular Gujarat was, on the other hand, impervious to such commercial influences. Much of Saurashtra is composed of arid undulating farmlands, while Kutch is surrounded by salty marshes. Neither region has any big rivers; the surface water sources that exist are seasonal. The basic geography therefore did not support intensive farming or a progressive peasantry inclined towards co-operative experiments. Maharashtra too was very much the same till almost the start of the twentieth century. The change was triggered by the construction of the Deccan irrigation works, beginning with the Nira Left Bank Canal in Pune district in 1885, followed by the completion of the Godavari and Pravara canal systems between 1911 and 1920 in Ahmednagar. These projects were taken up after a series of famines culminating in the 'Deccan Riots' of 1875, which saw indebted farmers in the region breaking into the homes of village moneylenders and burning mortgage deeds and other documents in their possession. The canals were originally conceived to provide protective irrigation cover, so that farmers could raise their normal subsistence crops of jowar and bajra in drought years. But what they ended up doing was converting western Maharashtra into a premier sugarcane-growing belt.

How this happened is well explained by Donald Attwood.[16] The canals did perform their protective role well in years when the rains failed. The problem for the colonial authorities, however, was in normal years, when there was no demand for the canal waters. The reason was simple. Irrigation entailed costs not just on the water, but also on levelling and drainage to ensure that all parts of the field were covered. In the heavy black soils of Maharashtra, more so, field preparation called for additional outlays on labour, bullocks, and better ploughs. While incurring these to productively utilize canal water made sense during famine, in ordinary years the farmer chose to rely exclusively on rain water. Also, there was no point spending so much money simply to grow coarse grains, which were intended for home consumption and had a limited market from where costs could be recovered. For the government this was nothing short of a disaster: if cultivators did not use irrigation for subsistence crops on a regular basis, how would the canals pay for themselves? The Deccan works, in 1899–1900, generated net revenues of only 1.4 per cent on capital invested, whereas it was 10 per cent in Punjab and 6.4 per cent for all of India.

The solution was eventually found in sugarcane, a cash crop that consumed ten times the water of a seasonal subsistence crop and required irrigation round the year. It was moreover a crop that, unlike millets, commanded a ready market and would justify the farmer's decision to invest in canal irrigation. The person who recognized these realities and proposed the solution was Sir Mokshagundam Visvesvaraya, then executive engineer for irrigation of Pune district, who attained greater fame later as the dewan of Mysore. In 1901, deposing before the Indian Irrigation Commission, he noted: 'Increase in the irrigation of ordinary crops will never pay in Bombay. Water is too costly to be profitably applied to them. If the Bombay works are ever to prove remunerative, perennial and other high class irrigation should be largely encouraged in ordinary years.'[17] Visvesvaraya accordingly came up with his idea of a 'sugarcane block system', wherein a cultivator would enter into a contract to take canal water for a certain block for six years at a fixed per acre rate. While one-third of the block was to receive irrigation for all twelve months of the year, suitable for cane cultivation, the other two-thirds would be given water during eight months (barring the summers) to raise seasonal crops. The blocks were allotted in multiples of 1.5 acres so as to induce even small farmers to grow cane and opt for intensive agricultural practices. The strategy worked. In 1890 only 300 acres of sugarcane were planted along the Nira Canal, but thirteen years later there were 8,500 acres. By 1922–3 the rate of return on capital had touched 8.3 per cent, mainly courtesy sugarcane.

Interestingly, it was not the Marathas but the Malis of Saswad in Pune district who were the first to take to sugarcane farming. The Saswad Malis were traditionally garden cultivators, supplying horticultural crops and vegetables to Pune city. When the Nira canals came up in the Baramati area around 1885, about a hundred of their families settled there, leasing in land from locals. They cultivated sugarcane, processed it into gur, and sold it in neighbouring urban markets through Gujarati Bania and Marwari traders who financed their operations. In due course the local Maratha landowners (from whom the immigrant Malis took land on lease) had also learnt the techniques of cane cultivation.[18] By 1936 there were six major canal systems in the Bombay Deccan, irrigating 242,000 acres, including 40,000 acres of sugarcane.[19] Western Maharashtra had been converted from a precarious subsistence farming region to a land of commercial crop agriculturists.

But being farmers with a progressive market orientation was not the same as being in control of the trade or agro-processing industry. The building of a rail link with Mumbai, we have seen, created a huge stimulus for milk production in Kheda; between 1846 and 1872 the number of buffaloes in the district rose by 36 per cent, while the milch animal population of Nadiad taluka went up by a further 28 per cent between 1872 and 1892–3.[20] However, the dairy industry that grew on the back of increased raw material availability was the preserve of European and indigenous mercantile capitalists. Kheda's first dairy plant was set up in 1900 by a Swede with a very English-sounding name, A.C. Strafford. Towards 1910–11 his British Express Dairy was reportedly sending about 100,000 pounds of cream daily to Mumbai. A German, A.M. Kohler, was more innovative: in 1911 he started a unit near Anand to manufacture casein, using the surplus skim milk that villagers disposed of after separating the cream for making ghee. In 1914, an Englishman proper, one G.R. Reeves, got into the act and his Indian Dairy Supply Company's plant at Nadiad was dispatching 24,000 pounds of pasteurized milk every day to Mumbai. But the biggest player was a Parsi, Pestonji Edulji Dalal, better known as Polson. In 1930 he established in Anand what was then India's largest dairy, which during the War years produced over 3 million pounds of butter annually under the 'Polson's' brand.[21] In southern Gujarat, too, the milk and cotton trade was overwhelmingly with Kutchi Bhatia and Parsi sheths. The cotton grower was linked to the exporter in Mumbai through a complex network of ginners and middlemen, who advanced him credit for supplying the kapas.

The situation was no different in Maharashtra, where sugarcane farmers owned at most gur-making units. In the late 1930s there were more than a hundred cane crushers powered by oil engines along the Pravara and Godavari canals. These establishments, crushing about 6,300 acres of cane, belonged mainly to big cultivators, who manufactured gur from not only their crop but also on behalf of other farmers.[22] Simultaneously, a sugar industry was taking shape in western Maharashtra from the 1920s. At the time of Independence there were thirteen mills producing over 1 lakh tonnes of sugar. Most were set up after 1932, when the government put high duties on imported sugar. Tariff protection aside, it was the policy to guarantee perennial irrigation water for earmarked cane areas of every factory – based on a recommendation by the Deccan Canals Financial Improvement Committee – that lured investors. Unlike in UP and Bihar, mills in Maharashtra were even encouraged to develop their own sugarcane plantations. These captive farms covered 36,000 acres, of which two-thirds were leased in from local landowners.[23] And like Kheda's dairies the mills were all owned by non-Marathas. They included the Ravalgaon Sugar Farm of Walchand Hirachand (Gujarati Jain Bania), Godavari Sugar Mills of Karamshibhai Jethabhai Somaiya (Lohana), Kolhapur Sugar Mill of Radhakrishna Ruia (Marwari), and Phaltan Sugar Works of V.S. Apte (Brahmin). It was only a matter of time before the tide would change through co-operatives.

Co-operative Capitalists

Why co-operatives? What prevented the rural local bosses of western Maharashtra and mainland Gujarat to take the plunge into industry through direct private initiative, as the Kamma landlords of Andhra Sugars or the Naidu mirasidars-turned-spinning mill owners of Coimbatore had done? We can cite three major factors why 'co-operative capitalism' specifically appealed to the Patidar and Maratha middle peasantry. The first is the business environment in which these communities were operating: western India, in comparison with southern India, already had an entrenched mercantile class holding sway over commodity and money markets. In a hostile world of Parsi, Marwari, Gujarati Bania, Lohana, and Bhatia magnates, it was a tall order for a person of rural farming background – howsoever big a landowner he may have been – to become a full-fledged industrialist purely on the basis of private entrepreneurship. The co-operative route offered a seemingly more practical alternative.

Secondly, there were strong techno-economic imperatives favouring this strategy. Both milk and sugarcane, being perishable commodities, had to be processed within hours of leaving udders and fields. Moreover, setting up a sugar mill or dairy involved huge investments in plant and machinery. The only way to recover the fixed costs was through high capacity utilization, which then demanded a reliable flow of raw material. A sugar factory with a capacity to crush 1,000 tcd required 150,000 tonnes to run for at least 150 days of the year. As against this the most that even a wealthy 100-acre grower recording good yields of 50 tonnes per acre could supply was 5,000 tonnes. Likewise, a progressive milk producer keeping 25–30 animals, each giving 10–15 litres daily, would have been able to meet only a fraction of the capacity of a modern dairy handling upwards of 10,000 litres every day. And, given the perishable nature of the raw material, it was important to secure supplies not simply in overall quantitative terms but in a timely and continuous manner.[24] Sheer techno-economic compulsions, therefore, made it necessary for the large aspirant rural entrepreneur to strike an alliance with small- and medium-sized growers. Further, for the venture to succeed and operate at optimal capacity, this alliance had to be of a stable and accommodative nature, responsive to smallholder interests.

That brings us to the third dimension of how objective social conditions in rural western India were particularly suited for forging such alliances. The Maratha-Kunbis were the largest community in Maharashtra, forming 31.2 per cent of its population according to the 1931 census. This proportion was even higher, at 36.9 per cent, in the Bombay Deccan (which mainly covers western

Maharashtra).[25] The predominance of a single intermediate caste in rural society – mostly comprising independent peasant proprietors – was a factor quite congenial to co-operative enterprise. This was all the more so in western Maharashtra which, during the early twentieth century, was the site of a vibrant non-Brahmin movement under the patronage of Chhatrapati Shahu (1874–1922), the ruler of the princely state of Kolhapur.[26] Although its immediate impact was in the domain of education and government jobs,[27] the movement's more durable legacy was the creation of a unified Maratha identity. The earlier distinction between elite Marathas, claiming descent from ninety-six exclusive Kshatriya clans, and ordinary Kunbi cultivating folk was sought be consciously blurred. During the 1921 and 1931 census surveys, concerted efforts were made, through newspaper articles and conferences, to persuade the broader Kunbi population to return itself as Maratha.[28]

The Patidars in Gujarat are not as numerically decisive, accounting for 12.2 per cent of the population, making them the state's second biggest caste after the Kolis, at 24.2 per cent.[29] However, they are its largest landowning community, having a reputation for hard work and hands-on experience in producing cash crops like cotton, tobacco, and indigo. Control over land, highly evolved commercial peasant skills, and reasonable numerical strength (compared to, say, the Malis in Maharashtra) made the Patidars natural village leaders, a status given added legitimacy during the freedom struggle. Kheda in 1918 and Bardoli taluka of Surat in 1928 were centres of historic land revenue refusal campaigns by peasants – campaigns that not merely catapulted Sardar Vallabhbhai Patel into the national centrestage but which were also a defining moment when, to quote Mahatma Gandhi, 'the Patidar peasant came to an unforgettable consciousness of his strength'. Above all, it transformed the Congress, enough for Gandhi to proclaim in 1931, perhaps with some degree of exaggeration, that the party was 'essentially a peasant organization'.[30] Till then the nationalist movement in Gujarat was led by Brahmins and Banias, with a sprinkling of big Patidar landlords, and based out of Mumbai. But after Kheda and Bardoli – which, as Hardiman emphasizes, were movements of the Patidar peasantry as opposed to landlords[31] – the Gujarat Congress became a veritable Patidar citadel. A similar rural Maratha takeover of the Congress in Maharashtra was witnessed from the mid 1930s,[32] gaining momentum during the Quit India movement of 1942. It threw up leaders like Chavan, Nanasaheb Ramchandra Patil, and Vasantdada Patil, who even ran a Prati Sarkar (parallel government) in 150 villages of Satara between August 1943 and May 1946.[33] These rural nationalist agitations set the stage for yet another factor behind the success of co-operatives in western India: state support and patronage for its chief backers in the post-Independence era. We shall return to this point a little later.

It was in Surat that the first significant agro-processing co-operatives were born. In 1919, at the initiative of Purushottambhai Ichharam Patel, thirteen farmers from Sonsak village of Olpad taluka formed a cotton-marketing society. They pooled their kapas, got it ginned and pressed by private parties, and jointly marketed the lint and seed. This proved far more remunerative than simply selling raw cotton to traders at prices dictated by them. Soon, other villages in Surat joined and by the mid 1930s the co-operative had installed its own ginning and baling facility by importing machinery from England. Later on, the Purushottam Farmers' Cooperative Ginning and Pressing Society, renamed after its founder, added a rice mill to pool, process, and market the paddy of its members. Till the 1980s Purushottam was a reputed global supplier of the finest quality cotton, inspiring similar co-operatives in Bharuch and Vadodara. But by then south Gujarat's cotton economy had gone into decline, due to a combination of repeated white-fly pest attacks and the commissioning of the Ukai-Kakrapar irrigation project.[34] These resulted in large-scale displacement of cotton by sugarcane and the setting up of a number of sugar factories. It is another thing that all these mills (eight in Surat district alone) were co-operatives promoted essentially by the same set of Patidars. Surat was also the birthplace of the first ever dairy co-operative: the Choryasi Taluka Milk Sale Cooperative Society, which came up in 1939 under the leadership of Lallubhai Patel against considerable opposition from Kutchi Bhatia traders.[35]

The Kheda milk union – the original 'Amul' – was started in December 1946 following the government's decision to grant Polson's dairy the sole monopoly to collect milk from the district for supplies to the Bombay Milk Scheme (BMS). It was an iniquitous arrangement, to protest against which farmers, guided by a young Congress worker Tribhuvandas Patel, resolved not to sell a single litre. The strike, blessed by Sardar Patel – who had himself earlier advocated co-operative processing and marketing of milk by farmers – lasted fifteen days, paralysing supplies to Mumbai and forcing the government to withdraw Polson's monopoly. By end 1948 the union was collecting 5,000-odd litres of milk daily from 430 farmers.[36] This translated into nearly 12 litres per farmer, showing that the co-operative's early members were from the better-off sections of the Patidar peasantry. As Amul's operations grew, running the dairy at full capacity impressed upon its enlightened leadership the need to look beyond the Charotar villages and recruit producers from lower castes. Maharashtra's first two sugar co-operatives – Pravara and Kopargaon (both in Ahmednagar district) – were founded in the early 1950s by Vithalrao Vikhe-Patil and Ganpatrao Rabhaji Autade, respectively. They, too, were among the bigger cane growers in their areas who, after experiencing extreme swings in gur prices, saw the wisdom of getting into sugar production and involving other farmers in the project. Autade had previously organized a co-operative sale and purchase union at Kopargaon to take on local Marwari and Gujarati Bania gur traders.[37]

A crucial element in the success of these ventures, as already alluded to, was the exceptional support they got from successive Congress governments in post-Independent India. Co-operative sugar mills were allowed to meet 70 per cent of their project costs through long-term loans from public financial institutions, with the Maharashtra government providing guarantees for their repayment. Even for the balance 30 per cent equity portion, the government undertook to subscribe up to two-thirds of the share capital, which mills could gradually redeem at face value. The repayment of loans and redemption of government equity was done by deducting a portion of the cane price payable to farmer-members over a period. Until now the Maharashtra government has cumulatively invested roughly Rs 1,200 crore as share capital alone in the state's co-operative sugar factories, of which around half is still to be redeemed.[38] In the case of milk co-operatives, substantial assistance came from international agencies – the World Bank and the European Community – and was channelled through the National Dairy Development Board (NDDB). Between 1970 and 1995 over Rs 1,700 crore was spent in dairy infrastructure under NDDB's Operation Flood programme. 40 per cent of this – bearing a 30 per cent grant component – went to GCMMF's affiliated unions.[39] Another indicator of this 'Gujarat bias' was NDDB being strategically headquartered at Anand and its indomitable chairman, Verghese Kurien, simultaneously holding office as chairman, GCMMF![40]

Apart from financial support aimed at bringing down their cost of capital, state patronage to co-operatives was dispensed at the level of policy-making. The Maharashtra government's land reforms of 1961 delivered a body blow to private mills by confiscating their captive sugarcane estates and transferring these to the Maharshtra State Farming Corporation. It rendered their operations unviable and most of the factories either closed down or relocated (e.g. the Somaiya family's Godavari Sugar Mill, which moved to Bagalkot in Karnataka). The other potent non-financial intervention weapon was import controls and licensing: before the 1990s it was a declared state policy to reserve all new sugar mills and dairies for the co-operative sector, which was combined with preferential allocation of cane area and milk sheds. For instance, by 1952, Amul had turned the tables on Polson's by obtaining the exclusive right to supply milk from Kheda to the BMS, thereby signing the Parsi company's death warrant. Further, NDDB was made the sole canalizing agency for all imports of milk powder and butter oil. To their credit, though, it must be said that the co-operatives in Maharashtra and Gujarat have made constructive use of these official sops to become, by and large, commercially sound entities accountable to their millions of rural stakeholders. Moreover, measures such as subsidizing project costs were effectively not very different from the tax holidays and liberal depreciation allowances given to private corporations. Also, being farmer-owned organizations, co-operatives could not have tapped public equity markets, which offered cheaper funds relative to debt.

One thing that the co-operatives have done, on which there are no two opinions, is bring the Maratha and Patidar communities into the industrial mainstream. Out of Maharashtra's 175 co-operative sugar factories there are at least 140 whose key promoters were Marathas.[41] Compare this to the pre-Independence period, when not a single Maratha industrial undertaking existed! As for GCMMF, the founders of its five premier milk unions – Kheda (Tribhuvandas Patel), Mehsana (Mansinhbhai Patel), Sabarkantha (Bhurabhai Patel), Surat (Jagjiwandas Patel), and Banaskantha (Galbabhai Patel) – were all Patidars. So were those of the smaller unions such as Baroda (Thakurbhai Patel), Panchmahal (Babubhai

Patel), and Bharuch (Thakurbhai Amin). In fact it is remarkable that some of the unions started after Kheda – Mehsana, Banaskantha, and Sabarkantha – today procure more milk than the trailblazer.[42] All the three fall in the drier northern Gujarat mainland, where the use of chemical fertilizers and tube-wells to harness groundwater has injected a fair bit of agrarian dynamism since the 1960s. Again, it is the Patidars who, through institutional innovations like co-operatively managed 'tube-well companies', have been the agents of change, resorting to intensive cultivation of jeera (cumin), mustard, castor, potatoes, and other cash crops.[43]

While Maratha–Patidar dominance in western India's co-operatives is an accepted fact, the presence of other communities cannot be over-looked. Indeed, Maharashtra's biggest sugar producer, the Warana co-operative in Kolhapur district, was the initiative of Vishwanath Vilasrao Kore, a Lingayat (see profile at the end of the chapter). Kolhapur has three other very well-managed factories: the Panchganga, the Datta Shetkari Shirol, and the Jawahar Shetkari co-operatives. The founders of the first two were Lingayats (Ratnappanna Kumbhar and S.R. Patil), whereas the last was started by a Jain, Kallappa Baburao Awade. The Lingayats, like the Malis, are a numerically small caste in Maharashtra, traditionally into agriculture and running tiny village grocery stores. But unlike the Malis they have not been averse to co-operatives, fearing overriding Maratha power.[44]

Gujarat has been home to a somewhat different phenomenon of Patidars disengaging themselves from the co-operative movement over the last two decades or so. Having used co-operatives as a launchpad for economic mobility and capturing positions of power, the Patidars have gone big time into private industry, vacating the co-operative space increasingly to Kolis, Baraiyas, and other lower intermediate peasant castes loosely clubbed under the 'Kshatriya' banner. The best illustration of this is the Kheda milk union –

the original baby of the Charotar Leva Patidars – whose current chairman, Ramsinhbhai Parmar, is a Baraiya. The Panchmahal, Baroda, and Gandhinagar unions, too, are headed by Kshatriyas, while the leadership of the Mehsana and Banaskantha unions is with the Chaudhary Patels, considered 'inferior' to the more elite Leva and Kadva Patidars.[45] This 'de-Patidarization' of co-operatives has gone hand in hand with the growing assertion of Kshatriyas (who add up to 40 per cent of Gujarat's population) in the state's politics and the Patidars' alienation from the Congress. Attempts by Congress leaders like Madhavsinh Solanki to stitch up a 'KHAM' electoral coalition of Kshatriyas, Harijans, Adivasis, and Muslims have drawn the Patidars steadily rightwards, starting with the shortlived Janata Dal (Gujarat) experiment of Chimanbhai Patel to the Bharatiya Janata Party (BJP) in the 1990s.

Private Enterprise

In principle, co-operatives are democratic bodies controlled and accountable to their members. In their actual working they are more like quasi-private family-run businesses. Take the first Pravara factory, which began in 1950-1 with a crushing capacity of 800 tcd. Over time, this was enhanced to 4,000 tcd. Alongside, a distillery, a chemical plant, and a kraft paper unit were added to utilize the molasses and bagasse byproducts from the mill. The group today also consists of a co-operative bank, a rural education society (that runs an engineering college, a college for arts, science and commerce, industrial training institutes, and a number of schools), and a 'deemed university', with a hospital and affiliated medical, dental, and nursing colleges. Initially, this whole conglomerate was headed by Vithalrao Vikhe-Patil. After his death the baton passed on to the son, Eknathrao (Balasaheb) Vikhe-Patil, who is the Congress MP from Kopargaon. Both Balasaheb and his son, Radhakrishna

Vikhe-Patil – the next in the line – were also with the Shiv Sena for five years before returning to the Congress fold in 2004. During this crossover period the father served as a minister in New Delhi, while the son was made agriculture minister of Maharashtra. That was the only time when the BJP–Shiv Sena combine succeeded in breaking into western Maharashtra by weaning away a section of disgruntled Congress sugar satraps.

Pravara is not the only instance where interlocked governance structures and cross-membership of boards have been used to confer certain families control over a wide network of co-operatives in an area. In 1962 a Congress legislator, Shankarrao Narayanrao Mohite-Patil laid the base for a similar 'co-operative kieretsu' through a 1,000 tcd sugar mill at Akluj (Solapur).[46] This factory, since expanded to 4,500 tcd with an attached distillery and chemical plant, is now part of a complex that has a co-operative dairy (which markets milk under the 'Shivamrut' brand), a poultry enterprise, a spinning mill, and assorted educational institutions. Again, it is a family affair: following the founder, his eldest son Vijaysinh Shankarrao Mohite-Patil took over, while the younger one Pratapsinh has a parallel sugar mill-based combine at Malshiras taluka. Vijaysinh is the minister for rural development and tourism in Maharashtra and was, for a short while, deputy CM as well.[47] Likewise, we have the finance minister, Jayant Patil, who presides over the Rajarambapu Cooperative group at Walwa in Sangli, established by his father (see joint case study with Warana later). Then, there is the Sanjivani group of the Shankarrao Genuji Kolhe family at Kopargaon and, of course, the chain of institutions created by the 'Sahakar Maharshi' (co-operation saint) and former CM, Vasantdada Patil. In the last case the leadership has spanned three generations, including his son Prakashbabu Patil and grandson, Prateek Patil. All three have been MPs from Sangli and headed the sugar mill that Vasantdada established in 1956, and which used to be one of the country's most efficiently run mills (not any longer). Further, Vasantdada's second wife Shalinitai Patil – who was known as the proxy CM and the power behind the throne – has her own Jarandeshwar co-operative factory at Koregaon (Satara) which, too, is not currently in very good condition.

The usefulness of co-operatives in carving out virtually family-owned business fiefdoms does not, however, mean that there is no history of 'pure' private entrepreneurship amongst the Marathas or Patidars. The man who set up Ahmedabad's second textile mill in 1864 (after the Nagar Brahmin, Ranchhodlal Chhotalal) was a Patidar by the name of Bechardas Ambaidas Laskari. The seed capital for the mill came from his father, an agriculturist who had made some extra money supplying groceries to the British army.[48] But the community's first real textile tycoon was Mafatlal Gagalbhai (1873–1944) who, like Bechardas, was from the lesser Kadva subcaste. Mafatlal belonged to one of the many Patidar families to have settled down in Ahmedabad by the early nineteenth century, taking to non-farming pursuits such as weaving and retail trading in textiles. After joining his father's small shop at the age of 13, Mafatlal worked part time in a textile mill, where his job was to weigh cotton bales and keep account of inventories. During this time he came in contact with Chandulal Mahadevia, a fellow Patidar weaving master, and Collinson Shorrock, a British textile machinery dealer. In 1905 the three jointly floated the Shorrock Spinning and Manufacturing Company in which the Englishman basically lent his name and helped in securing equipment on deferred payment from British suppliers. The timing was great. The swadeshi movement was at its peak and the unit, with 8,000 spindles and 200 looms, made enough profits for Mafatlal to buy out an existing mill at Nadiad in 1912, which was renamed the New Shorrock Mills. With World War I came even better times; in 1916, a mill owned by the erstwhile Muslim nawab rulers of

Surat was taken over. More acquisitions followed, including the Tatas' Standard Mills in 1927 and two mills controlled by the Jewish immigrant Sassoon family in 1949. The Mafatlals, by then under the founder's son Navinchandra, had emerged as India's pre-eminent textile group.[49] After Navinchandra's death in 1955 the group, led by his eldest son Arvind, forayed into new areas, setting up the country's first petrochemical cracker – National Organic Chemical Industries Limited (Nocil) – at Thane near Mumbai in 1968, and also its first private gas distribution concern, Gujarat Gas Company, in 1988.

Another early Patidar entrepreneur was Bhailalbhai Amin, a Charotar Leva from Virsad village of Borsad. Born to a landed family five years after Mafatlal, Amin studied at the Nadiad English School and was in college at Ahmedabad and Mumbai, making him one of the community's highly educated members. In 1907 he established Alembic Chemical Works, which has an unusual background: it was conceived by a chemistry professor, T.K. Gajjar, and his student, A.S. Kotibhaskar. In 1899 Gajjar quit teaching to pursue his main interest of 'applying science for industrial purposes'. He started a 'technological laboratory' in Mumbai that made chemicals used for polishing precious stones. Soon the professor and student were toying with the idea of a unit to make pharmaceutical formulations developed by them. They approached Bhailalbhai, who had worked at Gajjar's laboratory as a trainee and was keen on options outside farming. Alembic was thus born in Vadodara around the same time as P.C. Ray's Bengal Chemicals. By 1932 it was producing some twenty-eight pharmaceutical items. In 1942 the company went into production of liquor, taking advantage of the wartime disruption in supplies. After the War it exited this business which, nevertheless, led Alembic into bottle glass manufacturing and, later, consumer glassware ('Yera' brand). Another wartime diversification was Jyoti Limited. Originally a department within Alembic to fabricate tools and spare parts for its distilling and pharma plants, it was spun off into a company in 1943 to make hydraulic pumps and design chemical plants.[50] Under Bhailalbhai's third son Nanubhai Amin, Jyoti expanded its products to larger pumps and motors for industrial applications, switchgears, electronic relays and control systems. Meanwhile Alembic (headed by the eldest son Ramanbhai Amin) became a frontline pharma concern, pioneering basic fermentation manufacture of penicillin and erythromycin in India during the 1960s and 1970s, and owning brands like 'Althrocin', 'Wikoryl', 'Glycodin', and 'Zeet' cough and cold mixtures.

Yet Mafatlal and Bhailalbhai Amin were exceptions; excluding them, there were hardly any Patidar industrialists of note before Independence. In 1898 Ahmedabad had twenty-six textile units, of which Banias controlled twenty-two, Brahmins two, and Parsis and Patidars one each. Even in 1964 the position had improved only marginally: out of the total sixty-two mill companies, fifty-two were Bania-owned, eight by Patidars, and two by non-Gujaratis.[51] The Patidars were, in other words, just arriving on the scene, even while consolidating their social, political, and economic status through co-operatives. And of their early entrepreneurs Bechardas Laskari represents nothing more than a curious footnote in business history. The Mafatlals were India's third largest industrial house after the Birlas and the Tatas in as late as 1979, when the empire was divided between Navinchandra Mafatlal's sons: Arvind, Yogindra, and Rashesh. The 1990s have marked their precipitous decline. The Arvind Mafatlal group's textile flagship, Mafatlal Industries Limited, has gone sick. Nocil's petrochemicals business was sold to Reliance in 2004, while Gujarat Gas became a subsidiary of British Gas in 1997.[52] Yogindra Mafatlal's Indian Dyestuff Industries, which once marketed the popular 'Ranipal' fabric whitener, is also history. The group has of late been more in the news for a sex change operation that Yogindra's 48-year-old daughter Aparna (now

Ajay) underwent in 2003, allegedly to stake claim to the family's valued real estate assets in Mumbai. Only Alembic has survived and grown, but it is much smaller than the likes of Ranbaxy, Cipla, Nicholas Piramal, Dr Reddy's, Sun Pharma, Lupin, Matrix, and others, which started out much later. Jyoti Limited, too, is a pale shadow of its past.[53]

Among the dozen-odd domestic pharma concerns to have overtaken Alembic is one established in 1952 by a Patidar from Kathor in Kamrej taluka of Surat. A pharmaceutical science graduate from Ahmedabad's L.M. College of Pharmacy, Ramanbhai Patel began his career as a lecturer in the same college and was only 26 when he launched Cadila Laboratories. Today, his Zydus group (the flagship is now called Cadila Healthcare Limited) is the fourth largest Indian pharma major after Ranbaxy, Cipla, and Nicholas Piramal, in terms of profitability.[54] The other important industrialist from this early post-Independence phase, whom we shall discuss in more detail later, is Bhanubhai Ishwarbhai Patel. Bhanubhai's father, like Bhailalbhai Amin, was from a first generation of educated Patidar landlords – he studied in the same Nadiad High School – interested in exploring non-agricultural avenues. That took him to Mumbai, where the family started a small spare parts trading business, before they returned to Anand smelling opportunities after the new Gujarat state was formed in 1960. Bhanubhai's Elecon group is a leading manufacturer of industrial gears and material handling equipment such as wagon loaders, tipplers, and conveyors. An equally low-profile yet reputed engineering company, incorporated just after Independence, is the Mumbai-based Patel Engineering Limited of Pravin Arjunbhai Patel. A civil construction firm specializing in tunnelling and underground works for hydroelectric and transport projects, it has executed massive dam, road- and bridge-laying contracts both in India as well as in countries like the US, Greece, Bhutan, and Sri Lanka.[55]

In more recent times there has been a profusion of Patidar businessmen beyond pharma and engineering in areas like branded consumer goods. The most celebrated name here is Karsanbhai Khodidas Patel of the Rs 2,000-crore-plus detergent, soap, and chemicals giant, Nirma Limited (see case study). Apart from the Mehsana-born Karsanbhai, two other major Patidar-owned branded products entities are Sintex Industries Limited and Paras Pharmaceuticals: both based at Kalol near Ahmedabad. The former was founded by Natwarlal Bhikhabhai Patel, who took over the management of a textile unit (Bharat Vijay Mills) in 1956. Its growth took off with a product – plastic water storage tanks – that has become synonymous with its brand ('Sintex'). More than three decades after it was launched, Sintex retains a 60 per cent share in the segment, while also being the leader in prefabricated doors, windows, and similar processed plastic products.[56] Paras Pharma, promoted in 1980, is a closely held company of three brothers: Girish, Darshan, and Devendra Patel. It has in many ways done to multinationals like SmithKline Beecham what Nirma did to Hindustan Lever. But while Nirma is largely a single brand concern, Paras has a portfolio that is truly humongous: from 'Moov' pain relief ointment to 'Krack' foot cream, 'DermiCool' prickly heat powder, 'ItchGuard' and 'RingGuard' anti-fungal creams, 'BoroSoft' antiseptic cream, 'Livon' hair-conditioner and 'Set Wet' hair gel.

It is not Gujarat's mainland alone that has produced entrepreneurs from the community. Odhavjibhai Ravjibhai (O.R.) Patel is a Saurashtra Patidar who taught science in the not-so-known V.C. Technical High School at Morbi, a town about 60 km from Rajkot. In 1971 he set up a small facility to produce mechanical analog clocks. This outfit, the Ajanta Transistor Clock Manufacturing Company (later Ellora Time Limited), went on to be the world's most prolific wall clock manufacturer ('Ajanta' brand). The Rs

500 crore Orpat group (derived from O.R. Patel) today also makes calculators, telephones, compact fluorescent lamps and other electrical appliances under the 'Orpat' label, along with 'Ajanta' toothpaste and 'Oreva' vitrified tiles (named after the promoter's wife Revaben). O.R. Patel has a nephew, Manubhai Patel, whose Samay group has a near-identical product line ('Samay Quartz' clocks and 'Sogo' tiles). Gujarat's vitrified tile industry is, in fact, full of Patidars: be it 'Oreva' and 'Sogo' or Asian Tiles of Hasmukh Patel, Excel Ceramic of Ashokbhai Patel, and Suman Tiles of Devram Patel. Other industries with sizeable Saurashtra Patel presence include diesel engines (the Rajkot-based PM Diesels and Gujarat Forgings Limited, who jointly make 'Field Marshall' engines and pumpsets) and edible oil refining (Morvi Vegetable Products of Ashokkumar Patel and Sanjay Oilcake Industries of Mohanlal Patel). Bigger than these men is Govind-bhai Laljibhai Kakadia who, as a 10-year-old in 1968, left Patana village in Vallabhipur taluka to work as a diamond polisher in Bhavnagar. Eight years later, Kakadia had his own polishing unit doing job works for jewellers and traders in Mumbai. By the early 1990s his Sheetal Manufacturing Company had broken into a traditional Palanpuri Jain bastion, with factories in Bhavnagar and Surat and sourcing bases at Antwerp and London. The Sheetal group is currently one of the world's leading manufacturers of polished diamonds by volume and selling branded jewellery under the 'Kiah' label.

The biggest and most famous Saurashtra Patel industrialist though – and whose rise is not even a decade-old phenomenon – is Tulsi Ranch-hodbhai Tanti. A commerce graduate and mechanical engineering diploma holder, Tanti's father owned a cold storage unit at Rajkot. In the late 1980s Tulsi and his three younger brothers – Girish, Vinod, and Jitendra – moved into processing of polyester yarn and making furnishing fabrics. With erratic and costly power hitting their operations, the Tantis sought to ease the situation by installing a couple of windmills. The government had around that time announced gratuitous tax breaks for companies investing in renewable energy sources (see case study on Pioneer Asia in the previous chapter). Eyeing the potential from the business, the brothers incorporated Suzlon Energy Limited in April 1995 with a paid-up capital of Rs 1 crore. Shopping for technology took them to Europe. And as none of the large players were willing to provide it sans equity stake, they had to settle for a small German com-pany, Sudwind, in return for buying ten of its turbines. Using his contacts at Indian Petrochemicals Corporation Limited (IPCL), which supplied raw materials for his yarn business, Tanti got the then state-owned company to install the turbines with an aggregate generating capacity of 3.5 mega-watts (MW). In 1997, when Sudwind went bust, Suzlon hired its engineers to create a research centre based in Germany. Over the next few years the company rode on the state-assisted windmill investment boom by selling turbines and, along the way, acquiring a Dutch manufacturer of rotor blades and a Belgian company fabricating the crucial turbine gearbox components. By September 2005, when it went public, Suzlon had cumulatively commissioned over 1,500 MW, making it among the world's top ten wind energy companies.[57]

To the above list of Patidar industrialists one should add Chimanbhai Patel of *Sandesh* and the current union civil aviation minister, Praful Patel. *Sandesh*, a small-time paper taken over in 1958 by Chimanbhai, is now a prominent Gujarati daily and also the country's first media house to have gone public in 1994.[58] Originally from Nadiad, Praful Patel's father Manoharbhai, during the 1930s, migrated to Gondia in Maharashtra's Bhandara district, bordering Madhya Pradesh. There, he joined the tobacco trading business of his uncle Chhotabhai and cousin Jethabhai Patel.[59] When the War broke out Manoharbhai ventured into bidi manufacture, sensing the fortunes to be made by supplying the indigenous cheroot to weary soldiers. Within a decade Manoharbhai had emerged as a bidi king and his company, Chhotabhai Jethabhai Tobacco Products, the owner of the popular 'No. 27' brand. Today it remains the mainstay of the Rs 500 crore Ceejay group that Praful Patel – born to Manoharbhai and his third wife Shantaben – inherited in 1973, when he was just 16. Apart from bidi, the group includes Ceejay Healthcare (which ironically makes 'NuLife', a nicotine replacement therapy product to counter tobacco dependence!), Ceejay Finance and the Gondia Education Society. The latter manages the Manoharbhai Patel Institute of Engineering & Technology and a chain of twenty-four other colleges and fifty schools in and around Bhandara.

One aspect of Patidar enterprise on which we have not shed light so far is overseas migration. Broadly speaking, there were two waves of migration. The first was triggered by the severe drought of 1899–1900 – referred to as Chhappanio Dukal or the famine of 1956 in the Hindu Vikram Samvat calendar – and the plague epidemic that immediately followed. Many Patidars, who had previously not gone farther than Ahmedabad and Vadodara, began following the old trade link between Gujarat and Africa. They landed in Kenya, Uganda, Tanzania, Zambia, and Malawi, initially working as labourers and clerks in colonial establishments. Although the Patidars had little prior business experience – as against the Bhatias or Banias, who were already entrenched in East Africa – within fifty years they had also turned into a wealthy overseas trading community.[60] However, the political unrest and 'Africanization' drive unleashed first in the late 1960s by the Idi Amin regime in Uganda forced a second wave of migration, this time to the US and Britain. They found their niche in the motel industry which, in the US, was going through a lull. The twice-migrant Patidars bought old undervalued properties and turned them round by employing – in true peasant style – family labour and recruiting cheap workforce from relatives and friends back home. This strategy of Patidars keeping costs low by hiring other Patidars, and often helping the latter open franchises, has led to the 'Patel Motel' becoming a generic term.[61] Today, one in every four mid-sized motels and hotel properties in the US is owned by Patidars. The Asian American Hotel Owners Association's (AAHOA) 8,300-odd members control some 6,300 independent and 11,700 franchised properties, with an estimated market value of $40 billion. Most have names such as Mukesh (Mike) Patel, Dhansukh (Dan) Patel, Naresh (Nash) Patel, and Bakulesh (Buggsi) Patel. Some, like the Diplomat Hotel Corporation of Mike Patel, have extended into real estate, banking, commercial insurance, and related activities.

The impact of migration on domestic Patidar life cannot be underestimated. The new wealth from the first emigrants had a considerable role in bridging the gulf between the aristocratic Leva Patidars and their inferior brethren, and, as David Pocock has argued, hastened the transition from Kanbi to a more inclusive Patidar identity. There were spin-offs in business as well. To consolidate fibre supplies to his mills Mafatlal Gagalbhai had, as early as 1920, established ginneries in Uganda in partnership with his clansmen, who had taken to cotton growing and ginning there. Similarly, Cadila's first exports in the 1960s were facilitated through a connection that Ramanbhai Patel had forged with one Kanubhai Patel of Bombay Trading Stores at Kampala. More recently, there are instances of overseas Patidars investing directly in India. One such individual is Bhupendra Shantilal Kansagra, a twice-migrant to Kenya and the UK who has promoted the low-cost airline SpiceJet Limited.

The Marathas have not displayed the same enthusiasm for private capital. Whatever movement from co-operative to 'pure' private enterprise has occurred is of fairly recent origin and restricted to fields like wineries and education. Shamrao Chougule started out as a contractor who secured a big order for constructing 50,000 housing shelters after the massive Koyna earthquake of 1967. From there he got into structural steel fabrication and doing turnkey erection jobs for the armed forces. The work entailed frequent foreign trips and it was one such visit to France that induced Chougule to try out cultivating wine grapes (as opposed to normal table grapes) by grafting imported vines on to the rootstocks of local varieties. In 1984 he set up India's first winery at Narayangaon on the Pune-Nasik road. Chougule's Indage group today churns out wine and champagne under the 'Riviera-Pinot Noir', 'Riviera-Blanc de Blanc', 'Marquise de Pompadour' and 'Omar Khayyam' labels, which are even marketed overseas. The other well-known Maratha wine maker is Rajeev Samant, a postgraduate in industrial engineering from Stanford. In 1990 Samant chucked a job with Oracle Corporation at Silicon Valley to grow alphonso mangoes and tomatoes in his 30-acre family land at Nasik. A few years on he was planting grapes, which became the precursor to Sula Vineyards. But in sheer turnover terms – notwithstanding the various excise and soft loan sops showered on the industry courtesy Sharad Pawar – neither Indage nor Sula are significant.[62]

The business in which there are genuinely big-time private Maratha names is education. We have already talked about the schools and colleges established by sugar barons as adjuncts to the co-operative mills in their respective areas. These are largely managed by trusts (in which the leaders nominate themselves as lifelong trustees), with corpus funds created through deduction of cane payments from farmer-members. However, in recent times education has become a stand-alone business, independent of the co-operatives. We can single out at least four Maratha education magnates: D.Y. Patil, Patangrao Shripatrao Kadam, Datta Meghe, and Kamal Kishore Kadam. Their operations are not confined to a particular local area. D.Y. Patil, who hails from Ambap village of Kolhapur, runs around seventy-five educational institutions spread across Pune, Kolhapur, and Mumbai. They include a medical and dental college-cum-hospital that are part of the D.Y. Patil Vidyapeeth, a 'deemed university' at New Mumbai. The Sangli-born Patangrao Kadam's Bharati Vidyapeeth, again 'deemed' a university, is an even larger empire. It has nearly 150 educational institutions with campuses in Delhi, Mumbai, Pune, Solapur, Kolhapur, and Sangli. Both D.Y. Patil and Kadam have co-operative sugar mills to boot – one is at Gaganbavada in Kolhapur and the other is at Sonhira in Sangli – but these are subsidiary to their main education business. Datta Meghe, an ex-MP of Wardha and a rare Maratha stalwart from the Vidarbha region, similarly has a chain of medical, engineering, and polytechnic institutions mainly around Nagpur and Mumbai. Kamal Kishore Kadam is an education baron from Marathwada controlling the Mahatma Gandhi Mission, with engineering, medical, and management colleges and schools in Aurangabad, Nanded, Parbhani, New Mumbai, and Noida near Delhi. Both Patangrao Kadam and Kamal Kishore Kadam have fittingly also been education ministers of Maharashtra.

In sugar, there are some very early signs of private Maratha capital formation, especially in the Marathwada districts. Two major factories to have come up since 1999–2000 – each with 2,500 tcd capacity – are Natural Sugar & Allied Industries Limited of B.B. Thombare at Kallam taluka in Osmanabad and Gangamai Sugar Industries Limited at Sillod (Aurangabad) of P.H. Mulay. Thombare has a co-operative connection: he was the managing director of the Manjara Shetkari co-operative sugar factory at Chincholirao (Latur), founded by none other than Maharashtra's present chief minister Vilasrao Deshmukh! Another 2,500 tcd Maratha private sugar venture that started crushing from the 2002–3 season is Gurudatt Sugars Private Limited at Shirol in Kolhapur district, belonging to Bhagwanrao Ghatage. There are quite a few other smaller mills that have been commissioned over the last five or six years. Many of them are said to be benami or front-companies of politicians and leaders of existing co-operatives themselves. The exact antecedents of these units – who their real promoters are and whether they suggest an impending transition from co-operative capitalism to its 'pure' form – need to be ascertained to obtain a definitive picture of things to come.

We will next take up some representative case studies of industrialists from the communities of western India.

Case Studies

1. Nirma

Karsanbhai Patel comes from Ruppur village in Chansma taluka of Mehsana, where he was born on 7 January 1944.[63] In contrast to the fertile central and south Gujarat plains, this was an area generally dry and agriculturally underdeveloped till the advent of diesel engines and tubewells in the early 1970s. Karsanbhai was one of six children – two brothers and four sisters – of Khodidas Patel, a ten-acre farmer. 'Irrigation came to us only in 1975. We did not have chemical fertilizers either. Effectively, only a single agricultural season was possible, as double cropping would have depleted soil nutrients. To minimize risks, we used to grow many crops, including jowar, bajra, castor, cotton, mustard and occasionally wheat', recalls Karsanbhai.[64] Being aware that ten acres of rainfed land would not suffice for both sons, Khodidas was keen on their education, having himself passed the seventh standard. Karsanbhai studied up to class five at Ruppur's government school and, from the sixth to the tenth standard in a private institution at Chansma. For his intermediate and graduation he went to Ahmedabad, completing a BSc in chemistry from St Xavier's College in 1966.

While awaiting final year results in college, Karsanbhai got a call from the Kasturbhai Lalbhai group's New Cotton Mills to work as a chemist in their laboratory. After putting in three years, he joined the Gujarat government's geology and mining department as a senior chemist in 1969. It was there that he began a side business of making synthetic detergents after office hours and on weekends. Saturday being a half-day for government helped. 'I would procure the active agents (acid slurry and soda ash) and subsidiary chemicals like Tinopal (sodium tri-polyphosphate, used as a builder to remove water hardness) and CMC (carboxy methyl cellulose, an additive to prevent re-deposition of already removed dirt on the fabric) directly from the market. I used to mix them by hand in a bucket according to a formula of my own and then sieve and pack in polythene bags for sale', says Karsanbhai. The mixing and packing operations were carried out twice a week at a 10 x 12 ft rented space near his home. Initially, Karsanbhai marketed the product door-to-door all by himself on a cycle, but gradually a few relatives joined in. By 1972 the volumes had picked up sufficiently for the budding entrepreneur to quit his secure government job and take up production on a daily basis. A bigger 100-yard built-up site was chosen at an industrial estate in Ahmedabad's Rakhial area, for which Karsanbhai invested around Rs 21,000.

When Karsanbhai embarked on his project, the synthetic detergent industry – which uses petroleum-based surfactants like linear alkyl benzene (LAB) – was at an infant stage in the country. Washing was predominantly done by laundry soaps derived from vegetable oils. There were only two manufacturers of synthetic detergent powder. The Sarabhai group's Swastik Oil Mills was the first to market the 'Det' brand in 1957, followed two years later by Hindustan Lever's (HLL) 'Surf'. For the middle-class housewife there was no disputing the advantages of the new product: clothes could be washed easily after immersing in the powder-sprinkled water for 15-20 minutes, whereas the conventional route entailed overnight soaking and handling messy soap chips that performed poorly in hard water. The flip side was the cost. In 1969 'Surf' retailed at a stiff Rs 15 a kg. Partly, it had to do with the energy-intensive spray drying process employed by manufacturers. In spray drying, the acid slurry (the LAB that is 'sulphonated' by reacting with sulphuric acid) is mechanically blended with soda ash (sodium carbonate) and other additives (tri-polyphosphate, CMC and various fillers) in a turbo-mixer and passed through a homogenizer. The uniform mixture obtained is then sprayed into a current of hot air, due to which the moisture evaporates almost instantaneously and the powder granules fall to the bottom of the chamber.

'My process involved simple dry mixing of the chemicals by hand. There was no dissolving in water and no need for expensive spray-dryers and turbo-mixers. Also, because mine was a concentrate and not a granular powder, it had more detergent value', asserts Karsanbhai. The veracity of these superior quality claims is open to question, but what Karsanbhai certainly did was to introduce a new detergent-manufacturing concept that sought to reconcile modern synthetic chemistry with elemental Gandhian handicraft. And, he priced his product at Rs 2.50 per kg, against Rs 15 for 'Surf'. The ultimate vindication for his strategy came in 1987, when HLL launched 'Wheel', its own version of dry-mix concentrate detergent.

The innovation on the process side was complemented by imaginative marketing techniques and a focused advertising campaign. In 1972 Karsanbhai registered the brand 'Nirma' for the product, named after his second daughter Nirupama, who, fifteen years later, died tragically in a road accident. 'By 1975, I was selling in Gujarat, Rajasthan, Maharashtra and even Uttar Pradesh. Business was growing by 50 per cent every year and that was when I knew I could take on a multinational', he notes. The catchy jingle, *Dudh si safedi Nirma se aaye* (the milk-like whiteness from Nirma), was aired first on radio in 1975 and subsequently on television in 1982. 'I never hired any premier ad agency. For me, what mattered was that my brand and product attributes should be communicated in a straightforward way, so as to register firmly in the consumer's mind. I did not see any need for bluffing or getting superstars to endorse my brand. We did later engage models like Sangeeta Bijlani and Sonali Bendre, but at a time when they were not celebrities. One good thing those days was that there was just one national Doordarshan channel, which made it possible to mount a focused and cost-effective campaign. Today, with so many channels, it is difficult to be sure whether you are striking the right target', he avers.

Having become the market leader by the 1980s, the next major step was backward integration to produce the chemicals used in detergent making. Karsanbhai started by putting up a sulphuric acid plant in 1987–8 at Mandali (Mehsana district). But the real challenge lay in gaining control over the key ingredients, LAB and soda ash. 'I was consuming half of the LAB being produced domestically by Reliance, IPCL, and Tamil Nadu Petroproducts (TNPL). When in the mid-1980s, LAB prices suddenly rose from Rs 16,000 to over Rs 22,000 per tonne, I felt something must be done', he points out. In 1994 Nirma Limited went public to raise funds for its proposed investments. In December 1997 it commissioned a 75,000 tonnes per annum LAB plant costing Rs 630 crore at Alindra in Vadodara. This was followed in August 2000 by a Rs 1,140-crore, 650,000-tonne soda ash unit in Kalatalav, Bhavnagar. That was not all. Going further backwards, the company installed a seawater desalination plant adjoining the soda ash complex to meet the latter's salt and water requirement. In 2001 Nirma also acquired captive limestone quarries on long-term lease. It is now in the process of setting up coke ovens, which would give it control over all the three raw materials for soda ash (limestone, salt and coke). Likewise, the LAB plant is equipped with a 70 km pipeline to the Indian Oil Corporation's (IOC) Vadodara refinery, to enable production from the basic kerosene and normal-paraffin stage.

The most significant thing Karsanbhai's entry has done is that the size of India's synthetic detergent industry, which used to be hardly 10,000 tonnes a year, is now in the region of 2.5 million tonnes. His success has begot scores of regional clones – brands like 'Ghadi', 'Fena', and 'Friendly Wash' – that have adopted similar low-cost production and aggressive marketing techniques. In the process Nirma's market share has fallen, though volume-wise it is still No. 1, having produced 7.66 lakh tonnes of detergent in 2004–5 compared to HLL's 7.08 lakh tonnes.[65] Moreover, Nirma's operations are fully integrated: it is India's second biggest soda ash producer and one of the four companies that makes LAB.[66] 'In the early 1970s synthetic detergents made up less than 20 per cent of our fabric wash market, whereas it would now have crossed 80 per cent. For us, it implies that the earlier explosive growth phase, driven by replacement of laundry soap, is over. We will continue to see volumes go up 3–4 per cent annually, but that would be more from population growth and overall improvement in living standards', adds Karsanbhai.

That realization, in turn, has guided efforts in recent years to extend the 'Nirma' brand to more product categories. It took Nirma sixteen years after its powder first hit the market to come out with a detergent cake. In 1990 the company launched 'Nirma Super' – a spray-dried powder formulation – and two years later forayed into toilet soaps, where it is already in a distant No. 2 position behind HLL.[67] Then, as part of the same 'umbrella branding' strategy of leveraging more bang from the advertising rupee, it started marketing 'Nirma Shudh' salt in 2002, produced from the Bhavnagar chemical complex. With accumulated reserves and surpluses of Rs 1,800 crore and promoters' stake at over 77 per cent – giving the company substantial leeway to mobilize monies from the market – Karsanbhai is now looking at more capital-intensive investment avenues like power and infrastructure.[68] How much of these would actually materialize remains to be seen. In the meantime he has acquired Core Healthcare Limited – the country's leading intravenous fluids manufacturer – from its debt-stricken promoter Sushil Handa, and established a Nirma Education and Research Foundation. The latter runs an engineering college and a management institute in Ahmedabad

2. The Elecon Group

Uttarsanda, near Nadiad, is a typical Patidar-dominated village in the Charotar heartland, which was the epicentre of militant peasant nationalist protests beginning with Kheda in 1918. Ishwarbhai Bhulabhai Patel belonged to this very village and yet seemingly chose to be detached from the ferment of that period. He was Uttarsanda's first graduate, who did his schooling at Nadiad and college at Ahmedabad and Junagarh before moving to Mumbai around World War I. He started his career working on a monthly salary of Rs 50 for Greaves Cotton, then a British-owned company selling oil engines and textile machinery. In 1919 Ishwarbhai floated his own Milling Trading Company (MTC) to import spare parts for flour mills and sugar machinery. Simultaneously, he ventured into real estate with a fellow Patidar by the name of Hirabhai Ashabhai Patel. The two partners bought virtually half of Goregaon, which was totally virgin territory then. Over a period, as this Mumbai suburb was developed with the laying of roads, electric cables and a railway bridge, they made a killing, disposing of the land bit by bit: the existence of an I.B. Patel Road in Goregaon East is an enduring reminder of Ishwarbhai's adroit speculative ways.

Bhanubhai Patel, Ishwarbhai's son, was born on 17 March 1928 and spent his early years at Mumbai, graduating in arts from Ruia College. In 1951 Bhanubhai and his elder brother Shantilal (Shapurji) decided to take a leap into manufacturing. 'We were importing chains for sugar machinery and mills. The same chains could be used as components to make bucket elevators for industrial applications and we just had to do the basic steel work fabrication. So, we began with bucket elevators and screw belt conveyors, and it is these products (ELEvators and CONveyors) that gave our company its name, Elecon', reminisces Bhanubhai.[69] From a workshop in Goregaon making simple conveying equipment used in industrial sites, Elecon Engineering's sales rose steadily to touch around Rs 16 lakh, when it was converted into a private limited company in 1960.

But the real break came after a chance encounter Ishwarbhai had with Hirabhai Muljibhai (H.M.) Patel on a train journey. H.M. Patel was an illustrious civil servant (and father of the present NDDB chairperson Amrita Patel) who also happened to be a Charotar Patidar from Dharmaj in Petlad taluka. H.M. Patel was heading the Gujarat Electricity Board (GEB), having previously served as union finance secretary: a post he resigned in the wake of the Mundhra scandal revelations of 1957.[70] 'During the meeting, my father casually remarked on the labour problems we were facing in Mumbai. There was also a strong anti-Gujarati sentiment (fuelled by the Samyukta Maharashtra movement). It was then that H.M. Patel suggested we move to Gujarat, which, having been constituted as a separate state in May 1960, was keen to attract investments. To facilitate this the GEB had even built a thermal station at Dhuvaran, near Anand, and he assured us that there was plenty of power for which there were few takers', says Bhanubhai.

In 1962 Elecon Engineering transferred its manufacturing

facilities to Vallabh Vidyanagar, a town barely 6 km from Anand on the Vadodara–Ahmedabad highway that was being developed as an industrial hub by the Gujarat government.[71] Elecon was the first major concern to start operations in this area and, very soon, others – including Gujarat Machinery Manufacturers Limited of Ashok Patel – set up shop. For Ishwarbhai, who had by then retired from business, it was a homecoming of sorts. In his new innings as sarpanch (headman) of Uttarsanda, he was actively engaged in building schools, roads, and drainage infrastructure, for which it earned official recognition as a Gokul Gram (ideal village). Elecon meanwhile was undergoing a transition from a two-product company to an integrated manufacturer of bulk material handling equipment. In 1964 it set up a foundry, Prayas Castings Limited, to cater to the castings requirement of Elecon and its surrounding industries. The company also entered into foreign technological collaborations: with Strachen & Henshaw of the UK for manufacturing wagon tipplers (used for discharging materials from rail wagons), and with Weserhutte of Germany for open cast mining conveyors and stacker reclaimers.

The 1960s and 1970s were halcyon days for the public sector, when huge investments went into core sectors like iron and steel, power, coal and lignite mining, fertilizers, and cement. 'It was a good time for us. One of the biggest orders we bagged came after the 1974 oil shock, which forced the government to develop indigenous energy sources. We undertook work worth Rs 25 crore for the Neyveli Lignite Corporation in Tamil Nadu. It was to design, manufacture and erect a 70 km long shiftable conveyor system for their open cast mine, capable of handling up to 20,000 tonnes per hour of materials. This was the largest ever conveying system in the world outside Germany', Bhanubhai proudly recounts. Elecon was now supplying a range of bulk material handling equipment: integrated coal handling plants for power stations, ore crushers, belt conveyors, stackers, reclaimers, idlers and pulleys, wagon tipplers, and ship loaders.

In 1976 the company established a separate gears division. 'Since we were making the machines, it was a natural extension to supply the industrial gearboxes and transmission systems that drive these machines. So we started designing, supplying and servicing various kinds of gearboxes for material handling systems in coal and lignite mines, cement factories and steel, sugar and chemical plants. We also make the gearbox and electric motors used by elevator companies such as Kone, Schindler, and ThyssenKrupp', says Bhanubhai. In gears, too, the initial knowhow was procured from multinationals like Thyssen, though he claims 'we have absorbed and mastered all the technologies that we sourced'. In fact, gears today contribute well over 65 per cent to Elecon's top line and the company is India's foremost manufacturer of industrial gears. 'We have even delivered customized gearboxes for the satellites in our space programme and for strategic users like the Indian navy and the coast guard, who require powerful and yet low-noise transmission systems for effective patrolling', he adds.

Yet it was not always smooth sailing. Unlike companies hawking detergents or milk – which have a steady demand and business is more about rival brands vying for the housewife's attention – Elecon has been in a segment particularly vulnerable to the vagaries of the business cycle. Its customers being industrial buyers, Elecon's fortunes have waxed and waned depending upon investments taking place in core sectors from coal, iron, and steel to fertilizers, steel, and cement. 'We had a torrid time after the balance of payments crisis of 1991, when the government under the International Monetary Fund's (IMF) advice had to reduce deficits and it chose the easy route of slashing capital spending by state undertakings. The company was affected very badly', confesses Bhanubhai. Elecon had to shed a lot of its workforce and adopt all-round cost-cutting measures. But over the last couple of years, with India in the midst of a manufacturing investment boom, the going has been good. The Elecon group – also including Eimco Elecon India (a joint venture with Sandvik AB for making underground mining and tunnelling equipment, in which the Swedish partner holds 25.1 per cent) and Power Build Limited (which makes geared motors) – posted a turnover of over Rs 500 crore in 2004–5 and looks set for double-digit growth every year – till the next recession strikes.[72]

3. The Warana and Rajarambapu Co-operative Groups[73]

In the early nineteenth century the Utopian Socialist Robert Owen stirred Continental Europe's imagination with his New Lanark model industrial complex and Villages of Co-operation that envisaged self-sustaining communes of people working together on farm and in factory. Warananagar in Panhala taluka of Kolhapur may not be a beautifully restored Scottish World Heritage Site that New Lanark is today; nor is its architect Vishwanath Vilasrao Kore as celebrated worldwide the way Robert Owen is. Yet in design and essence Warananagar is very much what Owen would have aspired for, though in his lifetime not a single Village of Cooperation fructified, as the lure of acquisitiveness proved too powerful for the bond of romantic idealism. The New Lanark experiment was more successful, but by 1828 Owen had sold his entire stake in the mills because of growing friction with other wealthy philanthropist co-owners.

A visitor to Warananagar – which lies 10 km off the national highway at a point about 20 km from Kolhapur city – is led to a two-storey administrative building that is a mini-replica of New Delhi's Parliament House, with its circular structure, open corridors, stone pillars, and all that. Around this building, within a radius of 5 km, is a thriving network of co-operative institutions with a combined annual turnover exceeding Rs 800 crore. They include a sugar mill-cum-distillery (Rs 290 crore sales in 2004–5), a dairy (Rs 200 crore), a bank (Rs 223 crore of deposits as on 31 March 2005), a co-operative bazaar (with 42 branches and total sales of Rs 61 crore in 2004–5) and an education complex (comprising both Marathi- and English-medium pre-primary to high schools; an arts, science and commerce college; an industrial training institute; a pharmacy college and an engineering college). In addition there is the Warana Agricultural Goods Processing Cooperative Society or WAGPCOS (which exports mango, banana, and guava pulp and purees), a paper plant (that uses the bagasse from the sugar mill), a jute factory (that weaves gunny sacks for bagging sugar), a poultry society, a women's credit co-operative (deposits of Rs 20 crore), a Bhagini Mandal (where women undertake home-based production of papads and other edible items marketed through the Warana bazaar chain), a 200-bed Mahatma Gandhi Hospital, and a printing press. As if these were not enough, Warana also has a Wyayam Mandir (a centre for traditional wrestling and body-building), a military academy (a school imparting army training and 'love for the motherland') and a children's orchestra that performs every evening and has been showcased before elite audiences in India as well as abroad. Indeed, this is one place that, in Jawaharlal Nehru's dreams, has been 'convulsed by co-operatives'.

The man behind all this – Vishwanath Kore or 'Tatyasaheb' in popular reference – was strikingly enough not a Maratha, despite belonging to a land overwhelmingly Maratha. Born on 17 October 1914, he was from a Lingayat family which, apart from owning nearly 100 acres of land, had wholesale trading interests in grain, gur and cloth at Kolhapur.[74] Tatyasaheb was initiated into public life in 1935, when he joined the local village co-operative marketing society. Five years later he was elected president of the Kodoli municipality, of which Warananagar is a part. Tatyasaheb also participated in the

Quit India movement of 1942, which brought him close to leaders such as Y.B. Chavan and Vasantdada Patil. But for all that, he did not nurse overt political ambitions or use co-operatives to build a political power base, as the majority of Maratha sugar barons did. The story goes that when Y.B. Chavan was requisitioned by the centre as defence minister after the 1962 China war and asked to suggest a suitable replacement as CM of Maharashtra, he named Tatyasaheb. The latter, true to style, promptly refused, citing his inability to leave the precincts of Warana. It is the same incorruptible image that provided legitimacy for his leadership of its co-operatives, despite repeated takeover attempts mounted by the local Maratha legislator from Panhala, Yashwant Eknath Patil, allegedly through cynical exploitation of caste feelings.

The idea to start a sugar mill came after a crash in gur prices in 1951. Finding it unremunerative to manufacture gur, farmers took recourse to burning their standing cane crop. The commissioning of the Pravara factory at Ahmednagar inspired Tatyasaheb to mobilise growers in Kodoli towards establishing a similar co-operative mill. The Warana Co-operative Sugar Factory was registered on 27 September 1955 and commenced crushing from 1 November 1957. That was the spark for other institutions in Warana: the poultry society in 1963, the co-operative bank in 1966, the dairy in 1968, the Bhagini Mandal in 1974, the consumer co-operative in 1976, the paper plant in 1981–2, the engineering college in 1983, WAPCOS in 1987, and the women's credit society in 1989–90.

After Tatyasaheb's passing away on 13 December 1994, the reins of the empire were handed over to his son Vilasrao Kore. The latter, however, died barely four months later, on 5 April 1995. He was succeeded by Tatyasaheb's wife, Savitri 'Akka' (elder sister) Kore, who headed the sugar factory till she died on 28 March 2002. The Warana co-operative complex is presently identified with Vilasrao's younger son Vinay 'Savkar' (everybody's friend) Kore, who was first inducted into the mill's board in 1994. Unlike Tatyasaheb the new generation has not shown any marked aversion to politics. In 1995 Vilasrao's elder son Nipun Kore unsuccessfully contested the assembly elections as an independent from Panhala. Four years later Nipun's brother fought from the same seat and won, ending Yashwant Eknath Patil's unbroken 25-year reign. Vinay Kore repeated his success in 2004, after which he was made minister of horticulture and non-conventional energy in the Maharashtra government. In his short political career, Vinay Kore has displayed uncanny flexibility, oscillating from Sharad Pawar's Nationalist Congress Party (NCP) to the Shiv Sena and then back, before forming his own Jana Surajya Shakthi (JSS) party in 2004.

Some 30 km from Warananagar in Sangli's Walwa taluka is an equally large co-operative combine founded by a Maratha, Rajaram Anant Patil. A lawyer by training, 'Rajarambapu' (born on 1 August 1920) was 25 when he set up the Azad Vidyalaya school in his native village of Kasegaon. It was the seed for the Kasegaon Education Society, which now runs thirty-nine schools and colleges in and around Sangli, including the Rajarambapu Institute of Technology. Rajarambapu's first full-fledged co-operative venture, however, came in 1969 when he was the industries minister of Maharashtra. Today, besides education, his group's business straddles sugar and alcohol (net sales of Rs 210 crore in 2004–5), dairy (Rs 90 crore), and a co-operative bank (Rs 343 crore deposits as on 31 March 2005). After Rajarambapu died on 17 January 1984 his son, Jayant Patil, a civil engineer from Mumbai's VJT Institute, has spearheaded the group's diversification into new activities. The first of these is a solvent extraction-cum-refining unit, established in 1982 to process soybean grown by farmers in the region. This was interestingly promoted as a private limited company, Rajaram Solvex (annual sales of Rs 80 crore), with 4,000-odd farmer-shareholders and headed by Jayant's brother Bhagat Patil. The second is a textile complex spread over 70 acres in Walwa, consisting of a co-operative spinning mill and separate concerns for weaving, knitting, fabric processing, and garmenting (aggregate turnover of Rs 150 crore). Jayant Patil, like his father, has been a legislator from Walwa since 1990 and is currently Maharashtra's finance and planning minister.

While both the Warana and Rajarambapu co-operatives are effectively dynastic family businesses, they also happen to be fairly vibrant organizations responsible to their farmer-members. During the 2004–5 season (October–September), their sugar mills paid a cane price of Rs 1,350 per tonne, which is much higher than the statutory minimum price (SMP) of Rs 1,050 per tonne fixed by the government. If one includes the cost of harvesting and transport from the field to the factory (Rs 180 per tonne, which, in Maharashtra, is borne by the mills and not the farmers), the difference works out to almost Rs 500 per tonne or 45 per cent.[75] The two co-operatives have also implemented lift irrigation schemes on the Warana and Krishna rivers, by constructing pump houses on their banks and conveying this 'lifted' water to the command area. The Rajarambapu co-operative alone has thirty-one schemes across 30,000 acres, involving an investment of Rs 40 crore, in which the factory has put in Rs 12 crore and provided bank guarantees for the remaining sums borrowed by the farmers. The Warana factory, too, has sixty-five such schemes, each covering a couple of hundred growers.

These measures have led to a significant expansion in cane area and crushing capacities. The Rajarambapu factory began with a capacity of 1,250 tcd, which has since gone up to 4,000 tcd. During the 2002–3 season a second 2,500 tcd mill was commissioned, taking the co-operative's aggregate cane crushing capacity to 6,500 tcd. Similarly, the Warana plant's capacity has grown over the years from 1,000 tcd to 7,000 tcd. Recently, it has acquired, on a five-year lease, the 2,500 tcd Jarandeshwar factory at Koregaon (Satara district), promoted by Vasantdada Patil's wife Shalinitai. The dairies have also flourished: Warana procures 3.5 lakh litres of milk every day, while the Rajarambapu union does about 2 lakh litres and both have strong regional brands ('Warana' and 'Krishna'). Warana has even gone to the extent of installing computer kiosks in the seventy villages of its command area and connecting these through a wireless network to its main administrative office and business centres. This project – an initiative of Vinay Kore – has again benefited farmers who no longer have to come to the factory to know the exact date when labourers would be sent to harvest their cane, whether payments have been credited to their individual account, the balance amount due on their tractor loans, and so on.

8

The Paradox of Northern Farming Communities

In terms of sheer quantum of physical purchases and scale of commodity movement and storage, the operations of the Food Corporation of India (FCI) are perhaps without parallel anywhere in the world. The public sector behemoth organizes procurement of about 40 million tonnes (mt) of wheat and rice every year, or close to a fifth of the country's aggregate foodgrain output.[1] Much of this is concentrated over short time spans, calling for an enormous deployment of financial and logistical resources. The bulk of wheat, for instance, is bought between mid April and the first week of May. At its peak, daily purchases touch 1 mt or more, the equivalent of 1 lakh trucks or 435 rail rakes of 2,300 tonnes each. Payments are made within 72 hours and the grain that is procured and loaded into 50 kg jute bags travels an average distance of 1,500 km. Financing these operations is in itself big business, involving an annual working capital outlay of Rs 30,000 crore, met through a consortium of 61 banks.[2]

Jatland Capitalists

At the hub of all this activity are Punjab and Haryana, which together account for less than 2.9 per cent of India's geographical area and 4.4 per cent of its population, and yet contribute over 60 per cent of the foodgrains procured by FCI.[3] If the description 'capitalist farmers' applies more to anyone in the country, it is to their agriculturists, who are overwhelmingly Jat: Sikhs in Punjab, and Hindus in Haryana. Jat Sikhs make up an estimated 90 per cent of Punjab's farmer population; the rest comprising assorted communities like the Sainis, Kambohs, and Labanas. About half of Haryana's peasantry is similarly reckoned to be Jat, followed by Ahirs (Yadavs), Bishnois, and Gujjars.[4]

What is it that makes these farmers, or at least a section within them, belong to a class of capitalist farmers?[5] For one, they are – just as the Kammas in Andhra or the Patidars of rural Gujarat – commercial in orientation, producing principally for the market. Roughly 60 per cent of the wheat output of the two states is sold to the FCI alone, with the corresponding ratio for rice ranging from 50 per cent in Haryana to nearly 90 per cent in Punjab.[6] While foodgrains may be subsistence cereals for a large chunk of Indian farmers, in this case they are primarily cash crops.

Secondly, capitalist farmers are highly responsive to technical innovations and improved agricultural practices. This is manifest in the adoption of high yielding varieties (HYV), fertilizers, crop protection chemicals, and modern farm machinery. In the process the emphasis shifts from conventional low-input, risk-minimizing farming to yield and profit-maximizing 'agri-business', sustained by a regular absorption of new scientific knowledge. The agriculturists of the two states have been trailblazers in this regard, with practically their entire cropped area coming under HYVs. Per hectare fertilizer consumption, at 184 kgs for Punjab and 167 kgs for Haryana, is the highest among all states and way above the national average of 89.8 kgs.[7] And since 98 per cent of the gross cultivated area in Punjab and 86 per cent in Haryana is irrigated (the corresponding all-India figure is 40 per cent), it is possible to raise at least two crops a year.

On the mechanization front, every fifth tractor in the country today is operated by a farmer in Punjab or Haryana.[8] However, mechanization is not simply about using tractor-driven disc harrows and seed-cum-fertilizer drills for seed bed preparation and planting, or employing diesel engines and electrified tubewells for watering the fields. The real revolution in recent years has been in the realm of harvesting. In the old days, crops were harvested using sickles, after which threshing was done by bullock-drawn phalas (frames) treading out the grain from the bruised straw. This was followed by manual winnowing using pitchforks. Towards the 1970s the phala and pitchfork gave way to power threshers, which, in conjunction with sickle harvesting, helped bring down the average labour/animal requirement per hectare from 37 man-days and 14.2 animal-days to 30.9 man-days for wheat.[9] The bullock was, thus, done away with even at the post-harvesting stage. From the 1980s came harvester combines, which made threshers redundant as well. With combines, the produce of one hectare can be harvested, threshed, and cleaned – all at one go – in just about an hour, as against twelve hours using threshers or three to four days in the traditional system. One study for 2002–3 found around 82 per cent of paddy and over 72 per cent of the wheat grown in Punjab to be combine-harvested.[10] It is this technology that has reduced the marketing season for foodgrains to a bare month-long affair, unlike in the past, when the harvesting of wheat often extended to mid July and a good part of the standing crop suffered damage from the monsoon rains.

The third distinguishing characteristic of capitalist farmers is that they are self-cultivators, as opposed to the class of feudal zamindar landlords. The latter is a rentier – an absentee city dweller or bangladhari, who leases out his land to tenants. The capitalist farmer, on the other hand, is either a haldhari, who directly ploughs his field employing family and hired labour, or a chathadhari, who organizes the supply of labour and other inputs and usually supervises agricultural operations on the edge of his field holding an umbrella.[11] He is a hands-on manager who, rather than leasing out his land, tends to lease in additional land for self-cultivation. To the extent that they conform to the above attributes, the predominantly Jat cultivators of Punjab and Haryana – definitely sections among them – are very much the sort of capitalist farmers we encountered in coastal Andhra, Kongunad, and mainland Gujarat. It is these agriculturists who have been prime beneficiaries of the state-assisted diffusion of modern farming technologies since the mid 1960s. As the table below shows, while the country's foodgrain production has nearly doubled since 1970–1, it has trebled in the case of Punjab and Haryana. If we were to also include the Hindu Jats of western Uttar Pradesh (UP) and their Sikh counterparts who have 'colonized' the irrigated tracts of northern Rajasthan (mainly Ganganagar and Hanumangarh) and the Tarai area of Uttarakhand, the result is a geographically contiguous, extended 'Jatland' territory. It is this belt that has been the cradle of India's Green Revolution.

Foodgrains Output and Yields: Punjab, Haryana, and All-India

Year		Rice		Wheat		Foodgrains	
		Output	Yield	Output	Yield	Output	Yield
1970–1	Punjab	0.69	1764	5.14	2238	7.31	1860
	Haryana	0.46	1710	2.34	2074	4.75	1235
	All-India	42.22	1123	23.83	1307	108.42	872
2003–4	Punjab	9.66	3694	14.49	4207	24.73	3929
	Haryana	2.79	2749	9.13	3966	13.22	3085
	All-India	88.28	2077	72.11	2713	213.46	1731

Note: Output is in million tonnes; yield is in kgs per hectare.

Prior Legacy

The ascendancy of the Jats, however, pre-dates the Green Revolution. Even prior to Independence, undivided (pre-Partition) Punjab was home to a vibrant class of independent peasant-proprietors. In 1937 the Institute of Agrarian Reforms at Lahore estimated that more than half of the cultivated area in the province was tilled by the proprietors themselves. The cultivating owners in Punjab, at 17.07 lakh, outnumbered the tenant-cultivator population of 11.28 lakh. This was in marked contrast to the United Provinces (now UP) and Bihar–Orissa, where tenant-cultivator numbers, at 84.33 lakh and 61.29 lakh, far exceeded cultivating owners, at 10.91 lakh and 2.91 lakh, respectively.[12]

The comparatively low prevalence of tenancy relations and preponderance of peasant-proprietors was not only crucial in forging a distinct Jat identity,[13] but also found expression in the word zamindar in Punjab being used interchangeably with khudkasht or self-cultivator. This was emphasized by prominent community leaders such as Sir Chhotu Ram (1881–1945), who, in the *Jat Gazette* of 22 March 1935, noted: 'In some provinces zamindars are different from peasants. But in the Punjab the two are synonymous. Here the agriculturist who has proprietary rights in land is the one who actually ploughs it.'[14] The notion of the Jat's attachment to his land got official stamp of approval through the Punjab Land Alienation and Preemption Act of 1901, which classified the province's various castes and tribes into 'agriculturists' and 'non-agriculturists'. The latter were legally barred from owning or buying farmland, the ostensible purpose being to save the peasantry from expropriation by the moneylender and the Bania.

For the British the Jat represented 'the flower of Indian agriculture',[15] fulfilling the strategic role of supplying food and cash crops and generating land revenue for the treasury. Having apparently learnt from their past mistakes – notably the Permanent Settlement of Bengal in 1793 that created a parasitical breed of absentee landlords – the authorities were keen not to repeat them in a province annexed relatively late, in 1849. Thus, even while an intermediary feudal aristocracy was propped up, it was never at the cost of Punjab's proprietary cultivators.[16] On the contrary, colonial policy sought to strengthen this stratum through protective legislations like the Land Alienation Act and virtually 'manufacture' a class of progressive capitalist farmers out of them. The highpoint of these efforts was the 'canal colonies' of West Punjab (now part of Pakistan) that came up some thirty years after Arthur Cotton's grand anicuts on the Krishna and Godavari.

The colonies – mainly in Lyallpur, Sargodha (Shahpur), Montgomery, and Multan – brought over 10 million acres of flat, sandy loam plains under irrigation through a canal network linking the Jhelum, Chenab, and Ravi rivers. Simultaneously, an extensive rail and road infrastructure, previously non-existent, was laid.[17] The canal colonies (also known as the Bars) were India's bread basket before Independence; but apart from that they were an extraordinary exercise in social engineering. At their core were the 'colonists': largely peasants and yeomen farmers, carefully selected from among the more 'hardworking' and 'thrifty' castes and given individual holdings from half a square to five squares of 27.7 acres each.[18] The majority were Jat Sikhs from Amritsar, Ludhiana, Jalandhar, Hoshiarpur, and Gurdaspur. In the words of Malcolm Darling: 'Grit, skill in farming, and a fine physique are characteristics common to all, and in his new environment the Jat Sikh has reached a point of development probably beyond anything else of the kind in India. In less than a generation he has made the wilderness blossom like the rose. It is as if the energy of the virgin soil of the Bar had passed on to his veins and made him almost a part of the forces of nature which he has conquered.'[19]

The colonies, the first of which came up in 1885, were also a learning ground for refined agronomic practices and the introduction of farm machinery. Early experiments in the use of steam tractors, for example, were conducted in 1914 by Sardar Jogendra Singh, who was specially allotted 2,000 acres in Montgomery for this purpose.[20] The establishment of the Government Agricultural College and Research Institute at Lyallpur in 1907 was another important landmark, for it was there that Chaudhary Ram Dhan Singh, a Jat from Rohtak in present-day Haryana, bred his famous 'C-518' and 'C-519' wheats. These strains, released in the 1930s, were cultivated over wide areas in northern India and even crossed national frontiers into Canada and Mexico.[21] The canal colony model was later extended to the sand dunes of Ganganagar during the 1920s and the marshlands of the Tarai in the 1950s. The 'colonists' there, too, were the redoubtable Jat Sikhs. Today, Ganganagar and its adjoining districts irrigated by the massive Rajasthan Canal project produce much of the state's wheat and cotton.

Besides being the mainstay of its agrarian regime, the Jats formed the vanguard of the imperial army. About half of the British Indian army was recruited from the Punjab, earning its people the sobriquet 'martial races of India'.[22] A memorandum submitted by the All-India Jat Mahasabha to Michael O'Dwyer, lieutenant governor of Punjab, on 8 November 1916, stated: 'The Mutiny of 1857 marks the starting point at which the loyalty of our tribe came into prominent notice. During those dark days the Jats... maintained an attitude of singular loyalty to the Government. They not only refrained from taking part in the revolt, but... stood as a community by the side of the authorities... They promptly joined in large numbers the fresh levies which had to be raised to suppress the mutineers. The 14th Jat Lancers was raised wholly in 1857.'[23] In similar vein Chhotu Ram wrote: 'There is no doubt about my loyalty and my sense of duty. During the war I was your sepoy. In times of peace I was your paid servant. I fought in France, in Flanders, in Gallipoli, Egypt, Mesopotamia, China, Afghanistan, Abyssinia and South Africa... I turned the land red with my blood wherever I fought. When the war stopped I put the sword away and picked up the sickle and the blade. I filled the government's treasury with my earnings and produce.'[24]

The point to note is that at the dawn of Independence the Jats – more so the Sikhs – had arrived economically, socially, and politically as an upwardly mobile and assertive community of progressive peasant-proprietors. The post-Partition events, leading to the biggest ever land resettlement operation in history and culminating in the Green Revolution, merely reinforced this position. Partition forced Sikh-Hindu landholders in West Punjab to vacate an estimated 2.7 million hectares, against which there were only 1.9 million hectares in the Indian side abandoned by their Muslim counterparts. This gap – magnified by the loss of the canal colonies – made it impossible to fully compensate the returning émigrés for the lands left behind by them.[25] But the upside was that it presented an opportunity for land reforms and re-planning the countryside through consolidation of the hitherto fragmented holdings. The same canal colony farmer who had perfected his art in Montgomery and Lyallpur became the catalyst for agricultural modernization in Indian Punjab. Even when there was less land available, this was more than offset by the allotment of new holdings on a consolidated basis rather than those fragmented into five or ten bits. The scheme of compulsory aggregation of tiny scattered plots into compact blocks made investments in tractors and farm machinery viable. 'In 1950, Punjab had no tube-wells, but in 1978 it had 570,000 of them . . . Increase in agricultural production due to consolidation alone without any change in techniques was reported to be about 25 per cent.'[26] By the late 1960s the entire cultivable land in Punjab, Haryana, and western UP had been consolidated, rendering the area 'ready' for the Green Revolution and fortifying the hegemony of the self-cultivating middle peasant.

The bifurcation of Punjab and the creation of a separate province, Haryana, in November 1966 provided further impetus to this process, as the Jats became the dominant community in both states – to the detriment of the urban Hindu and Sikh petty bourgeoisie.[27] A reflection of this is that in the initial years after Independence, from 15 August 1947 to 23 January 1956, the chief ministers of Punjab were Brahmin (Gopichand Bhargava) or Khatri (Bhim Sen Sachar). Since then – barring a brief period between 21 June 1964 and 5 July 1966 – all its CMs, from Pratap Singh Kairon to Captain Amarinder Singh and now Parkash Singh Badal, have been Sikhs. And within them, the sole non-Jat was Zail Singh, a Ramgarhia, who held office from 17 March 1972 to 30 April 1977. Similarly, in Haryana, except for Bhagwat Dayal Sharma and Banarsi Das Gupta, whose combined tenure lasted two years, all the CMs have been Jat (Bansi Lal, Devi Lal, Om Prakash Chautala, Hukam Singh, Bhupinder Singh Hooda), Bishnoi (Bhajan Lal), or Ahir (Rao Birendra Singh).

The agrarian transformation achieved in the main 'Jatland' territory has been subsequently replicated in the rest of the Indo-Gangetic plain and even the mustard-soybean growing regions of southern Rajasthan and western Madhya Pradesh (MP) – albeit with differing degrees of success. The main communities to have gained from the abolition of zamindari and the spread of irrigation and Green Revolution technologies to these areas are the Yadavs, Kurmis, and Koeris.[28] The empowerment of these communities is exemplified by the rise of a host of provincial politicians within their ranks from the late 1970s, reaching its apogee in August 1990, when the V.P. Singh government at the centre accepted the Mandal Commission's recommendation to reserve 27 per cent of all government jobs for Other Backward Classes (OBCs). A tradition that began with Chhotu Ram co-founding the National Unionist Party in 1923 and carried forward by Charan Singh in western UP and Baldev Ram Mirdha in Rajasthan in later decades, became a generalized northern phenomenon by the end of the century through Devi Lal, Parkash Singh Badal, and the post-Lohia socialist formations of Lalu Prasad, Mulayam Singh Yadav, and Nitish Kumar.

The Incomplete Transition from Agriculture to Industry

But for all their exploits in the countryside and storming the corridors of power, the northern farming communities have not managed to leverage this clout to make the transition from prosperous agriculturists to successful businessmen-industrialists. Instances of them doing a Kamma, Naidu, Gounder, Maratha, or Patidar are few and far between.

Take the Jat Sikhs, arguably the most 'capitalist' among Indian farmers. The pre-eminent Sikh industrialists – Bhai Mohan

Singh of Ranbaxy, Raunaq Singh of Apollo Tyres, and Charanjit Singh (owner of Delhi's Le Meridien hotel and the erstwhile 'Campa' brand of soft drinks) – have been Khatris or Aroras. The contradiction between country and town is equally pronounced when one looks at Ludhiana, Punjab's industrial capital. Its bicycle majors – the Munjals of the Hero group, the Pahwas of Avon, or for that matter, the Kapurs of Atlas Cycles who manufacture out of Sonepat in Haryana – are all Khatri-Aroras. So are cycle tyres and tubes producers such as Mann Singh Chabra of Metro Tyres, O.P. Pahwa of Ralson India, and B.C. Maini of Hindustan Cycles & Tubes. The city's textile and woollen hosiery industry is completely Bania-Marwari dominated, whether it is the entrenched Oswal families or new-generation entrepreneurs like the terry-towel maker Rajinder Gupta of Abhishek Industries and Komal Kumar Jain of Duke (the country's largest selling T-shirt brand). The only substantial Jat Sikh industrialist of Ludhiana is Inder Mohan Singh Grewal of Upper India Steel, which manufactures special and alloy steels. However, its main competitors in the state – Shiv Parshad Mittal's Aarti Steels at Ludhiana and Amarjit Goyal's Modern Steels in nearby Mandi Gobindgarh – are bigger Bania outfits. Amarjit Goyal is also the promoter of Modern Dairies at Karnal. What is true of Ludhiana holds for the rest of Punjab as well. Kapurthala's best-known units are JCT and Jagatjit Industries Limited (JIL). Both are products of the 1940s that came up under the patronage of Jagatjit Singh, the ruler of Kapurthala. JCT is part of the M.M. Thapar group (Khatri). JIL, the flagship concern of the L.P. Jaiswal group (Bania), manufactures the 'Aristocrat' and 'Bonnie Scot' liquor range. It used to also control the malt beverage brands 'Viva' and 'Maltova' before they were sold to the British multinational GlaxoSmithKline in 2000. The Jaiswal family further owns Milkfood Limited, which has a dairy at Bahadurgarh in Patiala. The Khatri and Bania communities, simply put, exercise near-monopoly over big business in Punjab, with the presence of Jat Sikhs inversely proportional to their dominance in agriculture.

This is not to say there has been no engagement of Jat Sikhs with industry. On the contrary, it must be said that the community did have a fair share of businessmen at least in the initial part of the last century and well before the onset of the Green Revolution. Sir Sunder Singh Majithia is credited with establishing the first ever Indian-owned sugar mill in 1911 at Sardarnagar (Gorakhpur) in UP. All factories before this were controlled by British managing agency firms like Parrys, Begg Sutherland, and James Finlay & Company. The Majithias were landed aristocrats from Majitha village in Amritsar. Sunder Singh's father, Sardar Surat Singh Majithia, was a British loyalist who, for his services during the sepoy mutiny of 1857, was granted the Dumri estate in Gorakhpur which that the authorities confiscated from land-owning rebels. The family cultivated a 1,672 acre-farm on this estate, of which 738 acres were earmarked for sugarcane in 1936–7.[29] Their Saraya Sugar Mills had a capacity of 2,000 tcd – against the then prevailing standard of 400–500 tcd – making it the country's largest factory at that point in time.

The other celebrated Majithia was Sardar Dyal Singh (1848–98). A jagirdar who diversified into real estate and trade in diamonds and precious stones, Dyal Singh Majithia founded *The Tribune* in 1880, around the same period as *The Hindu* in Madras, *Amrit Bazar Patrika* in Calcutta, and *Kesari* in Pune. He was a liberal, profoundly influenced by the Brahmo Samaj, reflected perhaps in the fact that all the editors of *The Tribune* till 1945 were from Bengal![30] Dyal Singh was also the driving force behind the setting up of the Punjab National Bank in 1894, in which he held 25 per cent of the initial shares and remained its chairman till his death. In his will, Dyal Singh Majithia bequeathed assets worth Rs 30 lakh – including properties at Lahore, Karachi, and Amritsar – to

The Tribune and two others trusts for starting a college and library. All these testify to a pretty lucrative business career.

The lead given by the Majithias was emulated by others. The Simbhaoli Sugar Mills in Ghaziabad district (UP) was founded in 1933 by Raghbir Singh Sandhanwala from the ruling family of Rajasansi: the estate on which the Amritsar airport currently stands. Another Jat Sikh who joined the sugar bandwagon in the 1930s – the stimulus for which was the clamping of a 185 per cent duty on Javanese sugar in 1932[31] – was Sardar Bahadur Ranjit Singh of Akoi village in Sangrur. He promoted the Rai Bahadur Narain Singh Sugar Mills at Laksar (Hardwar) in 1932 and was a member of the constituent assembly that drafted India's constitution. The Laksar factory was named after his father, a contractor in Lutyens' Delhi, who constructed the magnificent parliament building. Narain Singh was also one of the main developers of the Connaught Place area in the 1920s, along with the writer Khushwant Singh's father Sir Sobha Singh (a Khatri Sikh).

But the most successful of all Jat Sikh industrialists, who transcended sugar and real estate, was Indra Singh. Coming from Dumna village in Ropar, where his family held large landed properties, Indra Singh gave up a railway engineer's job in the Central Provinces (now MP) to become a contractor and shift to Jamshedpur on the eve of World War II. That was the time when the Tatas were keen on developing a cluster of user industries in the vicinity of their steel plant. With their encouragement Indra Singh took over two struggling units in 1939 – Indian Steel & Wire Products (ISWP) and Jamshedpur Engineering & Machine Manufacturing Company – which grew to be flourishing concerns. ISWP was a manufacturer of rods, galvanized and barbed wires, nails, bolts, rivets, and like products; the latter produced castings for jute mills. The huge profits made during the War enabled Indra Singh to purchase two cotton mills in Jalgaon (Maharashtra) and

Madras, besides a cement company at Sylhet (now in Bangladesh). During the 1950s his group bought a majority stake in the Metal Corporation of India and also acquired interests in road transport, collieries, and insurance.[32] In its heyday the Indra Singh group figured among the top industrial houses of the country. The Monopolies Inquiry Commission of 1965 ranked it thirty-fifth in the list of seventy-five premier houses, with group assets of Rs 1,940 lakh and a turnover of Rs 777 lakhs. A subsequent report of the Industrial Licensing Policy Inquiry Committee in 1969 likewise ranked it thirty-third out of seventy-three.[33] Indra Singh's son was the high profile Sikh politician Baldev Singh, who became Independent India's first defence minister (and, for some strange reason, a reference point in old 'Sardarji jokes').

From the above we can discern two broad strands common to the early Jat Sikh businessmen. The first is that, except for Dyal Singh Majithia, their operations were outside Punjab. Two, they were mostly from the princely order or the landed gentry, who received titles, jagirs, and even mill licences in exchange for support to the empire. Theirs was an exclusive club of members, often linked through kinship ties that hardly admitted ordinary farmers-turned-entrepreneurs – unlike what we saw in the southern and western peasant communities. To illustrate, Raghbir Sandhanwala's son, Major Harinder Singh (a former revenue minister of Punjab), was married to Bhajan Kaur, whose mother was the daughter of Sir Sunder Singh Majithia. One of Harinder Singh's daughters, Jasjit Kaur, is the wife of the present chairman of Simbhaoli Sugar, Gurmit Singh Mann, who happens to be the grandson of Kripal Singh Majithia (son of Sir Sunder Singh). Further, the deputy managing director of Simbhaoli, Gurpal Singh (son of another daughter of Harinder Singh, Yadvinder Kaur) is married to the niece of the former Punjab CM, Captain Amarinder Singh, who is a scion of the Patiala dynasty.[34]

Furthermore, not all these groups have consolidated their head start or even survived, let alone becoming forerunners to the large-scale entry of Jat Sikhs into industry. The House of Indra Singh has ceased to exist; its ailing flagship, ISWP, was in 2003–4 acquired by Tata Steel. The Majithias are a spent force. The Saraya factory has crushed little cane in recent seasons and only its distillery is chugging along by producing country liquor. The only company to have shown some dynamism is Simbhaoli,[35] which, with a 20,000 tcd capacity, is UP's eighth largest sugar producer after Shishir Bajaj's Bajaj Hindusthan, K.N. Saraogi's Balrampur Chini, Dhruv Sawhney's Triveni Engineering, the K.K. Birla group, Vijay Goel's Dhampur Sugar, Ajay Shriram's DCM Shriram Consolidated, and Siddharth Shriram's Mawana Sugars. The latter are all Bania–Marwari owned, barring Triveni (Khatri). The Laksar sugar mill, now under Hardev Singh Akoi, is a middle-rung player. The Akois also manage the classy Imperial Hotel in Delhi, though the family cannot be said to be what it was during the heady days of Rai Bahadur Narain Singh.

The position is worse with respect to non-Sikh Jats and other northern agrarian communities. There are just a handful of Hindu Jat industrialists whom we can name: the real estate king, Kushal Pal Singh of DLF (see separate case study), the beleaguered Rita Singh of the Mesco group, and M.P. Singh of Venus Sugar with a modest 3,500 tcd plant at Majhawali in Moradabad (UP). Before them, there was Seth Chhaju Ram (1861–1943), a Haryanvi Jat from Alakhpura village in Bhiwani who went to Kolkata in the 1880s and initially kept accounts and drafted letters for Marwari businessmen. By the turn of the century Chhaju Ram was himself trading heavily in jute and company stocks, ending up as the biggest shareholder in twenty-four companies. These included ten of Andrew Yule, for whom he was the chief authorized jute broker. Chhaju Ram is supposed to have helped G.D. Birla establish his jute mill in 1919, in which he was a director. But unlike a Birla, a Sarupchand Hukumchand, or a Surajmull Nagarmull, the Jat Seth never promoted his own mill. While living in Calcutta – where he owned twenty-one mansions in Alipur and Burrabazar – Chhaju Ram maintained links with his clansmen, setting up Jat schools in Rohtak and Hissar and financing the activities of Chhotu Ram and the Jat Mahasabha. Also, in Hissar, he 'purchased five villages, i.e Sheikhpura, Moth, Kumhar-Ki-Dhani, Jamni and Kagsar'.[36] The business ventures established by this jute magnate-philanthropist unfortunately did not outlive him. None of Chhaju Ram's eight children – five of them died before him – took over from where he left off.

Rita Singh, on her part, began with a small dairy and khandsari (cottage sugar) unit at Hapur near Delhi, before getting into the export of leather garments. Her meteoric rise was in the early 1990s when the Mesco group forayed into footwear retailing, aviation, shipping, and putting up a pig iron plant and integrated steel complex in Orissa. The projected investments of around Rs 3,500 crore – for which funds were raised from the public and financial institutions – did not fructify, partly because of the prolonged recession plaguing the economy in the mid 1990s. In the process the Mesco empire went bust and Rita Singh herself landed behind bars on charges of defrauding the institutions and issuing fake company shares. To compound her woes, she fought and lost the 1996 parliament elections on a Congress ticket from Hapur.

Among non-Jats the only significant business enterprise is the Rs 400 crore VRS Foods, which sells milk products under the 'Paras' brand and is India's leading exporter of edible casein. The company's Ghaziabad dairy is also North India's biggest in the private sector after Nestle's plant at Moga in Punjab. It was started in the early 1960s by a Gujjar, Chaudhary Ved Ram, who was an ordinary dudhiya (milk contractor) in Bulandshahr, UP. But VRS is an oddball – like K.P. Singh of DLF or Inder Grewal of Upper India Steels. The region's other major milk processors – which, besides Milkfood and Modern Dairies, include Mahaan Foods of Rajiv Goyal (Bania), JK Dairy (Bania), Cepham Milk Specialities of Dewan Chand Pruthi (Khatri), and Sterling Agro Industries of Kuldip Saluja (Khatri) – are all from non-agrarian communities. There are no big Jat, Gujjar, or Yadav names in oilseeds processing or other agro-industries either. MP has seen its soybean output soar tenfold in the past two decades, just as Rajasthan has experienced a similar revolution in rapeseed-mustard.[37] Yet, over 90 per cent of the solvent extraction and refining units in the two states are controlled by Banias and Marwaris, with a sprinkling of Khatris.[38] The same is the case with real estate. If one leaves out DLF, the large property developers around Delhi and other northern centres are all Banias/ Marwaris (Sushil Ansal of Ansal Properties & Infrastructure, Pradeep Jain of Parsvnath Developers, Rohtas Goel of Omaxe, and Pankaj Bajaj of Eldeco Infrastructure) or Khatris (Ashok Sarin of Anant Raj Industries). Amidst this rather gloomy picture, though, there is an unlikely entrepreneur in an unusual industry: the Yoga evangelist Baba Ramdev. Born as Ram Kishan Yadav at Mahendragarh in Haryana, this politically connected, television-savvy seer has, in an amazingly short period, become a brand presiding over a vast empire, including a Rs 100 crore Patanjali Yog Peeth near the holy town of Hardwar.

A sector in which the involvement of northern farming castes is strikingly low is the media. Strange, given that newspapers and journals have been powerful vehicles for communities to articulate their positions and challenge the hegemony of entrenched groups. Many of the prime vernacular dailies and television channels in the South were promoted by intermediate-caste people with considerable political backing, as with *Eenadu* (Kamma), *Daily Thanti* (Nadar), and *Sun TV* (Isai Vellalar). But in the North, the big media houses belong to Bania-Marwaris (*Dainik Jagran* of Mahendra Mohan Gupta, *Dainik Bhaskar* of Ramesh Chandra Agrawal, *Navbharat Times* of Bennett, Coleman, *Hindustan* of K.K. Birla, *Amar Ujala* of the Agarwal-Maheshwari families, *Rajasthan Patrika* of Gulab Kothari, Zee TV of Subhash Chandra) or Khatris (*Aaj Tak* and *Punjab Kesri*). The exceptions are *The Tribune* and *Ajit*: a Punjabi daily run by a Saini-Sikh, Barjinder Singh Hamdard, competing with the Punjab Kesri group's *Jag Bani*. There have been few serious attempts by prominent Jat, Yadav, or Gujjar politicians to start newspapers or encourage initiatives in this direction, despite the potential for a captive readership base. Chhotu Ram's *Jat Gazette*, an Urdu weekly printed from Rohtak, had a circulation of 500–700 copies between 1923 and 1926. Even with limited marketing efforts, it boasted of a loyal reading public of lawyers, teachers, sepoys, and peasant-proprietors.[39]

Plausible Explanations for Tepid Business Inclinations

The lacklustre participation of northern agrarian communities in industry is ascribed, among other things, to 'cultural factors'. As the former union agriculture minister Ajit Singh puts it, farming for the Jat is a traditional knowledge-based occupation that comes naturally to him, the way the Bania takes to trade. There is a lot of pride in being a zamindar, 'as he is the Lord and Master of what he surveys'. The Bania's trade, on the other hand, is looked down upon as involving *hera-pheri* (dubious deal-making).[40] Making a similar point is Rana Gurjeet Singh, an industrialist and Member of Parliament (MP) from Jalandhar: 'From the moment a Jat is born, his mother feeds him lot of milk and ghee. From day one, he is conditioned to be a farmer, warrior, wrestler or kabaddi player, and not a businessman'.[41] On a subtler plane, H.S. Shergill draws attention to the Jat's historical attachment to his land. 'After

Partition, both Jat and Khatri Sikhs were allotted land. But since they were never really cultivators, the Khatri-Sikhs gradually disposed of their land and moved to the cities, where they truly belong. This was not the case with Jat Sikhs. They were agriculturists in the canal colonies and continued to be even after coming here. You cannot separate a Jat from his land; those who settle abroad, too, will do everything to retain land in their villages', he points out. Even if he does not farm, 'you will rarely see a Jat opening a kirana (grocery) store, which, for the Bania, comes instinctively.' The Jat instead uses that money to pay an agent to help him migrate to Canada or Britain, even if the neighbourhood kirana shop makes better financial sense and has a lower risk. Alternatively, he may buy a truck or a taxi (which he will tend to drive himself) or take up a job in the army and other service professions, while holding on to his land – tilled by his family.[42]

Another explanation for farming classes in the North not venturing into industry is linked to agriculture being a comparatively remunerative activity till the 1980s, which rendered diversification 'unnecessary'. That was the high noon of the Green Revolution, when yields were on the rise with the introduction of the new dwarf seed varieties. Farmers therefore saw a future in agriculture both for themselves and their descendants. 'There was no need to look for career options outside agriculture then. I don't recall many people from my community approaching my father (Chaudhary Charan Singh) for job recommendations', says Ajit Singh. The situation has changed in the last ten to fifteen years. With crop yields stagnating or showing no dramatic improvements – alongside an increasing fragmentation of landholdings, declining water tables, rising costs of labour, fuel and other inputs – 'the law of diminishing returns has set in, which is forcing our farmers to diversify', feels Captain Kanwaljit Singh, Shiromani Akali Dal leader and former finance minister of Punjab.[43] The major impediment here, however, is again the specific socio-cultural milieu: the absence of the 'right' bent of mind and possessing the 'right' kind of skills.

'The Jats have not been trained to start industries. You will find few engineers, chartered accountants, and business management professionals in their ranks', observes Ajit Singh, who is an exception himself. The former minister is a mechanical engineer from the Indian Institute of Technology, Kharagpur, who went to the US in 1964. There he did his master's in industrial engineering from the Illinois Institute at Chicago and worked with IBM and Xerox Corporation, before returning in 1981. 'Till recently, UP did not even have engineering colleges, save the Roorkee University, the Harcourt Butler Institute at Kanpur and a couple of others in Allahabad and Gorakhpur. And since these were virtually national-level institutes, it was not easy for our boys to get admission. This is unlike the South or Maharashtra, which always had a profusion of government and private technical educational institutions', he adds.

Insightful though these views are, they provide only partial answers to why the region's dominant farming communities have been unable to make the transition to industry. The proposition about farmers not considering alternatives earlier because of agriculture being a reasonably paying profession is valid so long as there is scope for growth and making productive investments within the existing field of activity. But once a large farmer has expanded the scale of his enterprise by buying or leasing in more land and intensifying cultivation through mechanization and undertaking land improvements (to the extent the laws and state of public infrastructure permit), he has hit an investment ceiling. He would, then, automatically look for avenues outside agriculture to invest surplus profits. Economic diversification becomes an objective necessity for the rural capitalist.[44]

In such a scenario it is not willingness to invest in trade and industry that matters as much as whether the avenues for making such investments exist. A crucial determinant here is the environment confronting capitalist farmers who aspire to traverse from the field to the boardroom. This environment, we have observed in earlier chapters, was relatively conducive in the South, where traditional mercantile communities like the Chettiars and Komatis exercised no decisive stranglehold over business. The bulk of Chettiar capital was, in fact, invested overseas in Sri Lanka and South East Asia. There was always, then, a 'Vaishya vacuum' in the domestic arena that could, from time to time, be filled even by Syrian Christians and Muslim traders of Arab descent. In an open field of this sort it was not impossible for the Kamma or Gounder 'capitalist-farmer' to turn a 'farmer-capitalist'.[45]

In the North conditions have been altogether different. The Banias, Marwaris, and Khatris have been ubiquitous in commodity and money markets; this has made the entry point for affluent capitalist farmers not terribly inviting even in areas such as agro-processing. The capital that grew with the Green Revolution may be eager for self-expansion through conversion into industrial capital; but the outlets are few and precarious.[46] While in the West the Patidars and Marathas circumvented the problem through farmer-controlled co-operatives – which they used as a stepping stone for making further inroads into industry – this strategy has found little state backing in the northern states. Co-operatives in UP produce only 13–14 per cent of the state's sugar and procure below 2 per cent of its milk. Also, unlike Maharashtra and Gujarat, the northern political class has been indifferent towards promoting viable co-operatives because of which they are run more like extension arms of government departments.[47] Their dismal performance is even justified by leaders like Captain Kanwaljit Singh, who blindly asserts that 'Jat Sikhs are individualistic by nature and cannot excel collectively.'

As a result, most of the agricultural surpluses are squandered on conspicuous consumption and extravagant spending on social ceremonies, or invested in petty businesses like transport, petrol pumps, shopping complexes, cinema theatres, and marriage halls in Chandigarh and Ludhiana. Some writers have gone on to trace the roots of militancy and the separatist Khalistan movement in Punjab to the frustrations of the Sikh agrarian elite in furthering its industrial agenda.[48] The invocation of religious feelings is seen as reflecting underlying tensions between the Jat Sikh-dominated agricultural capital and a Hindu majority holding sway over trade and industry. Some of these were expressed in the Akali Dal's famous Anandpur Sahib Resolution of 16–17 October 1973, which cited the 'hard fact that the levers of economic power continue to be in the hands of big traders, capitalists, and monopolists'. To curb their power, the resolution even demanded that 'all key industries should be under public control', while calling for 'complete nationalization of the wholesale trade in foodgrains through the establishment of state agencies'.[49]

A pointer to how the extant environment influences the investment behaviour of communities is the numerous success stories scripted by overseas businessmen of Jat Sikh origin. Prominent among them is Didar Singh Bains from Nangal Khurd village in Hoshiarpur, whose father went to the US in 1948 as a farm labourer. Bains joined him in 1958 and, four years later, had saved enough to buy 25 acres of land in California. Over time he became America's biggest peach grower, owning 10,000 acres and growing 50,000 tonnes of the fruit worth $13 million every year. The Greater San Joaquin Valley is today home to some 3,000 Jat Sikh 'mega farmers' who produce much of California's peaches, raisins, grapes, prunes, almonds, and pistachios. Most of them – like Bains and the 13,200-acre Charanjit Singh Batth (the state's No. 1 raisin producer) – started off as farm hands, who became landed through community connections. Bains is known to have personally sponsored over 500 Sikh immigrants, many of whom worked in his orchards. Later he enabled them to start their own businesses by co-signing loans (there is a parallel here with the 'Patel Motel' phenomenon noted in the previous chapter). Some immigrant labourers, like the Tut brothers (Amarjit, Ranjit, Surjit, and Pritam), became truck drivers and subsequently transport tycoons, only to return to farming. The prod for this came from their father, Sadhu Singh. The old man, a resident of Paragpur village in Jalandhar, is said to have advised them in plain Jat-speak: *mitti lavo mitti* (literally: buy mud; in other words, 'get land').[50] The other Jat Sikh émigrés to have made it big include Darshan Singh Dhaliwal and Avtar Lit. Originally from Rakhra village near Patiala, Dhaliwal's Bulk Petroleum Corporation is the largest petrol retailer in the US, with more than 1,000 stations in eleven states. The Wisconsin-based billionaire was also in the news for contributing Rs 5 crore towards relief work following the December 2004 tsunami disaster and running a round-the-clock langar (community kitchen) for over three weeks in Nagapattinam (Tamil Nadu). Avtar Lit owns Sunrise Radio, the UK's premier radio broadcasting service catering to its Asian population.

These examples basically demonstrate that a community facing entry barriers in business at home – given the overbearing presence of entrenched groups across industries – is able to overcome them in less hostile environs abroad. For the upwardly mobile Jat Sikh farmer in Ludhiana, domestic land ceiling laws and poor public infrastructure are deterrents to up-scaling his agricultural operations. Nor can he diversify into other fields, already the domain of Banias and Khatris. But the same agriculturist in California has succeeded in reproducing his activity on a vastly expanded canvas to emerge as a full-fledged agro-industrialist, just as single truck or petrol pump owners have metamorphosed into transport and gas retail magnates. Incidentally, many of these émigré businessmen were also ardent supporters and financiers of the Khalistan cause during the 1980s.[51]

A New Dawn for Punjab?

The separatist movement in Punjab was mercilessly suppressed and by the early 1990s the centre had restored its writ in the troubled province. The strong-arm methods employed were, nevertheless, tempered by measures to resolve the apparent tensions between the state's agricultural elite and traders. Some early results can be seen on the ground, but they still pale in comparison with the transition achieved by the agrarian communities in the South and West.

An area where Jat Sikhs have made a considerable dent over the past couple of decades is the arhat or grain commission agency business, a traditional Bania–Khatri bastion. A survey by the author in Khanna – Asia's biggest wholesale grain market, handling about 3.2 lakh tonnes (lt) of paddy and 1.2 lt of wheat every year – during the 2005–6 rabi procurement season revealed that 105 out of its 290 licensed arhatias were Jat Sikhs.[52] In 1985 they numbered just 13, according to Harbans Singh Rosha, president of Khanna's Arhatia Association, who entered the trade in 1987. The oldest Jat Sikh-owned arhat business in Khanna is that of Jaswant Singh Gill, whose father, a lambardar (village head-man), set it up in 1960. 'We were the only ones then. In the last 5–10 years, all new shops are of Jat Sikhs', informs Gill.[53] Significantly, out of the 105 arhatias from the community, 80 are farmers-cum-commission agents, similar to the early Kamma tobacco dealers of coastal Andhra. Rosha, who transacts 3,500 tonnes of paddy and 2,500 tonnes of wheat annually, cultivates 30 acres himself in Bugga village, Patiala.

'Arhat is the easiest business for a Jat Sikh to do. Our relatives are farmers, so sourcing grain is no problem. On the marketing side, too, there is no risk. If there are no private buyers, we still have FCI and other state agencies that pay us a fixed 2.5 per cent dami (commission fee) on the minimum support price at which grain is procured from farmers. And they disburse this money within seventy-two hours', affirms Paramjit Singh, a farmer-turned-arhatia. In addition, there is money to be made from financing the credit needs of farmers.[54] Some arhatias, like Rosha, have graduated to become rice or wheat flour millers. Khanna alone has 54 rice mills, of which 18 belong to Jat Sikhs. Another field survey of 30 rice mills in Moga found 4 of them were owned by Jat Sikhs.[55] But these are essentially small 'shellers', engaged in custom milling of ordinary paddy for government agencies. The bigger mills or branded basmati rice players of North India are all again either Khatris – Satnam Overseas, LT Overseas, Lakshmi Energy & Foods, and Amar Singh Chawal Wala (see Chapter 3) – or Bania-Marwaris such as Anil Kumar Mittal of KRBL ('India Gate'), Sanjay Jhunjhunwala of REI Agro ('Mr Miller'), and Harnarain Aggarwal of Shivnath Rai Harnarain ('Shrilalmahal').

Apart from arhatias and grain millers, there are cases of Jat Sikhs entering large industry since the late 1980s. Among them are Rana Gurjeet Singh and Harbhajan Singh Cheema. Both are interestingly big farmers from Uttarakhand's Tarai belt who went into seed production and then set up paper plants using agro-residues, before diversifying into sugar and textiles. (We shall examine them in detail later). Then, there are agro-entrepreneurs like Malvinder Singh Bhinder and Satbir Singh Nijjer, whose companies were established as joint ventures with Punjab Agro Industries Corporation (PAIC). Bhinder, a US-returned mechanical engineer, started Agro Dutch Industries in 1994 for the cultivation, processing, and canning of mushrooms. From an initial capacity of 3,000 tonnes per annum, it has expanded to 36,000 tonnes, making it one of the world's largest integrated mushroom manufacturers. Nijjer Agro Foods

– promoted by a postgraduate researcher from the University of California, Davis – makes tomato paste and chilli purees and sauces, sourcing the raw materials from its own farms as well as through contract cultivation. The performance of these companies has been mixed.[56] Nevertheless, they have prompted others to launch similar concerns. One of them is P.S. Chatha, whose Chatha Foods Private Limited at Lalru in Patiala district makes processed meat and frozen ready-to-eat products under the 'Swiss Naturen' brand. 41-year-old Mandip Singh Lally grows seed potatoes in 2,200 acres near Jalandhar – of which 400 acres is family land; the rest being leased – and also owns four cold storages. He is now setting up a Rs 42 crore plant to produce frozen French fries and flakes, which will be 'cheaper and of better quality' than what the US fast-foods chain McDonald's is currently selling in India. 'They are importing the fries at Rs 150 per kg and selling to the consumer for Rs 300. My product will be available for Rs 75 per kg', he claims. Mandip plans to do contract farming of Kufri Chipsona – a special low-sugar, processing-grade variety bred by the Central Potato Research Institute, near Shimla – in over 8,000 acres and import a plant from Holland for 4 million euros. 'I conceived of the project five years ago, only to discover how difficult it is for a zamindar to start an industry. I had the raw material, the technology, and I was myself investing Rs 20 crore, and yet the bankers kept raising questions about my not having a business background, firm marketing tie-ups, and so on', complains Mandip.[57] Eventually, the Punjab National Bank agreed to lend Rs 20 crore, with PAIC chipping in with equity participation of Rs 2 crore.

Yet another crop of new Jat Sikh businessmen happen to be the relatives and friends of politicians, enjoying better access to institutional finance and other forms of state support. Not all of them have, however, turned out to be successes. Bubli Brar, daughter of former CM Harcharan Singh Brar, had a thriving stud farm business, Dashmesh & Hargobind Racing, before venturing into mushroom cultivation and telecom cable manufacturing in the late 1980s. Both outfits – Dashmesh Haegans Agro Tech and Telephone Cables Limited – have closed down. Other failed ventures promoted by the kin of ex-CMs include Japson Pharmaceuticals of Jasjit Singh Dhaliwal (son of Surjit Singh Barnala), Harpartap Steels of Gurinder Singh Kairon (son of Pratap Singh Kairon), and National Agro Chemical Industries of Gurpratap Singh Kairon (Pratap Singh Kairon's grandson, whose brother Adesh Pratap is also the son-in-law of Parkash Singh Badal). Most of these were started with liberal financial assistance from government institutions like PAIC and the Punjab State Industrial Development Corporation (PSIDC).[58]

A slightly better case is that of Jarnail Singh Wahid, considered 'close' to the Badal family. A member of the Shiromani Gurdwara Prabandhak Committee (SGPC),[59] he owns Wahid Sandhar Sugars, a 5,000-tcd plant at Phagwara, originally promoted in 1933 by Gokul Chand Narang. This mill was taken over by a Marwari, Abhey Oswal, before Wahid acquired it in 2000. Another politically connected industrialist is the Congressman Kewal Singh Dhillon, who went to Liberia during the early 1970s and returned in the ensuing decade to partner Pepsico. His Dhillon Kool Drinks & Beverages used to be one of the US soft drinks giant's largest franchisee manufacturer-cum-distributors in India, though now it is reduced to a mere contract bottler for Pepsico in Punjab. Dhillon also had a cinema theatre at Chandigarh, which has since been converted into a multiplex-cum-retail mall ('Fun Republic') in partnership with Subhash Chandra's Zee group.

It would seem from all this that some sort of industrial transformation is under way in the community, reminiscent of the mini renaissance witnessed during the time of the Majithias, the Sandhanwalas, and the Indra Singhs. Whether this points to a genuine resurgence or will falter like the earlier one and presage a fresh wave of frustration and divisive politics, only time will tell. What is clear is that none of the new businessmen are in the same big league as Lanco, Nirma, Sakthi, Dr Reddy's, and LMW.

The Ramgarhias

The business community which hasn't featured so far in our analysis is the Ramgarhias: a loose cluster of Sikh artisan castes, mainly comprising Tarkhans (carpenters), Lohars (blacksmiths), and Rajs (masons).[60]

As businessmen, the Ramgarhias have carved out a special niche for themselves in the interstitial zone between big industry and kulak agriculture. Ludhiana's cycle majors and producers of tyres and tubes may all be Khatris, but those supplying components – from cups, hubs and axles to rims, handle bars, brake sets, mudguards, bells, chain covers, and freewheels – are mostly Ramgarhias. Many of them, like Bhogal Sons of Mohinder Singh Bhogal, KW Engineering Works of Karam Singh and Wasan Singh, Gemco Cycles of Gurdial Singh Mankoo, Kular Cycles Industries of Ajit Singh Kular, and Vishvkarma Industries of Tara Singh Gharyal are established names in both domestic as well as global markets. Likewise with the city's textile industry, where the big yarn and knitwear tycoons are Bania–Marwaris, even as the bulk of hosiery and knitting equipment comes from Ramgarhia-owned firms. They include GSL Textile of Ghansham Singh Lotey – a producer of carding machines, draw frames, cutters, fabric-raising and shearing machines, and pilot testing and simulation plants for yarns – and Swarup Mechanical Works of Narpal Singh. The latter is India's largest manufacturer of industrial sewing machines ('Revo' label), being the first to introduce high-speed bag closing and overlock machines. Besides, there are Ramgarhia makers of hosiery circular knitting machines like TS Mechanical Works of Teja Singh and STM Knitting Machinery Works of Surinder Singh.

The community has played a similar role *vis-à-vis* Punjab's agriculture. While the Green Revolution's principal protagonist was the Jat Sikh farmer, its unsung heroes are the numerous Ramgarhia fabricators of drills, threshers, chaff cutters, spray pumps, reapers, and combines. Among them are the harvester-combine makers Nacchattar Singh's Standard Combines at Barnala, and Amarjeet Singh's Kartar Agro Industries at Bhadson (Patiala). Then, we have the Ludhiana-based Sukhdev Singh's National Agro Industries (which pioneered production of seed drills in the country and, lately, also 'zero-till' fertilizer-cum-seed drills), and Amar Agricultural Implements Works of Amar Singh Tatter (a prominent thresher manufacturer). Others include Kalsi Metal Works of Manmohan Singh Kalsi (a leading regional player in agricultural pumps, electric motors, and tubewell fittings), and Virdi Tubewell Boring Company of Swaran Singh Virdi.

The Ramgarhias are also active in industries such as foundries and machine tools. Ludhiana has a number of grinding machine and mechanical power press units like Riat Machine Tools of Kirpal Singh Riat and Mankoo India Private Limited of Mohinder Singh Mankoo, just as Batala in Gurdaspur is home to a cluster of Ramgarhia-owned foundries and manufacturers of lathes, boring-cum-turning mills, and planing machines. There are, in addition to these, some unique industrial concerns like Chanan Singh Wilkhu's Sutlej Motors, and Dhiman Engineers of Tarlochan Singh Dhiman. Starting with a small carpentry shop producing wooden bullock-carts in 1935, the Jalandhar-based Sutlej Motors went into making bodies for trucks and buses towards the late 1950s. The company is today India's No. 1 bus and coach body builder, while being the trendsetter in luxury coaches and airport buses (in which it is ranked among the world's top three). Dhiman

Engineers from Nakodar (Jalandhar) is a manufacturer and supplier of confectionery machines – including lollypop, bubble gum, candy, and toffee forming, processing, and wrapping plants – to big domestic and multi-national brands. The community has also produced auto-component makers like Guru Nanak Auto Enterprises (GNA) at Goraya, Jalandhar, and the GS Auto group of Ludhiana. The former, founded by Sardar Amar Singh, is the country's largest integrated supplier of rear axle shafts, while the latter specializes in suspension components and radiators (see end-chapter case study). Thakur Uday Singh of Namdhari Seeds, the Bangalore-based vegetable hybrid seeds breeder, and the footwear industry's once rising star Ajay Kalsi of Phoenix International, are Ramgarhias too.

A distinct aspect of the above enterprises is that the majority were set up as tiny carpentry or smithy units by men of humble rural artisan stock. As fabricators of ploughs and other hand-made agricultural implements, the Ramgarhias were tied to the Jat Sikh peasantry in an unequal jajmani (patron–client) relationship.[61] Being categorized as 'non-agriculturists' under the Punjab Land Alienation Act, the community could not own land, blocking an important avenue of upward mobility. It is the building of the canal colonies and railroad networks from the latter half of the nineteenth century that opened up opportunities for them to move out of the Punjab countryside. The British found it expedient to employ these local artisans to forge, cast, repair, and manufacture the simple parts and tools they required in bulk, which would otherwise have been imported at a premium.[62] The Ramgarhias were recruited in large numbers, with many even going to East Africa to build the Kenya–Uganda railways.[63] Just as the canal colonies exposed Jat Sikhs to capitalist farming, these imperial infrastructure projects provided a learning ground for Punjab's artisan castes to upgrade their traditional skills and adapt them to new production tasks and environments.

This experience proved valuable later, when the growth of Ludhiana's knitwear and bicycle industries during World War II and post-Partition period transformed erstwhile rural artisans and metal workers into ancillary suppliers, job-shop owners, and fabricators of industrial parts, components, and machine tools. The Green Revolution provided a similar impetus for them to become farm machinery manufacturers. The Ramgarhias have, thus, penetrated into businesses that evinced little participation from either the mainstream trading communities or the Jat Sikhs. A vital element to this has been their ability to replicate existing (often imported) machinery and recondition them to local needs, thereby reducing start-up costs.[64] The absence of strong laws to protect proprietary designs and knowhow – besides the policy to 're-serve' production of various components and farm machinery (ex-cluding tractors) for small-scale units – has further facilitated these processes.

But for all this none of the Ramgarhia-owned companies have grown to be truly big: most of the concerns named have annual sales below Rs 50 crore, with only the GNA and GS Auto groups in the Rs 100-crore-plus league. Some, notably the textile equipment makers, have been affected by liberalization, which has made it cheaper for knitwear firms to install imported fabrication machinery incorporating sophisticated electronic and numerical control devices, in place of the earlier Ludhiana contraptions working on simple mechanical principles. Ramgarhia capitalists have also not managed to rise beyond their ancillary industry or components supplier status. Isolated efforts by Bhogal Sons and Standard Combines to become full-fledged branded bicycle or tractor manufacturers have not really borne fruit. This mirrors the community's position in Punjab politics, where they are reconciled to playing second fiddle to the Jat Sikhs. Given the latter's traditional association with the Akalis, the Ramgarhias generally vote for the Congress which, in turn, has occasionally propped up leaders from their ranks. The most famous – and possibly the only significant – Ramgarhia politician was the former Punjab CM Zail Singh, who was also India's president during 1982–7.

We shall round up this chapter with select cases studies of successful businessmen from the communities surveyed.

Case Studies[65]

1. DLF Universal Limited

Delhi Land and Finance (DLF) was incorporated on 18 September 1946. Its founder, Chaudhary Raghvendra Singh (1910–2000), was the son of Rai Bahadur Lal Chand, a prominent lawyer of Rohtak and the 'first Jat graduate'. Lal Chand was also a contemporary of Sir Chhotu Ram, having set up joint legal practice with him and being one of the key figures of the Unionist Party.[66] Raghvendra Singh, too, did law at Lahore's Government College, before joining the provincial civil service, which he left after becoming secretary of the Punjab State Road Transport Authority. The Chaudhary's decision to enter business – unusual for a person of his community background – was guided by the country's impending partition and his perception that the population influx arising from it would create a huge demand for housing in Delhi. While the idea was good, the problem was to find the money to finance the proposed real estate venture; not being from a business family setting was an added handicap.

It was in this context that Raghvendra Singh evolved his 'land bank-partnership model'. Since land had to be acquired from farmers without the money to pay them, the model involved the farmers giving their land on credit. His company would then develop and sell the real estate and use the proceeds to pay back the farmers. But it did not stop there: 90 per cent of the money that the farmers received would be redeposited with the company, against which interest was to be credited to them on the third of every month. This would include a component of the profits made by the company. The model succeeded, partly due to no defaults taking place in interest payments, but also by virtue of the community connections that Raghvendra Singh was able to leverage to his advantage. The farmers were mostly Jats and his land bank was essentially a tool for mobilising community savings to build a private business.

The above model was used by DLF to develop its first residential colonies across some 5,800 acres in Delhi during the initial period after Independence. These included Hauz Khas, Greater Kailash I & II (originally Yaqudpur and Bahapur villages), Kailash Colony (Zamrudpur), South Extension (Kotla Mubarakpur), and Shivaji Park (Madipur). The party, however, ended with the Delhi Development Authority (DDA) Act of 1957 which gave the state-owned DDA the sole right to acquire land for property development. The effective nationalisation of the capital's real estate business meant that DLF could now only develop the land it had acquired before the act came into force. The original DLF became DLF Housing & Construction Private Limited, with its focus shifting to ordinary building construction. Even this underwent a change, when DLF Housing was merged into a new entity, American Universal Electric (India) Limited, created on 4 July 1963 to manufacture fractional horsepower motors. Raghvendra Singh's family held a 50 per cent share in it, the rest being with the Michigan-based American Universal Electric. The family also invested 50 per cent in Willard India, which made automotive and industrial batteries.

By this time Kushal Pal Singh, who was married to the DLF

founder's eldest daughter Indira, had come into the scene. Originally from Bulandshahr, his father was a lawyer with an agriculture background, similar to that of Raghvendra Singh. Born in 1931, Kushal Pal Singh joined the Royal Military Academy at Sandhurst, UK, and then the Deccan Horse Regiment, from where he retired in 1961 as a captain. At that point his father-in-law's real estate business was in limbo. Nor were the two industrial ventures doing well; the family was eventually forced to exit from them. The foreign partner's stake in American Universal Electric (India) was bought out and the company was converted into DLF Universal Electric Limited on 18 June 1980 and finally to DLF Universal Limited on 28 May 1981. The entire fractional horsepower motor business was taken over by General Electric (GE). In 1977 the family also sold its stake in Willard India. The wheel had turned full circle. It was decided that DLF would go back to its original business of real estate, the development of residential colonies and commercial complexes, and the leasing of assets.

A major impediment though was the law: following DDA's example, virtually all states had enacted legislations creating public sector monopolies in township development. Kushal Pal Singh's concerted lobbying to 'get the law opened up' struck a sympathetic chord with Rajiv Gandhi. At the instance of his mother Indira Gandhi, the Haryana government under Bhajan Lal gave DLF the licence in 1980 to develop the Gurgaon area in Delhi's outskirts. The challenge now was to get the land. Although Raghvendra Singh had hung up his boots around 1972, Kushal Pal Singh decided that his 'model' was to be deployed all over again in a 'more aggressive and articulate manner'. It was not easy, as the times had changed and the new generation of farmers was more educated. Unlike in the past, when a family patriarch's word was all, each individual now had to be persuaded to part with family land. And since the Hindu Undivided Family law required the consent of all adult members and getting the married daughter to sign up wasn't easy (because the eldest male karta would invariably refuse to share the sale proceeds with her), it meant going to the in-laws and paying them off. There was no escape from all this as the property had to be purchased on a clean title and due diligence was necessary to pre-empt any scope for litigation.

'It was a painful exercise starting from 1980 to 1997, during the course of which we acquired 3,500 acres. The average landholding in Haryana being 4–5 acres, it meant dealing with 700-odd families with 5–6 members each. I was involved in buying every piece of land and would have personally visited the houses of 70–80 per cent of the families. I sometimes had to go to places as far as Alwar (in Rajasthan) to meet the girl's in-laws', recalls Kushal Pal Singh. In business, he points out, one has to 'wear different caps at the same time', which calls for dealing with a sophisticated clientele simultaneous with drinking buffalo milk in the company of rustic farmers and patwaris (land record-keepers). 'I have occasionally mediated in family disputes and even helped in arranging marriage alliances', he says. A helpful factor here was the proposed 'master plan' for the National Capital Region, which would have given the government blanket powers to acquire land from farmers. 'They were aware of it and figured out that I would be a better partner than the authorities, who would probably have paid them a pittance', he notes.

The other idea of Raghvendra Singh that was persisted with was the land bank. 'There was no alternative because commercial banks those days were prohibited from lending for real estate development. The other source was inter-corporate deposits, but it would have entailed borrowing at 24–30 per cent through brokers for short 6–12 months duration. Moreover, one could not roll over these deposits, which was not so with the corpus money provided by farmers', states Kushal Pal Singh. But the end result was that Gurgaon turned DLF into India's prime realty firm. The land that it bought in the early 1980s at Rs 80–100 a square yard has appreciated to well over Rs 40,000. There was a time when Gurgaon had to be desperately marketed as 'Qutub Enclave' in order to get people in; today the 3,000-acre DLF City is prime residential space that also hosts the plush corporate offices of multinationals from GE, Pepsi, Coke, and Nestle to ICI, Dupont, and Cargill. What was once dusty territory in Sikandarpur Ghosi and Chakkarpur villages now house Phases I and IV of DLF City, which have luxury condominiums with names like Silver Oaks, Beverly Park I, Ridgewood, Windsor, Regency, Richmond Park, and Hamilton Court. Phase II was originally part of Sarhaul and Shahpur villages; today, it has the more grandiloquent Oakwood, Belvedere Tower, and Beverly Park II complexes. Belvedere Park in Phase IV is similarly carved out from Nathupur, just as Wazirabad village has become Phase V, overlooking a golf course and hosting the likes of Princeton, Carlton, Aralias, Westend Heights, Royalton Towers, Icon, and Pinnacle.

In the last few years DLF has spread its wings beyond Delhi and its vicinity to Jaipur, Kolkata, Pune, Bangalore, Hyderabad, Kochi, and other centres. In June 2005 it snapped up an eighteen-acre plot of a sick, state-owned textile mill in Mumbai's Lower Parel for a successful bid of Rs 702 crore. With the land value of its properties under development in sixty-four locations across India estimated at around Rs 80,000 crore, Kushal Pal Singh was rated by *Forbes* magazine as the country's fifth richest man in 2005.[67]

2. The Rana and Cheema Groups

Rana Gurjeet Singh is originally from Bahar Majra village in Nawanshahr district of Punjab. His grandfather, Rana Ujjagar Singh, was a farmer who, in 1910, went to New Zealand as a labourer. He had three sons, including Rana Daljit Singh, Rana

Gurjeet's father. Rana Ujjagar Singh died in 1940 and about five years later his sons returned to India. They briefly experimented with road construction in Nangal (Ropar), but decided to go back to their ancestral profession and settle down in the Tarai area of the present Uttarakhand state in 1949. This region, lying below the Shivalik ranges in Nainital, was a jungle-filled marshland prone to waterlogging and inhabited mainly by aboriginal tribes – the Tharus and Buksas – and nomadic herdsmen. However, recognizing the inherent fertility of its soil, perennially irrigated by streams flowing from the Himalayas, the government had initiated an ambitious programme for reclamation of the Tarai, starting in 1948.[68] This, together with the advantage of larger holdings, attracted many Jat Sikh settlers, who were even allotted forest land free to convert into farmland. Rana Gurjeet's father and uncles were among the first colonist-farmers of the Tarai and he himself was born on 19 April 1952 in Bazpur Tehsil of what is now Udham Singh Nagar district of Uttarakhand.

The family initially undertook ordinary crop cultivation on about 1,800 acres and then, towards the mid 1960s, went into seed farming. They would source the breeder material from the Govind Ballabh Pant University of Agriculture & Technology – which had come up in 1960 – and multiply them into foundation and certified seeds. The establishment of the Tarai Development Corporation (TDC) in 1969 was a major enabler as it procured the breeder material on behalf of the farmers and marketed the certified seeds multiplied by them. It was a semi-co-operative whose three stakeholders were the state government, the Agricultural University, and the farmers. Rana Daljit Singh was, in fact, twice director of TDC. 'Seed cultivation was hugely profitable. If wheat fetched Rs 150 per quintal those days, we used to get Rs 225 for the seed', informs Rana Gurjeet. By then, the government had clamped an individual landholding ceiling of 12.5 acres, though it was still possible to lease in forest land on a three-year renewable basis. The family took 4,000-odd acres on lease, on which they produced seeds of wheat, paddy, maize, peas, gram, and lentils under their own 'Rana' brand. The base for capital accumulation had been fully laid.

In 1989 Rana Gurjeet Singh migrated to Punjab and diversified into industry by setting up a 30 tonnes per day Kraft paper unit that used wheat straw, paddy husk, and sugarcane baggase as raw material. The plant, at Fatehpur village of Ropar, cost Rs 5 crore; he put in Rs 1.30 crore, the rest came from PAIC and banks. In 1991 PAIC obtained a licence to start a sugar mill, for which it sought a joint venture partner. Given the uncertain environment prevailing in Punjab, there were no takers for the advertisement. 'I took a calculated gamble and went ahead with putting up a 2,500 tcd unit for Rs 40 crore, out of which my contribution was Rs 6 crore', says Rana Gurjeet. The Rana Sugars factory at Buttar Seviyan village in Amritsar began crushing in December 1993. 'All through, I used to receive ransom calls from extremist groups. The then CM, Beant Singh, organized a whole Central Reserve Police Force (CRPF) battalion for me', he adds. This was followed by a 35,000-spindle, 100 per cent export-oriented cotton yarn venture – Rana Polycot – at Lalru in Patiala, which began operating in September 1996. The collaborator here was PSIDC.

Today, the Rana group companies have a combined turnover of Rs 250 crore, with the flagship, Rana Sugars, earning a profit after tax of Rs 20.67 crore on net sales of Rs 132.46 crore during 2004–5. The sugar mill's capacity has been expanded to 5,000 tcd, along with the addition of a 15 MW cogeneration plant and a 60 kilolitre per day potable alcohol distillery. Rana Polycot has extended its operations to garmenting and the manufacture of blended yarns. The group also has interests in construction and infotech, with plans under way to build a mini steel plant and power project in

Orissa. How much of these investments will actually take off is, of course, another matter. Rana Gurjeet has, in the meantime, cut his teeth in politics as well, winning the 2004 parliament polls from Jalandhar as a Congress candidate.

Harbhajan Singh Cheema's career path bears close resemblance to that of Rana Gurjeet. Born in 1942 at Cheema Kalan in Amritsar district, Harbhajan's father Bhag Singh was in the army till 1945, after which the family went to the Tarai. They too started off with normal crop farming before going into branded seed production by taking 2,500 acres of forest land on lease. Like the Rana family, the Cheemas were shareholders of TDC. A minor difference is that Harbhajan Singh moved into industry earlier and his first projects – a 50 tonne per day Kraft paper factory at Bazpur in 1981 and a 150 tonne duplex board plant at Kashipur in 1988 (both agro residues-based) – were in the Tarai itself. These were part-financed by the UP Finance Corporation and other state undertakings. The Bazpur plant, with an initial capacity of 15 tonnes, cost Rs 1.5 crore, with the Cheemas investing Rs 50 lakh. Harbhajan Singh's subsequent ventures have, however, all been in Punjab. They include Cheema Spintex, a 100 per cent export-oriented 35,000-spindle textile unit (set up jointly with PSIDC, again in Lalru, Patiala), and Cheema Printpac at Mohali, which uses the paper board from the Kashipur mill to make packaging cartons. Harbhajan Singh has also invested in politics, successfully contesting the 2002 assembly elections from Kashipur in Uttarakhand on an Akali Dal platform.

3. The GS Auto Group

Gurmukh Singh Ryait was a Ramgarhia Sikh, born in 1900 at Hedon Bet village of Ludhiana's Machhiwara block. He had little education, possessed no land, lost his parents early, and at the age of 12 began working as an apprentice in a smithy shop. Later, he had his own tiny workshop to fabricate hand-made agricultural tools. He remained there till about 1930, when a fight with local Jat Sikhs forced him to leave the village. The conflict was apparently over the construction of a gurdwara, for which his efforts to secure land were blocked by the village elite. Gurmukh Singh then went to the Montgomery canal colony (now in Pakistan) before returning to Ludhiana in 1937, though not to the same village. The family was still struggling; of his sons – Bhagat Singh, Kirpal Singh, Jagat Singh, Madan Singh, and Mohan Singh – only the third could complete his matriculation. He set up shop again, this time to produce bicycle parts along with farm implements and in 1948 established Gurmukh Singh & Sons.

In 1954 Gurmukh Singh's eldest son Bhagat Singh went to Asansol (West Bengal) along with a team of small entrepreneurs. During the visit, organized by the National Productivity Council, they were taken to the bicycle plant of Sen Raleigh Industries. The domestic industry was then in a nascent stage. Both the Raleigh unit as well as TI Cycles' facility at Ambattur, near Madras, had come up in 1949 as British joint ventures. Apart from them, there was the Birlas' Hind Cycles at Mumbai. The Heroes, the Atlases, and the Avons were yet to arrive. There was some local manufacturing of cycle parts and accessories, basically for the replacement market. 'It was at the Raleigh factory that my father came across a hub-making machine. Till then, we were producing cycle parts using small lathe-type machines and ordinary presses that would fabricate one hub every 10 minutes, whereas this machine turned out one per minute. Although my father had studied only up to class five, he was very good with his hands and could copy any machine. He not only did that, but made an improvised version of it', notes Ranjodh Singh, son of Bhagat Singh.

The machine generated good revenues for the fledgling Gurmukh Singh & Sons right through the 1960s. 'It was a huge contraption that I still remember seeing as a small boy. We sold it around

1972 to Bhogal Sons', recalls Ranjodh. But before that the family concern had forayed into auto parts. That was sometime in 1958, when Chevrolet had its mini-buses running on Indian roads. The components in these were largely imported. 'At that point, there was a shortage of wheel boards, which the American auto major had, for some reason, stopped importing. We therefore started making wheel boards for the same mini-buses and, from there on, moved to supplying centre-bolts and spring-pins for the replacement market. From the early 1970s we began producing auto components for original equipment manufacturers (OEM)', he adds.

Since then the GS Auto group (named after its founder) has grown into a Rs 100-crore-plus organization making various forged, cast and machined suspension components, and radiators.[69] Its OEM client base includes Maruti Udyog, Delphi Automotive Systems, Mahindra & Mahindra, Tata Motors, Ashok Leyland, Hindustan Motors, and Punjab Tractors. The group also runs the Ramgarhia Educational Complex at Ludhiana, comprising a chain of schools, a girls' college, and a recently opened Ramgarhia Institute of Information Technology.[70] The complex was Gurmukh Singh's own initiative, as was the Ramgarhia gurdwara at Ludhiana, for which he is said to have raised money by selling a prized shaping machine. 'It was my grandfather's dream to set up a gurdwara, which people in his village had not allowed earlier', says Ranjodh Singh.

9

A Note on the Minorities

This chapter, as the title indicates, does not attempt comprehensiveness. Our objective is to trace certain general historical patterns of business entrepreneurship amongst the country's two major religious minorities – Muslims and Christians – while bringing into light developments in the more recent period.

The traditional Muslim business gentry, as we know, was mainly recruited from the three commercial communities of the Sindh–Kutch–Kathiawar region: the Memons, Khojas, and Dawoodi Bohras. For all their complex theological differences – the Memons are Sunnis, while the other two are Ismaili Shias – they were essentially Hindu trading castes, notably Lohanas, who embraced Islam sometime around the fourteenth century. These sects retained many Hindu practices even after conversion, especially inheritance laws that discouraged dispersal of assets and, to that extent, were friendlier towards capital accumulation goals. Nor were they apparently hindered by Koranic injunctions against usury.[1]

The other significant Muslim business community was the Chinioti Sheikhs. Hailing from Chiniot, a small town near Lyallpur

(Faisalabad) in today's Pakistan, their ancestors were Khatris and Aroras who again converted roughly the same time as the Memons, Khojas, and Bohras. Besides these two Sindhi–Gujarati and Punjabi groups, there were the Konkani Muslims descended from immigrant Arab mariners and merchants. Like the Parsis, they had a long association with shipbuilding and were attracted to Mumbai as it developed into a premier port and commercial hub. In the early part of the nineteenth century quite a few prominent Konkani Muslim families – the Roghays, Kurs, and Ghattays – had amassed fortunes exporting cotton to China in partnership with the Parsis. Muhammad Ali Roghay, who was given the title 'Nakhoda' (shipmaster) for the fleet of vessels he commanded, entered the China trade by tying up with the Readymoney family.[2] Even prior to the Konkani magnates was the legendary Mulla Abdul Ghafur who, in 1701, controlled a quarter of the entire shipping tonnage of Surat, which was then still India's busiest port. Having prospered from the Red Sea trade, Ghafur even ingratiated himself with Yemeni high society, owning one of the largest mansions in Mocha and gaining special privileges at the customs.[3]

In many ways, the above Muslim business groups were no different from the old Parsi and Hindu Vaishya hereditary merchant communities we studied in Chapter 2. Originally from Thatta in southern Sindh, the Memons first migrated to the Kutch-Kathiawar region of Gujarat, where they settled in small and medium-sized towns such as Bhuj (Kutch), Jetpur (Rajkot), Dhoraji and Kutiyana (Porbandar), and Bantva and Vanthali (Junagadh). From these nondescript centres, they then forged long-distance mercantile connections covering virtually the subcontinent by the first half of the nineteenth century – just as the Marwaris had done earlier. Describing the working of their 'moving companies', an official report of that time said: 'Some of them will have shops in the great centres of trade, Bombay and Calcutta, and others in different places in the interior. Each member then acts as a correspondent and agent for all the others, and puts what business he can in their way...At the end of the season when all return to their native Gujarat, the profits from the different shops are pooled and divided among them in varying proportion. By this method they obtain all the advantages which are recognized as attaching to co-operative trading.'[4] The community came to dominate the entire rice trade of eastern India, from Orissa and Bengal up to the Arakan coast of Burma. In this, their past Hindu ethnic links seemingly helped: it was largely the credit funnelled through Multani (Shikarpuri Lohana) bankers that the Memons used to trade produce all over the Bombay Presidency, Central India and the East, Burma included.[5]

At the end of the nineteenth century the Memons and Khojas had established diasporic networks extending beyond India to the ports of the Red Sea and Persian Gulf, East and South Africa, Ceylon, China, and the Far East. The Chinioti Sheikhs, by comparison, had a limited operational spread and, in that sense, were more akin to their Hindu Khatri counterparts. Even while venturing outside their home bastion of Punjab, neither of the two was in the league of the Marwaris, Parsis, Gujarati Banias, Bhatias, Memons, or Khojas in the pre-Independence period. The Chiniotis' main sphere of influence outside Punjab was Kolkata's flourishing market for hides and skins and manufacture of leather and rubber goods, besides small pockets at Kanpur and Madras.

But despite the enormous merchant wealth they accumulated, Muslim businessmen, irrespective of denomination, rarely invested in industry in British India. From this perspective they were a marked contrast to communities which had aggressively diversified into manufacturing well before Independence: the Parsis and Bhatias (from the 1850s to 1870s), Gujarat Banias/Jains (1880s–1890s) and Marwaris (post-World War I). There were a handful of exceptions to this conspicuous trend. One of them was Currimbhoy Ebrahim, a Khoja merchant prince with extensive dealings in opium, cotton, yarn, silk, and tea with China, and whose family had made voyages to Zanzibar and East Africa much earlier. In 1888 he founded Currimbhoy Mills, precursor to a textile combine that at the end of the War included thirteen companies, including nine mills in Mumbai. The Currimbhoy group was in fact the biggest Indian-owned business house after the Tatas in 1931–2.[6] It went bust during the Depression, being that period's most distinguished casualty.

The other notable industrialist was Adamjee Haji Dawood. In 1922 this Memon rice trader from Jetpur set up Asia's largest match factory at Rangoon (Burma), just before Wimco (Swedish Match) entered the scene. A jute factory at Belur, near Kolkata, followed six years later. There was also Ahmed Ebrahim Bawany, yet another Jetpuri Memon to make it big in Burma, first as a piece-goods importer and then via establishing a large hosiery mill at Rangoon in 1931. The political instability after World War II forced Bawany to leave Burma for his homeland and start Kathiawar Industries Limited at Junagadh. A joint venture involving other leading local Memons for manufacturing cement, leather goods, salt, ghee, and margarine, it had the nawab of Junagadh as a co-promoter. Similar initiatives at encouraging modern Muslim entrepreneurship through the joint-sector route were also taken by the nizam of Hyderabad. His government, in 1929, constituted an Industrial Trust Fund (ITF) with an initial capital of Rs 1 crore, which grew to over Rs 5 crore by 1948. A key beneficiary of the ITF was Mir Laiq Ali, the 'Rockefeller of Hyderabad' who, with Abdulkarim Babu Khan, owned or ran the Sirpur Paper Mills, Singareni Collieries, Nizam Sugar Factory, Hyderabad Roller Flour Mills, Deccan Airways, and Hyderabad Construction Company. Another nizam-era capitalist was Muhammad Vazir, whose Vazir

Sultan Tobacco Company in 1930 created the first indigenous cigarette brand, 'Charminar'.[7]

But on the whole there was no mistaking the general Muslim indifference, if not aversion, to industry in undivided India. It is beyond the present book's scope to delve into the many complex and interrelated reasons for this. What we do know is that there was an influential section within the Muslim bourgeoisie which, by the 1930s, had become distinctly uncomfortable with the prospect of an Independent India under the Congress – a party seen as mainly harbouring Marwari business interests. The fear of being subsumed by Marwari and Gujarati Hindu/Jain capital may have been psychological; either way, the idea of a separate Muslim nation that could provide more conducive space for a business class aspiring to full-scale industrial transition had crystallized by the time Mohammad Ali Jinnah had moved the Pakistan Resolution of 1940 in Lahore. In this they were egged on by the British colonial authorities. This is not to say that Muslim big business was less 'nationalistic' than its Hindu counterpart. Umer Sobani, Adamjee Dawood, and other pre-eminent Memon industrialists were indeed active participants in Annie Besant's Home Rule League. In 1918, when Mahatma Gandhi sought Sobani's contribution to the Tilak Swaraj Fund, the latter is said to have handed over a blank cheque to the Mahatma, who wrote it out for Rs 100,000.[8] Support for the Muslim League and Pakistan came only at a later stage, when the same bourgeoisie began smelling opportunities that an independent 'Muslim' state could potentially present by forestalling competition from entrenched Bania–Marwari capital. A similar motive guided Mir Laiq Ali who, as prime minister under the nizam between November 1947 and September 1948, did everything in order to secure Hyderabad's independence from India. It proved as disastrous as the nawab of Junagadh's attempt to cede his Hindu-majority state to Pakistan.

To understand the opportunities arising from the creation of Pakistan one needs only to account for the fact that, prior to Partition, western Punjab's entire money market was controlled by non-Muslims (mostly Hindus and Khatri Sikhs), who also owned 167 out of the 215 indigenous factories in Lahore. Likewise in Karachi, '80 per cent of the landed property belonged to non-Muslims... Even with respect to foreign trade carried on in the port, 87 per cent of the concerns were controlled by non-Muslims.'[9] With Partition, there was a veritable vacuum that Muslim capital could therefore fill; and fill it did. The early birds to have capitalized on this gold rush were predictably the Memons, Khojas, and other immigrant business communities. In the 1960s the Memons constituted 0.16 per cent of Pakistan's population, yet controlled every fourth private factory there.[10] Their high noon period was during Field Marshall Ayub Khan's reign (1958–69), when a few diversified conglomerates with interests in jute, textiles, sugar, cement, paper, vegetable oil, chemicals, banking, and insurance came to dominate Pakistan's economy. They included the Adamjees (whose founder, Adamjee Haji Dawood, played a G.D. Birla-like role in the Muslim League), Bawanys, Dawoods, Karims, Dadas, Haroons, and the Rangoonwala-Bengali enterprise. Among the big Khojas were the Habibs (their Habib Bank lent Rs 8 crore to the Pakistan government in 1948, when the nascent state did not have a central bank) and the Fancy group. The 1971 war with India and the carving out of a separate Bangladesh from East Pakistan, and thereafter Zulfiqar Ali Bhutto's socialist dispensation, caused a setback to the established Memon and Khoja houses. The Adamjees (who were the world's biggest jute barons then), the Dawoods, and the Bawanys lost their mills in East Pakistan, while the Habib Bank and the Adamjee family's Muslim Commercial Bank (MCB) were nationalized. Since then, the Gujarati–Sindhi ethnic groups have been steadily marginalized, if not swamped, by the Chiniotis and various homegrown Punjabi communities. At the time of Partition the Chiniotis were basically rooted in leather and hides. As late as 1970 there were only five Chinioti groups in Pakistan's forty-two leading industrial families; but by 1997 there were at least fourteen. Pakistan's No. 1 conglomerate now is the Nishat house of Mian Mohammad Mansha, a Chinioti. He benefited substantially from the privatization programme of the prime minister, Nawaz Sharif – a Punjabi tycoon himself, who controlled the Ittefaq group – in the 1990s. Mansha's prized acquisition was the MCB, a bank belonging to the Adamjees before nationalization. Besides Nishat, the other major Punjabi combines include the Saigol, Crescent, Chakwal, Colony, Monnoo, and Sapphire groups.[11]

While Pakistan did turn out to be the promised land for a significant section of the Muslim bourgeoisie, it is not that their co-religionists in India have suffered a decline in business fortunes. On the contrary, the record of Muslim entrepreneurship in Independent India is far from dismal and can legitimately be cited as a shining illustration of the country's secular and pluralistic traditions. For a start, take the old merchant communities. The owner of India's third largest information technology (IT) enterprise after HCL and TCS – Wipro Limited – is a Khoja, Azim Hasham Premji. Wipro was originally called Western India Vegetable Products Limited and set up by his father, Mohammad Hussain Hasham Premji, in 1945 to produce vanaspati (hydrogenated vegetable oil) and laundry soaps. The senior Premji was supposedly invited by Jinnah (a fellow Khoja) to be Pakistan's first finance minister – an offer he declined. The Stanford-educated Azim, who had to take over after his father's sudden demise in 1966, expanded Wipro's operations from vanaspati to toilet soaps, baby care products, lighting, hydraulic components, medical equipment, and finally computer hardware and IT services.

Habil Fakhruddin Khorakiwala, who runs the pharmaceutical

major, Wockhardt Limited, is a Dawoodi Bohra. His father, Fakhruddin Taherbhai Khorakiwala, started it in 1959 as a partnership firm, Worli Chemicals. The Khorakiwala family also controls the Mumbai-based department store chain Akbarallys, established way back in 1897.[12] A more recent Bohra businessman is Siraj Lokhandwala of Lokhandwala Construction, a leading real estate and residential property developer in Mumbai. Among Memons, we have Abdul Razzak Allana's Allana group, which happens to be India's top exporter of agricultural and processed foods, from coffee to frozen buffalo meat.

Two industries where Muslims have, for obvious reasons, had a dominant presence are meat (apart from Allanasons, there is Sirajuddin Qureshi's Hind Agro Industries) and leather (the Kanpur-based Mirza International of Irshad Mirza, and the Chennai-based T. Abdul Wahid & Co. of Thadey Abdul Wahid, Farida group of Mecca Rafeeque Ahmad, KAR group of K. Ameenur Rahman, Presidency Kid Leather of Zackria Sait, Forward group of Asgar Ali Dhala, and M.A. Khizar Hussain & Sons). But to limit them to just these traditional sectors would be to ignore entrepreneurs spanning a whole range of other businesses: from cheroots (Mustak Hossain's Pataka Biri Manufacturing Company), edible oils (Hamza Abdul Kader's Liberty Oil Mills), and bread making (Harvest Gold Foods India Limited, belonging to the husband-and-wife team of Adil Hassan and Taab Siddiqi), to real estate (Lokhandwalas, the Bangalore-based Prestige group of Irfan Razack); logistics (Asgar Shakoor Patel's Patel Roadways and Patel On-Board Couriers Limited); menswear (Mohamed Yusuf Noorani's Zodiac Clothing Company); retail (Mohammed Abdullah's Homes Stores India, which operates the 'Sabka Bazar' chain); pharma (Wockhardt, Yusuf Khwaja Hamied's Cipla Limited, Meraj Manal's Himalaya Drug Company, Hakeem Abdul Hameed's Hamdard Wakf Laboratories); IT (Wipro, Cranes Software International of Asif

Khader and Mukkaram Jan); and media (Khalid Abdul Hamid Ansari's Mid-Day Multimedia Limited, which publishes *Mid Day* and *Inquilab* dailies).[13]

Some of these have pretty interesting histories. Yusuf Hamied's father Khwaja Abdul Hamied did a doctorate in chemistry from Berlin University in 1927 and it took him almost a decade to mobilize resources to start the Chemical, Industrial & Pharmaceutical Laboratories, which eventually became Cipla. An ardent nationalist on the lines of Prafulla Chandra Ray, it was Khwaja Hamied who drew the blueprint for a publicly funded industrial research body in 1942, leading to the birth of the Council of Scientific and Industrial Research (CSIR). The company he founded has grown to be India's second largest pharma concern after Ranbaxy. The 100-year-old Hamdard Laboratories has two branches, with the Indian one being under Hakeem Abdul Hameed and his sons, and the other in Pakistan started by his brother Hakeem Mohammed Said. Both Hamdard Laboratories India and Hamdard Laboratories Pakistan were companies that were converted into 'Waqf' (Trusts) in 1948 and 1953, respectively, and both make Unani herbal products like 'Rooh-Afza' cold drink concentrate, 'Safi' blood purifier and 'Sualin' cough-and-cold mixture.

The above examples are suggestive of Muslim entrepreneurship, more than surviving the ravages of Partition. Further, the post-Independence period has witnessed a widening of its base beyond the old Gujarati–Sindhi merchant groups to include communities such as the Ansaris and Qureshis. The Ansaris are traditionally weavers, many of whom, to escape retribution following the failed 1857 revolt, moved from the Indo-Gangetic plain to settle along towns on the Agra-Mumbai route. As the decline of Mumbai's textile mills from the 1960s spurred the growth of a decentralized powerloom industry to meet the demand for grey fabric, it created a class of master weavers-turned-power loom owners in Bhiwandi, Malegaon, and other peripheral urban clusters of Maharashtra. The Ansaris today not only control a large chunk of the business in these major power loom centres, but have since around the late 1970s also made inroads as middlemen and wholesale traders in the Varanasi-Mau handloom belt of Uttar Pradesh. A similar transition from ordinary butchers and meat sellers to owners of integrated abattoir-cum-meat processing plants has taken place within the Qureshis: Sirajuddin Qureshi of Hind Agro being a notable example.

Needless to say, the emergence of this new, often assertive, Muslim bourgeoisie has fuelled business rivalries with established Hindu mercantile interests. These tensions have often assumed communal overtones, making the likes of Bhiwandi, Malegaon, and Mau sensitive trouble spots. Also, unlike the old Muslim gentry, the leadership of the new bourgeoisie has tended to back non-Congress formations like the Samajwadi Party, or build independent power bases.[14] What is more, the Ansaris, and to a lesser extent Qureshis, have taken to education and the modern professions, facilitating the formation of a genuine Muslim middle class with no feudal trappings.[15] Another community to have prospered from trade and education are the Navayaths of Bhatkal, a picturesque coastal town in Uttara Kannada district of Karnataka. The Navayaths, like the Konkani Muslims, are considered products of the integration of immigrant Arabs with locals, and predominantly into small businesses spread across the southern states and Mumbai. In recent decades many – doctors, engineers, and other professionals, among them – have gone to the Persian Gulf, the US, and the UK, while not totally severing their umbilical cord with Bhatkal. The Anjuman Hami-e-Muslimeen – a trust running a clutch of schools and colleges at Bhatkal, founded by community members in 1919 – has had a catalysing influence in this regard.

Even more remarkable are the Malabar Muslims or Moplahs of Kerala, whose rise as a full-fledged business community has its genesis in the migration boom to the Gulf since the oil price shocks of the 1970s. Between 1972–3 and 1999–2000 annual foreign remittances to Kerala are estimated to have gone up from Rs 7.47 crore to Rs 13,652.14 crore, with Muslims making up over half of the emigrants and 47 per cent of the transfers.[16] A barely documented impact of this monetary flow – nearly a quarter of Kerala's net state domestic product – is the stimulus it has given for a new generation of Muslim businessmen. Leading the pack are M.A. Yusuffali – his Emke group manages a huge retail conglomerate (Lulu Hypermarkets) with branches all over the Middle East, besides garment factories in Kenya and Indonesia and meat-processing units at Kochi, Mumbai, and Sahibabad (near Delhi) – and P. Mohammed Ali of Galfar Engineering & Contracting LLC, a construction giant based in Oman. Both these non-resident Indian (NRI) tycoons are also the major investors in Cochin International Airport Limited, the country's first non-government airport venture. Another such NRI with trading and construction interests in the United Arab Emirates – he also has plantations, educational institutions, and car dealerships (Indus Motors) in Kerala – is P.V. Abdul Wahab of the Peevees group. Apart from them, there are hosts of others who have sprung up or grown quite big over the past two or three decades. Their areas of operation are varied: jewellery retailing (M.P. Ahammed's Malabar Gold); wheat flour and steels castings (P.K. Ahammed's Peekay group); edible oil refining (N.K. Mohammed Ali's Parisons group); cattle-feed manufacture and vehicle dealership (P.P. Koya's Koyenco group), cargo transport (V.K. Moidu Hajee's Kerala Roadways); spices and condiments (M.E. Meeran's Eastern group); real estate (Rafi Mather's Mather Projects and Constructions); hotels (Ahmed Usman Sait's Abad group); travel and ticketing services (K.V. Abdul Nazar's Akbar Travels of India); and IT (Javad K. Hassan's NeST group). Most of these men are from the northern Malabar districts of Malapuram and Kozhikode (besides parts of Thrissur): a historically backward region of the state that has undergone remarkable transformation due to the Gulf bonanza and resurgent Muslim capital.[17] Some of this upward mobility has also been facilitated by the Indian Union Muslim League (IUML), which has off and on ruled Kerala as part of Congress-led coalitions and exercised lien over the industries portfolio. For the record: P.V. Abdul Wahab is an IUML MP; P.P. Koya is brother-in-law of the ex-industries minister P.K. Kunhalikutty (their wives are sisters); M.K. Muneer, the owner of the Malayalam news channel *IndiaVision*, is the son of the former chief minister C.H. Mohammed Koya.

In contrast to the Moplahs, there has been a perceptible decline of Muslim entrepreneurship in old centres like Hyderabad. The companies that Mir Laiq Ali set up with the nizam's patronage have all closed down, been nationalized, or sold for their scrap value. A similar fate has befallen the Alladin family's Hyderabad Allwyn (a fairly reputed refrigerator maker till the 1970s) and Hyderabad Asbestos Cement Products (taken over by the Birlas), and Vazir Sultan Tobacco (now an ITC affiliate). Another group to have gone downhill is that of Mustafa Rashid Shervani who, in 1948, started a nickel-chromium electroplating unit at Allahabad, Great Eastern Electroplaters Limited (GEEP). It went on to also manufacture flashlights and dry cell batteries under the 'Geep' brand, which, in the late 1990s, was acquired by the US multi-national Gillette.[18]

Among Christians the most prolific are the Syrian Christians of central Kerala – a community with unique hybrid features. In terms of literacy they are arguably as advanced as the Brahmins or Kayasthas; there is no corner in India (extending to the Gulf, West Africa, the US, and the UK) where one doesn't find nurses, teachers, pastors, secretarial assistants and higher-end professionals from their ranks. As farmers they have a commercial orientation and flair for cropping innovations comparable to the Kammas, Gounders, and

Patidars. And, in the absence of a well-defined indigenous Vaishya class in Kerala, it is they who historically performed this role. Only in more recent times has their commercial and financial monopoly come under assault from the Moplahs and the Ezhavas. The land reforms carried out in Travancore from the early nineteenth century benefited the Syrian Christians more than anyone else, the Ezhavas included.[19] Relaxed rent obligations and the creation of an active land market were propitious for the accumulation of agricultural surpluses. While the Ezhavas, by and large, confined themselves to coconut, the Syrian Christians took to intensive farming of paddy in the coastal plains of Alappuzha and Kottayam (especially the low-lying Kuttanad tract) and plantation crops (rubber and spices) in the midlands and high ranges of Kottayam, Idukki, and Wayanad. By the early part of the twentieth century there were substantial landholders with capital principally being channelled into trading, organized moneylending, and rubber estates.[20]

The Kandathil and Chalakuzhi families epitomize the trajectory described above. In 1888 Kandathil Varghese Mappillai, a moneylender who taught Malayalam at Kottayam's Church Missionary Society (CMS) College, launched *Malayala Manorama* with a capital of Rs 1 lakh. After Varghese Mappillai died in 1904 the business passed to his nephew Kandathil Cherian (K.C.) Mammen Mappilai. The latter, in 1912, founded the Travancore National Bank, which, twenty-five years later, combined with the Quilon Bank (controlled by C.P. Mathen of the Chalakuzhi family) to form the Travancore National and Quilon Bank Limited. Even before the merger, the two banks between them commanded a working capital of Rs 3.5 crore. From banking, K.C. Mammen Mappillai expanded into insurance (Guardian of India Insurance Company), besides promoting large plantation concerns in association with other wealthy Syrian Christian groups (Associated Planters Limited and Young India Agencies).[21] Significantly, the Kandathil family's foray into industry did not materialize till well after Independence. In 1946 Mammen Mappillai's youngest son K.M. Mammen Mappillai opened a tiny toy balloon unit at Tiruvottiyur in Chennai. From rubber balloons and squeaking toys this undertaking – Madras Rubber Factory – diversified into manufacturing industrial gloves, contraceptives, tread-rubber, and finally tyres. MRF Limited today is India's leading tyre company, while *Manorama* remains the No. 1 Malayalam daily.[22]

While the Travancore National and Quilon Bank crashed within a year of its amalgamation, there are other Syrian Christian banking ventures that have managed to survive and even grow: Federal Bank Limited (established as a chit auction business in 1931, before its takeover when on the verge of liquidation by Kulangara Paulo Hormis in 1945), Catholic Syrian Bank (incorporated in 1920), and South Indian Bank (roughly the same time).[23] All three are based in the Aluva-Thrissur belt. Then, we have non-banking financial intermediaries such as Muthoot which, too, began as a small-time money-lending and chit fund operation at Kozhencherry, an hour's drive from Kottayam. Around 1939 the business was split between the two brothers, M. George Muthoot and Mathew M. Thomas (Muthoot Pappachan). Both groups today have a nationwide presence in virtually identical lines – from lending against gold to providing vehicle finance, hire purchase, and merchant banking services, running hotels, and developing real estate. A relatively new entrant in finance is C.J. George's Geojit Financial Services Limited which, over the last decade, has risen to be a well-established stock and commodity exchange broking firm.

Linked somewhat to finance is gold, a commonly employed loan collateral and pawning instrument in the South. Here again, there is a profusion of Syrian Christian jewellery retailing houses, mostly Thrissur-based: the Alappats, Alukkas, Chemmanurs, Manuelsons, and Joscos. The Alappats, in fact, happen to be one of the original promoters of South Indian Bank. Other notable businessmen from the community include M.A. Abraham (his Chennai-based Aban group has interests in offshore oil drilling and engineering construction), Kochouseph Chittilappilly of V-Guard Industries (which produces voltage stabilizers, wiring cables, and other electrical appliances) and M.C. Jacob (Anna Aluminium, Kitex Garments, Sara Spices). As for non-Syrian Christian business houses, rather few seem identifiable. In Chapter 6 we did take note of a few Nadar Christian combines, especially the A.V. Thomas plantation empire. The only other comparable entrepreneur is Gracias Saldhana, whose Glenmark Pharmaceuticals Limited is among the country's top twenty drug companies.[24]

10

Conclusion

On 25 November 1949, at the penultimate sitting of the Constituent Assembly which drafted Independent India's constitution, Bhimrao Ramji Ambedkar noted:

> we are going to enter into a life of contradictions. In politics we will have equality and in social and economic life we will have inequality. In politics we will be recognizing the principle of one man one vote and one vote one value. In our social and economic life, we shall, by reason of our social and economic structure, continue to deny the principle of one man one value. How long shall we continue to live this life of contradictions? How long shall we continue to deny equality in our social and economic life? If we continue to deny it for long, we will do so only by putting our political democracy in peril. We must remove this contradiction at the earliest possible moment or else those who suffer from inequality will blow up the structure of political democracy which this Assembly has so laboriously built up.[1]

Ambedkar is known by many as the man who chaired the Drafting Committee elected by the Assembly; and by all as someone who gave voice and articulate expression to the country's vast Dalit populace, unprivileged and unlettered by custom and circumstances.

More grudgingly acknowledged has been Ambedkar's stature as an original thinker and scholar par excellence: his concept of 'graded inequality' as an organizing principle of Indian society is as insightful a contribution to the sociological lexicon as the terms 'dominant caste' and 'sanskritisation' coined by M.N. Srinivas. Well over half a century since he talked about the impending 'life of contradictions', Ambedkar's prognosis stands vindicated. Independent India has seen Dalits becoming chief ministers, governors, even president (K.R. Narayanan) and chief justice (K.G. Balakrishnan). Since the coming in of the 73rd constitutional amendment legislation, Dalits have also gained formal access to political power in village panchayats and local bodies. The day may not be distant when India has a Dalit prime minister as well. The democratic process and adherence to the 'one man one value' principle has led to a significant political empowerment of Dalits and other historically underrepresented sections of the Brahminical *ancien regime*. With all its limitations and flaws, diversity has become enshrined in the polity and here India probably scores over every Western political democracy.

This book's concern has been with diversity in the economic and business sphere. The central point conveyed is that capitalism in India has evolved a long way since Independence and today is fairly well diversified not just in terms of production profile (spanning a whole range of industries) but also social base. Capital is not the privileged bastion of a few mercantile castes the way it was; its base has expanded to incorporate a wide spectrum of communities. However, this 'inclusive capitalism' has been more a feature of southern and, to some extent, western India. Take, for instance, the sugar industry in the South, which cannot possibly be identified with any particular community. Thus, we have EID Parry (Nattukottai Chettiar), Sakthi Sugars, Bannari Amman Sugars and Dharani Sugars (Gounders), Thiru Arooran Sugars (Mudaliar),

Ponni Sugars (Brahmin), Rajshree Sugars (Naidu), Andhra Sugars and KCP Sugar (Kammas), GMR Industries (Komati), Gayatri Sugars (Reddy), Kothari Sugars (Gujarati Bania/Jain) and Empee Sugars (Ezhava).[2] A similar diversity in ownership exists for the major media houses: Sun TV (Isai Vellalar),[3] *TV9* (Raju), *Eenadu* (Kamma), *Malayala Manorama* (Syrian Christian), *Asianet* (Nair), *Daily Thanthi* (Nadar), *The Hindu* and *Dinamalar* (Brahmins), *Deccan Chronicle* (Reddy), and *Deccan Herald-Prajavani* (Idiga).

This is not so in the North, where businessmen tend to be uniformly Bania–Marwaris or Khatris. The Jats (both Hindu and Sikh), Yadavs, Gujjars, and other intermediate castes produce the bulk of its sugarcane, paddy, wheat, cotton, oilseeds and milk, but rarely does one find sugar millers, branded rice makers, grain exporters, textile tycoons, solvent extractors, and dairy processors from these communities. There is only one Jat Sikh-owned company (Simbhaoli Sugar Mills) figuring in the region's top ten sugar manufacturers, just as VRS Foods (Paras) is the sole dairy whose promoter happens to be a Gujjar. Nor have these politically powerful castes produced media barons comparable to a Ramoji Rao, a Kalanithi Maran, and a Sivanthi Adityan. The social churning resulting from competitive electoral politics – accentuated in the post-Mandal era – has not extended itself into the business arena and there is an almost neat convergence of caste and class. Generation after generation of entrepreneurs – from the Birlas, Shrirams and Thapars to the Jindals, Mahindras, and Munjals, right up to Sunil Mittal, Naresh Goyal, and Kishore Biyani – have been bred from the same Bania or Khatri community stock. Things are better in the West, where the co-operative movement has enabled peasant castes like the Marathas and Patidars to make a successful entry into industry.

In our discussions we have referred to a number of factors behind this mixed bag. Education – more specifically, exposure to

English and the technical disciplines – is certainly one of them. The intermediate castes in the South and West have had better access to modern education – something that, we saw, goes back to the colonial period, and which was further facilitated by the role of progressive princely regimes (Baroda, Kolhapur, Travancore) and Christian missionaries (as it was for the Nadars). This, more than anything else, helped in integrating town with countryside and familiarizing village families to the values and mores of townsmen. It led to the formation of a middle class that, even while retaining its rural roots, generated a regular stream of engineers, doctors, bureaucrats, lawyers, writers, and accountants. Awareness and demand for education, in turn, spurred the setting up of schools, colleges, and vocational training institutions through private and co-operative community initiatives. Affirmative action from the state – backed by popular movements, whose leaders came from the same upwardly mobile strata – only reinforced this process. Non-Brahmin mobilizations in the Madras and Bombay Presidency areas from the turn of the last century, in fact, had a dual impact. Firstly, they created a middle class with a reasonably broad social base. Secondly, by re-defining and tweaking conventional social hierarchies, they forced the Brahmins and other upper castes to explore alternative career paths and become entrepreneurs themselves in the bargain. It is from the resultant socially heterogeneous middle class, comprising both Brahmins and non-Brahmins, that a new 'type' of industrialist emerged and flourished especially after Independence: people whose fathers may have been agriculturists, schoolteachers, or government babus, not shopkeepers or merchants.

This kind of social churning and thirst for education embracing the town and countryside has not been witnessed in the North until quite recently. Although the first stirrings of change are visible, a truly broad-based and representative middle class is still far from taking shape. Neither has the idea of affirmative action fully permeated the popular imagination. Little surprise, then, that reservations for Other Backward Classes in government jobs ('Mandal I') and seats in educational institutions ('Mandal II') have met with fierce resistance from the region's socially narrow urban middle class and media. This is unlike in the South and the West, where the 'social justice' problem was sorted out several decades ago and reservations are an accepted reality of life.

Besides education and affirmative action, the factor that has contributed to a considerable 'democratization of capital' in the South is the absence of stranglehold over business by traditional mercantile and banking communities. Not that they did not exist; but the Chettiars and Komatis were nowhere as overbearing in the money and commodity markets as the ubiquitous northern Bania. The latter's universe encompassed the entire business chain: from village-level moneylending and primary sourcing of produce to wholesale brokerage and bill discounting, and manufacture and marketing of final products. In such a hostile environment, it was difficult for outsiders to penetrate the system. The Ramgarhias of Punjab represent a unique case of artisan castes adapting their skills in the modern age to become fabricators of cycle and auto parts, machine tools, textile equipment, and farm machinery. However, given the power of entrenched business interests, these men could never advance to the next stage of controlling textile mills or manufacturing branded bicycles and tractors. Breaking through the socio-business hierarchy called for countervailing support from the state – conscious policy intervention of the sort that proved decisive in the success of sugar and dairy co-operatives promoted by the dominant rural Maratha-Patidar communities of western India. The South, by contrast, benefited from a historical Vaishya vacuum, which conferred a relatively open social space for private enterprise. An entrepreneur could under the circumstances be a Chettiar, Brahmin, Kamma, Gounder, Nadar, Syrian Christian, or

Muslim. So, when the post-Independence era heralded a step-up in public investments in irrigation, power, transport, and other core sectors under successive five-year plans, it spawned contractors and aspirant industrialists who were recruited from a variety of community backgrounds. Not that caste was obliterated in business; the point is that it turned out to be less of an impediment in the South than in other parts.

In our discussions, we delineated three general trajectories of industrial transition by communities. The first was the conventional Bazaar-to-Factory route, involving the various Bania and Vaishya groups dealt with in Chapter 2. The second, from Office to Factory, referred to the Brahmins, Khatris, Kayasthas, the Bengali bhadralok, and other scribal castes with a distinct urban 'middle class' orientation. These sections traditionally dominated the bureaucracy and white-collar professions and, as noted in Chapter 3, their entry into business in phenomenal proportions was essentially a post-1947 development. The later chapters examined a third pathway: from Field to Factory, covering those communities classified as Shudras in the classical Hindu chaturvarna scheme. This wide-ranging category included landowning peasant castes like the Kammas, Reddys, Gounders, Jats, Patidars, and Marathas, and also 'lower Shudras' such as Nadars, Ramgarhias, and assorted rural service-provider communities. Alternatively, they may be viewed as constituting the 'rural middle class', whose political, social and economic empowerment was one of the epochal features of the last century. Their journey into corporate boardrooms, howsoever uneven across regions, paralleled a similar transition achieved by the urban scribal castes. Both these urban and rural middle-class-led trajectories have undermined the time-honoured association of 'business communities' with an exclusive Vaishya order.

The group that has, nevertheless, been bypassed in this churning of capital and widening of its social base are the Dalits. In our study we did not come across a single Dalit industrialist even in the South. Recent reports suggest the rise of a nascent Dalit bourgeoisie, concurrent with the Bahujan Samaj Party (BSP) becoming a formidable force and occasionally ruling Uttar Pradesh via coalitions since the 1990s, and currently with a clear majority of its own. There is mention of one Hari Kishen Pippal, the owner of a 125-bed hospital in Agra who once contested assembly elections on a BSP ticket. Likewise, Agra has Devki Nandan Sone, who runs a budget hotel called 'Taj Plaza', and Arun K. Singh, a university lecturer-turned-proprietor of a commercial complex in the heart of the city. Then, there are small-scale Dalit establishments engaged in the manufacture and export of shoes, horse-riding equipment, and leather upholstery.[4] Some of this entrepreneurial zeal is also reflected through organizations like the Pune-based Dalit Indian Chamber of Commerce and Industry (DICCI) and Delhi's Dalit Vyapar Welfare Association (DVWA), which have made access to start-up loans and reserving a fixed percentage of government contracts the focal point of their lobbying efforts. These demands were also articulated in the 'Bhopal Declaration' adopted by activists and delegates at a conference in January 2002. A subsequent task force set up by the Madhya Pradesh government recommended 'supplier diversity' in public contracts, departmental purchases, and allotment of liquor licences. It further mooted tax breaks for automobile manufacturers, pharmaceutical companies, and other industries linked to their awarding dealerships and distributorships to Dalit businessmen.[5] But it's still early days. DICCI's 100 or so members in Maharashtra have annual turnovers between Rs 50 lakh and Rs 4 crore, while DVWA's 500-strong constituents each do business of up to only Rs 20 lakh.[6] It will obviously take some time for a genuine Dalit capitalist class to storm India Inc.

A couple of more points may be in order before we end. The first has to do with the ephemeral dimension of caste identities in business. As communities get entrenched in economic space and capital accumulates and reproduces on an expanding scale, the atomistic calculations of individual capitalists tend to override the ideals of collective enterprise. We saw this most clearly *vis-à-vis* the Nadars, an extremely close-knit community that, in the face of social persecution, created a network of institutions to organise its members and advance their common corporate interests. One of the stated objectives of the Nadar Mahajana Sangam, formed in 1910, was 'to encourage and promote commercial and industrial enterprise among the members of the community'. The Tamilnad Mercantile Bank, too, was started in 1921 to finance Nadar entrepreneurs; till as late as 1962 it was known as the Nadar Bank. But by the mid 1990s, the ownership had passed on to a Marwari group (the Ruias of Essar), which then offloaded its controlling stake in the bank to a California-settled Mudaliar (C. Sivasankaran). The Sangam could do nothing to prevent the original Nadar promoters from selling out to 'outsiders' when offered a good price for their shares. An analogous explanation can be given for the co-operative movement in Gujarat and Maharashtra losing its vibrancy over the years. With private enterprise becoming an increasingly viable and preferred option among Patidars and Marathas, these communities – or, at any rate, the upwardly mobile sections that provided their leadership – have shown a waning interest in co-operative businesses. All these indicate how sharpening internal differentiation and stratification exert a weakening influence on community solidarity, with well-to-do members being drawn towards new functional and class alignments cutting across caste lines. A Kamma sugar magnate ultimately identifies his interests with other mill owners and not with fellow Kamma cane growers or workers. While community feelings continue to be strong among less successful members,[7] these, if at all invoked by the elite, usually take opportunistic forms.[8]

What is true for caste also holds for regional and other ethnic identities. At a certain stage of its growth the emergent bourgeoisie finds it expedient to play up subnational pride and invest in provincial political formations. The Dravida Munnetra Kazhagam, the Telugu Desam, and the Akali Dal – for that matter even the Congress in Maharashtra and Gujarat – were manifestations of this trend. The Congress at the centre was seen to be favouring 'monopoly big-business capital' over 'non-monopoly regional capital', which did not enjoy as much leverage in New Delhi to secure industrial licences and related concessions.[9] But as the capital accumulation process intensifies, the lines between the national and regional bourgeoisie are progressively blurred. A corresponding realignment also takes place at the political plane, with provincial demagogues and erstwhile rabble-rousers developing high stakes at the centre. In India the dismantling of the licence-control raj has happened almost simultaneously with coalition politics becoming the order of the day. It is perhaps no simple coincidence that regional parties are propping up national governments these days, just when the likes of GMR and GVK are starting to build international airports in Delhi and Mumbai, and a Rajshree Sugars is planning to erect factories in Bihar.

Notes

1. Introduction

1. Gadgil 1951, Gadgil 1959, Lamb 1955.
2. Tripathi 1984, Timberg 1978.
3. On this, see Granovetter 1985, Landa 1981.
4. Landa's argument that personalistic exchange relations and reputation matter mainly in societies with an underdeveloped legal infrastructure is possibly overstated. The preference for dealing with 'people like us' is also reflected in the appointment of country managers of multinational subsidiaries and similar racial considerations that impinge on strategic business decisions. The spilling over of business relations into sociability and vice versa may be less apparent, but is not totally absent even in countries with advanced legal systems. As Granovetter (1985) points out, litigation everywhere is a last resort and disputes are 'frequently settled without reference to the contract or potential or actual legal sanctions' (p. 496).
5. Gadgil (1959) has noted that for describing business activity in India 'it is necessary to pay attention to the castes and communities engaged in it'. In a situation where society is highly stratified into caste and subcaste groups, permitting little mobility between one occupation and another, 'the history of rise and development of modern business

becomes, to a large extent, the history of the activities of members of certain groups' (p. 16).

6. Kautilya 1992, pp. 242–50.
7. See Tripathi and Mehta 1984, and Divekar 1984. Also Gadgil 1959, p. 19.
8. In her study on Hokkien-Chinese middlemen in South East Asia, Landa (1981) has mapped a 'calculus of relations', ranking traders as 'insiders' and 'outsiders' in descending order of trustworthiness. Within insiders, there is a further subgradation comprising 'near kinsmen from family', 'distant kinsmen from extended family', 'clansmen', 'fellow villagers from China', and 'fellow Hokkiens', while outsiders include 'non-Hokkiens' (Teochews, Cantonese, etc.) and 'non-Chinese' (Malays, Europeans, etc.). Transactions involving 'insiders' were based on credit, whereas dealings with 'outsiders' were strictly in cash.
9. If arranged marriage from within the community is a general norm in India, impressionistic evidence suggests it is more so among businessmen. This is natural, given the predominance of family-owned businesses that guard against potential wealth dilution via marriage alliances with outsiders. To quote Rajshree Pathy, a sugar baroness from Coimbatore's Kammavar Naidu community: 'The PSG family produces girls, the Lakshmi Mills family produces boys, they marry each other and live happily ever after' (Aditi Phadnis, 'Lunch with BS: Rajshree Pathy', *Business Standard*, 7 December 2005). For a deeper sociological account of marriages and relational patterns within business families, see Dutta 1997, pp. 59–123.
10. The two classic readings on the country's industrial history are Bagchi 1972 and Ray 1979. Both these cover the pre-1947 era. The other grand work – Hazari 1966 – is of 1960s vintage. Even the recently published, Tripathi 2004, offers a skimpy coverage of post-Independence business trends.
11. Gadgil (1951 and 1959) and Lamb (1955) mainly deal with these communities, although the former does also mention the Punjabi Khatris. More focused contributions include Timberg 1978, Goswami 1985, Rudner 1994, Mahadevan 1978, Ito 1966, Guha 1984, Desai 1968, Markovits 2000, and Papanek 1973. Also, see Iyer 1999.

12. In Piramal 1997, and Piramal 1999, the industrialists are all Parsi, Marwari, or Gujarati Bania/Jain.
13. McDonald 1998, p. xviii. This is a rare business biography, not really worshipful of its subject.
14. Take, for instance, Sanjay Subrahmanyam, 'Big Bucks, But Still No Bang', *India Today*, 30th Anniversary Issue, 26 December 2005, pp. 334–5. The author here sweepingly states that there is very little evidence of the emergence of major entrepreneurs from outside the bazaar and even the new actors 'belong in their vast majority to the older merchant communities (Baniyas, Khojas, Memons, Marwaris and Sindworkies)'.
15. Notable in this genre are Hardgrave 1969, Owens and Nandy 1978, Saberwal 1976, Upadhya 1988, Rutten 1995, and Chari 2004.
16. The only serious, even if tentative, attempt in this direction is Baru 2000.
17. The exceptional scholar who has taken a more nuanced approach – even if his work concerns the pre-Independence era – is Raman Mahadevan. See Mahadevan 1991, Mahadevan 1992, Mahadevan 1984, and 'The South Side', *Businessworld*, 3 January 2000, pp. 54–8.
18. For an account of early provincial industrialization in the Tamil heartland, see Baker 1984, pp. 334–420.
19. The Mahishyas (Owens and Nandy 1978) are an example of a 'weak' business community that has failed to outgrow its smallness. True, there are many engineering shops and foundries in Howrah, near Kolkata, belonging to members of this traditional cultivating caste. Yet one does not know of any major Mahishya industrialist today. The Gounders of the Coimbatore region are a study in contrast: of peasants turning into big-time knitwear entrepreneurs (Chapter 5, and Chari 2004). In between these two, in terms of success rate, are the Ramgarhias of Punjab (Chapter 8, and Saberwal 1976).

2. The Old Merchant Communities

1. Marx and Engels 1977: p. 112.
2. Letter to Purshotamdas Thakurdas, quoted in Ray 1979, p. 304.

3. See, for example, Ray 1979, pp. 292–338, Markovits 1985, Mukherjee 2002, and Chibber 2004, pp. 85–109.
4. This aspect is brought out well by Ray 1984. Also see Iyer 1999.
5. Ray 1984.
6. On the links between fiscal policy, trade, and usury capital in princely states, see Sharma 1984 and Hardiman 1996, pp. 18–42.
7. For regional details of Marwari migration, see Timberg 1978, pp. 179–228.
8. Timberg 1978, pp. 47, 130–53.
9. Goswami 1989.
10. Timberg 1978, pp. 197–201.
11. The above details are mainly from Desai 1968 and Guha 1984. Also see Siddiqi 1982.
12. Gupta 1979.
13. Before the outbreak of the Civil War, India's share in raw cotton imported into Britain averaged just 20 per cent, which jumped to 75 per cent during 1861–4. On this, and also Roychand's rise and fall, see Tripathi 2004, pp. 100–10.
14. Markovits 2000, pp. 57–109.
15. Ibid., pp. 110–55.
16. Mahadevan 1978.
17. Raman Mahadevan, 'The South Side', *Business World*, 3 January 2000, pp. 54–8.
18. Farooqui 1995.
19. On how the Depression had lasting positive consequences for Indian industry, while badly hitting British interests, see Markovits 1985, pp. 41–67.
20. On the Marwari entry into the jute industry, see Goswami 1989.
21. Letter to Ambalal Sarabhai, 30 April 1930. Quoted in Ray 1979, p. 72.
22. The major Tata companies are Tata Motors (Rs 1,348.99 crore profit after tax (PAT) on net sales of Rs 19,279.20 crore for the year ended 31 March 2005), Tata Steel (Rs 3,545.24 crore and Rs 15,998.61 crore), Tata Consultancy Services (Rs 1,831.42 crore and Rs 8,027.58 crore), Tata Power (Rs 587.95 crore and Rs 4,954.72 crore), VSNL (Rs 756.37 crore and Rs 3,303.04 crore), Tata Tea

(Rs 235.90 crore and Rs 3,039.53 crore), Tata Chemicals (Rs 340.55 crore and Rs 3,008.14 crore), Voltas (Rs 52.25 crore and Rs 1,477.07 crore), Indian Hotels (Rs 100.70 crore and Rs 1,313.53 crore), Titan Industries (Rs 34.40 crore and Rs 1,081.96 crore), Tata Infotech (Rs 79.78 crore and Rs 959.85 crore), Tata Teleservices Maharashtra (Rs –527.86 crore and Rs 807.47 crore), and Rallis (Rs 33.50 crore and Rs 565.87 crore).

23. The Godrej group includes Godrej Industries (Rs 71.06 crore and Rs 1,950.60 crore), Godrej Consumer Products (Rs 86.07 crore and Rs 562.67 crore), Godrej & Boyce Manufacturing Company, and Godrej Agrovet Limited. The Wadia companies comprise Britannia Industries (Rs 148.77 crore and Rs 1,587.57 crore), Bombay Dyeing (Rs 26.56 crore and Rs 1,011.20 crore), Bombay Burmah Trading Corporation (Rs 6.75 crore and Rs 145.77 crore), and National Peroxide (Rs 14.27 crore and Rs 75.33 crore). The Pallonji group's main construction concerns are Shapoorji Pallonji & Co Ltd and Afcons Infrastructure. The group's only listed company is Forbes Gokak Ltd (Rs 19.37 crore and Rs 1,086.90 crore). Eureka Forbes Ltd and other businesses are privately held. Thermax reported a net profit of Rs 68.28 crore on net sales of Rs 1,229.10 crore for the year ended 31 March 2005.

24. For the year ended 31 March 2005 Great Eastern made a PAT of Rs 845.68 crore on net sales of Rs 2,157.12 crore. The corresponding figures were Rs 83.87 crore and Rs 388.96 crore for Varun Shipping, Rs 70.14 crore and Rs 1,002.34 crore for Marico, and Rs 170.91 crore and Rs 1,711.51 crore (total consolidated income) for Kotak Mahindra Bank. Godavari Sugar's net sales amounted to Rs 365.27 crore.

25. For the year ended 31 March 2005 SPIC earned a PAT of Rs 10.39 crore on net sales of Rs 2,427.75 crore, while being Rs 27.99 crore and Rs 1,214.83 crore for Sical, and Rs 15.87 crore and Rs 733.92 crore for Tamilnadu Petroproducts. Raja Sir Annamalai Chettiar's eldest son, M.A. Muthiah Chettiar, was also known by the title of 'Raja Sir'. The latter's son, M.A.M. Ramaswamy, owns Chettinad Cement Corporation (Rs 27.96 crore and Rs 387.35 crore), besides being a prominent racing baron and horse breeder. The PAT and

net sales numbers for the Murugappa group companies were Rs 146.87 crore and Rs 2,236.69 crore for EID Parry, Rs 95.60 crore and Rs 1,521.82 crore for Tube Investments, Rs 17.09 crore and Rs 1,200.05 crore for Godavari Fertilisers, Rs 48.36 crore and Rs 357.69 crore for Carborundum Universal, and Rs 30.78 crore and Rs 229.92 crore (income) for Cholamandalam DBS.

26. The PAT and net sales for the Hinduja group companies in India were Rs 271.41 crore and Rs 4,258.40 crore for Ashok Leyland, Rs 210.15 crore and Rs 1,385.15 crore (total income) for IndusInd Bank, Rs 184.43 crore and Rs 607.58 crore for Hinduja TMT, Rs 17.90 crore and Rs 436.14 crore for Gulf Oil Corporation, and Rs 13.08 crore and Rs 222.67 crore for Ennore Foundries.

27. For the year ended 31 March 2005 Blue Star reported a PAT of Rs 39.16 crore on net sales of Rs 916.80 crore, with the corresponding numbers being Rs 95.92 crore and Rs 824.46 crore for Finolex Industries, Rs 61.68 crore and Rs 655.90 crore for Finolex Cables, Rs 27.93 crore and Rs 210.56 crore for Ador Welding, Rs 19.03 crore and Rs 498.13 crore for Shopper's Stop, Rs 79.26 crore and Rs 1,270.15 crore for Exide, Rs 25.82 crore and Rs 441.45 crore for Prism Cement (year ended 30 June 2005), Rs 34.80 crore and Rs 622.63 crore for Unitech, Rs 31.82 crore and Rs 1,104.72 crore for Mirc Electronics, Rs 18.32 crore and Rs 481.26 crore for Man Industries, and Rs 39.58 crore and Rs 719.80 crore for Gokaldas Exports.

28. For the year ended 31 March 2005 the PAT and net sales figures stood at Rs 117.38 crore and Rs 1,960.81 crore for Arvind Mills, Rs (–) 8.26 crore and Rs 406.74 crore for Arvind Products, Rs 12.55 crore and Rs 724.45 crore for Atul, and Rs 1.77 crore and Rs 171.68 crore for Anil Products. The same were Rs 73.57 crore and Rs 1,578.16 crore for HCC, Rs 7.72 crore and Rs 257.88 crore for Walchandnagar Industries (year ended 30 September 2005), and Rs 25.36 crore and Rs 179.21 crore for Indian Hume.

29. Since 2005 the Reliance group has been split between Dhirubhai's two sons, Mukesh and Anil. Mukesh's companies include RIL (Rs 7,628.23 crore and Rs 66,010.47 crore) and Indian Petrochemicals Corporation Limited (Rs 785.73 crore and Rs 8,171.00 crore),

while Anil has Reliance Energy (Rs 520.14 crore and Rs 4,050.53 crore), Reliance Capital (Rs 105.81 crore and Rs 295.69 crore), and Reliance Infocomm Limited (unlisted entity).

30. For the year ended 31 March 2005 Torrent Pharma earned a PAT of Rs 48.76 crore on net sales of Rs 530.78 crore, with these being Rs 107.03 crore and Rs 1,314.35 crore for Torrent Power AEC, Rs 39.96 crore and Rs 950.22 crore for Torrent SEC, and Rs 121.58 crore and Rs 15,005.34 crore for Adani Exports.
31. The 31 March 2005 year-ending PAT and net sales were Rs 174.59 crore and Rs 2,673.28 crore for Asian Paints, Rs 72.42 crore and Rs 772.33 crore for Pidilite, Rs 156.00 crore and Rs 1,351.89 crore for United Phosphorus, Rs (–) 2.16 crore and Rs 218.90 crore for Excel Industries, Rs 23.07 crore and Rs 404.70 crore for Excel Crop Care, Rs 79.45 crore and Rs 526.52 crore for Deepak Fertilisers, Rs 10.06 crore and Rs 328.42 crore for Deepak Nitrite, Rs 8.79 crore and Rs 650.28 crore for Garden Silk (end June 2005), Rs 39.40 crore and Rs 184.60 crore for Kothari Products, Rs 25.80 crore and Rs 2,679.79 crore for Vishal, and Rs 44.86 crore and Rs 1,110.77 crore for Shah Alloys.
32. www.geskey.com/achievements.html.
33. Dan Bilefsky, 'Indians Unseat Antwerp's Jews as the Biggest Diamond Traders', *The Wall Street Journal*, 27 May 2003. According to official statistics, India's exports of gems and jewellery during 2004–5 (April–March) were valued at $15.68 billion (Rs 70,245 crore), while corresponding imports of roughs and other raw material stood at $ 11.58 billion (Rs 52,234 crore).
34. For the year ended 31 March 2005 Rajesh Exports earned a PAT of Rs 43.09 crore on net sales of Rs 4,246.81 crore, while being Rs 30.82 crore and Rs 1,149.65 crore for Su-Raj Diamonds, Rs 22.53 crore and Rs 1,094.86 crore for Asian Star, Rs 12.03 crore and Rs 564.73 crore for Classic Diamonds, Rs 12.06 crore and Rs 558.27 crore for Shrenuj, and Rs 10.21 crore and Rs 1,371.16 crore for Gitanjali Gems.
35. For the year ended 31 March 2005 Hindalco reported a PAT of Rs 1,284.79 crore on net sales of Rs 9,919.68 crore, while amounting to Rs 880.43 crore and Rs 9,314.82 crore for Grasim (including

UltraTech), Rs 58.40 crore and Rs 3,170.75 crore for Aditya Birla Nuvo, Rs 122.55 crore and Rs 2,472.30 crore for Century Textiles, Rs 33.52 crore and Rs 1,421.96 crore for Kesoram, Rs 52.56 crore and Rs 955.13 crore for Century Enka, and Rs 56.93 crore and Rs 678.35 crore for Indo Gulf.

36. During the year ended 31 March 2005 the PAT and net sales numbers were Rs 224.50 crore and Rs 3,059.08 crore for Chambal Fertilisers, Rs (–) 9.88 crore and Rs 2,892.46 crore for Zuari, Rs 12.01 crore and Rs 355.33 crore for Oudh Sugar and Rs 14.01 crore and Rs 329.65 crore for Upper Ganges Sugar (both ending 30 June 2005), Rs 27.34 crore and Rs 624.58 crore for HT Media, Rs 18.55 crore and Rs 531.96 crore for Sutlej Industries, Rs 15.88 crore and Rs 294.72 crore for Texmaco, Rs 41.79 crore and Rs 1,050.62 crore for Hindustan Motors (15 months ended 30 June 2005), Rs 13.68 crore and Rs 724.54 crore for National Engineering, Rs (–) 3.53 crore and Rs 831 crore for Orient Paper, Rs 9.74 crore and Rs 407.96 crore for Hyderabad Industries, and Rs 86.39 crore and Rs 1,131.12 crore for Birla Corporation.

37. The net sales and PAT figures for the major Shriram companies during the reference period were Rs 104.73 crore and Rs 1,864.53 crore for DSCL, Rs 59.36 crore and Rs 1,146.40 crore for SRF, Rs 24.84 crore and Rs 532.26 crore for DSIL, Rs 63.51 crore and Rs 551.33 crore for Mawana Sugars (year ended 30 September 2005), Rs 6.36 crore and Rs 368.38 crore for Usha International, and Rs 0.19 crore and Rs 196.16 crore for Siel. The corresponding levels were Rs 20.42 crore and Rs 2,079.08 crore for J.K. Industries (year ended September 2005), Rs 38.53 crore and Rs 657.55 crore for JK Paper (30 June 2005), Rs 28.75 crore and Rs 486.78 crore for JK Lakshmi, Rs 85.34 crore and Rs 1,460.11 crore for Raymond, and Rs 6.30 crore and Rs 329.41 crore for J.K. Cement

38. For the year ended 31 March 2005 CESC earned a PAT of Rs 147.20 crore on net sales of Rs 2,352.64 crore, with these being Rs (–) 7.76 crore and Rs 1,534.85 crore for CEAT, Rs 42.25 crore and Rs 1,230.27 crore for KEC, Rs 12.36 crore and Rs 912.07 crore for PCB (18 months), Rs 41.63 crore and Rs 142.04 crore for Harrisons Malayalam, Rs 9.50 crore and Rs 113.60 crore for Saregama, Rs

13.66 crore and Rs 398.78 crore for NRC, and Rs 20.18 crore and Rs 183.37 crore for Star Paper. The corresponding figures were Rs 798.65 crore and Rs 6,196.39 crore for Bajaj Auto, Rs 140.39 crore and Rs 881.97 crore (year ending 30 September 2005) for Bajaj Hindusthan, Rs 13.66 crore and Rs 649.63 crore for Bajaj Electricals, Rs 184.78 crore and Rs 1,511.48 crore for Mukand, and Rs 2.72 crore and Rs 856.12 crore for Force Motors.

39. The PAT and net sales for the year ended 31 March 2005 were Rs 29.07 crore and Rs 582.08 crore for Shree Cement, Rs 60.42 crore and Rs 562.20 crore for Graphite India, Rs 29.88 crore and Rs 500.02 crore for West Coast Paper, Rs 20.73 crore and Rs 291.06 crore for Rama Newsprint, Rs 25.40 crore and Rs 443.39 crore for AP Paper, and Rs 10.34 crore and Rs 185.62 crore for Shree Umaid Mills.

40. For the year ended 31 March 2005 Modipon earned a PAT of Rs 11.87 crore on net sales of Rs 533.46 crore, while being Rs 65.15 crore and Rs 682.56 crore for Godfrey Phillips, Rs 21.03 crore and Rs 675.12 crore for DCW, Rs 30.18 crore and Rs 565.64 crore for GHCL, Rs 31.25 crore and Rs 449.36 crore for Dalmia Cement Bharat, and Rs 28.19 crore and Rs 485.64 crore for OCL India. Bennet, Coleman & Co. is an unlisted company that made a PAT of Rs 514.38 crore on net sales of Rs 1,808.40 crore during the year ended 30 June 2004.

41. For the year ended 31 March 2005 JSW Steel recorded a PAT of Rs 870.11 crore on net sales of Rs 6,675.14 crore, with the corresponding numbers standing at Rs 245.85 crore and Rs 3,118.23 crore for Jindal Stainless, Rs 515.70 crore and Rs 2,577.35 crore for Jindal Steel & Power, Rs 99.37 crore and Rs 2,313.85 crore for Jindal Saw (end September 2005), Rs 76.80 crore and Rs 708.46 crore for Jindal Poly Films, Rs 28.51 crore and Rs 425.88 crore for Jindal Photo, Rs 84.88 crore and Rs 769.42 crore for Maharashtra Seamless, Rs 8.94 crore and Rs 100.79 crore for Jindal Drilling, Rs 10.60 crore and Rs 1,122.25 crore for Surya Roshni, and Rs 16.14 crore and Rs 797.07 crore for Prakash Industries. The same stood at Rs 590.15 crore and Rs 6,116.71 crore for Essar Steel, Rs 9.86 crore and Rs 1,045.12 crore for Essar Oil (15 months), Rs 456.27

crore and Rs 999.74 crore for Essar Shipping, Rs 118.92 crore and Rs 735.05 crore for Essar Power, Rs 427.68 crore and Rs 5,653.83 crore for Videocon Industries (15 months ended September 2005), Rs 27.19 crore and Rs 1,129.47 crore for Videocon Appliances (end September 2005), Rs 48.42 crore and Rs 4,705.08 crore for Ruchi Soya, Rs 16.83 crore and Rs 1,366.89 crore for National Steel, Rs 11.71 crore and Rs 1,075.87 crore for MP Glychem, Rs 6.11 crore and Rs 809.90 crore for Ruchi Infra, Rs 1.85 crore and Rs 292.64 crore for Ruchi Strips, Rs 518.09 crore and Rs 3,074.97 crore for GACL, Rs 378.39 crore and Rs 3,902.06 crore for ACC, and Rs 28.72 crore and Rs 541.84 crore for Kalpataru Power Transmission Limited.

42. The 31 March 2005 annual PAT and net sales figures were Rs 695.92 crore and Rs 5,934.19 crore for Ispat Industries, Rs (–) 1.50 crore and Rs 99.50 crore for Gontermann-Peipers, Rs 914.50 crore and Rs 7,252.47 crore for Sterlite Industries, Rs 2.06 crore and Rs 350.66 crore for Sterlite Optical Technologies, and Rs 42.19 crore and Rs 368.81 crore for Malco (end June 2005).

43. For the year ended 31 March 2005 Bharti Airtel made a PAT of Rs 1,497.79 crore on net sales of Rs 8,002.78 crore, with these being Rs 391.99 crore and Rs 4,338.01 crore for Jet Airways, Rs 312.32 crore and Rs 1,307.93 crore for Zee Telefilms, Rs 90.20 crore and Rs 816.60 crore for Essel Propack (end December 2005), Rs 38.55 crore and Rs 1,084.01 crore for Pantaloon (end-June 2005), Rs 198.71 crore and Rs 1,986.93 crore for Patni (end December 2005), Rs 58.04 crore and Rs 787.12 crore for Polaris, Rs 89.25 crore and Rs 1,195.97 crore for Alok, Rs 42.45 crore and Rs 706.83 crore for Abhishek (15 months), Rs 33.83 crore and Rs 1,038.49 crore for Welspun Gujarat, Rs 39.47 crore and Rs 469.57 crore for Welspun India, and Rs 0.24 crore and Rs 262.47 crore for Welspun Syntex.

44. The 31 March 2005 year-end PAT and net sales figures are Rs 18.41 crore and Rs 733.94 crore for Rajasthan Spinning, Rs 41.15 crore and Rs 455.03 crore for HEG, Rs 1.09 crore and Rs 248.65 crore for Maral, Rs 7.48 crore and Rs 357.38 crore for Malwa Cotton, Rs 120.76 crore and Rs 1,850.86 crore for Mahavir Spinning, Rs

19.61 crore and Rs 177.60 crore for Vardhman Acrylics, Rs 20.33 crore and Rs 604.99 crore for Nahar Industries, Rs 16.04 crore and Rs 444.78 crore for Nahar Spinning, Rs 25.35 crore and Rs 448.91 crore for Nahar Exports, and Rs 70.21 crore and Rs 1,874.79 crore for Indo Rama Synthetics.

45. During the twelve months ended 31 March 2005 Nicholas Piramal registered a PAT of Rs 164.05 crore on net sales of Rs 1,308.18 crore, while these were Rs 4.66 crore and Rs 303.84 crore for VIP Industries, Rs 9.67 crore and Rs 265 crore for Blow Plast, Rs 396.20 crore and Rs 1,230.06 crore for Sun Pharma, Rs 119.19 crore and Rs 1,170.27 crore for Jubilant Organosys, Rs 78.97 crore and Rs 557.43 crore for India Glycols, Rs 84.36 crore and Rs 1,161.13 crore for Lupin, Rs 30.07 crore and Rs 325.54 crore for Panacea, Rs 125.06 crore and Rs 813.37 crore for Balrampur Chini, Rs 87.99 crore and Rs 977.09 crore for Dhampur (end September 2005), Rs 153.35 crore and Rs 2,682.13 crore for Bhushan Steel, Rs 50.08 crore and Rs 1,550.26 crore for Usha Martin, Rs 3.68 crore and Rs 1,467.94 crore for Surana Corporation, Rs 3.94 crore and Rs 489.71 crore for Surana Industries, Rs 49.80 crore and Rs 1,397.47 crore for Lloyds Steel, Rs 29.62 crore and Rs 790.33 crore for Shree Precoated, Rs 23.65 crore and Rs 814.10 crore for Supreme Industries and Rs 36.60 crore and Rs 1,347.03 crore for Supreme Petrochem (both end June 2005), Rs 58.85 crore and Rs 1,982.56 crore for Eicher Motors, Rs 30.47 crore and Rs 581.96 crore for Havell's, Rs 25.17 crore and Rs 999.01 crore for Simplex Infrastructures, Rs 10.55 crore and Rs 734.67 crore for TCIL, and Rs 174.44 crore and Rs 560.66 crore for Mercator Lines.

3. Brahmins, Khatris, and Babus

1. *Godaan* (original Hindi version), New Delhi: Star Publications (P) Ltd, 2005 reprint.
2. Tripathi and Mehta 1984, p. 155.
3. Khatri family names include – apart from Khanna and Thapar – Anand, Bagga, Bahri, Bahl, Bhalla, Bhasin, Chadha, Chopra, Dhawan, Gujral, Handa, Kapoor, Kochhar, Kohli, Malhotra, Mehra, Nayyar,

Oberoi, Puri, Sahni, Sarin, Sehgal, Sethi, Suri, Talwar, Tandon, Trehan, Wahi, and Walia. Traditionally, the Khatris are considered superior to the Aroras (Ahuja, Aneja, Batra, Chawla, Kaura, Khurana, Nagpal, Narang, Narula, Saluja, Taneja, and Tuteja), although these distinctions have narrowed considerably in recent times. For our purposes the term Khatri encompasses Aroras as well as Soods and Punjabi Bhatias. As per the 1931 Census, around 89 per cent of Khatris and 85 per cent of Aroras were Hindus, with the rest being Sikhs. Khatris and Aroras together made up 5 per cent of the total Sikh population. Khatri Sikhs typically have names like Bedi, Bindra, and Sodhi. All the ten Sikh Gurus, from Guru Nanak to Guru Gobind Singh, were Khatris. The majority (over 63 per cent) of Sikhs are Jats.

4. Grewal 1984, p. 216.
5. Bayly 2002, pp. 383–4, 443, 448. Sheo Prasad was also one of the promoters of Kanpur's Victoria Mills in 1885.
6. Ray 1984, pp. 256–7.
7. *Monopolies Inquiry Commission* 1965. The Report's data pertains to 1963–4. In its rankings, based on total assets of individual houses, the Thapars were placed at No. 6, Mahindras at No. 33, Martin Burn at No. 3, Seshasayees at No. 24, TVS at No. 27, Amalgamations at No. 28, and Kirloskars at No. 36.
8. While Brahmins and Kayasthas have a 'traditional' association with knowledge, literacy levels among Khatris, too, had already crossed 25 per cent in 1911. Further, 8 per cent of Khatris reportedly knew English: a pretty high figure for that time (Grewal 1984, p. 217). Also see Kumar 1997.
9. The above details are mainly from Divekar 1984.
10. Tripathi and Mehta 1990, pp. 37–54.
11. Ray 1979, p. 149.
12. These are largely from Tripathi and Mehta 1990, pp. 131–46. For the year ended 31 March 2005, Kirloskar Brothers earned a profit after tax (PAT) of Rs 64.22 crore on net sales of Rs 1,296.80 crore. The corresponding numbers were Rs 173.89 crore and Rs 1,181.23 crore for Kirloskar Oil Engines, Rs 21.83 crore and Rs 497.75 crore

for Kirloskar Ferrous Industries, and Rs 1.53 crore and Rs 261.21 crore for Kirloskar Pneumatic. The Shantanu Kirloskar branch controls all these companies, while Kirloskar Electric (Rs 0.8 crore PAT on net sales of Rs 284.44 crore) is with the line of Laxmanrao's youngest son Ravi. Mysore Kirloskar has folded up. The group also has joint ventures with the US-based Copeland Corporation for airconditioning and refrigeration compressors, and with the Japanese auto giant Toyota for cars (Kirloskar Copeland and Toyota Kirloskar Motors).

13. For the year ended 31 March 2005, Garware Polyester reported a PAT of Rs 19.31 crore on net sales of Rs 854.73 crore, while these stood at Rs 13.26 crore and Rs 225.14 crore for Garware-Wall Ropes. Garware Offshore Services of Ashok Garware made a PAT of Rs 10.58 crore on total income of Rs 32.72 crore for the year ended 31 December 2005. Chandrakant Garware's Garware Paints has closed down, while his other company, Garware Synthetics is loss-making.
14. During 2004–5, 23 million tonnes (mt) of iron ore of Goa-origin was exported, with Sesa Goa (controlled by the Japanese trading house, Mitsui) doing 4.2 mt, Dempo 3.8 mt, and Salgaonkar 2.7 mt. (Prakash Kamat, 'International Mining Meet in Goa from Sept 28', *The Hindu BusinessLine*, 14 September 2005.)
15. Camlin and Ugar Sugar are the only listed companies from the above lot. For the year ended 30 September 2005 Ugar Sugar recorded a PAT of Rs 11.57 crore on net sales of Rs 334.53 crore, while the corresponding end-March 2005 figures for Camlin and D.S. Kulkarni were Rs (–) 5.02 crore and Rs 201.42 crore and Rs 3.68 crore and Rs 53.60 crore, respectively.
16. Washbrook 1977, p. 275.
17. The Iyers, who mainly worship Shiva, and the Vaishnavite Iyengars constitute the two broad streams of Tamil Brahmins. The renowned farm scientist M.S. Swaminathan is a Monkombu Iyer, with his initials standing for Monkombu Sambasivan.
18. Baker 1984, pp. 284–5. In 1930 S.N. Subba Iyer, one of Madurai's largest Kallidaikuruchi firms, had a personal capital of just Rs 3–4 lakh, supplemented by Rs 6 lakh of deposits and Rs 2 lakh loans from

the Imperial Bank. Working with Rs 1.5 lakh in cash and the rest lent out, he used to do a daily turnover of Rs 2–3 lakh and handle hundis valued up to a crore in a single year.

19. This information is courtesy S. Muthiah, 'Pioneering an Industrial Empire', *The Hindu*, Chennai, 9 January 2006 and Mahadevan 1984, p. 234.
20. Mahadevan 1991, pp. 192–3. The 1940s were a golden age for industry in Kerala, basically powered by immigrant investors, including Chinubhai Madhowlal (Travancore Rubber Works and Travancore Plywood Industries) and the Ogales (Travancore Ogale Glass Manufacturing Company). Apart from these, Travancore Titanium Products (British), Travancore Rayons (Chettiar), Travancore Cements (Iyer Brahmin), and Punalur Paper Mills (British) were the big projects to have taken off during this decade. C.P. Ramaswamy Aiyar has probably not got his due, and certainly not in the way Sir M. Visvesvaraya and other modernizers are celebrated.
21. See Note 7.
22. Seshasayee Paper registered a PAT of Rs 6.58 crore on net sales of Rs 385.56 crore for the year ended 31 March 2005, while these stood at Rs 6.02 crore and Rs 89.30 crore for Ponni Sugars and Rs 1.90 crore and Rs 30.48 crore for High Energy Batteries.
23. Mahadevan 1984, pp. 234–5.
24. For the year ended 31 March 2005 Sundaram-Clayton posted a PAT of Rs 117.75 crore on net sales of Rs 3,742.34 crore. The corresponding numbers were Rs 69.77 crore and Rs 989.89 crore for Sundram Fasteners, Rs 28.65 crore and Rs 778.97 crore for Wheels India, Rs 4.16 crore and Rs 198.57 crore for TVS Srichakra, Rs 18.47 crore and Rs 150.18 crore for India Nippon Electricals, and Rs 10.16 crore and Rs 132.77 crore for Sundaram Brake Linings. Sundaram Finance had a PAT of Rs 88.89 crore on total income of Rs 717.62 crore, with net current assets of Rs 4,715.71 crore and deposits of Rs 787.83 crore.
25. Mahadevan 1992, p. 355.
26. S. Muthiah, 'Looking Back', *The Hindu*, 13 September 2003 (125 years-Special Supplement). For the year ended 31 March 2004 Kasturi and Sons registered a PAT of Rs 44.75 crore on net sales of

Rs 453.31 crore. According to the Audit Bureau of Circulations, the daily net paid circulation of *The Hindu* during July–December 2004 was 10,47,121.

27. For the year ended 31 March 2005 TTK Prestige posted a PAT of Rs 4.05 crore on net sales of Rs 182.43 crore, while these stood at Rs (–) 2.07 crore and Rs 153 crore for TTK Healthcare.
28. Mahadevan 1991, pp. 194–5. Indo-Commercial Bank was nationalized in 1969 through its amalgamation with Punjab National Bank.
29. For the year ended 31 March 2005, India Cements recorded a PAT of Rs (–) 0.42 crore on net sales of Rs 1,152.31 crore, with the corresponding figures for Chemplast Sanmar being Rs 25.68 crore and Rs 523.20 crore. In 1985 the Seshasayee-promoted Mettur Chemical was sold to Chemplast and later merged with it. Sanmar Shipping earned a PAT of Rs 6.08 crore on net sales of Rs 107.69 crore for the year ended 31 March 2004.
30. Gordon G. May's 164-page *Royal Enfield: The Legend Rides On* (www.royalenfieldbooks.com, 2005) provides a good coffee-table history of the bike's fifty-year ride in India. During the year ended 31 March 2005 Easun Reyrolle Limited made a PAT of Rs 3.57 crore on net sales of Rs 51.24 crore, while these amounted to Rs 2.09 crore and Rs 120.02 crore for WS Industries.
31. For the year ended 31 March 2005 Shriram Transport Finance Company Limited earned a PAT of Rs 49.32 crore on total income of Rs 346.69 crore, while the corresponding numbers were Rs 46.84 crore and Rs 342.93 crore for Shriram Investments Limited, Rs 23.10 crore and Rs 181.19 crore for Shriram City Union Finance, and Rs 11.35 crore and Rs 30.54 crore for Shriram Overseas Finance.

32. Ramesh Pai's elder brother, Tonse Anant (T.A.) Pai, was the chairman of Syndicate Bank before it became one of the fourteen banks to be nationalized in 1969. The existing shareholders then incorporated ICDS. The Syndicate Bank link remained nevertheless, with the Pai family members holding top executive positions even post-nationalization. The joke about Syndicate Bank employees was that most of them privately worked for ICDS soliciting deposits. T.A.

Pai also became the first chairman of the nationalised Life Insurance Corporation (LIC) in 1970 and subsequently a union minister over 1972–7. He had a big role in the growth of Dhirubhai Ambani's Reliance Industries, both as a banker and as Industries Minister.

33. For the year ended 3 March 2005 McDowell earned a PAT of Rs 14.14 crore on net sales of Rs 1,236.58 crore, while amounting to Rs (–) 4.54 crore and Rs 578.38 crore for United Breweries, Rs (–) 28.08 crore and Rs 393.18 crore for Herbertsons, and Rs (–) 24.88 crore and Rs 112.53 crore for Shaw Wallace. Shaw Wallace and Herbertsons were earlier controlled by Manohar Chhabria and Kishore Chhabria, respectively.
34. Jaiprakash Associates Limited, the holding company of the group, reported a PAT of Rs 206.69 crore on net sales of Rs 3,049.47 crore for the year ended 31 March 2005. The corresponding numbers were Rs 2.55 crore and Rs 225.70 crore for Mohan Meakin, and Rs 33.77 crore and Rs 995.66 crore for Flex Industries. For a brief early history of the Dyer breweries, see Collet 2005.
35. Divekar 1984, pp. 95–6. The best examples of this ritual flexibility are the liquor and bidi barons discussed earlier. No less significant are the 'Udupi hotels' started by Shivalli Brahmins all over India, whose distinct cuisine was perfected by Brahmin cooks at Udupi's famous Sri Krishna temple. Some of them have evolved into chains like the Dasaprakash and Woodlands restaurants. The owners of MTR Foods Limited ('MTR' brand of spices, powders and ready-to-eat products) are also Udupi Brahmins. It was started as a restaurant by the name of Mavalli Tiffin Room in Bangalore by Yajnarayana Maiya in 1950. Likewise, the makers of 'Bedekar's pickles' are Chitpavan Brahmins.
36. Tandon 2000, p. 74.
37. The Brahmin association with IT, howsoever appealing in theory, is perhaps a trifle overstated. Apart from Infosys, the other major Brahmin software firm is Ashank Desai's Mastek Limited (PAT of Rs 58.64 crore on net sales of Rs 567.01 crore for the year ended 30 June 2005). IT is, in fact, one industry with a fairly diverse community spread, encompassing Bania-Marwaris (Patni Computer Systems of Narendra Patni and Polaris Software of Arun Jain), Khatris (Moser

Baer of Deepak Puri), Parsis (TCS of the Tatas), Rajus (Satyam Computer Services of B. Ramalinga Raju) and Nadars (HCL of Shiv Nadar).

38. For the year ended 31 March 2005 Infosys earned a PAT of Rs 1,891.67 crore on net sales of Rs 7,129.65 crore, with these being Rs 22.09 crore and Rs 722.34 crore for Orchid Chemicals, Rs 34.54 crore and Rs 1,873.64 crore for Dishman Pharma, Rs 197.54 crore and Rs 712.56 crore for Biocon, Rs (–) 35.23 crore and Rs 320.28 crore (total income) for Deccan Aviation, Rs 36.35 crore and Rs 459.82 crore for Blue Dart, and Rs 2.81 crore and Rs 1,085.20 crore for Sai Service Station.
39. These details are mainly courtesy Ray 1979, pp. 283–4 and Tripathi 2004, pp. 195.
40. Ray 1979, pp. 143–4.
41. For the year ended 31 March 2005 Triveni Engineering recorded a PAT of Rs 99.46 crore on net sales of Rs 964.64 crore. The corresponding end-September 2005 figures for Saraswati Industrial Syndicate were Rs 17.26 crore and Rs 404.71 crore, respectively. The Narang group's lone functional factory at Basti was recently taken over by Bajaj Hindusthan.
42. For the year ended 31 March 2005 Crompton Greaves registered a PAT of Rs 116.87 crore on net sales of Rs 2,056.23 crore, with these being Rs 8.39 crore and Rs 595.72 crore for JCT and Rs (–) 163.33 crore and Rs 309.04 crore for JCT Electronics. The corresponding end-June 2006 numbers were Rs 168.13 crore and Rs 1,802.41 crore for Bilt and Rs 62.98 crore and Rs 731.24 crore for Greaves Cotton. Bilt is part of the L.M. Thapar group, while Crompton Greaves and Greaves Cotton are with B.M. Thapar, and JCT and JCT Electronics with M.M. Thapar.
43. See Datta 1986. Partition might have also helped in another way: foreclosing competition from an aspirant Muslim bourgeoisie. In the 1931 Census, Muslims formed 56 per cent of undivided Punjab's population.
44. For the year ended 31 March 2005 M&M earned a PAT of Rs 681.54 crore on net sales of Rs 7,636.66 crore, with these being Rs 102.39 crore and Rs 954.19 crore for Tech Mahindra, Rs 54.83

crore and Rs 521.87 crore for Mahindra Ugine, and Rs 0.35 crore and Rs 123.35 crore for Mahindra Gesco.

45. For the fifteen months ended September 2005, Escorts Limited made a PAT of Rs 39.09 crore on net sales of Rs 1,269.13 crore, while the corresponding annual end-March 2005 figures for Goetze India were Rs 21.86 crore and Rs 462.55 crore. Rajan Nanda's wife, Ritu, is the daughter of the Hindi film star Raj Kapoor. As an agent for the Life Insurance Corporation of India, she holds the *Guinness Book* record of selling 17,000 policies in a single day. H.P. Nanda's autobiography (Nanda 1992) makes good reading, while Swraj Paul's memoirs (Paul 1998) throws light on his failed attempt at buying out Escorts.
46. For the year ended 31 March 2005 Hero Honda earned a PAT of Rs 810.47 crore on net sales of Rs 7,421.65 crore, while these stood at Rs 7.83 crore and Rs 524.68 crore for Munjal Showa, Rs 25.98 crore and Rs 246.10 crore for Munjal Auto Industries, and Rs 2.26 crore and Rs 430.36 crore for Atlas Cycles Haryana. For a good overview of the development of the Indian cycle industry, see Singh 1990.
47. For the year ended 31 March 2005 Apollo Tyres registered a PAT of Rs 61.78 crore on net sales of Rs 2,236.35 crore, with these at Rs 4.36 crore and Rs 144.40 crore for Bharat Gears.
48. Bhandari 2005 and Karkaria 1992 are hagiographic accounts, but give useful details. For the year ended 31 December 2005 Ranbaxy made a PAT of Rs 261.71 crore on net sales of Rs 5,281.59 crore, with the corresponding end-March 2005 figures at Rs (–) 159.86 crore and Rs 699.78 crore (total income) for Max India and Rs 28.17 crore and Rs 606.57 crore for EIH.
49. Satnam Overseas made a PAT of Rs 15.74 crore on net sales of Rs 526.35 crore for the year ended 31 March 2005, while these were Rs 4.97 crore and Rs 360.72 crore for LT Overseas, and Rs 18.05 crore and Rs 407.65 crore for Lakshmi Energy. LT Overseas was originally Lalchand Tirathram Rice Mills, a partnership between two brothers from Bhikiwind in Amritsar. In 1976 the younger brother, Tirathram Arora, broke away and formed Satnam Overseas.

Raghunath Arora and Jugal Kishore Arora are the sons of Lalchand and Tirathram, respectively.

50. The 82-year-old Lala Jagat Narain was shot dead by Sikh extremists in September 1981. Four years later, his successor and son Ramesh Chandra Chopra met with the same fate. TV Today Network Limited, the only listed firm of the India Today Group, earned a PAT of Rs 16.42 crore on net sales of Rs 139.07 crore for the year ended 31 March 2005, while these stood at Rs 32.90 crore and Rs 98.43 crore for Television Eighteen.
51. Incidentally, the man who financed many of Raj Kapoor and B.R. Chopra's early films was Aroon Purie's father V.V. Purie, who, in 1967, incorporated Thomson Press India Limited at Faridabad before *India Today's* launch. For the year ended 31 March 2005 Balaji Telefilms recorded a PAT of Rs 41.30 crore on net sales of Rs 196.75 crore, with these being Rs (–) 16.97 crore and Rs 48 crore for Mukta Arts.
52. For the year ended 31 March 2005, Subros earned a PAT of Rs 19.94 crore on net sales of Rs 590.88 crore, while these were Rs 48.27 crore and Rs 778.04 crore for Rico Auto, Rs 20.29 crore and Rs 505.19 crore for Omax Autos, and Rs 16.67 crore and Rs 298.66 crore for Sona Koyo. Amtek Auto and its subsidiaries' PAT for the year ended 30 June 2005 stood at Rs 159.35 crore on net sales of Rs 1,660.53 crore. The late Lalit Suri's hotels include Kolkata's Great Eastern, which he acquired from the West Bengal government in November 2005.
53. For the year ended 31 March 2005 Samtel Color registered a PAT of Rs 64.53 crore on net sales of Rs 918.86 crore. The corresponding figures were Rs 59.79 crore and Rs 1,280.30 crore for Moser Baer, Rs 94.66 crore and Rs 2,091.71 crore for Uttam Galva, Rs 33.30 crore and Rs 1,409.21 crore for PSL, Rs 55.07 crore and Rs 855.89 crore for Berger Paints and Rs 100.61 crore and Rs 1,790.01 crore for Punj Lloyd.
54. Goswami 1989, pp. 292.
55. Bagchi 1992, p. 193.
56. Goswami 1989, pp. 295–6.

57. These details are from Kling 1966.
58. Sinha 1992, pp. 80–2.
59. Bagchi 1992, p. 161.
60. Goswami 1989, p. 303.
61. According to the Audit Bureau of Circulations, the daily net paid circulation of *Ananda Bazar Patrika* and *The Telegraph* during July–December 2004 stood at 11,06,408 and 376,408, respectively.
62. For the year ended 31 March 2005 NDTV registered a PAT of Rs 35.41 crore on net sales of Rs 176.13 crore. These were Rs 155.80 crore and Rs 1,536.95 crore for Dabur India and Rs 20.53 crore and Rs 234.80 crore for Dabur Pharma.
63. The above numbers were Rs 9.59 crore and Rs 417.33 crore for TIL, Rs (–) 34.40 crore and Rs 253.18 crore for IFB Industries, and Rs 1.83 crore and Rs 105.99 crore for IFB Agro Indusries.
64. For the eighteenth months ended 31 March 2005 BPL recorded a PAT of Rs (–) 74.04 crore on net sales of Rs 413.90 crore, with the corresponding twelve months-ending figures at Rs 44.76 crore and Rs 256.69 crore for Hotel Leelaventure, Rs 25.72 crore and Rs 116.55 crore for Subex Systems, Rs 34.75 crore and Rs 453.06 crore for Sobha Developers, Rs 2.97 crore and Rs 72.59 crore for Menon Pistons, and Rs 3.03 crore and Rs 26.66 crore for Menon Bearings. For a biased biography of Rajan Pillai, see Pillai and Kutty 2001. Bhave 2005 is an interesting account of the Menon group's founder and his journey from Kodungallur in Kerala to establishing a successful auto castings enterprise at Kolhapur just after Independence.
65. For the year ended 31 March 2005 Elder Pharma earned a PAT of Rs 20.39 crore on net sales of Rs 285.35 crore.

4. Kammas, Reddys, and Rajus

1. The state of Andhra Pradesh, formed in 1956, encompasses three regions: coastal Andhra, Telangana, and Rayalaseema. Within coastal Andhra, there are (a) the four 'delta districts' with large alluvial plains formed by the division of the Godavari and Krishna rivers into various branches before entering the Bay of Bengal;

and (b) the five 'non-delta districts' of Srikakulam, Vizianagaram, Visakhapatnam, Prakasam, and Nellore. Rayalaseema comprises the four southern districts of Chittoor, Kadapa, Anantapur and Kurnool, while Telangana includes Mahabubnagar, Nalgonda, Ranga Reddy, Hyderabad, Medak, Warangal, Khammam, Nizamabad, Karimnagar, and Adilabad. Telangana belonged to the erstwhile nizam's Hyderabad state, whereas the other two regions were part of the British-governed Madras Presidency.

2. Rajahmundry district was renamed Godavari in 1859 and further bifurcated into East Godavari and West Godavari districts in 1925.
3. Rao 1988, pp. 27–8.
4. Lady Hope 1900, p. 73.
5. Ibid., p. 70.
6. Rao 1988, p. 26.
7. Lady Hope 1900, p. 96.
8. Rao 1988, p. 28.
9. More conservative estimates of output made by Rao 1988 for 1878–9, 1880–1, and 1890–1 put the surplus ratio between 22 per cent and 34 per cent (p. 54). Even discounting for official exaggeration, there is no doubt that the district had turned significantly grain surplus.
10. Lady Hope 1900, pp. 73–4.
11. Rao's estimate of the surplus ratio for the same year is lower, at 50 per cent. See Rao 1985, p. A-62.
12. Figures are for 2003–4. Compiled from *Statistical Abstract of Andhra Pradesh* 2005.
13. Quoted in Lady Hope 1900, pp. 111–12.
14. Reddy 1989, pp. 269–70. The district boundaries have been altered since the 1921 Census. While Godavari was bifurcated in 1925, Guntur was split in 1970, after a new district, Prakasam, headquartered at Ongole, was carved out of it.
15. Washbrook 1977, pp. 68–91.
16. Duvvury 1986, p. PE-46.
17. Rao 1988, p. 56.
18. Rao 1985, p. A-63.
19. Ibid., p. A-64.

20. Ranga, 'Some Facts Concerning the Development of the Tobacco Trade of Madras', *Indian Journal of Economics*, vol. III, 1926–7. Quoted in Duvvury 1986, p. PE-48.
21. Duvvury 1986, p. PE-50.
22. Ibid., p. PE-52. The 1 lakh hectare figure includes the FCV area in Prakasam district, which, till February 1970, formed part of Guntur. Prakasam is actually today the largest Virginia tobacco-growing district, accounting for 57,000 hectares out of the total 96,000 hectares covered in AP during 2003–4. After Guntur started receiving water from the Nagarjuna Sagar project, a significant portion of its tobacco acreage gave way to cotton, from the mid 1970s. On this, see Reddy 1985.
23. During 2003–4, the average per hectare lint yield in Guntur was 594 kgs, against 384 kgs for AP and 307 kgs for India.
24. Board of Revenue, 1903. Quoted in Rao 1985, p. A-63.
25. Ranga, *Economic Organization of Indian Villages*, Vol. I: Deltaic Villages, Bezwada: Vani Press, 1926. Quoted in Upadhya 1988, p. 1377.
26. Washbrook 1977, p. 94.
27. Quoted in Upadhya 1988, p. 1381.
28. Duvvury 1986, p. PE-47.
29. Rao 1985, p. A-66.
30. Upadhya 1988, p. 1378.
31. Ibid.
32. *Monopolies Inquiry Commission* 1965.
33. We shall study this community – essentially Kammas who migrated to the Tamil region centuries ago – in detail in the next chapter. The Coimbatore Naidus, it will be seen, made the transition to industry earlier than the Kammas of coastal Andhra.
34. For the year ended 31 March 2005, the KCP Limited group reported a PAT of Rs 16.02 crore on net sales of Rs 230.46 crore, while the corresponding figures for KCP Sugar and Jeypore Sugar were Rs 41.07 crore and Rs 305.51 crore and Rs 15.11 crore and Rs 162.13 crore, respectively.
35. VBC Ferro Alloys earned a PAT of Rs 8.68 crore on net sales of Rs 128.20 crore for the year ended 31 March 2005.

36. Sarvaraya is headed by S.B.P.B.K. Satyanarayana Rao, who was Union Minister of State for Agriculture during 1999–2000.
37. Upadhya 1988, p. 1378.
38. Satyanarayana, p. 78.
39. To these the group has now added an integrated 'IMAX' 3-D theater, along with a five-screen multiplex-cum-retail complex in Hyderabad, over-looking the Tank Bund.
40. Rama Naidu successfully contested the 1999 parliament elections on a TDP ticket from Bapatla. The 2004 elections saw him lose from the same seat to NTR's daughter, Purandeswari, who fought as a Congress candidate. Purandeswari's husband, Daggubati Venkateswara Rao, happens to be Rama Naidu's brother's son.
41. In April 2002 Subhash Chandra's Zee Telefilms became the main shareholder in Padmalaya Telefilms through a 64 per cent acquisition in its holding company. During the year ended 31 March 2005 Padmalaya Telefilms reported a net loss of Rs 3.17 crore on net sales of Rs 20.81 crore.
42. Duvvury 1986, p. PE-51.
43. Ibid., p. PE-57.
44. According to the Tobacco Board, India exported 137,731 tonnes of un-manufactured tobacco in 2004–5, valued at Rs 952.55 crore. Of the 137,731 tonnes, FCV tobacco constituted 105,417 tonnes (77 per cent). Nearly half of the country's FCV production is exported. While ILTD's share in FCV exports is below 30 per cent, it buys up the bulk of the leaf used domestically, given its parent's total domination of the Indian cigarette market.
45. During the year ended 31 March 2005 Navabharat Ferro earned a PAT of Rs 106.83 crore on net sales of Rs 520.64 crore.
46. Out of AP's nine CMs before NTR, six were Reddys: Neelam Sanjeeva Reddy (two terms, from 1 November 1956 to 10 January 1960, and from 12 March 1962 to 28 February 1964), Kasu Brahmananda Reddy (29 February 1964 to 24 September 1971), Marri Chenna Reddy (6 March 1978 to 10 October 1980), Tanguturi Anjaiah (11 October 1980 to 23 February 1982), Bhavanam Venkatram (24 February 1982 to 19 September 1982) and Kotla Vijaya Bhaskara Reddy (29 September 1982 to 8 January 1983). The others were

one Brahmin (P.V. Narasimha Rao, from 25 September 1971 to 18 January 1973), one Velama (Jalagam Vengala Rao, from 10 December 1973 to 5 March 1978) and one Dalit (Damodaram Sanjeevaiah, from 11 January 1960 to 11 March 1962).

47. The CPI won 41 seats in the Andhra region of the composite Madras legislative assembly, compared to the Congress' 50. In the elections to the Hyderabad state, the CPI garnered 36, against 44 for the Congress. On the Kamma-Reddy peasantry's support for CPI, see Reddy 1989, pp. 268–81.
48. Srinivasulu 2002, pp. 7–10.
49. Reddy 1989, pp. 313–14.
50. According to the Audit Bureau of Circulations, *Eenadu's* daily net paid circulation during July–December 2004 was 985,278.
51. Eenadu Television is a division of Ushodaya Enterprises Limited, which, for the year ended 31 March 2003 reported a net loss of Rs 29.50 crore on net sales of Rs 418.44 crore.
52. Upadhya 1988, pp. 1433–7.
53. Among the non-coastal districts Chittoor has the highest concentration of Kammas, at 10.7 per cent of the 1921 Census population (Ram Reddy, p. 270). NTR's son-in-law and former CM, Nara Chandrababu Naidu, comes from Naravaripally village in Kuppam taluka of Chittoor.
54. Progressive Construction recorded a PAT of Rs 19.01 crore on net sales of Rs 479.88 crore for the year ended 31 March 2004.
55. For the year ended 31 March 2005, Madhucon Projects reported a PAT of Rs 19.71 crore on net sales of Rs 306.06 crore.
56. For the year ended 31 March 2005, Divi's Laboratories earned a PAT of Rs 66.03 crore on net sales of Rs 347.38 crore, while being Rs 1.56 crore and Rs 164.37 crore for Natco Pharma, and Rs 7.43 crore and Rs 79.26 crore for Krebs Biochemicals.
57. Suven Life Sciences reported a PAT of Rs 3.80 crore on net sales of Rs 60.78 crore during the year ended 31 March 2005. The corresponding numbers for Vimta Labs were Rs 14.12 crore and Rs 52.20 crore, respectively.

58. For the year ended 31 March 2005 Amara Raja posted a PAT of Rs 8.69 crore on net sales of Rs 218.68 crore, while this was Rs 10.16 crore and Rs 266.13 crore for Heritage Foods. Nuziveedu's PAT for the fiscal ended 31 March 2003 was Rs 49.08 crore on net sales of Rs 131.20 crore, while the same for Devi Sea Foods stood at Rs 5.01 crore and Rs 179.09 crore.
59. Srinivasulu 2002, p. 3. The figure is a rough approximation from the 1921 Census, when caste enumeration was last done for the districts of the Madras Presidency and the nizam's domain that were merged into AP. In that census, the Reddys were clubbed with the Kapus and their combined share assessed at 15.2 per cent.
60. Washbrook 1977, p. 71.
61. Satyanarayana 1992, p. 77. One of the best examples of a Rayalaseema Reddy making a fortune from mining, allegedly by not very honourable means, is the present chief minister, Yeduguri Sandinti Rajasekhara Reddy (YSR). On this, see Balagopal 2004. YSR used the profits from mining of barites (used for petroleum refining) in Kadapa to also bag lucrative construction contracts at the Tehri Dam in Uttaranchal.
62. For the year ended 31 March 2005 GVK Industries (which runs the Jegurupadu power plant) reported a PAT of Rs 49.60 crore on total income of Rs 304.70 crore. During the same fiscal Taj GVK Hotels & Resorts earned a PAT of Rs 22.09 crore on net sales of Rs 115.47 crore, while these figures for Novopan Industries were Rs 4.83 crore and Rs 119.40 crore, respectively.
63. During the year ended 31 March 2005 Deccan Chronicle Holdings reported a PAT of Rs 32.05 crore on net sales of Rs 165.65 crore, with these being Rs 9.34 crore and Rs 301.26 crore for Gayatri Projects. According to the Audit Bureau of Circulations, *Deccan Chronicle's* net daily paid circulation for July–December 2004 was 402,351.
64. For the year ended 31 March 2005 DRL recorded a PAT of Rs 32.91 crore on net sales of Rs 1,835.88 crore, while the corresponding numbers were Rs 3.25 crore and Rs 1,416.73 crore for Aurobindo Pharma, Rs 56.71 crore and Rs 1,054.73 crore for IVRCL, and

Rs 49.20 crore and Rs 592.70 crore for Apollo Hospitals. Besides Pratap C. Reddy, the other person who had a part in the company's promotion was P. Obul Reddy, owner of Dynavision Limited (which made 'Dyanora' televisions) and former head of the Madras Telugu Academy.

65. Reddy 1989, p. 269.
66. During the year ended 31 March 2005 Madras Cements reported a PAT of Rs 55.92 crore on net sales of Rs 731.74 crore. The corresponding figures for Ramco Industries were Rs 30.11 crore and Rs 298.67 crore, while amounting to Rs 8.21 crore and Rs 149.38 crore for Rajapalayam Mills and Rs (–) 67.93 crore and Rs 220.51 crore for Ramco Systems, respectively.
67. Nagarjuna Fertilizers posted a PAT of Rs 29.53 crore on net sales of Rs 1,270.85 crore for the year ended 31 March 2005. The corresponding numbers stood at Rs 24.57 crore and Rs 286.71 crore for Nagarjuna Agrichem, Rs 711.64 crore and Rs 3,520.85 crore for Satyam Computer, Rs 28.34 crore and Rs 188.18 crore for VisualSoft, and Rs 20.11 crore and Rs 115.43 crore for Megasoft (year ended 31 December 2005).
68. For the year ended 31 March 2005 NCC reported a PAT of 57.27 crore or net sales of 1,188.50 crore, while this was Rs 5.34 crore and Rs 111.29 crore for DCL.
69. For the year ended 31 March 2005 Pennar Industries posted a PAT of Rs (–) 4.94 crore on net sales of Rs 348.81 crore, while the same for the VH group's flagship Venky's (India) Limited amounted to Rs 16.67 crore and Rs 342.93 crore, respectively.
70. GMR Industries Limited (sugar and ferro-alloys divisions) recorded a PAT of Rs 18.70 crore on net sales of Rs 297.81 crore for the year ended 31 March 2005. The corresponding figures for GMR Infrastructure Limited (including power and roads) were Rs 111.84 crore and Rs 992.91 crore. In the mid 1980s, the still-to-emerge G.M. Rao was made a director in Vysya Bank by its chief executive and fellow-Komati Ramesh Gelli (who went on to promote the failed Global Trust Bank). He built up a controlling holding in Vysya Bank, when a rights issue was not subscribed. In 2002 Rao sold his 50 per cent stake to the Dutch finance major ING for Rs 380 crore. It is now called ING Vysya Bank.

71. This term is borrowed from Washbrook 1977, p. 77.
72. Personal interview, 20 October 2005, Tanuku.
73. Hazari 1966, pp. 253–5.
74. For the year ended 31 March 2005 Andhra Sugars made a PAT of Rs 43.63 crore on net sales of Rs 432.03 crore, while these stood at Rs 11.27 crore and Rs 197.12 crore for APL and Rs 11.10 crore and Rs 85.23 crore for Jocil, respectively.
75. Personal interview, 18 October 2005, Hyderabad.
76. Originally, Eastern Generation of the UK held 30 per cent, which was sold to NRG Energy, US, before passing on to Genting. The Malaysian connection with new Andhra industrialists is something that calls for investigation. Lanco, GVK, GMR, and Madhucon have interestingly all had Malaysian partners in their infrastructural ventures.
77. During the year ended 31 March 2005 Lanco Kondapalli Power Private Limited earned a PAT of Rs 108.74 crore on net sales of Rs 559.70 crore, while amounting to Rs 9.25 crore and Rs 183.92 crore for Lanco Infratech, and Rs 20.94 crore and Rs 286.08 crore for Lanco Industries.
78. Personal interview, 19 October 2005, Hyderabad.

5. Kongunad Naidus and Gounders

1. According to the Office of the Textile Commissioner, Union Ministry of Textiles, TN mills manufactured 952.60 million kgs of cotton yarn in 2003–4, which is 45 per cent of the all-India output of 2,120.71 million kgs. Out of the 218 member mills from TN belonging to the Southern India Mills' Association (SIMA), 90 (41 per cent) are in Coimbatore district. From these, and discounting for SIMA's Coimbatore-centric disposition, we can assume that Coimbatore mills produce around 15 per cent of the country's cotton yarn. The 45 per cent share for knitwear exports is based on data from the Apparel Export Promotion Council's (AEPC) office at Tirupur, which is part of Coimbatore district. The estimates for pumps and motors are from the Southern India Engineering Manufacturers' Association (SIEMA).

2. Baker 1984, pp. 30, 201. It is the laying of the railways from the 1860s that really helped integrate Coimbatore and its adjoining environs into the commercial mainstream.
3. The average yearly rainfall in the Cauvery delta (Tiruchirappalli, Thanjavur, Thiruvarur, Nagapattinam) is 1,101 mm, while it is 814 mm for the southern districts (Pudukkottai, Theni, Madurai, Sivaganga, Virudhunagar, Ramanathapuram, Thoothukudi, Tirunelveli), 849 mm for the north-western districts (Dharmapuri, Salem, Namakkal, Perambalur), 1,109 mm for the north-eastern districts (Tiruvallur, Kanchipuram, Vellore, Tiruvannamalai, Villupuram, Cuddalore), 1,457 mm for Kanyakumari, and 1,857 mm for the Nilgiris. These figures are from World Bank 2004, pp. 20–1.
4. The Grand Anicut or Kallanai ('stone bund') across the main Cauvery stream is attributed to the Chola king Karikalan and dates back to the second century. It is considered the world's oldest water diversion structure still in use and, in fact, was a base engineering model for Sir Arthur Cotton when he designed his famous Godavari–Krishna anicuts (see the previous chapter).
5. The valley mirasidar's general detachment from the countryside was evident in the gradual replacement of the traditional waram system of proportionate crop sharing with kuthagai or fixed grain-rents from the start of the twentieth century. Kuthagai land lease-deeds commonly stipulated conditions such as 'the grain to be delivered at the lessor's house in Egmore (a Chennai suburb)'. Quoted in Baker 1984, p. 181.
6. Subramaniam 1982, p. 3.
7. Baker 1984, pp. 210–11.
8. Ibid., pp. 267–70.
9. Personal interview, 22 March 2005, Coimbatore.
10. Baker 1984, pp. 270.
11. The Kaleeswarar Mills, promoted by P. Somasundaram Chetty, with the backing of the A.L.A.R. Chetty family, came up a year later in 1906.
12. Perumal 1977, pp. 13–29.
13. Mahadevan 1992a, p. 16.

14. Perumal 1977, p. 19.
15. The links between the two families were further cemented through the marriage of K.K. Naidu's daughter Padmavathi, with P.S.G. Naidu's grand-son G.V. Doraiswamy Naidu in 1933.
16. Another partner, B. Rangaswamy Naidu, who married Kuppuswamy Naidu's daughter Ranganayaki, also founded his own Rajalakshmi Mills. All these details are from Subramaniam 1982 and Perumal 1977.
17. Mahadevan 1992a. It is estimated that between 1928 and 1934, at the height of the Depression, about Rs 45 lakhs was invested in the mill industry in Coimbatore (p. 18).
18. Personal interview (note 9).
19. Mahadevan 1992a has shown how the Congress-led boycott of yarn produced by British companies badly affected sales of mills under the management of Binny and Co. and A. & F. Harvey. The number of wholesale indenters of Binny's in the Madras region fell from around 400 to a mere 40 by mid 1931 (p. 26).
20. Some of the traditional handloom weaving castes like the Devanga Chettiars (not to be confused with the moneylending Nattukottai Chettys) and Kaikola Mudaliars (as opposed to Vellala Mudaliars) were also involved in setting up mills in the region in the early stage. The promoters of the Dhanalakshmi and Ramalinga Choodambika mills in Tirupur during 1932–3 – M. Nanjappa Chetty and S. Kulli Chetty – were Devangas. Similarly, the owners of the well-known silk garment retail houses like Nalli and Kumaran Silks happen to be from the Telugu-speaking Padmashali weaving community.
21. This point was suggested to me by Raman Mahadevan. For a lucid account of the presence of European expatriate firms in South India, see Mahadevan 1992.
22. Baker 1984, pp. 351–2.
23. Mahadevan 1992, p. 348.
24. *Monopolies Inquiry Commission* 1965 and *Industrial Licensing Policy Inquiry Committee* 1969.
25. V. Rangaswamy Naidu's son P.R. Ramakrishnan is married to Rajeswary, the daughter of Velagapudi Ramakrishna, the founder of the KCP group. The latter are Kammas from coastal Andhra (see

Chapter 4). P.R. Ramakrishnan and Rajeswary Ramakrishnan's son, R. Prabhu, is the Congress Member of Parliament from the Nilgiris.

26. They include the PSG College of Technology, PSG Institute of Management, PSG Institute of Medical Sciences and Research, the PSG Hospital, and a host of schools.
27. The old Naidu industrial groups have had a tradition of producing motor rallyists, from the late S. Karivardhan (son of G.K. Sundaram) to Narain Karthikeyan, J. Anand (grandson of D. Balasundaram, the founder of Textool Company), and Arjun Balu of Sri Balasubramania Mills (grand-nephew of K.K. Naidu).
28. Another struggling Naidu family textile concern is the Sri Ramakrishna Coimbatore Mills. Its promoters, the SNR group, also manage a chain of institutions under the Sri Ramakrishna banner, including an engineering college, an institute of technology, a dental college, a college of nursing, a college of pharmacy and a 350-bed hospital.
29. Personal interview, 24 March 2005, Coimbatore. For the year ended 31 March 2005 Rajshree Sugars earned a PAT of Rs 16.79 crore on net sales of Rs 190.03 crore.
30. Lakshmi Mills reported a PAT of Rs 4.34 crore on net sales of Rs 146.27 crore for the year ended 31 March 2005. The corresponding figures for LMW stood at Rs 73.34 crore and Rs 990.77 crore, respectively. Lakshmi Mills is under G.K. Sundaram, while LMW is with the family of G. Kuppuswamy Naidu's elder son G.K. Devarajulu.
31. 'Coimbatore's wealth creators', *The Hindu*, 2 February 2004, Coimbatore.
32. These details are courtesy Perumal 1974.
33. Personal interview, 24 March 2005, Coimbatore.
34. SIEMA.
35. Coimbatore has 5 universities, 25 engineering colleges, and 90 arts and science colleges. In addition, there are several institutions offering vocational and engineering diploma courses. G.D. Naidu, in particular, was a passionate advocate of higher education that emphasised practical training. The Government College of Technology and the Government Polytechnic of Coimbatore were both privately started by him in 1945, which he subsequently donated. The Industrial Labour Welfare Association that he founded a year

later (now G.D. Naidu Charities) has trained over 35,000 students in short-term courses in automobile servicing and maintenance, radio and television repairs, etc.

36. Personal interview, 23 March 2005, Coimbatore. L.G. Varadaraj's brother L.G. Balakrishnan was the husband of G.D. Naidu's daughter Sarojini.
37. For the year ended 31 March 2005 LGB registered a PAT of Rs 16.93 crore on net sales of Rs 416.64 crore. The corresponding figures were Rs 21.39 crore and Rs 285.26 crore for Elgi Equipments, Rs 42.75 crore and Rs 448.97 crore for Pricol, Rs 11.22 crore and Rs 367.52 crore for Super Spinning, Rs 8.10 crore and Rs 238.74 crore for Precot Mills, and Rs 11.32 crore and Rs 124.46 crore for Elgitread. R. Jagadish Chandran's Premier Mills posted a PAT of Rs 13 crore on net sales of Rs 152.93 crore during the year ended 31 March 2004.
38. Just for the record, Jagadish Chandran's wife Sabitha is the daughter of G.K. Sundaram's elder brother G.K. Devarajulu. Another example of the way inter-industrial group familial connections are forged is Nandini Rangaswamy, who is the daughter of L.R.G. Naidu's youngest son L.G. Nityanand. Her husband G. Rangaswamy is the son of G.R. Govindarajulu and grandson of P.S.G. Rangaswami Naidu. Nandini Rangaswamy heads Chandra Textiles and also manages the educational institutions under the G.R.G Trust.
39. Personal interview, 24 March 2005, Coimbatore. The KG group has established a link with the PSG family through the marriage of B. Srihari (son of G. Bakthavathsalam's brother K.G. Baalakrishnan) with Deepika, the sister of Narain Karthikeyan. For the year ended 31 March 2005 KG Denim earned a PAT of Rs 5.25 crore on net sales of Rs 198.25 crore, while the same for Sri Kannapiran Mills stood at Rs 10.82 crore and Rs 156.93 crore.
40. See, for instance, Prahalad 2005, pp. 265–86.
41. The Kaleeswarar Mills was the first Indian-owned mill to be set up in Coimbatore (also see note 11).
42. The above numbers are from the AEPC's office at Tirupur (note 1). According to its director, D.G. Reddy, the value of indirect exports, wherein the product shipped out is actually manufactured

in Tirupur, would be to the tune of Rs 1,200 crore per year. In addition, 'non-quota' exports, i.e. of goods and to countries not covered under the Multi-Fibre Agreement, are another Rs 600–700 crore. If one includes these figures, which are not registered in the AEPC database, the overall annual knitwear exports from Tirupur in 2004 would have 'easily exceed Rs 6,000 crore' (personal interview, 23 June 2005, Tirupur).

43. Chari 2004, p. 170. Also, see note 20.
44. Chari 2004, pp. 185–91. Also, Vijayabaskar 2001, pp. 65–71.
45. Knitting and weaving both entail conversion of yarn into fabric. But as against weaving, in which the cloth is made in two dimensions (warp and weft), knitting is done in a single dimension: one strand of yarn is looped back into itself. This imparts the unique elasticity to knitted cloth and distinguishes T-shirts from ordinary shirts. For an overview of knitwear production operations, see Chari 2004, pp. 55–75.
46. Vijayabaskar 2001, p. 77.
47. Ibid., pp. 92–5. Chari has alluded to a couple of big landholding Gounder families entering the knitwear industry through the familiar route of investing surpluses from agriculture. These ventures were dismal failures in contrast to the 'non-elite' Gounder ex-worker route. Chari's field surveys conducted over 1996–8 identified 42 per cent of SIHMA-affiliated owners to be Gounder ex-workers, with 'other Gounders' accounting for another 14 per cent (pp. 109–40).
48. C. Vijayakumar, 'A Study of the Hosiery Entrepreneurs at Tiruppur, Tamil Nadu', 1986. Quoted in Vijayabaskar 2001, p. 94.
49. Banerjee and Munshi 2004. According to TEA, Tirupur has about 2,500 knitting and/or stitching units, 750 dyeing and/or bleaching units, 300 printing units, 100 embroidery units, and 200 other (compacting, calendaring, etc) units.
50. Chari 2004, pp. 236–7. Before Verona arrived on the scene, an average company exported a case a day, while he did 7,000 dozens daily.
51. Personal interview, 23 June 2005, Tirupur. Ramasamy is also president of Tirupur's Kongu Vellala (Gounder) Association.

52. Personal interview, 24 June 2005, Tirupur.
53. For the year ended 31 March 2005 Shanthi Gears posted a PAT of Rs 19.12 crore on net sales of Rs 121.71 crore. These numbers were Rs 1.12 crore and Rs 169.29 crore for Dharani Sugars, and Rs 1.74 crore and Rs 40.62 crore for KMCH.
54. Personal interview, 6 April 2005, Salem.
55. Personal interview, 23 June 2005, Tirupur.
56. V. Sridhar, 'Tirupur's Crisis', *Frontline*, 26 August 2005, pp. 116–21.
57. Unless otherwise mentioned, these are based on company inputs and personal interviews at Coimbatore with M. Manickam (22 March 2005), S.V. Balasubramaniam (24 March 2005), and G. Rajendran (23 March 2005).
58. Another famous Pollachi Gounder who bit the dust in the 1967 parliament elections from neighbouring Gobichettipalayam constituency was C. Subramaniam. As the Union Food and Agriculture Minister, he was one of the prime architects of India's Green Revolution in the mid 1960s. Incidentally, after losing the elections, C. Subramaniam worked in ABT, where he was employed for five years on a monthly salary of Rs 2,500! (See Alladin 2001, p. 65.)
59. For the year ended 30 June 2005 Sakthi Sugars earned a PAT of Rs 23.54 crore on net sales of Rs 730.37 crore. Another listed company, Sakthi Finance, reported a PAT of Rs 1.95 crore on total income of Rs 29.11 crore for the year ended 31 March 2005.
60. For the year ended 31 March 2005, Bannari Amman Sugars reported a PAT of Rs 43.61 crore on net sales of Rs 487.32 crore. During the same period the corresponding PAT and total income for Bannari Amman Spinning and Shiva Texyarn was Rs 11.53 crore and Rs 75.63 crore, and Rs 5.08 crore and Rs 97.58 crore, respectively. Shiva Distilleries posted a PAT of Rs 7.05 crore on income of Rs 172.78 crore for the year ended 31 March 2004, while the total income from the wheat business (Coimbatore Agro Industries and Annamallai Industries) was Rs 35 crore.

6. Nadars and Ezhavas

1. The term 'dominant caste', coined by M.N. Srinivas, refers to a caste that is both numerically strong in a village or local area as well as wields preponderant power through control over land. See Srinivas 2002.
2. Srinivas 2002a, 'A Note on Sanskritization and Westernization' and '*Varna* and Caste', pp. 42–69.
3. Heilbroner 1986, p. 213. For assertion of Kshatriya status by the Jats and the Marathas, see Datta 1999 and Deshpande 2004.
4. Robert Caldwell, *The Tinnevelly Shanars*. Quoted in Hardgrave 1969, p. 21.
5. Before the advent of sugarcane to facilitate factory-scale production of sugar, palmyra was the main source of sweetener and alcohol. Tamil Nadu accounts for about 60 per cent of the palmyra trees in the country.
6. Hardgrave 1969, pp. 24–31.
7. Ibid., pp. 55–70.
8. Modern Kerala consists of the former princely states of Travancore and Cochin (barring Kanyakumari, which was ceded to Tamil Nadu in 1956 due to its predominantly Tamil-speaking population), besides British Malabar that was part of the Madras Presidency. The Ezhavas of Malabar are also known as Tiyyas.
9. Osella and Osella 2000, p. 52. Also see the Alummoottil website, www. alummoottil.com, where it is claimed that 'many self acclaimed "upper caste" Nairs served as attendants, administrators, assistants and accountants for the family'.
10. Osella and Osella 2000, p. 66.
11. Hardgrave 1969, pp. 109–29. To fight the case, the Nadars established a fund of Rs 42,000, collected from community members throughout Tamil Nadu.
12. Ibid., pp. 133–40.
13. Osella and Osella 2000, pp.155–6. Between 1881 and 1931 the percentage of Travancore's Ezhavas reporting their occupation as toddy-tapping in census surveys fell from 25 to 4. Whether this

decline was real or a result of wrong disclosure in response to the movement against toddy is not clear.

14. Quoted in Hardgrave 1969, pp. 47–8.
15. Ibid., p. 51.
16. Baker 1984, p. 101.
17. Hardgrave 1969, p. 53.
18. The London Missionary Society in southern Travancore had even direct stakes in coffee plantations, which were used to fund its operations. In 1877 there were eight plantations owned by ex-missionaries covering 863 acres (Tharakan 1998, p. 12).
19. The poligars were holders of individual territories, each consisting of few villages, granted to them by the Telugu Nayak rulers in return for military service and tribute. On the rebellion by the poligars of Tirunelveli and its suppression by the Company, see Seylon 2004.
20. Baker 1984, pp. 255–6.
21. Hardgrave 1969, pp. 97–105.
22. Ibid., p. 151.
23. Between 1921–2 and 1926–7 match imports fell from 13.68 million gross to 6.13 million gross, while domestic production increased from less than 1 million gross to 10.5 million gross. See Ray 1979, pp. 151–61.
24. On this see Chandrasekhar 1997.
25. In July 2005 Swedish Match divested its 74 per cent stake in Wimco to the cigarette major ITC Ltd.
26. The Ayya Nadar group (headed by the founder's two elder sons, A. Grahadurai and A. Vairaprakasam) sells 'Camel' safety matches, as opposed to the 'Kaka' (crow) brand of Shanmuga Nadar's Sri Kaliswari group. The latter's business now is, however, predominantly in fireworks ('Cock' label).
27. Personal interview, 17 August 2005, Sivakasi.
28. Litho printing involves the transfer of images (words or artwork) from a metal plate surface to paper, based on the simple principle that oil and water do not mix. The surface is treated so that it has non-image areas that absorb ink. During printing, the plate is kept

moist so that the oily ink is repelled by the wet areas and adheres to the image area. In offset printing the image from the plate is first transferred ('offset') to an intermediary rubber-surfaced blanket cylinder and from there to the paper. It produces consistently high image quality because the blanket cylinder's flexibility preserves the delicate plate and also conforms to the surface of textured papers.

29. The premium diary – incorporating 140 grams of silver on its cover logo and bookmark and additional features like special cotton-laced paper and imported acrylic-coated cloth – sold about 300 copies in 2004.
30. Personal interview, 18 August 2005, Sivakasi.
31. The group also has a 14,000-spindle textile mill at Srivilliputhur (Virudhunagar), Silver Spring Spinners India Private Limited, which specialises in manufacture of technical and fire-retardant yarns used in industrial garments.
32. Personal interview, 17 August 2005, Sivakasi.
33. ITC owns the 'Aim' brand, apart from 'Ship' and 'Homelites' matches that it acquired from Wimco (note 25).
34. Hatsun Foods was renamed Hatsun Agro Products Limited in 1995. For the year ended 31 March 2005 it made a PAT of Rs 0.74 crore on net sales of Rs 449.19 crore.
35. M.S.P. Rajah married the daughter of Ayya Nadar. All this information is courtesy M.S.P. Rajah's son Ramesh P. Rajah, who is also the president of the Coffee Exporters Association of India (personal interview, 5 September 2005, Bangalore).
36. In April 2004 Rajagopal Nadar was sentenced to ten years' rigorous imprisonment on charges of abducting and murdering the husband of an employee's daughter. The latter had spurned the hotelier's advances to marry her.
37. For the year ended 30 June 2005 HCL Infosystems posted a PAT of Rs 227.71 crore on net sales of Rs 7,747.32 crore, while the corresponding numbers for HCL Technologies were Rs 618.72 crore and Rs 3,351.20 crore, respectively. Shiv Nadar is also associated with the IT education player NIIT, whose main promoters are Rajendra S. Pawar and Vijay K. Thadani. NIIT Limited earned a PAT of Rs 34.82 crore on net sales of Rs 398.37 crore during the year ended 31

March 2005, with these amounting to Rs 58.54 crore and Rs 543.20 crore for NIIT Technologies (a software services provider).

38. Jeffrey 2000, p. 79.
39. According to the Audit Bureau of Circulations (ABC), *Daily Thanthi's* net paid circulation during July–December 2004 was 796,900, against *Dinamalar's* 582,688. Though not a member of ABC, *Dinakaran* reportedly sells 300,000–350,000 copies.
40. When the Dravida Munnetra Kazhagam (DMK) split in 1977, Adithanar aligned with the breakaway All-India Anna DMK (AIADMK) of M.G. Ramachandran, while Kandasamy founded *Dinakaran* on a pro-DMK platform. Sun Network's promoter happens to be the grand-nephew of the DMK chief M. Karunanidhi.
41. Personal interview, 17 August 2005, Madurai.
42. Hardgrave 1969 has shown how the Nadars were initially united behind the anti-Brahmin, pro-British Justice Party, which fitted in with their support for the Raj and was reaffirmed in successive resolutions of the Sangam till the 1930s. The decisive break came after 1937 when the Congress government in Madras under C. Rajagopalachari threw open temples to all castes. Kamaraj being made president of the Tamilnad Congress Committee in 1940 only speeded the community's shift towards the Congress, which, by then, was clearly emerging as the new ruling power worth courting (pp. 173–201).
43. A. Ganesh Nadar, 'Endless Excitement: TMB is Back in the News – and Controversy', *Rediff On The Net*, 27 July 1999.
44. 'Nadar Bodies want TMB Board Dissolved', *The Hindu BusinessLine*, 3 December 2003.
45. Cited in Jeffrey 2001, p. 163.
46. Isaac and Tharakan 1986, p. 3. The relatively egalitarian pattern of land ownership in Travancore is also borne out by the fact that towards the end of the nineteenth century only one family paid more than Rs 10,000 in annual land revenue and fourteen over Rs 500. In Malabar, forty 'great houses' held about 28 per cent of the land and paid more than Rs 500,000 or over one-sixth of the region's total assessment (Jeffrey 2001, p 163). Kerala's Communist-inspired land reforms, thus, had their real impact in the erstwhile Malabar districts.

47. Isaac 1984, pp. 23–4.
48. This statement, made by M.L. Janardhana Pillai and N.C. John in an open address to the dewan of Travancore in 1928, is quoted in Isaac 1984, p. 45. The alleged lack of a level playing field led to the Indian coir manufacturers forming the Alleppey Chamber of Commerce in 1929, distinct from the European-dominated Travancore Chamber of Commerce.
49. Isaac 1984, p. 69.
50. During 2004–5 (April–March) India's export of coir and coir manufactures stood at Rs 455.11 crore (ministry of commerce). The other community with a major presence in coir is the Syrian Christians, whose leading exporters are N.C. John & Sons, the Palm Fibre group of Mathew Joseph, and D.C. Mills of K.J. Dennis.
51. Osella and Osella 2000, p. 51.
52. In Kerala every taluka (sub-district) has 2–3 'ranges' and each 'range' contains 30–40 shops.
53. Proof of this is that till recently the revenue realized per unit of liquor officially sold in the state ruled higher than the unit sale price itself (interview with senior excise official who chose to be anonymous, 24 August 2005, Thiruvananthapuram)!
54. Personal interview, 13 August 2005, Cherthala. Syrian Christians account for the rest, though they are mostly confined to the hilly districts of Idukki and Kottayam.
55. Osella and Osella 2000, p. 59.
56. Of the twenty-one reformed Ezhava temples that Sree Narayana Guru consecrated by 1909, seventeen were in Travancore and only two each in Cochin and Malabar district. The SNDP till date has not succeeded in sinking deep roots in northern Kerala.
57. For the year ended 31 March 2005 Jyothy Laboratories recorded a PAT of Rs 33.27 crore on net sales of Rs 265.35 crore.
58. These details are from M.L.N. Swamy's nephew Moola Bhaktavatsala, owner of Sharada Movies in Bangalore (personal interview, 10 August 2005, Bangalore). Also see Chapter 4 on B.N. Reddy.
59. Personal interview, 17 August 2005, Sivakasi.
60. Personal interview, 22 August 2005, Kozhikode.
61. *Mathrubhumi's* average daily net paid circulation during July–

December 2004 was 948,089, against 1,373,079 for *Malayala Manorama* (Audit Bureau of Circulations).

62. In 1988 a move by some shareholders led by M.D. Nalapat (son of the writer-poet Kamala Das alias Surayya) to offload 20 per cent in *Mathrubhumi* to Bennett Coleman invited charges of 'Malayali pride' getting hurt. It got 'resolved' when one set of Jains (Bennett Coleman) sold the disputed shares to another (Veerendra Kumar), who became the dominant shareholder.
63. Personal interview, 10 August 2005, Bangalore.
64. Venkataswamy 1975, pp. 15–19.
65. During July–December 2004 *Deccan Herald's* average daily net paid circulation was 161,232, compared to the *Times of India's* 346,761 (Karnataka numbers). The corresponding figures for *Prajavani* and *Vijay Karnataka* were 448,583 and 626,279, respectively (all editions). Vijay Sankeshwar's English daily *Vijay Times* (started in 2002), sold 97,502. In June 2006 the *Times of India* group (Bennett, Coleman) acquired Sankeshwar's entire newspaper business – Vijayanand Printers – for Rs 200 crore.
66. Guruswamy did not have children and had adopted his younger brother K.N. Anjanappa's son K.A. Nettakallappa. The latter predeceased Guruswamy.
67. Personal interview, 9 August 2005, Bangalore.

7. Patidars and Marathas

1. The GCMMF is primarily a marketing body for the twelve district unions that collect milk from farmers through 11,600-odd village societies. Technically, therefore, it is owned by the unions, with farmers having in-direct control though elected representatives to the societies and the unions. Roughly a fifth of the milk procured by the unions is sold locally under their own brands (e.g. 'Sumul' milk sold by the Surat Union). It is the remaining surplus milk that is marketed by GCMMF under the 'Amul' stable. For the year ended 31 March 2005, GCMMF registered net sales of Rs 2,922.53 crore. Inclusive of local sales by individual unions, the total turnover would be in the region of Rs 4,000 crore.

2. The unions' daily procurement in 2004–5 averaged 57.13 lakh litres (58.89 lakh kgs) or 21.49 lakh tonnes for the whole year. This accounts for 31.9 per cent of Gujarat's officially estimated milk production of 67.45 lakh tonnes for the year.
3. The average per kg fat price paid by GCMMF unions in 2004–5 ranged between Rs 205 and Rs 225. For milk with 6 per cent fat (and assuming a weight-volume conversion factor of 1.028 kg to a litre), the corresponding per litre prices work out to Rs 12.64 and Rs 13.88, respectively. For 8 per cent fat, these numbers would go up to Rs 16.86 and Rs 18.50 per litre.
4. A price of Rs 13 per litre may not seem much, when a farmer maintaining a herd of buffaloes near a city could probably realize Rs 19–20 for the same milk. But then the cost of feed, labour, and various overheads would be higher in city outskirts relative to rural areas. GCMMF's real beneficiary is the milk producer in the hinterland who, on his own, cannot access distant urban markets for a perishable product. For him the village society is an avenue for marketing milk round the year at a steady price that more than covers his immediate costs. The co-operative also provides cattle feed, artificial insemination, veterinary and extension support, which again cannot be easily availed of by the urban milk producer.
5. It was 47 per cent in 2000. See Harish Damodaran, 'A Tale of Two Milk Districts', *The Hindu BusinessLine*, 9 December 2001.
6. These figures are derived from the websites of Fonterra (www.fonterra.com) and DFA (www.dfamilk.com).
7. Estimates are average for the 2000–1, 2001–2 and 2002–3 crushing seasons (October–September). We have not considered subsequent seasons, since these coincided with a severe drought in Maharashtra, which would give a distorted picture.
8. For 2000–1 to 2002–3, the mean sugar recovery rate in Maharashtra was 11.62 per cent, while being 9.59 per cent in UP and 10.37 per cent for all-India.
9. Y.B. Chavan was CM of the bilingual Bombay state from 1 November 1956 and remained so even after Maharashtra was formed on 1 May 1960 till 19 November 1962. Vasantdada Patil had two terms: from 17 May 1977 to 18 July 1978 and from 2 February 1983 to

1 June 1985. Sharad Pawar was CM thrice: from 18 July 1978 to 17 February 1980, from 26 June 1988 to 25 June 1991, and from 6 March 1993 to 14 March 1995.

10. Kutch district alone occupies 23 per cent of Gujarat's area with just 3 per cent of its population (2001 Census). The Saurashtra region includes Surendranagar, Bhavnagar, Amreli, Rajkot, Jamnagar, Porbandar, and Junagarh districts.
11. The Rajkot union's daily procurement in 2004–5 averaged 1.35 lakh litres, against 57.13 lakh litres for Gujarat on the whole. Almost 80 per cent of the milk came from the five unions of Mehsana (13.69 lakh litres), Banaskantha (9.53), Sabarkantha (8.18), Kheda (7.34), and Surat (6.13).
12. Gujarat produces 1.1 million tonnes (mt) of sugar every year (average for 2000–1 to 2002–3), which is behind Maharashtra (6.2 mt), UP (5.2 mt), Tamil Nadu and Karnataka (1.7 mt each).
13. Khandesh covers Nandurbar, Dhule, and Jalgaon districts. Marathwada includes Aurangabad, Jalna, Beed, Parbhani, Hingoli, Nanded, Latur, and Osmanabad, while Vidarbha consists of Buldhana, Akola, Washim, Amaravati, Yavatmal, Wardha, Nagpur, Chandrapur, Bhandara, Gondia, and Gadchiroli. The other distinct region of Maharashtra is Konkan, which embraces the coastal districts of Thane, Mumbai, Raigarh, Ratnagiri, and Sindhudurg. During British rule, western Maharashtra, Konkan, and Khandesh were part of the Bombay Presidency, whereas Marathwada and Vidarbha were under the Hyderabad state and Central Provinces, respectively.
14. Hardiman 1981, p. 261.
15. Ibid., p. 262.
16. Attwood 1993, pp. 49–67.
17. Quoted in ibid., p. 59.
18. On the Saswad Mali pioneers, see Baviskar 1980, pp. 22–3.
19. Attwood 1993, p. 75.
20. Rutten 1995, p. 75.
21. Kamath 1996, pp. 28–34.
22. Attwood 1993, p. 80.
23. Baviskar 1980, p. 24.

24. This condition does not apply to, say, a flour miller, who can buy wheat in bulk during the harvest season and store it in his warehouse for use throughout the year. In milk and sugarcane, the risk of spoilage and depletion of sucrose content automatically reduces the time between production of the raw material and its processing. That, by itself, necessitates greater co-ordination of farm and factory operations, making these industries highly amenable to co-operative ownership of processing facilities.
25. These figures are taken from Lele 1990, pp. 116–21. The share of Maratha-Kunbis was 38.7 per cent in Konkan, 32.4 per cent in Marathwada and 23 per cent in Vidarbha.
26. The protest against Brahmin dominance in all walks of life, through privileged access to Western education and jobs, had its roots in the Satyashodhak Samaj founded in the 1870s by Jotirao Phule (1827–90), a Mali by caste. As writers like Lele and Omvedt have shown, the movement, which had a universalistic humanist character in Phule's time, later became basically a tool for Maratha assertion. See Omvedt 1976.
27. See Deshpande 2004. In 1894 Brahmins occupied 104 jobs in Shahu's government, against 18 by non-Brahmins. By 1922 Brahmins were only 69, non-Brahmins 168, and untouchables 1. Over this period the number of Brahmin students in Kolhapur's schools rose from 2,522 to 2,722, whereas they shot up from 8,088 to 21,027 for non-Brahmins and from 264 to 2,162 for untouchables.
28. Deshpande 2004, p. 27.
29. 1931 census figures cited in Shah 1990, p. 63.
30. Quoted in Hardiman 1981, pp. 1–2.
31. Ibid., pp. 243–55.
32. Between 1936–7 and 1937–8, Congress membership in Maharashtra soared from 45,925 to 163,880, driven by the spurt in rural area numbers, from 29,516 to 126,598 (Lele 1990, p. 161).
33. On this, see Omvedt 1988.
34. Shah 1996, pp. 96–105.
35. George 1996, pp. 237–54.
36. Shah 1996, pp. 172–3.
37. Baviskar 1980, pp. 26–39.

38. Discussion with officials of the Maharashtra State Cooperative Sugar Factories Federation, 19 December 2005, Mumbai. The 70:30 debt-equity scheme was formulated in the 1950s for mills with 800 tcd capacity. When the minimum viable capacity norms were revised upwards, to 1,250 tcd in the 1960s and to 2,500 tcd after 1975, the debt component was reduced to 65 per cent and 50 per cent, respectively, for both new as well as expansion projects. For the Pravara factory, the total investment was Rs 41 lakh, in which the farmers and the state government put in Rs 6 lakh of equity each. For the remaining, Rs 20 lakh was borrowed from the Industrial Finance Corporation of India and Rs 9 lakh as short-term loans from the State Bank of India.
39. World Bank 1998, p. 21. Also Patel 1997, p. 37.
40. Verghese Kurien's contribution to Amul is similar to that of D.R. Gadgil, who was the main guiding spirit behind the Pravara experiment. The former was a Syrian Christian from Kerala and the latter a Chitpavan Brahmin. Their being given a lead part in managing the affairs of the co-operatives says a lot about the far-sightedness and professional candour of peasant leaders like Tribhuvandas Patel and Vikhe-Patil.
41. Computed from the List of Sugar Factories in Maharashtra, Mumbai: Maharashtra Rajya Sahakari Sakhar Karkhana Sangh.
42. See note 11.
43. Dubash 2002, pp. 69–155. For an account of the working of tubewell companies in Mehsana, see Shah 1996, pp. 121–47.
44. The yeomen Mali cultivators, referred to earlier, set up a sugar mill near Akluj in Solapur district way back in 1933. Though formally not a co-operative, the Saswad Mali Sugar Factory Limited was organized pretty much on those lines, with every shareholder being a cane grower and supplying one acre of crop for each share held. This principle was subsequently adopted by the co-operatives in Maharashtra, even as the factory that pioneered it remained outside the fold of a movement, seen as being overtly Maratha-dominated (Baviskar 1980, pp. 25–6).
45. The Mehsana union's founder was a Chaudhary Patel. The Patidars descend from a landowning peasant community known as 'Kanbi',

a name incidentally stemming from the same root as the Maratha Kunbis. For a background on the various divisions among Patidars, see Pocock 1972, pp. 52–69.

46. This is a term Shah 1996 has used to describe co-operatives in Surat, which are linked through complex interlocking of governance structures akin to the system in Japan's giant industrial corporations (pp. 66–7).
47. Pratapsinh Shankarrao Mohite-Patil, too, had a brief stint with the saffron alliance, successfully contesting a parliamentary byelection from Pandharpur in 2003 on a BJP ticket. The fact that the BJP–Shiv Sena combine has had to import 'rebel' Maratha barons to make a dent in western Maharashtra demonstrates how deep the Congress' roots are in the region, courtesy the freedom movement and co-operatives.
48. Tripathi 2004, pp. 105–6.
49. For an early history of the group, see Tripathi and Mehta 1990, pp. 105–15.
50. Ibid., pp. 116–30.
51. Shah 1990, p. 94.
52. Mafatlal Industries posted a net loss of Rs 6.32 crore on net sales of Rs 130.84 crore for the year ended September 2005.
53. For the year ended 31 March 2005 Alembic Limited recorded a PAT of Rs 52.05 crore on net sales of Rs 524.46 crore. The corresponding figures for Alembic Glass Industries and Jyoti Limited were Rs (–) 2.88 crore and Rs 54.34 crore and Rs (–) 2.94 crore and Rs 85.11 crore, respectively.
54. For the year ended 31 March 2005 Cadila Healthcare reported a PAT of Rs 117.90 crore on net sales of Rs 1,243 crore.
55. Patel Engineering registered a PAT of Rs 41.55 crore on net sales of Rs 777.94 crore during the year ended 31 March 2005.
56. Sintex Industries posted a PAT of Rs 53.91 crore on net sales of Rs 658.72 crore during the year ended 31 March 2005.
57. The end-March 2005 yearly PAT and net sales figures for Suzlon were Rs 365.33 crore and Rs 1,942.48 crore, respectively.
58. For the ended 31 March 2005 The Sandesh Limited reported a PAT of Rs 6.71 crore on net sales of Rs 663.08 crore. The main rivals to

Sandesh are *Gujarat Samachar* of Shreyans Shah (Jain) and *Divya Bhaskar* of Ramesh Chandra Agrawal (Marwari). Interestingly, the prominent Marathi daily *Sakal* (average daily net paid circulation of 830,654 during July–December 2004) is also a takeover product. In 1985 its ownership passed from the Parulekar family (Brahmin) to that of the Maratha strongman Sharad Pawar.

59. The Patidars of Kheda have traditionally controlled the trade in non-virginia (bidi) tobacco, which has made them rather lukewarm to growers' co-operatives. Patidar non-participation – unlike in dairy or sugar, where the business was dominated by Banias, Parsis or Bhatias – is seen by some to have been crucial behind the failure of tobacco growers co-operatives. The fact that tobacco constitutes only 10–15 per cent of the cost of bidis (the main raw material, labour, is available cheaper outside Gujarat, while the tendu leaves are grown in Madhya Pradesh and Orissa) is an added factor militating against integrated co-operatives. On this, see Shah 1996, pp. 86–96.
60. Pocock 1972, p. 63.
61. For a comprehensive study on Patidar migration and settlement patterns in the US, see Bhakta 2002.
62. For the year ended 31 March 2005 Champagne Indage Limited earned a PAT of Rs 5.49 crore on net sales of Rs 37.49 crore. A more significant recent Maratha tycoon is Avinash Bhonsle, an irrigation contractor and owner of Pune's Sun-n-Sand five-star property. Bhonsle first struck gold by bagging contracts for the Krishna Valley Project during the mid-1990s under the BJP–Shiv Sena coalition regime.
63. Chansma now comes under Patan district that was formed from parts of Mehsana and Banaskantha in 2000.
64. Personal interview, 27 December 2005, Ahmedabad.
65. HLL's production is inclusive of third-party processing of 3.47 lakh tonnes. Figures are taken from Nirma's Annual Report for the year ended 31 March 2005 and HLL's for the year ended 31 December 2004.
66. The major domestic soda ash producers are Tata Chemicals (8.75 lakh tonnes capacity), Nirma (6.5), Gujarat Heavy Chemicals (5.25), and Saurashtra Chemicals (3.5). In July 2005 Nirma bought

a controlling stake in Saurashtra Chemicals from the S.K. Birla group. If the latter's capacity is added, Nirma would be the largest soda ash manufacturer. In LAB, Reliance has a capacity of 1.45 lakh tonnes (including IPCL's 45,000 tonnes), followed by IOC (1.2 lakh), TNPL (1 lakh), and Nirma (75,000). During 2004–5 Nirma produced 542,378 tonnes of soda ash and 105,598 tonnes of LAB (more than installed capacity), of which captive consumption stood at 252,296 tonnes and 69,509 tonnes, respectively.

67. During 2004–5 Nirma produced 97,859 tonnes of toilet soap, against HLL's 2.94 lakh tonnes (inclusive of 15,707 tonnes of third-party processing) for 2004.
68. For the year ended 31 March 2005 Nirma Limited posted a PAT of Rs 281.93 crore on net sales of Rs 2,098.18 crore.
69. Personal interview, 5 January 2006, Anand. Bhanubhai died on 1 February, less than a month after this interview.
70. The Mundhra financial scam – the first ever to surface in independent India – involved the state-owned Life Insurance Corporation (LIC) purchasing shares in six companies of Haridas Mundhra, a Kolkata Marwari, bypassing its investment committee. Besides H.M. Patel, it also led to the then finance minister, T.T. Krishnamachari, demitting office. H.M. Patel later on went to become finance minister in the Janata Party government at the centre.
71. Sardar Patel is credited with having inspired two great ideas that transformed Kheda. The first is, of course, Amul. The second is Vallabh Vidyanagar, originally conceived as an educational township encompassing a large number of institutions within a compact area serving Charotar's rural populace. It is often said about the Patidars in the US that many of them are from families who once sold milk to Amul and whose children later studied engineering and medicine in Vallabh Vidyanagar. The industrial estate adjoining its boundaries was meant to house units providing practical training for students from the various colleges in the township.
72. For the year ended 31 March 2005 Elecon Engineering Company Limited earned a PAT of Rs 10.04 crore on net sales of Rs 280.78 crore, while the corresponding figures for Eimco Elecon stood at Rs 8.75 crore and Rs 97.22 crore, respectively. In 1967, after Ishwarbhai's

death, Bhanubhai's elder brother Shapurji promoted his own Rolcon Engineering Company Limited for manufacture of steel roller chains and sprockets. It has not been as successful, posting a meagre Rs 0.48 crore PAT on net sales of Rs 16.03 crore in 2004–5.

73. This case study is based on field visits to Sangli and Kolhapur during 15–18 December 2005.
74. The Lingayats can be considered as the primary indigenous trading community of southern Maharashtra and northern Karnataka. Besides the promoters of the Warana, Panchganga, and Datta Shetkari Shirol co-operatives in Kolhapur, Vijay Sankeshwar of *Vijay Karnataka* (see previous chapter) and Neelkanth A. Kalyani are also Lingayats. The last named industrialist is the founder of India's No. 1 auto forgings combine – the Rs 5,000 crore Kalyani group. The companies under its fold include Bharat Forge (Rs 161.63 crore PAT on Rs 1,166.87 crore net sales in 2004–5), Kalyani Steels (Rs 51.11 crore and Rs 771.24 crore), Kalyani Brakes (Rs 33.51 crore and Rs 365.77 crore), and Automotive Axles (Rs 36.86 crore and Rs 354.74 crore).
75. The official SMP is the price that the farmer receives at the factory gate. Since in most states (other than Maharashtra), the onus for harvesting and bringing the cane to the mill lies with the farmer, it is he who has to bear the expenses involved. The actual price he gets would, therefore, be the SMP (or factory-gate price) minus the cost of harvesting and transport.

8. The Paradox of Northern Farming Communities

1. India's foodgrain production amounted to 213.46 mt in 2003–4, including 88.28 mt of rice and 72.11 mt of wheat. Of this, 22.83 mt of rice and 16.80 mt of wheat were procured for the central pool. Compiled from *Agricultural Statistics* 2005.
2. 'FCI to Float Bonds to Raise Rs 1,000 Crore', *The Hindu BusinessLine*, 18 January 2005.
3. Of the 22.83 mt of rice procured in 2003–4, Punjab's share was 8.66 mt and Haryana's 1.33 mt. In wheat, the corresponding figures in

the total (16.80 mt) were 9.24 mt and 5.11 mt (*Agricultural Statistics* 2005).

4. These are ballpark numbers, as no caste-based census has been carried out after 1931 and changes in demographic profile post-Partition make any extrapolation exercise for north-west India problematic. The 90 per cent estimate for Punjab is by H.S. Shergill of Panjab University, Chandigarh (personal interview, 13 February 2005). In the 1931 census, Jats formed two-thirds of the Sikh population. If one interpolates this with the fact that non-Jats (both Sikhs and Hindus) in Punjab are mostly urban-based or landless labourers, Shergill's figure seems reasonable. By the same count, Jats are seen to constitute a quarter of Haryana's population. This, along with their being mainly rural-based, gives credence to the estimated 50 per cent share of Jats in the state's farming community.
5. For a useful sum-up of the debate surrounding the subject, see Rutten 1995, pp. 1–50. The Agricultural Census data for 1995–6 puts 'large' operational holdings – 10 hectares (24.71 acres) and above – at 80,000 in Punjab and 40,000 in Haryana. Shergill reckons that Punjab alone has some 10,000 farmers with holdings in excess of 100 acres. Taking an average return of Rs 10,000 per acre from growing two irrigated crops a year, a farmer with 100 acres would rake in an annual profit of Rs 10 lakh, not to count income from dairying and various non-farming sources.
6. During 2003–4 Punjab produced 14.49 mt of wheat and 9.66 mt of rice, while the same for Haryana stood at 9.13 mt and 2.79 mt, respectively (*Agricultural Statistics* 2005).
7. Figures are for 2003–4 and expressed as nitrogen, phosphorous, potash, or NPK (*Agricultural Statistics* 2005).
8. The country's total agricultural tractor population in 2003 was assessed at 23.61 lakh, including 2.99 lakh in Punjab and 1.94 lakh in Haryana ('Detailed Statistical Tables of Agricultural Machinery & Implements', *17th Livestock Census* 2005). Official data also shows cumulative tractor sales in India over a fifteen-year period from 1989–90 to 2003–4 at 29.14 lakh, of which Punjab and Haryana accounted for 3.62 lakh and 2.68 lakh, respectively.
9. Alam 1998, pp. 373–4.

10. Ahuja 2004.
11. Haldhari literally means wielder of the plough, while chathadhari and bangladhari refer to umbrella-holder and mansion-dweller, respectively. This neat categorization of farmers was made for me some years back by the former union minister of state for agriculture, Hukum Deo Narayan Yadav.
12. Singh 2001, p. 26.
13. On this, see Datta 1999.
14. Quoted in ibid., p. 97.
15. Darling 1978, p. 117.
16. Singh 2001, p. 23.
17. Between 1872–3 and 1932–3, total rail track mileage in Punjab shot up from 410 to 5,500, while that of metalled roads rose from 1,036 to 3,904 (Calvert 1936, p. 107). For a detailed background of the canal colonies, see Ali 1989. Also, Randhawa 1983, vol. III, pp. 282–94.
18. One of the officially stated aims for the largest Chenab Colony project was 'to colonize the area in question with well-to-do yeomen of the best class of agriculturists, who will cultivate their own holdings with the aid of their families and the usual menials, but as much as possible without the aid of tenants, and will constitute healthy agricultural communities of the best Punjab type'. Quoted in Ali 1989, p. 13.
19. Darling 1978, p. 117. Darling was a member of the Indian Civil Service who served as financial commissioner of Punjab.
20. Randhawa 1983, vol. III, pp. 366–75.
21. Ibid., p. 345.
22. Ali 1989, p. 4.
23. Quoted in Datta 1999, p. 77.
24. Quoted in ibid., pp. 100–1. Chhotu Ram played a key role in enlisting soldiers during World War I from Rohtak, as honorary secretary of the District Recruitment and War Committee.
25. Randhawa 1986, vol. IV, pp. 1–17.
26. Ibid., pp. 26–37.
27. Sikhs are 59.9 per cent of Punjab's population as per the 2001 census, of which Jat Sikhs presumably constitute two-thirds. Jats

form the single largest community in Haryana with an estimated share of 25 per cent, ahead of the Dalits, who, according to the census, account for 19.3 per cent. Bifurcation essentially caused a splintering of the urban bourgeoisie in the previously unified Indian Punjab province.

28. For an insight into the enactment of the Zamindari Abolition and Land Reforms Bill in UP, see Singh 1986.
29. Amin 1984, pp. 131–4.
30. Madan Gopal, 'Sardar Dyal Singh Majithia's Vision', *The Tribune*, 9 September 2003, Chandigarh. According to the Audit Bureau of Circulation's (ABC) data for July–December 2004, *The Tribune*'s average net daily paid circulation stood at 246,379.
31. Tariff protection led to a spurt in the number of sugar mills in India from 29 in 1931 to 137 in 1936–7. In UP alone there were fifteen mills in 1930, which rose to 75 by 1937 (Amin 1984, p. 111).
32. See Tripathi 2004, pp. 237–8 and Hazari 1966, p. 256.
33. *Monopolies Inquiry Commission* 1965 and *Industrial Licensing Policy Inquiry Committee* 1969.
34. All this information is courtesy Gurmit Singh Mann (personal interview, 23 April 2005, New Delhi).
35. For the year ending 31 March 2005 Simbhaoli Sugar Mills reported a profit after tax (PAT) of Rs 11.86 crore on net sales of Rs 390.20 crore.
36. Malik 1994, pp. 36–70.
37. Between 1980–1 and 2003–4 soybean production in MP went up from 0.35 mt to 4.71 mt, while the corresponding increase for rapeseed-mustard in Rajasthan was from 0.25 mt to 2.74 mt. During 2003–4 MP produced 60 per cent of India's soybean, with Rajasthan's share in rapeseed-mustard amounting to 44 per cent (*Agricultural Statistics*, various years).
38. For a complete list, see *SEA Handbook* 2005, pp. 43–7.
39. Datta 1999, p. 159. As per ABC figures for July–December 2004 the average daily net paid circulation of *Ajit* was 298,571, against 269,744 for *Jag Bani*. The corresponding numbers were 21,61,446 for *Dainik Jagran*, 20,08,778 for *Dainik Bhaskar*, 984,812 for

Hindustan, 935,783 for *Rajasthan Patrika*, 864,095 for *Punjab Kesri*, and 619,624 for *Amar Ujala*.

40. Personal interview, 11 February 2005, New Delhi.
41. Personal interview, 25 February 2005, Jalandhar.
42. Personal interview, 13 February 2005, Chandigarh.
43. Personal interview, 16 February 2005, Chandigarh.
44. On this, see Rutten 1995, pp. 348–61.
45. These terms are taken from Sau 1988.
46. Ibid.
47. Batra 1996 has shown how lack of interest amongst political leaders has contributed to the poor functioning of the co-operative sugar factory at Baghpat, which happens to be the pocket borough of Ajit Singh, and earlier of his father Charan Singh.
48. This is hinted at in Sau 1988. For more explicit, though slightly crude, formulations on these lines, see Purewal 2000.
49. Quoted in Purewal 2000, p. 87.
50. Ramesh Vinayak, 'Firmly Rooted', *India Today*, 11 October 2004. Also, Kaur 2003a, pp. 36–42.
51. Besides Didar Singh Bains, they included Ganga Singh Dhillon, Gurmit Singh Aulakh, Jagjit Singh Chohan, Tarsem Singh Purewal, Gian Singh Sandhu, and Talwinder Singh Parmar. All of them were Jat Sikhs who had strong social and familial connections in rural Punjab (Purewal 2000, p. 136).
52. The survey was conducted on 21–22 April 2005.
53. Personal interviews, Khanna.
54. A state government-commissioned study in 1997 showed that arhatias meet 61 per cent of seasonal agricultural operation loans availed by farmers. For an overview of their operations, see Harish Damodaran, 'Grains Market Still Under Sway of Commission Agents', *The Hindu BusinessLine*, 12 May 2000.
55. Kaur 2003.
56. Agro Dutch Industries recorded a PAT of Rs 17.90 crore on net sales of Rs 144.47 crore for the year ending 31 March 2005. Nijjer Agro made a net loss of Rs 7.29 crore on sales of Rs 38.85 crore for the year ending 31 March 2004, while returning a PAT of Rs 0.46 crore on net sales of Rs 43.84 crore in the next fiscal.

57. Personal interview, 22 April 2005, Jalandhar.
58. See P.P.S. Gill, 'PSIDC in Debt Snarl: Standing Dues Touch Rs 1,050 Crore', *The Tribune*, 1 June 2002, Chandigarh.
59. The SGPC administers all Sikh shrines in Punjab, Haryana, and Himachal. The Jat Sikh-dominated body has failed in its attempts to take over gurudwaras in Delhi and other centres, which are controlled by Khatris and other petty-bourgeois sections in the community. See Purewal 2000, pp. 127–8.
60. The forging of a composite Ramgarhia identity among Punjab's different artisan castes professing the Sikh faith (on the lines of the Kshatriyas of Gujarat) is an early-twentieth-century phenomenon. The increasing popularity of the term accompanied a steady improvement in the economic status of Tarkhans, many of whom returned themselves as Ramgarhias in the 1921 and 1931 censuses. Subsequently, other Sikh artisan groups also claimed to be Ramgarhias. On this, see McLeod 2003, pp. 216–36.
61. Ibid.
62. Tewari 1998.
63. Ramgarhias form 90 per cent of the migrant Sikh population in East Africa. Many of them, like the Gujarati Patidars, subsequently moved to Britain, following the Africanization drive of the 1960s. See Bhachu 1990.
64. Tewari 1998. An indicator of the community's overall mechanical disposition is the website, www.ramgarhiakom.com, which has, among others, a special monthly section featuring detailed drawings and descriptions of anvils, hammers, mallets, tongs, chisels, swages, pincers, and other tools.
65. Unless otherwise mentioned, these are based on company inputs and personal interviews with Kushal Pal Singh (10 March 2005, New Delhi), Rana Gurjeet Singh (25 February 2005, Jalandhar), Harbhajan Singh Cheema (12 April 2005, Chandigarh), and Ranjodh Singh (22 April 2005, Ludhiana).
66. Datta 1999, pp. 90, 203.
67. For the year ended 31 March 2005 DLF Universal Limited made a PAT of Rs 83.70 crore on total income of Rs 630.20 crore. The

estimate of DLF's land assets is by the global property consultant Cushman & Wakefield.

68. For useful details on the reclamation and colonization of the Tarai, see Randhawa 1986, vol. IV, pp. 51–60.
69. For the year ended 31 March 2005 GS Auto International reported a PAT of Rs 0.63 crore on net sales of Rs 61.44 crore.
70. There is a Ramgarhia Educational Council at Phagwara too, started in 1929 by Mohan Singh Hadiabadi, which manages more than a dozen schools and college, including the Ramgarhia Institute of Engineering & Technology. The Goraya-based GNA group also runs a GNA Institute of Management & Technology.

9. A Note on the Minorities

1. Tirmizi 1984, pp. 64–5. Under Muslim law, the agnatic heirs (through the male lineage) were entitled only to a residual share of the deceased's property, once the spouse and other specified blood relations (including parents and sisters) had received their fixed portions. The Memons and Khojas were, however, granted a special exemption to follow the agnatic patrilineal pattern as per Hindu custom, which excluded women from succession. Although the Shariat Act of 1937 diluted this engrafted provision considerably, it did not dispense with the power to dispose of property by testament which is enjoyed by these communities.
2. Tripathi 2004, pp. 78–9.
3. Gupta 1979 gives a good working profile of Abdul Ghafur.
4. Quoted in Ray 1984, p. 252.
5. Ibid., pp. 253–4.
6. Markovits 1985, p. 190. Also Tripathi 2004, pp. 124–5.
7. Khalidi 2006, pp. 142–3. The official *Indian Sugar Industry – 1939 Annual* publication listed the promoter of the Nizam Sugar Factory at Bodhan as 'H.E.H. The Nizam's Industrial Trust Fund represented by the Hyderabad Construction Co Ltd' (Appendix 1, p. 28).
8. Tirmizi 1984, p. 64.

9. C.N. Vakil, *Economic Consequences of Divided India.* Quoted in Papanek 1973, p. 64.
10. Levin 1974, p. 235.
11. The above details are from Levin 1974 and Shahid-Ur-Rehman, *Who Owns Pakistan?* (http://richpaki.tripod.com).
12. For the year ended 31 March 2005 Wipro earned a PAT of Rs 1,619.82 crore on net sales of Rs 8,160.56 crore. The corresponding figures (ending 31 December 2005) for Wockhardt were Rs 257.10 crore and Rs 1,458.20 crore, respectively.
13. For the year ended 31 March 2005 Cipla's PAT stood at Rs 409.61 crore on net sales of Rs 2,181.26 crore, while amounting to Rs 26.09 crore and Rs 255.76 crore for Mirza International, Rs 8.89 crore and Rs 156.22 crore for Zodiac Clothing, Rs 46.03 crore and Rs 163.26 crore for Cranes Software, and Rs 0.23 crore and Rs 112.02 crore for *Mid-Day*.
14. Prominent names figuring in this context are Abu Azmi, a Mumbai-based restaurant magnate and Samajwadi Party politician, and Badruddin Ajmal, an exporter of attar and perfumery extracts to the Middle East, who has floated the Assam United Democratic Front. Others are Mukhtar Ansari, a don and independent legislator from Mau, and a former UP minister Haji Yaqoob Qureshi, best known for offering a Rs 51-crore reward to kill the Danish cartoonist who caricatured the Prophet Mohammed in the *Jyllands-Posten* daily in late 2005.
15. On this point, see Asghar Ali Engineer, 'Muslim Middle Class and its Role', *Secular Perspective*, 16–31 May 2001.
16. Zachariah, Kannan and Rajan 2002, pp. 13–45, 199–227.
17. A symbol of this prosperity is Perinthalmanna, a remote one-horse town of Malapuram that today boasts four 'super-speciality' hospitals! On Malapuram's growth, see E.P. Unny, 'Calling the Believers', *The Sunday Express*, 19 March 2006.
18. Mustafa Rashid Shervani's son, Saleem, is a former union minister.
19. See Chapter 6.
20. For an overview of early Syrian Christian entrepreneurship, see Isaac and Tharakan 1986, and Mahadevan 1991. The latter has shown that

Syrian Christian capital, right until the 1940s, tended to be invested primarily in plantations and banking. Even in traditional industries like coir and cashew processing, the early local capitalists who really mattered were K.C. Karunakaran (Ezhava) in Alappuzha and the Kollam-based Thangal Kunju Musaliar (Muslim), respectively.

21. Mahadevan 1991, pp. 170–4. The Travancore National and Quilon Bank collapsed in 1938, with the dewan C.P. Ramaswamy Aiyar apparently using his informal connections in the Madras commercial circles to engineer a run on it. Mammen Mappillai's squabble with Ramaswamy Aiyar also resulted in *Manorama*'s almost decade-long closure from 1938.
22. During the year ended 30 September 2005 MRF recorded a PAT of Rs 40.31 crore on net sales of Rs 2,966.20 crore. According to the Audit Bureau of Circulations' data for July–December 2004, *Malayala Manorama's* average net daily paid sales stood at 1,373,079.
23. As on 31 March 2005 Federal Bank had outstanding deposits of Rs 15,192.88 crore, with the corresponding figures being Rs 8,492.32 crore for South Indian Bank and Rs 4,021.11 crore for Catholic Syrian Bank. Of the three, it is only the last-named bank that has sought to assiduously preserve its community identity. The Catholic church under the archbishop of Thrissur even lobbied successfully to foil a takeover attempt mounted by a Bangkok-based NRI, Surchan Chansri Chawla, in the mid 1990s. By contrast the biggest shareholders in Federal Bank and South Indian Bank now are foreign institutional investors.
24. For the year ended 31 March 2005 Geojit Securities registered a PAT of Rs 10.42 crore on net sales of Rs 54.43 crore, with these standing at Rs 51.66 crore and Rs 289.54 crore for Aban Offshore Limited, Rs 2.63 crore and Rs 73.84 crore for Kitex Garments, and Rs 107.14 crore and Rs 612.05 crore for Glenmark.

10. Conclusion

1. The entire proceedings of the Constituent Assembly Debates from 9 December 1946 to 24 January 1950 are available at the website of the Parliament of India (Lok Sabha), http://parliamentofindia.nic.in/ls/debates/debates.htm.

2. Thiru Arooran Sugars was founded in 1954 by Vadapathimangalam Tyagaraja Mudaliar. For the fifteenth months ended 30 September 2005 the company earned profits after tax (PAT) of Rs 10.64 crore on net sales of Rs 300.15 crore.
3. During the year ended 31 March 2005 Sun TV Limited recorded a PAT of Rs 77.97 crore on net sales of Rs 290.31 crore. It is part of Kalanithi Maran's Sun Network, which is the largest satellite television broadcaster in the South, running fourteen channels, including 'Sun TV' and 'KTV' in Tamil, 'Surya TV' and 'Kiran TV' in Malayalam, 'Gemini TV' in Telugu, and 'Udaya TV' in Kannada. The group also has stakes in the print media (a Tamil daily, *Dinakaran*, and an eveninger, *Tamizh Murasu*) and FM radio. Kalanithi Maran is the grandnephew of the present Tamil Nadu chief minister and DMK supremo M. Karunanidhi. The Isai Vellalars (Melakarars) – the community to which they belong – have traditionally been temple musicians and dancers, and are listed under Other Backward Classes.
4. Suman K. Jha, 'Not Caste in Stone', *The Week*, 28 May 2006, pp. 12–17.
5. See *Task Force Report on Bhopal Declaration* 2003.
6. Seetha, 'Wanted Next: A Dalit Business Class', *Daily News & Analysis*, Mumbai: 30 May 2006.
7. This aspect is well highlighted by Lamb 1955: 'Many poor Parsis attend Parsi schools and inhabit Parsi subsidized tenements along with their fellows; (on the other side) wealthy Parsis have been attending cosmopolitan educational institutions for the last hundred years' (p. 108).
8. See the case studies on the Sakthi group and DLF in Chapters 5 and 8, respectively.
9. On the apparent conflict between 'national' and 'regional' capital and its political implications, see Baru 2000.

Note on Numbers and Spellings

Unless specified otherwise, the events and developments in this book cover the period up to 2005. Figures pertaining to sales, profits, and other size magnitudes of companies or industries are expressed mainly in rupees (Rs) crore. One crore equals 10 million and one rupee represents 0.02 US dollars at an average exchange rate of Rs 44.10 to the dollar for 2005.

The names of many cities and towns in India and its neighbourhoods have undergone change or modification in recent times. Thus, Bombay is now formally called Mumbai, just as Madras has become Chennai, Calcutta is Kolkata, Baroda is Vadodara, Benares is Varanasi, Trichnapoly (Trichy) is Tiruchirapalli, Tinnevelly is Tirunelveli, Tuticorin is Thoothukudi, Ramnad is Ramanathapuram, Cochin is Kochi, Trivandrum is Thiruvananthapuram, Calicut is Kozhikode, Trichur is Thrissur, Alleppey is Alappuzha, Quilon is Kollam, Cuddapah is Kadapa, Vizag is Visakhapatnam, Masulipatnam is Machilipatnam, Burma is Myanmar, Ceylon is Sri Lanka, Malaya is Malaysia, and Lyallpur is Faisalabad. In this book, the old and new names have been used interchangeably, depending on the context.

Glossary

Abkari	Liquor contractor with vending rights for a defined area.
Adda	Informal meeting ground for intellectual brainstorming (usually over tea and cigarettes) peculiar to Bengal, specially Kolkata.
Amani	System of direct collection of revenues from cultivators by government officials (see *ryotwari*).
Amarakam	Revenue system of renting out villages jointly to farmers and assigning collection to prominent landowners.
Arhatia	Commission agent who aggregates produce from farmers at the market and supplies it to traders and other buyers. (An agent performing this simple intermediary role, for which he charges a commission at a fixed percentage of the purchase price, is a *kutcha arhatia*. An agent who is not just a middleman bringing together the principal buyer and seller, but also trades produce on his own account, is called a *pucca arhatia*.)
Arishtam	Alcohol-based ayurvedic concoction.
Avarna	Castes outside the Hindu *chaturvarna* fold, traditionally regarded as untouchables. The modern term used is Dalit.
Ayurveda	Ancient system of medicine native to India.

Bajra Pearl millet.
Banian Knitted undershirt. Also, a colloquial term for guaranteed brokers to European agency houses in colonial India.
Benami Property or assets held nominally by someone 'fronting' for the real owner.
Bhadralok Educated urban middle class of Bengal, mainly of upper-caste Hindu (Brahmin, Kayastha, Vaidya) background.
Bidi Indigenous cheroot.
Chakiri Dried coconut husk.
Chakram Spiral-shaped fire cracker.
Charatta Coconut shell.
Chaturvarna Traditional four-layered Hindu social order comprising Brahmins, Kshatriyas, Vaishyas, and Shudras.
Chena Malayalam term for elephant yam.
Cholam *Jowar* or sorghum.
Chootu Native torch made from coconut leaf bundles.
Cumbu *Bajra* or pearl millet.
Dakshina Alms given to teachers or Brahmins in return for blessings.
Dalit See *Avarna*.
Dami Commission fee charged by a *pucca arhatia*.
Desi Indigenous.
Dudhiya Milk contractor or vendor.
Fatka Indigenous futures and hedging contracts in raw jute evolved by Marwari traders in Kolkata.
Firman Decree issued by an Islamic ruler.
Gumastha Working partner or factor for a principal (see *shah*).
Gur Jaggery.
Havaldar Non-commissioned officer in the Indian army equivalent to a sergeant.
Hera-pheri Fraudulent activity.
Hundi Indigenous bill of exchange.
Ijara Revenue farming rights secured from the state.
Inam Land grant free from revenue obligations or held at reduced assessment, with the grantee being the *inamdar*.

Jagirdar	Holder of a specified tract of land on which he exercises rights over the collection and appropriation of revenue. The bestowing of a *jagir* was normally conditional upon the grantee maintaining troops and offering other services to the sovereign.
Jajmani	Traditional village-based system of exchange, binding various artisanal and service castes (blacksmith, carpenter, weaver, etc.) to the dominant landowning castes through hereditary patron–client relations.
Jowar	Sorghum.
Kangani	Labour contractors employed by plantation owners in Ceylon and South East Asia for recruitment and supervision of migrant workers from India.
Kaniyatchikaran	Tamil landed elite holding ownership rights or individual shares in whole villages, with these entitlements extending to wastelands, grazing grounds, and other non-cultivable assets. (Same as *mirasidar*.)
Kanungo	Custodian and keeper of land records (see *patwari*).
Kapas	Raw cotton.
Karta	Eldest male member or patriarch of a Hindu joint family.
Kashayam	Ayurvedic herbal decoction.
Khandsari	Cottage sugar in crystalline, unrefined form.
Kharif	Summer–monsoon crop sown in June–July and harvested from October.
Khudkasht	Independent peasant-proprietor.
Kirana	Local shop selling basic provisions.
Kist	Payment of revenue instalment.
Mahamai	Communal tax paid by Nadars to a common fund.
Mantravadam	Sorcery or black magic.
Mirasidar	See *kaniyatchikaran*.
Modi	Supplier of provisions to the army.
Mulki	Native of the old nizam-ruled Hyderabad State.
Munshi	Accountant or clerk.
Munsif	Village headman or subordinate magistrate.
Nawab	Muslim governor of a province.

Neera	Unfermented sap obtained from tapping the palmyra or coconut palm.
Oolium	Corvee labour obligation to the sovereign.
Papad	Flatbread made from pulse flour dough served as meal accompaniment.
Pappan	Elephant keeper or mahout.
Pan masala	Mouth freshener; a mixture of areca nut, spices, lime, and essence.
Panchayati Raj	Local three-tier government system at village, block, and district levels.
Pannaiyar	Landlord from southern Tamil Nadu.
Patta	Land title deed.
Patwari	Village accountant and record-keeper who reports to the *kanungo*.
Pedhi	Traditional Gujarati family business firm.
Peshwa	Brahmin prime ministers to Maratha kings who became de facto rulers by the mid-eighteenth century.
Pettai	Fortified settlements established by Nadars.
Phala	Threshing frame.
Poligar	Local military chieftain, derived from the Tamil word *palayakkarar*.
Rabi	Winter crop sown in November-December and harvested from March.
Ryotwari	Land revenue system based on direct levy and collection of tax from each *ryot* or individual cultivator (see *amani*).
Savakar	Moneylender; also called sahukar.
Savarna	Upper-caste Hindus. Technically, the term covers all the four *varnas* (including Shudras), with those outside its purview being *avarnas* or untouchables.
Sepoy	Foot-soldier.
Shah	Principal partner or capitalist in a business firm (see *gumastha*).
Sheth	Wealthy businessman or proprietor of a firm.
Shroff	Traditional banker or money changer.
Shudra	The lowest order in the *chaturvarna* hierarchy, inclusive

of cultivators, artisans, and other non-untouchable worker castes.

Subedar Junior commissioned officer in the Indian army.

Swadeshi Movement to promote consumption of Indian-made goods.

Taluka Administrative unit or subdivision below a district.

Tehsil The same as *taluka.*

Thottam Compact agricultural plots ('gardens') irrigated by open wells.

Udai Thorny scrub bush used as firewood.

Unani Graeco-Arabic system of medicine with similarities to Ayurveda.

Uravinmurai Local-level Nadar community organization.

Varna See *chaturvarna.*

Vaidyan Ayurvedic practitioner.

Vaishnav Adherent of the cult of the Hindu god Vishnu.

Vaishya Merchant strata in the classical *chaturvarna* scheme.

Vanaspati Hydrogenated vegetable oil.

Zamindari Revenue system instituted by the British in which a zamindar or hereditary tax collector paid an annual lump sum for his estate, often consisting of several villages. The estate lands were tilled by tenants, who had to fork out a share of the produce as rent to the zamindar.

Bibliography

Books and Articles

Ahuja, S.S. 2004. *A Study of Socio-Economic Impact of the Combine Harvesters*, Ludhiana: Punjab Agricultural University.

Alam, Anwar 1998. 'Harvesting and Threshing of Wheat for Better Straw Utilisation' in S. Nagarajan, G. Singh, and B.S. Tyagi (ed.), *Wheat: Research Needs Beyond 2000 AD*, New Delhi: Narosa Publishing House, pp. 369–79.

Ali, Imran 1989. *The Punjab under Imperialism: 1885–1947*, New Delhi: Oxford University Press.

Alladin, M. Ibrahim 2001. *Nachimuthu Mahalingam: A Living Legend*, Coimbatore: Rukmini Offset Press.

Amin, Shahid 1984. *Sugarcane and Sugar in Gorakhpur: An Inquiry into Peasant Production for Capitalist Enterprise in Colonial India*, New Delhi: Oxford University Press.

Attwood, Donald W. 1993. *Raising Cane: The Political Economy of Sugar in Western India*, New Delhi: Oxford University Press.

Bagchi, Amiya Kumar 1972. *Private Investment in India, 1900–1939*, Cambridge: Cambridge University Press.

——— 1992. 'European and Indian Entrepreneurship in India, 1900–30' in Rajat Kanta Ray (ed.), *Entrepreneurship and Industry in India, 1800–1947*, New Delhi: Oxford University Press, pp. 157–96.

Baker, Christopher John 1984. *An Indian Rural Economy, 1880–1955: The Tamilnad Countryside*, New Delhi: Oxford University Press.

Balagopal, K. 2004. 'Andhra Pradesh: Beyond Media Images', *Economic and Political Weekly*, vol. 39, no. 24, 12 June.

Banerjee, Abhijit and Munshi, Kaivan 2004. 'How Efficiently is Capital Allocated? Evidence from the Knitted Garment Industry in Tirupur', *The Review of Economic Studies*, vol. 71, issue 1, January.

Baru, Sanjaya 2000. 'Economic Policy and the Development of Capitalism in India: The Role of Regional Capitalists and Political Parties' in Francine R. Frankel *et al.* (ed.), *Transforming India: Social and Political Dynamics of Democracy*, New Delhi: Oxford University Press, pp. 207–30.

Batra, S.M. 1996. 'Dominant Classes and Cooperative Leaders in Western Uttar Pradesh' in B.S. Baviskar and Donald W. Attwood (ed.), *Finding the Middle Path: The Political Economy of Cooperation in Rural India*, New Delhi: Sage Publications India Pvt. Ltd, pp. 323–41.

Baviskar, B.S. 1980. *The Politics of Development: Sugar Cooperatives in Rural Maharashtra*, New Delhi: Oxford University Press.

Bayly, C.A. 2002. *Rulers, Townsmen and Bazaars: North Indian Society in the Age of British Expansion 1770–1870*, New Delhi: Oxford University Press.

Bhachu, Parminder 1990. 'Twice Versus Direct Migrants: East African Settlers in Britain', *ISSR-1010 Working Paper Series*, Los Angeles: Institute for Social Science Research, UCLA.

Bhakta, Govind B. 2002. *Patels: A Gujarati Community History in the United States*, Los Angeles: UCLA Asian American Studies Center Press.

Bhandari, Bhupesh 2005. *The Ranbaxy Story: The Rise of an Indian Multinational*, New Delhi: Penguin Books India.

Bhave, Savita 2005. *Casting a Destiny: The Biography of Chandran Menon* (translation from the Marathi by Nandu Dange), Pune: Ameya Prakashan.

Calvert, H. 1936. 'The Wealth and Welfare of the Punjab', Lahore: *Civil and Military Gazette*, Punjab Civil Secretariat.

Chandrasekhar, C.P. 1997. 'The Economic Consequences of the Abolition of Child Labour: An Indian Case Study', *The Journal of Peasant Studies*, vol. 24, no.3, pp. 137–79.

Chari, Sharad 2004. *Fraternal Capital: Peasant-Workers, Self-Made Men and Globalization in Provincial India*, New Delhi: Permanent Black.

Chibber, Vivek 2004. *Locked in Place: State-Building and Late Industrialization in India*, New Delhi: Tulika Books.

Collet, Nigel 2005. *The Butcher of Amritsar: General Reginald Dyer*, New Delhi: Rupa & Co.

Darling, Malcolm Lyall 1978. *The Punjab Peasant in Prosperity and Debt*, Delhi: South Asia Books (reprint).

Datta, Nonica 1999. *Forming an Identity: A Social History of the Jats*, New Delhi: Oxford University Press.

Datta, V.N. 1986. 'Punjabi Refugees and the Urban Development of Greater Delhi', in R.E. Frykenberg (ed.), *Delhi Through the Ages: Selected Essays in Urban History, Culture and Society*, New Delhi: Oxford University Press, pp. 442–62.

Desai, Ashok V. 1968. 'The Origins of Parsi Enterprise', *The Indian Economic and Social History Review*, vol. 5, no. 4, pp. 307–17.

Deshpande, Prachi 2004. 'Caste as Maratha: Social Categories, Colonial Policy and Identity in Early Twentieth-century Maharashtra', *The Indian Economic and Social History Review*, vol. 41, no. 1, pp. 7–32.

Divekar, V.D. 1984. 'Business Elements and Business Class in Maharashtra: A Historical Analysis' in Dwijendra Tripathi (ed.), *Business Communities of India*, pp. 83–108.

Dubash, Navroz K. 2002. *Tubewell Capitalism: Groundwater Development and Agrarian Change in Gujarat*, New Delhi: Oxford University Press.

Dutta, Sudipt 1997. *Family Business in India*, New Delhi: Sage Publications India Pvt. Ltd.

Duvvury, Nata 1986. 'Commercial Capital and Agrarian Relations: A Study of Guntur Tobacco Economy', *Economic and Political Weekly*, vol. XXI, no. 30, Review of Political Economy, pp. PE-46 to PE-57.

Farooqui, Amar 1995. 'Opium Enterprise and Colonial Intervention in Malwa and Western India, 1800–1824', *The Indian Economic and Social History Review*, vol. 32, no. 4, pp. 447–73.

Gadgil, D.R. 1951. *Notes on the Rise of the Business Communities in India* (with staff of Gokhale Institute of Politics and Economics, Pune), New York: Institute of Pacific Relations.

– – – 1959. *Origins of the Modern Indian Business Class: An Interim Report*, New York: Institute of Pacific Relations.

George, Shanti 1996. 'Beyond Anand: Comparing the Kheda and Choryasi Dairy Cooperatives' in B.S. Baviskar and Donald W. Attwood (ed.), *Finding the Middle Path: The Political Economy of Cooperation in Rural India*, New Delhi: Sage Publications India Pvt. Ltd, pp. 237–54.

Goswami, Omkar 1985. 'Then Came the Marwaris: Some Aspects of the Changes in the Pattern of Industrial Control in Eastern India', *The Indian Economic and Social History Review*, vol. 22, no. 3, pp. 225–49.

——— 1989. 'Sahibs, Babus, and Banias: Changes in Industrial Control in Eastern India, 1918–50', *The Journal of Asian Studies*, vol. 48, no. 2, pp. 289–309.

Granovetter, Mark 1985. 'Economic Action and Social Structure: The Problem of Embeddedness', *American Journal of Sociology*, vol. 91, no. 3, pp. 481–510.

Grewal, J.S. 1984. 'Business Communities of Punjab' in Dwijendra Tripathi (ed.), *Business Communities of India*, pp. 209–24.

Guha, Amalendu 1984. 'More About the Parsi Sheths: Their Roots, Entrepreneurship and Comprador Role, 1650–1918' in Dwijendra Tripathi (ed.), *Business Communities of India*, pp. 109–50.

Gupta, Ashin Das 1979. 'Gujarati Merchants and the Red Sea Trade, 1700–1725' in Blair B. Kling and Michael N. Pearson (ed.), *The Age of Partnership: The Europeans in Asia before Dominion*, Honolulu: University of Hawaii Press, pp. 123–58.

Hardgrave Jr., Robert L. 1969. *The Nadars of Tamilnad: The Political Culture of a Community in Change*, Berkeley and Los Angeles: University of California Press.

Hardiman, David 1981. *Peasant Nationalists of Gujarat: Kheda District 1917–1934*, New Delhi: Oxford University Press.

——— 1996. *Feeding the Baniya: Peasants and Usurers in Western India*, New Delhi: Oxford University Press.

Hazari, R.K. 1966. *The Structure of the Corporate Private Sector: A Study of Concentration, Ownership and Control*, Bombay: Asia Publishing House.

Heilbroner, Robert L. 1986. *The Worldly Philosophers: The Lives, Times,* *and Ideas of the Great Economic Thinkers*, New York: Simon & Schuster, Inc.

Isaac, T.M. Thomas 1984. 'Class Struggle and Industrial Structure: A Study of Coir Weaving Industry in Kerala, 1859–1980', unpublished PhD thesis, Thiruvananthapuram: Centre for Development Studies.

———**and Tharakan, P.K. Michael** 1986. 'An Enquiry into the Historical Roots of Industrial Backwardness of Kerala: A Study of the Travancore Region', *Working Paper 215*, Thiruvananthapuram: Centre for Development Studies, May.

Ito, Shoji 1966. 'A Note on the Business Combine in India with Special Reference to the Nattukottai Chettiars', *The Developing Economies*, vol. 4, no. 3.

Iyer, Gopalkrishnan R. 1999. 'The Impact of Religion and Reputation in the Organisation of Indian Merchant Communities', *Journal of Business and Industrial Marketing*, vol. 14, no. 2, pp. 102–17.

Jeffrey, Robin 2000. *India's Newspaper Revolution: Capitalism, Politics and the Indian-Language Press*, New Delhi: Oxford University Press.

———2001. *Politics, Women and Well-Being: How Kerala Became 'A Model'*, New Delhi: Oxford University Press.

Kamath, M.V. 1996. *Milkman from Anand: The Story of Verghese Kurien*, Delhi: Konark Publishers Pvt. Ltd.

Karkaria, Bachi J. 1992. *Dare to Dream: A Life of Rai Bahadur Mohan Singh Oberoi*, Penguin Books India.

Kaur, Rupinder 2003. *Rice Processing Industry in Punjab*, New Delhi: National Council of Applied Economic Research, November.

Kaur, Surjit 2003a. *Amongst the Sikhs: Reaching for the Stars*, New Delhi: Roli Books Pvt. Ltd.

Kautilya 1992. *The Arthashastra* (Edited, Rearranged, Translated and Introduced by L.N. Rangarajan), New Delhi: Penguin Books India.

Khalidi, Omar 2006. *Muslims in Indian Economy*, Gurgaon: Three Essays Collective.

Kling, Blair B. 1966. 'The Origin of the Managing Agency System in India', *The Journal of Asian Studies*, vol. 26, no. 1, pp. 37–47.

Kumar, Ravinder 1997. 'Urban Society and Urban Politics: Lahore in 1919' in Indu Banga (ed.), *Five Punjabi Centuries: Polity, Economy,*

Society and Culture, c. 1500–1990, New Delhi: Manohar Publications, pp. 180–219.

Lady Hope 1900. *General Sir Arthur Cotton: His Life and Work*, London: Hodder and Stoughton.

Lamb, Helen B. 1955. 'The Indian Business Communities and the Evolution of an Industrialist Class', *Pacific Affairs*, vol. 28, no. 2, pp. 101–16.

Landa, Janet T. 1981. 'A Theory of the Ethnically Homogeneous Middleman Group: An Institutional Alternative to Contract Law', *The Journal of Legal Studies*, vol. 10, no. 2, pp. 349–62.

Lele, Jayant 1990. 'Caste, Class and Dominance: Political Mobilization in Maharashtra' in Francine R. Frankel and M.S.A. Rao (ed.), *Dominance and State Power in Modern India: Decline of a Social Order*, vol. II, New Delhi: Oxford University Press, pp. 115–211.

Levin, Sergey 1974. 'The Upper Bourgeoisie from the Muslim Commercial Community of Memons in Pakistan, 1947 to 1971', *Asian Survey*, vol. 14, no. 3, pp. 231–43.

Mahadevan, Raman 1978. 'Immigrant Entrepreneurs in Colonial Burma: An Exploratory Study of the Role of Nattukottai Chettiars of Tamil Nadu, 1880–1930', *The Indian Economic and Social History Review*, vol. 15, no. 3, pp. 329–58.

——— 1984. 'Entrepreneurship and Business Communities in Colonial Madras, 1900–1929: Some Preliminary Observations' in Dwijendra Tripathi (ed.), *Business Communities of India*, pp. 225–39.

——— 1991. 'Industrial Entrepreneurship in Princely Travancore: 1930–47' in Sabyasachi Bhattacharya *et al.* (ed.), *The South Indian Economy: Agrarian Change, Industrial Structure and State Policy c. 1914–47*, New Delhi: Oxford University Press, pp. 159–207.

——— 1992. 'The Pattern of Industrial Control in Colonial Madras: Some Critical Observations on the Relative Position of Indian and Foreign Capital, 1930–50' in Arun Ghosh *et al.* (ed.), *Indian Industrialization: Structure and Policy Issues*, New Delhi: Oxford University Press, pp. 333–64.

——— 1992a. 'Process of Manchesterisation in Colonial South India: A Study of the Pattern of Textile Investment and the Growth of Indigenous Capitalists in Coimbatore 1914–45', unpublished paper presented at the 12th European Conference on Modern South Asian Studies, Berlin, September.

Malik, Shiva N. 1994. *Seth Chhaju Ram: A Life with a Purpose*, Hissar: Aman Prakashan.

Markovits, Claude 1985. *Indian Business and Nationalist Politics, 1931–1939: The Indigenous Capitalist Class and the Rise of the Congress Party*, Cambridge: Cambridge University Press.

———2000. *The Global World of Indian Merchants, 1750–1947: Traders of Sind from Bukhara to Panama*, Cambridge: Cambridge University Press.

Marx, Karl and Engels, Frederick 1977. *Manifesto of the Communist Party*, Selected Works, vol. I, Moscow: Progress Publishers.

McDonald, Hamish 1998. *The Polyester Prince: The Rise of Dhirubhai Ambani*, New South Wales: Allen & Unwin Pty Ltd.

McLeod, W.H. 2003. *Exploring Sikhism: Aspects of Sikh Identity, Culture, and Thought*, New Delhi: Oxford University Press.

Mukherjee, Aditya 2002. *Imperialism, Nationalism and the Making of the Indian Capitalist Class 1920–1947*, New Delhi: Sage Publications India Pvt. Ltd.

Nanda, H.P. 1992. *The Days of My Years*, New Delhi: Penguin Books India.

Omvedt, Gail 1976. *Cultural Revolt in a Colonial Society: The Non-Brahmin Movement in Western India 1873–1930*, Bombay: Scientific Socialist Education Trust.

———1988. 'The Satara Prati Sarkar' in Gyanendra Pandey (ed.), *The Indian Nation in 1942*, Calcutta: K.P. Bagchi & Company, pp. 223–61.

Osella, Filippo and Osella, Caroline 2000. *Social Mobility in Kerala: Modernity and Identity in Conflict*, London: Pluto Press.

Owens, Raymond Lee and Nandy, Ashis 1978. *The New Vaisyas: Entrepreneurial Opportunity and Response in an Indian City*, Durham, North Carolina: Carolina Academic Press.

Papanek, Hanna 1973. 'Pakistan's New Industrialists and Businessmen: Focus on the Memons' in Milton B. Singer (ed.) *Entrepreneurship and Modernization of Occupational Cultures in South Asia*, Durham, North Carolina: Duke University Press, pp. 61–106.

Patel, Amrita 1997. 'Operation Flood: The Next Step', *Dairy India 1997*, New Delhi, pp. 37–9.

Paul, Swraj 1998. *Beyond Boundaries: A Memoir*, New Delhi: Penguin Books India.

Perumal, Nilkan 1977. *The Life of A Textile Pioneer*, Coimbatore: The Kuppuswamy Naidu Charity Trust for Education & Medical Relief.

——— 1974. *An Industrial Scientist*, Coimbatore: Life Book Depot.

Pillai, Rajmohan and Kutty, K. Govindan 2001. *A Wasted Death: The Rise and Fall of Rajan Pillai*, New Delhi: Penguin Books India.

Piramal, Gita 1997. *Business Maharajas*, New Delhi: Penguin Books India.

– – – 1999. *Business Legends*, New Delhi: Penguin Books India.

Pocock, David F. 1972. *Kanbi and Patidar: A Study of the Patidar Community of Gujarat*, London: Oxford University Press.

Prahalad, C.K. 2005. *The Fortune at the Bottom of the Pyramid: Eradicating Poverty through Profits*, Wharton School Publishing, Delhi: Pearson Education (Singapore) Pte. Ltd., Indian Branch.

Purewal, Shinder 2000. *Sikh Ethnonationalism and the Political Economy of Punjab*, New Delhi: Oxford University Press.

Randhawa, M.S. 1983/1986. *A History of Agriculture in India* (vols III & IV), New Delhi: Indian Council of Agricultural Research.

Rao, G.N. 1985. 'Transition from Subsistence to Commercialized Agriculture: A Study of Krishna District of Andhra, *c.* 1850–1900', *Economic and Political Weekly*, vol. XX, nos 25–6, Review of Agriculture, pp. A-60 to A-69.

——— 1988. 'Canal Irrigation and Agrarian Change in Colonial Andhra: A Study of Godavari District, *c.*1850–1890', *The Indian Economic and Social History Review*, vol. 25, no. 1, pp. 25–60.

Ray, Rajat Kanta 1979. *Industrialization in India: Growth and Conflict in the Private Corporate Sector 1914–47*, New Delhi: Oxford University Press.

——— 1984. 'The *Bazar*: Indigenous Sector of the Indian Economy' in Dwijendra Tripathi (ed.), *Business Communities of India*, pp. 241–67.

Reddy, V.N. 1985. 'Pattern of Commercial Farming in Guntur District',

Economic and Political Weekly, vol. XX, nos 51–2, Review of Agriculture, pp. A-137 to A-152.

Reddy, G. Ram 1989. 'The Politics of Accommodation: Caste, Class and Dominance in Andhra Pradesh' in Francine R. Frankel and M.S.A. Rao (ed.), *Dominance and State Power in Modern India: Decline of a Social Order*, vol. I, New Delhi: Oxford University Press, pp. 265–321.

Rudner, David West 1994. *Caste and Capitalism in Colonial India: The Nattukottai Chettiars*, Berkeley: University of California Press.

Rutten, Mario 1995. *Farms and Factories: Social Profile of Large Farmers and Rural Industrialists in West India*, New Delhi: Oxford University Press.

Saberwal, Satish 1976. *Mobile Men: Limits to Social Change in Urban Punjab*, New Delhi: Vikas Publishing House Pvt. Ltd.

Satyanarayana, A. 1992. 'Industrialisation in Colonial Andhra, 1914–47', unpublished paper presented at Nehru Memorial Museum and Library, New Delhi, December.

Sau, Ranjit 1988. 'The Green Revolution and Industrial Growth in India: A Tale of Two Paradoxes and a Half', *Economic and Political Weekly*, vol. 23, no. 16, pp. 789–96.

Seylon, Raman N. 2004. 'Study of Poligar Violence in Late 18th Century Tamil Country in South India', *African and Asian Studies*, vol. 3, nos 3–4, pp. 245–72.

Shah, Ghanshyam 1990. 'Caste Sentiments, Class Formation and Dominance in Gujarat' in Francine R. Frankel and M.S.A. Rao (ed.), *Dominance and State Power in Modern India: Decline of a Social Order*, vol. II, New Delhi: Oxford University Press, pp. 59–114.

Shah, Tushaar 1996. *Catalyzing Cooperation: Design of Self-governing Organisations*, New Delhi: Sage Publications India Pvt. Ltd.

Sharma, G.D. 1984. 'The Marwaris: Economic Foundations of an Indian Capitalist Class' in Dwijendra Tripathi (ed.), *Business Communities of India*, pp.185–207.

Siddiqi, Asiya 1982. 'The Business World of Jamsetjee Jejeebhoy', *The Indian Economic and Social History Review*, vol. 19, nos. 3&4, pp. 301–24.

Singh, Charan 1986. *Land Reforms in UP and the Kulaks*, New Delhi: Vikas Publishing House Pvt. Ltd.

Singh, Himmat 2001. *Green Revolutions Reconsidered: The Rural World of Contemporary Punjab*, New Delhi: Oxford University Press.

Singh, Sukhpal 1990. 'Bicycle Industry since Independence: Growth, Structure and Demand', *Economic and Political Weekly*, 25 August, pp. M-98 to M-109.

Sinha, Narendra Krishna 1992. 'Indian Business Enterprise: Its Failure in Calcutta' in Rajat Kanta Ray (ed.), *Entrepreneurship and Industry in India, 1800–1947*, New Delhi: Oxford University Press, pp. 70–82.

Srinivas, M.N. 2002. 'The Dominant Caste in Rampura' in *Collected Essays*, New Delhi: Oxford University Press, pp. 74–92.

———. 2002a. *Caste in Modern India and Other Essays*, Mumbai: Media Promoters & Publishers Pvt. Ltd.

Srinivasulu, K. 2002. 'Caste, Class and Social Articulation in Andhra Pradesh: Mapping Differential Regional Trajectories', *Working Paper 179*, London: Overseas Development Institute, September.

Subramaniam, K.G. 1982. *My Philanthropic Friend: Karadivavipudur Shri K. Krishnaswamy Naidu*, Coimbatore: Kalaimani Printing Industries.

Tandon, Prakash 2000. *Punjabi Saga (1857–2000)*, New Delhi: Rupa & Co.

Tewari, Meenu 1998. 'Intersectoral Linkages and the Role of the State in Shaping the Conditions of Industrial Accumulation: A Study of Ludhiana's Manufacturing Industry', *World Development*, vol. 26, no. 8, pp. 1387–1411.

Tharakan, P.K. Michael 1998. 'Coffee, Tea or Pepper? Factors Affecting Choice of Crops by Agro-Entrepreneurs in Nineteenth Century South-West India', *Working Paper 291*, Thiruvananthapuram: Centre for Development Studies, November.

Timberg, Thomas A. 1978. *The Marwaris: From Traders to Industrialists*, New Delhi: Vikas Publishing House Pvt. Ltd.

Tirmizi, S.A.I. 1984. 'Muslim Merchants of Medieval Gujarat' in Dwijendra Tripathi (ed.), *Business Communities of India*, pp. 59–67.

Tripathi, Dwijendra and Mehta, M.J. 1984. 'Class Character of the Gujarati Business Community' in Dwijendra Tripathi (ed.), *Business Communities of India*, pp. 151–71.

Tripathi, Dwijendra 1984. (ed.), *Business Communities of India: A Historical Perspective*, New Delhi: Manohar Publications.

———**and Mehta, Makrand** 1990. *Business Houses in Western India: A Study in Entrepreneurial Response, 1850–1956*, New Delhi: Manohar Publications.

Tripathi, Dwijendra 2004. *The Oxford History of Indian Business*, New Delhi: Oxford University Press.

Upadhya, Carol Boyack 1988. 'The Farmer-Capitalists of Coastal Andhra Pradesh', *Economic and Political Weekly*, vol. 23, nos 27 (pp. 1376–82) and 28 (pp. 1433–42).

Venkataswamy, K. 1975. *The Story of Deccan Herald*, Bangalore: Privately printed.

Vijayabaskar, M. 2001. 'Industrial Formation under Conditions of Flexible Accumulation: The Case of a Global Knitwear Node in Southern India', unpublished PhD thesis, Thiruvananthapuram: Centre for Development Studies.

Washbrook, D.A. 1977. *The Emergence of Provincial Politics: The Madras Presidency, 1870–1920*, New Delhi: Vikas Publishing House Pvt. Ltd.

Zachariah, K.C., Kannan, K.P. and Rajan, S. Irudaya (ed.), 2002. *Kerala's Gulf Connection: CDS Studies on International Labour Migration from Kerala State in India*, Thiruvananthapuram: Centre for Development Studies.

Official and Industry Publications

Agricultural Statistics at a Glance 2005. New Delhi: Directorate of Economics & Statistics, Ministry of Agriculture, Government of India.

17th Indian Livestock Census: All India Summary Report 2005. New Delhi: Department of Animal Husbandry & Dairying, Ministry of Agriculture, Government of India.

Report of the Monopolies Inquiry Commission 1965. New Delhi: Manager of Publications, Government of India.

Report of the Industrial Licensing Policy Inquiry Committee 1969. New Delhi: Ministry of Industrial Development, Trade and Company Affairs, Government of India.

SEA Handbook on Indian Vegetable Oil Industry and Trade 2005: Mumbai: The Solvent Extractors' Association of India.

Statistical Abstract of Andhra Pradesh 2005. Hyderabad: Directorate of Economics and Statistics, Government of Andhra Pradesh.

Task Force Report on Bhopal Declaration, 2003. Bhopal: Government of Madhya Pradesh, January.

World Bank 1998. *India: The Dairy Revolution*, Washington: Operations Evaluation Department, June.

———2004. *Tamil Nadu Agricultural Development*, Final Report, Washington: Agriculture and Rural Development Department, November.

Index